The Public Speaker/ The Public Listener

Second Edition

Andrew D. Wolvin

University of Maryland
College Park and University College

Roy M. Berko

Communic-aid Consulting

Darlyn R. Wolvin

Prince George's Community College

Roxbury Publishing Company
Los Angeles, California

Library of Congress Cataloging-in-Publication Data

The public speaker/the public listener / Andrew D. Wolvin, Roy M. Berko, Darlyn R.
   Wolvin. —2nd ed.
     p. cm.
     Includes bibliographical references and index.
     ISBN 1-891487-12-4
     1. Public speaking. I. Berko, Roy M. II. Wolvin, Darlyn R. III. Title.
PN4121.W535 1999
808.5'1—dc21   98-21409
                                                            CIP

THE PUBLIC SPEAKER/THE PUBLIC LISTENER

Publisher and Editor: Claude Teweles
Developmental Editors: Elsa Van Bergen, Sacha Howells
Production Editors: Joyce Rappaport, Susan Converse Winslow
Production Coordinator: C. Max-Ryan
Production Assistant: Kate Shaffar
Typography: Synergistic Data Systems
Cover Design: Marnie Deacon Kenney
Cartoons: Tim Wallace

Printed on acid-free paper in the United States of America. This paper meets the standards for
recycling of the Environmental Protection Agency.

ISBN: 1-891487-12- 4

ROXBURY PUBLISHING COMPANY
P.O. Box 491044
Los Angeles, California 90049-9044
Tel: (310) 473-3312 • Fax: (310) 473-4490
Email: roxbury@crl.com

Contents

About the Authors

Andrew D. Wolvin is a professor and founding chair of the Department of Speech Communication at the University of Maryland—College Park. He has his Ph.D. from Purdue University. In addition to his many publications, he is a noted authority on listening behavior and has been the President of the International Listening Association and the Eastern Communication Association. He is a member of the Educational Policy Board of the National Communication Association. A professional speaker, he serves as a speech coach and trainer to a number of federal agencies, private corporations, and trade associations in Washington, D.C.

Roy M. Berko is the managing director of Communic–aid, a speech communication consulting organization. He has served as the associate director of the National Communication Association. He formerly was on the faculties of George Washington University, Towson State University, and Lorain County Community College. He holds a doctorate from Pennsylvania State University, an M.S. from the University of Michigan, and a B.A. from Kent State University. He has received seven national teaching awards, including being selected as a *Teacher on Teaching* by the NCA and was honored as the first recipient of the *Outstanding Teacher Award* by the Community College Section of NCA. He has authored or coauthored over 25 communication and education textbooks, appeared on such programs as *Good Morning America* and *Fox Morning News*, and was the communication expert for ABC-TV (Cleveland, Ohio). He has made regular appearances on National Public Radio.

Darlyn R. Wolvin is a professor and chair of the Department of Speech Communication and Theatre at Prince George's Community College, Largo, Maryland. She did her undergraduate and graduate work at the University of Nebraska—Lincoln. She has published widely and has been the president of the Eastern Communication Association and has served in a number of leadership positions in the National Communication Association.

Acknowledgements

No book of this scope is possible without the support and assistance of many individuals. We appreciate all that we have learned through the years from our speech communication colleagues, audiences, and students, for it is really their influence that has shaped our understanding of public speaking and public listening.

We are grateful to *Joanna Goldstein*, George Washington University, for unearthing the materials incorporated in the rhetorical history and cultural sections of this text, as well as for her tenacity in searching out, interviewing, and writing many of the speaker profiles.

We recognize the work of *Colleen Ryan* for her development of the profiles of notable American speakers in the first edition of the text, some of which were carried over into this edition.

Special thanks to *Joan Aitken*, University of Missouri—Kansas City, for developing the electronic ancillaries that accompany this book. Without her creativity, instructional knowledge, and computer skills, that important adjunct would not have been possible.

Appreciation to *Tim Wallace* for combining his knowledge of the field of communication and his creative abilities to craft the cartoons used in this edition.

Appreciation to *David Bodary*, Sinclair Community College, for his textual input and counsel on the Presentational Graphics section of the text.

A special remembrance to the late *Barbara Finegan* for her development of the *Instructor's Resource Manual* that accompanied the first edition of this text. Her spirit of advice and warmth will always be with us.

We are also grateful to the experts in our field for the constructive comments that aided in the development of this manuscript:

Joan Aitken, University of Missouri—Kansas City
Kenneth Albone, Rowan University
David Bodary, Sinclair Community College
Stanley Crane, Hartnell Community College
Sam Edelman, California State University—Chico
Ellen Hay, Augustana College
Marjorie Morris, Hinds Community College
Kathy Thompson, Alverno College

We acknowledge and appreciate the efforts of Claude Teweles for his support and advice on this project.

We hope that this text helps you to become a competent public speaker and listener. If so, all of our efforts will have proved to be worthwhile.

A.D.W.
R.M.B.
D.R.W.

Preface

Public communication plays a role in almost everyone's life. We are asked to present our ideas to audiences in educational, work, social, and political settings. We listen to political and public addresses, class lectures, sermons, business presentations, and informal talks.

The authors recognize that most people spend more time as public listeners than as public speakers. Therefore, in contrast to books that give little or no attention to the role of the listener, and almost all to speaking, this text centers on both aspects of the practice of public communication.

The Public Speaker/The Public Listener is intended to help students to develop their understanding and skills as public communicators—both as speakers and listeners.

A Message to the Student of Public Speaking and Listening

Like it or not, you are and will be a participant in the public communication arena. Whether in your role as a student, worker, or member of democratic society, you will find yourself presenting and listening to speeches. Research shows that being educated and trained in public communication increases a person's ability to speak and listen.[1]

This improvement encompasses such areas as clarity of statements, use of materials, and ability to capture attention and present ideas effectively.[2]

There is also an increase in the ability to present "lucid ideas in an organized fashion."[3]

Public speaking students learn to listen more effectively in classroom lectures, ask questions, summarize opinions, and distinguish facts from opinions.[4]

We have provided you with the resources and techniques to be an effective public speaker. In addition, we have included some historical background to help you understand how the principles of speaking and listening developed, the role of public communication in life, and how to appreciate public communicators.

We hope to encourage you to be effective and responsible communicators, because we believe that only through public discourse can we, as both listeners and speakers, ensure the durability of thoughtful deliberation on the issues and policies that affect our way of life as global citizens.

We have taken care to write directly to you, using a conversational tone, provocative examples, and an easily mastered format. At the same time, we have developed our ideas with the most recent scholarly research in mind. We have included both cartoons and photos to enhance the visual aspects of the material, and we have enhanced the textual presentation with sidebars that contain additional advice and ideas. Vocabulary terms appear in bold type for easy identification. You also will learn from the experiences of others through the profiles of celebrities and speech professionals.

The Structure of the Book

The 14 chapters of this book have been divided into sections which are double numbered—providing the chapter and section number. This format enables teachers to assign either a whole chapter or a section of a chapter at a time.

Stress is placed throughout the book on historical and contemporary issues while focusing on theory and skills. Special attention is paid to ethnic, racial, and gender issues.

What's New in This Edition

Based on the input of our reviewers and users, these enhancements have been made for this edition:

- The materials on public listening have been expanded.

- A chapter on what makes for a listenable speech has been added.

- The sidebars have been updated.

- Cartoons and new photos have been added for visual attention.

- New profiles of celebrities and communication professionals have been added.

- Additional material on race, ethnicity, and gender as they affect public communication have been blended into the materials.

- Research references have been updated.

- New sections have been added on such topics as the willingness to listen, plagiarism, fabrication, presentation graphics, computer-based retrieval systems, researching via the Internet, mind mapping, listener anxiety, and the effect of gender on the listenable speech.

On-Line Service

Instructional materials for the second edition of *The Public Speaking/ Public Listening* are available on-line. Edited and developed by Joan E. Aitken with the resources of the University of Missouri-Kansas City, the web site includes text materials, assignments, and other support for a virtual university course. By purchasing a CD, students can access on-line information. Online chat capability allows students to engage in live talk with other students studying public speaking around the country. A customized Internet search engine enables students to conduct online research for speech preparation. To find out more about these resources, see Aitken's web site at http://

cctr.umkc.edu/user/jaitken/index.html. (Note: The last "period" in the sentence denotes the end of the sentence and is not part of the web site address.)

Notes

1. David R. Seibold, Sami Kudsi, and Michael Rude, "Does Communication Training Make a Difference?: Evidence of a Presentation Skills Program," *Journal of Applied Communication Research*, May 1993, p. 120; Michael Kramer and J. S. Hinton, "Outcomes of the Public Speaking Basic Course," an unpublished paper presented at the Speech Communication Association Annual Convention, San Diego, CA, November, 1996, p. 16; Rebecca Rubin and Elizabeth E. Graham, "Communication Correlates of College Success: An Exploratory Investigation," *Communication Education*, 37, January, 1988, p. 14.
2. Siebold, p. 120.
3. Rubin, p. 14.
4. Ibid.

CHAPTER ONE

The Public Communicator: A Perspective

Chapter Outline

Learning Outcomes

After reading this chapter you should be able to:

- *Understand why you need to be an effective public speaker.*

- *Appreciate what can be learned from the rich heritage of public speaking.*

- *Recognize the role of nationality and culture on public speaking and public listening.*

- *Understand the process of public communication and how the speaker's needs, the listener's needs, and the context of the communication interrelate.*

$\mathbf{W}$hen you decided to register for this course in public speaking, you may have been thinking, "I like to get up and speak to audiences, so this class should be no problem." Maybe, though, your thoughts were more in the line of "Me, get up before a class and give a speech? No way!" If that was your response, feel some comfort in realizing that for most of us there is an element of uncertainty, or in some cases out-and-out fear, when it comes to **public speaking**—the act of communication that occurs between one person and an audience.

Some people actually do enjoy speaking before groups. If that were not true we would not have politicians, teachers, media performers, and religious leaders. On the other hand, research shows that 61 percent of the people in the United States are afraid of giving speeches.[1]

One of the purposes of this book, and the course you are taking, is to teach you the skills necessary to prepare and present an effective speech or to reinforce the skills you already have. People who are confident of their public speaking abilities naturally have more positive attitudes about communicating to an audience than those who lack these skills.

1.1 You and Public Speaking

A study aptly titled "Do Real People Ever Give Speeches?" revealed that, although many of us try to avoid public speaking, people at all levels do indeed give presentations.[2] In fact, 55 percent of the respondents gave at least one speech to 10 or more people every two years; 71 percent of these speakers gave at least four speeches during that time. People with more education and income give speeches more frequently. Knowing this, a person who wants a high-income job is wise to get a solid education and prepare to become an effective speaker.[3] And it is not only the business world which requires public speaking. Your participation in a class, club, volunteer activity, or political situation may call on your public communication skills.

No matter what your career choice, most college graduates enter occupations that require some form of speaking before groups, whether within the organization, at conferences or conventions, or as a representative of the company. Businesses are acutely aware of this requirement. A survey of Fortune 500 companies revealed that presentation skills were identified as "somewhat important" for secretarial staff and hourly wage workers; "important" for supervisors and technical staff; and "very important" for sales staff, executives, middle managers, and human resource staff.[4] Eighty-two percent of the Fortune 500 companies responding to this survey indicated that presentation skills are so important that they provide speech training in order to increase employee performance.

Public speaking occurs both within the organization to groups of employees, and to various groups outside, such as potential customers. Because communication is so central to productivity and effectiveness, many organizations offer public speaking training for their employees. One such company with an intricate communication plan is Honeywell. Honeywell's corporate communication department has established a speakers bureau with a specific public communication objective: to identify appropriate speaking platforms, negotiate media interviews, publish speakers' remarks, and provide opportunities to reach customers and prospects.[5]

Interest in effective public communication also is reflected in the growth of speakers' agents who book speakers for the annual sales meetings, conventions, and other large meetings that companies and organizations often sponsor. A former chief executive officer of Chrysler Corporation stresses that public speaking is "the best way to motivate a large group."[6] The speaking industry is lucrative. Well-known celebrities can command $25,000 or more for a speech.[7]

Skill in public speaking also is important in the academic arena. Students are asked to do classroom presentations of research projects, reports, experiments, and studies. Outside of class you might give a report to a student organization, make a proposal to your fraternity or sorority, represent a political candidate, or give a speech as part of a job interview.

Public communication is the lifeblood of political, legal, advertising, and promotional work. But you do not have to work in one of the media professions to be pressed into delivering a message effectively. During Operation Desert Storm, a military leader served as a highly effective communicator. The world was riveted to the television screen for regular briefings by General Norman Schwarzkopf, commander of the U.S. forces in the Persian Gulf. It was clear how much public speaking skills can accomplish. Schwarzkopf's success, though resounding, was not unique.

Public speaking has a long and colorful history. Being aware of this tradition allows us to realize that public speaking customs and processes are based on many trials and errors, theories, imitations of great speakers, and research into effective speaking.

Rate Your Presenting Skills

Labeling each of these statements as true or false will tell you if you know what it takes to be a powerful presenter:

1. Visuals will keep the audience's attention better if you use a variety of type fonts and sizes.
2. Memorizing a speech isn't a good idea.
3. Each visual should include no more than two key concepts.
4. Casually leaning back on one hip tells an audience that you're less formal and thus more believable.
5. To get an audience to think creatively, project information on the right side of a screen.

Answers: 1. *False*. Audiences react better to consistency, so use no more than one to two fonts. Also, it's best to use a sans serif because it's easier to read in the larger sizes you need for the screen. **2**. *True*, but some experts recommend that you memorize the first minute or two to help you build confidence by starting strong. **3**. *False*. Limit each visual to only *one* key concept or risk confusing an audience with too much to recall at once. **4**. *False*. It signals—nonverbally—that you wish you didn't have to be there. **5**. *True*. Research also shows that you should put the image or the words as high on the screen as you can get them.

Source: *Communication Briefings*, February, 1998.

1.2 You and Public Listening

Just as public communication depends upon skilled public speakers, so, too, does public communication depend upon skilled public listeners. As Dale's Cone of Learning (below) illustrates, public listeners process information (and learn) through many sensory channels. Think about it. Most of us spend a large portion of our public communication time as listeners. We may act as students listening to lecturers, react to speeches and sermons, attend civic and political events; we are receivers of many kinds of messages. We listen in person, and we receive information via technology. We hear speeches on television and radio, especially on channels such as CNN and C-Span. Political speeches, whether in the form of news broadcasts or the actual presentation itself, allow each of us to be the individual receiver of a political speech. In fact, we are the recipients of so many speeches that the phenomenon has been termed "Information Fatigue Syndrome."

To cope with information overload, it has become too easy just to "check out" and not participate in much of the communication in which we find ourselves. It is easy to dismiss a lecture with "this is boring," or to hit the remote and turn the channel to something more exciting when a speech comes on. But to be an educated political and social consumer, we need to assume an active role in the communication process.

Public communication education generally has focused on the speaker and how he or she should prepare a message. But this approach seems too narrow and unrealistic. The concept of **participative communication** appears more appropriate. This concept centers on a "balanced approach to the power relationship in communication, an ideal of both speaker and listener,

Dale's Cone of Learning

Source: Experience and learning. (Developed and revised by Bruce Nyland from material by Edgar Dale.) As printed in Mastering Meetings by the 3M Management Team, McGraw-Hill, 1994. Printed by permission.

Analyze your audience and satisfy its needs.

message-maker and message-receiver, sharing together the responsibility of creating meaning. . . . In participative communication, speaker and listener become collaborators, members of the meaning cooperative, joint builders of the edifice of public knowledge."[8]

After election to his first term as president, Bill Clinton called together a wide-ranging group of experts to participate in a forum in Little Rock, Arkansas, and asked them to give short issues presentations on the state of the U.S. economy. This approach to communication is not common. The American culture, in general, does not perceive leadership strength in terms of listening. Leaders are measured by the forcefulness of their own presented messages. Nevertheless, President Clinton listened and used the information he received to formulate his agenda for action.

To be a public listener, you must adopt strategies for listening actively. "Since a piece of communication is designed to get a response from you, you ought to ask yourself what it is doing to and for you as you listen."[9] An expert on public listening recommends that the public listener listen "defensively," understanding his or her own response to the communication and actively adapting that response to the communicator's objective. The "defensive" public listener must be able to concentrate all of his or her time, energy, and attention on the message itself.

Profile: Bill Moyers, Journalist and "Public Listener"

Any discussion of public speaking would be incomplete without a look at the role of listening in communication. Public speakers, particularly good ones, can wield considerable power in society.

Effective public listeners—those who are educated about public speaking and dedicated to listening—are equally important in determining the outcomes of significant events. Journalist Bill Moyers exemplifies the very best qualities of a "public listener."

At age 15, Moyers dove into journalism as a cub reporter for the *Marshall News Messenger*, in Marshall, Texas. He graduated from the University of Texas and has worked in broadcasting for over 20 years, devoting most of his energy to uncovering and scrutinizing the social, political, and international issues facing the United States. A *Television Quarterly* survey of critics recently named Moyers among the top 10 journalists who have had the most significant influence on TV news.

Moyers has produced over 125 programming hours, including *Special Report: After the War; God and Politics; Facing Hate with Elie Wiesel*, and *The Arab World*. His best-selling book, *Listening to America*, and his current PBS television series of the same name point to his understanding of the importance of listening in public communication. To watch him as he leads discussions is to witness active, effective public listening. Fully engaged in the communication event, he often leans toward his guests with interest. He sits back, chin in hand, and concentrates as he sorts out difficult issues and arguments. Most of all, his face tells speakers that he is committed to listening to what they have to say. Moyers's furrowed brow and tilted head seem to welcome the spoken word and encourage his guests.

Bill Moyers does not sit back and "just listen." He "sits up and listens." As a result, his insightful questions and attentive manner focus his viewers' eyes and ears on America's social, political, and international problems and triumphs.

Public listeners, then, become communication partners with their speakers: ". . . listening makes public speaking a reciprocal activity. . . . When both speakers and listeners work at making the speech transaction succeed, public speaking reaches its full potential as a partnership in communication."[10] In Chapter 2 we will explore the power of listening in greater detail.

1.3 The Historical Roots of Public Speaking

You might be asking yourself, after reading the title of this section, "Why should I care about the historical roots of public speaking? How will this make me a better speaker or listener?" This information may not make you a better public speaker or listener in the traditional sense of skills, but it will give you an understanding of how and why certain ideas are presented in this book. Theories of how to be an effective public speaker and listener did not appear out of the blue. They have been developed over many thousands of years. Accepting that we learn from the past and carry that information into the future, we realize the importance of understanding the history of public speaking and the theory behind it. To be an educated person means to possess more than the skills needed to do something. (And won't you be proud when the final question on the TV quiz show *Jeopardy* is "The person whose speech

❖ ❖ ❖ ❖

'On Woman's Right to Suffrage' played a vital role in gaining American women the right to vote," and you know the answer?)

"Give me liberty or give me death." "Ask not what your country can do for you, ask what you can do for your country." "We have nothing to fear, but fear itself." "Four score and seven years ago. . . ." "Read my lips. . . ." A review of lines from famous public speeches is a review of the history of people—of our conflicts, our ideals, our dreams, and our despairs.

The art of public speaking has a rich tradition in the study of **rhetoric**, or persuasive discourse.[11] *The Instruction of Ptah-hotep and the Instruction of Keg' emni*, an ancient book discovered on the banks of the Nile River in Egypt, advises a young Egyptian man how to become governor of a city and counselor to a king. In these instructions, effective speechmaking, the presentation of speeches, is recognized as a chief means to achieving social control. In ancient Greece, where the popular assembly was very powerful, the prominent statesman Pericles advocated and practiced skill in speechmaking. He trained as an orator with Zeno of Elea, noted as one of the first teachers of the art of speechmaking. The funeral oration Pericles delivered as a memorial to the first Athenian soldiers who fell in the Peloponnesian War in 431 B.C. is considered one of the great eulogies of all time. Another outstanding orator was Demosthenes, remembered for his seaside practice of speaking with pebbles in his mouth in order to perfect his delivery. Demosthenes delivered his speech "On the Crown," urging loyalty and honesty in politics, in Athens in 330 B.C. It is still considered a model of speechmaking.

During the middle years of the fifth century B.C., education was very much in the hands of a group of teachers known as the **sophists**, the first speech teachers to take money for their work. In preparing Athenians for civic life, they focused on the ability to speak effectively with **eloquence**, or with a memorable style. The Greek philosopher Plato was concerned about the sophists' approach to speech education. He attacked them for encouraging the deception of listeners and for stressing superficial knowledge. Responding to Plato's charges, the philosopher Aristotle wrote *The Rhetoric*, probably the most significant work in the history of public speaking. Aristotle's work, divided into three books dealing with the speaker, the audience, and the speech, insisted on worthwhile content and provided a thorough explanation of audience control. *The Rhetoric* today forms the foundation for our understanding of the process of persuasive speech.

In the classical Roman era, Cicero emerged as a prominent rhetorician and orator. In addition to his memorable speeches, he is noted for clarifying the classical **canons of rhetoric**, the aspects of the speechmaking process. The five Ciceronian canons, still useful to a student of public speaking, included:

- *Invention*, gathering the materials for the speech.

- *Disposition*, organizing the materials into the speech form.

- *Elocution*, practicing clear pronunciation of language.

- *Memory*, developing a command of the materials.

- *Action*, delivering the speech.

Cicero's scholarly written work *The Orator* stressed a liberal education as the foundation for developing speaking abilities.

Another significant figure in Roman speech history is Quintilian, whose *Institutes of Oratory* (dated about 95 A.D.) is an exhaustive manual for teachers, offering a plan for the education of the perfect orator. Stressing the need for teachers to adapt to the individual abilities of their students, Quintilian insisted on high ethical standards. Indeed, he defined the perfect orator as "the good man trained in speaking."

From Quintilian's time to about 1500 A.D., the Catholic Church was an important center of public communication. Most of the population of the Western world was not able to read or write, so people depended on the clergy to enlighten them and to pass on religious teachings and traditions through the spoken word. St. Augustine's *On Christian Doctrine* was an especially dominant effort to return rhetoric to the teachings of the Greeks and Romans.

As the English language developed, English rhetoric in the 1500s and beyond emerged from the classical Ciceronian tradition. Bishop Richard Whateley's *Rhetoric* of 1828 was an important text based on Aristotle's, Cicero's, and Quintilian's ideas. Some other specialized approaches to the study of speechmaking emerged. One approach, characterized by Henry Peacham's *Garden of Eloquence* (1577), stressed the use of figurative, ornamental language. Another approach, typified by John Walker's *Elements of Elocution* (1781), focused on the mechanics of speech delivery.

British eloquence flourished during the 18th century—the golden age of oratory in the British Parliament. The American Revolution occasioned speeches about the British position and the colonial position—notably by William Pitt, the Earl of Chatham, who argued that the British had no right to tax the colonies, and by Edmund Burke, who urged conciliation with the American revolutionaries. Speakers in Parliament would often present discourses lasting two or three hours, reflecting phenomenal command of the issues and of the English language.

These British rhetorical traditions underpinned educational practices in early American schools. Public speaking was included as part of the curriculum when Harvard was founded in 1636. Though some schools based their oratorical training on the Ciceronian canons, which combined speech content and delivery, other teachers of elocution focused solely on the speaker's delivery. Early colonial speakers of note included Patrick Henry, whose famous "Give me liberty or give me death" speech was delivered before the Virginia Convention of Delegates in 1775, and Jonathan Edwards, a New England preacher whose sermon "Sinners in the Hands of an Angry God" painted a vivid portrait of sin, hell, and punishment.

One of the greatest periods of American oratory occurred during the years leading to the Civil War. In 1830 Daniel Webster, a senator from Massachusetts, presented a masterful reply to Senator Robert Hayne of South Carolina on issues that were beginning to divide the North and the South. John Calhoun of South Carolina was an eloquent champion of the South, and Henry Clay of Kentucky emerged as the "Great Compromiser" in the historic debates over Southern secession. Charles Sumner, another senator from Massachusetts, became a militant spokesman for the abolition of slavery. His speech "The Crime Against Kansas," which he delivered in 1856, provoked the nephew of an opposing senator to physically attack him on the Senate floor. Abraham Lincoln, "The Great Emancipator," accomplished a great deal through his oratorical skills as president. His commemorative "Gettysburg Address" remains one of the most eloquent speeches of all time.

❖ ❖ ❖ ❖

Other American speakers took their place in the history of influential public communication. One of the most famous female orators was Susan B. Anthony, noted for her antislavery and temperance stands. Her eloquent speech "On Woman's Right to Suffrage" played a vital role in gaining women the right to vote in the United States. William Jennings Bryan's famous speech "The Cross of Gold," delivered at the Democratic National Convention in Chicago in 1896, favored free coinage of silver. The method of fighting economic problems it advocated won him a presidential nomination. Attorney Clarence Darrow presented eloquent courtroom speeches, notably his plea against capital punishment in the Leopold and Loeb case in 1924. Humorist Will Rogers was highly popular on the speaking circuit during the 1920s and 1930s.

Photo: Courtesy of University of Missouri—Kansas City, Communication Studies Department

As happened in South Africa with Desmond Tutu, when nations confront crises, spokespersons emerge to respond to those events.

World War II brought about another era of compelling oratory. Adolf Hitler's oratorical control over the German masses contributed greatly to his rise to power. President Franklin D. Roosevelt utilized the radio to speak reassuringly to people alarmed about domestic economic pressures and the dangers of the war in Europe. Britain's prime minister, Winston Churchill, will always be noted in history as an eloquent speaker. His oft-repeated messages of hope and inspiration included such famous phrases as "blood, sweat and tears" and "their finest hour." His warning about the "Iron Curtain" significantly influenced subsequent military and foreign policy in the Western world.

Public communication, as practiced in the United States today, has been shaped by the powers of many contemporary speakers. President John F. Kennedy was one of the first to understand the significance of television as a communication medium and how to use it to his advantage. Religious leaders such as the Reverend Billy Graham learned to adapt their oratorical style to the medium of television. The Reverend Martin Luther King, Jr, eloquently reached out to many Americans as a leader in the fight for civil rights. Public spokespersons Gloria Steinhem and Bella Abzug are credited with stimulating the women's movement; Barbara Jordan was a eloquent spokesperson for the downtrodden; Caesar Chavez rallied the nation with his impassioned appeals on the part of migrant workers.

The history of public communication truly is the history of ideas and their expression by competent speakers living in the midst of important human events. As nations confront crises, domestic or foreign, spokespersons emerge to respond to those events. By studying their responses, scholars of public communication can help us come to an understanding of the components in this complex process.

1.4 Cultural Influences in Public Speaking

Research shows that culture affects the way people use, present, and regard public speaking. The American tradition is different from that of the Japanese, for example, for reasons going far beyond geographical borders. The term culture is often understood as nationality. In fact, **nationality** refers to the nation in which one was born, now resides, or has lived or studied in long enough to become familiar with the customs of the area. Nationality identifiers are classifications such as Japanese, Mexican, or Canadian. Culture goes beyond that. A **culture** is a a shared system of values and interpretation.[12] Culture identifiers include American Indian/Native American, African American/black, and gender—male or female.

Cultural differences in public speaking and listening may be understood by first examining the Western approach to developing arguments. The typical pattern is to state a sequence of aspects:

- The *situation* (background materials).
- *Problem* (undesirable condition of things).
- *Solution* (the desirable condition).
- *Evaluation* (a check to see that the solution is good).

Though it is difficult to generalize about all members of any particular nation or culture, research in public speaking allows for the identification of some tendencies among peoples of common groups. Some examples of these several characteristics which have been documented include:

Germans tend to communicate even more directly than Americans, expecting that frankness, honesty, and directness will govern the communication. German orderliness is a matter of not wasting time, getting directly to the point, omitting pleasantries.[13] Czech writers and speakers closely follow the German patterns.[14]

The Chinese concept of self makes it difficult for Chinese speakers and writers to be direct, to express a point of view. The Confucian concept of self, on which the Chinese self is based, presents individualism as problematic. Arguments often are delayed, include narration, and use statements that seem unconnected to the ears of the Western listener. Chinese public communication relies greatly on appeals to history, tradition, and authority, and frequently refers to historical and religious texts, as well as proverbs.

"Cultural norms in Japan do not value talkativeness and the Japanese tend not to be outspoken."[15] Japanese speakers tend to be less forceful and dynamic than American speakers as they do not wish to draw attention to themselves.[16]

Among the Native American Indians, the Navajos have a great tradition of rhetoric. Navajo speech is based on "thinking publicly."[17] "Rhetoric, for the Navajo, is functional as a means to restore and maintain order, balance, and harmony."[18] The Navajo uses public discussion as a means to maintain or restore harmony, because speech is based on the assumption that all people are rational beings capable of persuasion. Therefore, all of the information needed for decision making is presented. This is in contrast to the Euro-American tradition of only exposing that information which can be used to sway the listener to reach the solution proposed by the speaker (thus denying the listener any chance of selecting one of the other possible conclusions).

Speaking to Diverse Groups

Today's business audiences include an increasing percentage of foreign-born people—both employees and foreigners on temporary assignments. Speaking to these culturally diverse groups requires special preparation and understanding. Some tips are:

- Start by finding out how many foreign-born folks will be in the audience. Ask where they are from and how well they handle the English language. Keep in mind that English taught in foreign classrooms won't qualify them to handle "words" such as, "Waddayathink?"

- When speaking, slow down and use natural pauses. "Speaking slower . . . with natural pauses . . . will allow everyone . . . a chance to absorb . . . your message."

- Avoid causing them the shame of losing face. *How*:

  —Don't call on them unless you're sure they'll understand what you'll be asking.
  —Be sure to give the instructions for an activity twice.

- Use as many visuals as possible.

- Be careful about using culturally specific examples, such as "touchdown" or "the Cosby show." Use universal themes, such as the desire for success or the importance of good friendship.

Source: *Communication Briefings,* as adapted from *Power Speaking: How Ordinary People Can Make Extraordinary Presentations,* by Dr. Frederick Gilbert, Frederick Gilbert Associates, 1233 Harrison Ave., Redwood City, CA 94062.

In slavery-era America, slaves gathered around the campfire to listen to tales, just as in Africa they had listened to the *griot* (storyteller) spin tales of the creation or recreate stories of tribal conquests, births, and deaths. In later years, African Americans moved from the campfire to inside the church to see and hear the minister interpret biblical passages with old proverbs, stories, and song.[19] Black rhetoric includes a highly significant tradition of storytelling and a highly charged ritual of the call-response pattern of the black religious and secular gatherings.[20] The minister often uses a drum beat rhythm; changes pitch; or adds popping, clicking, and clapping sounds to dramatize the events in the story. Services are accompanied by song and dance and are often enlivened by sound effects. The members of the audience respond like a chorus. They interpose comments at convenient intervals, add their own sound effects, and sing the songs of the tale along with the minister.[21] This is in stark contrast to the traditional Euro-American speech event in which the audience sits silently—maybe laughing or applauding when they are amused or are in agreement but generally appearing "polite" and giving passive attention to the speaker.

Even males and females in the United States are noted for having different styles in presenting speeches. Researchers have found that females tend to use more words to make their point.[22] Men are more direct as they clearly state what they want, while women are more likely to use questions and indirect references.[23] They even vary as listeners. Men are generally more interested in visual stimulation and physical details, while women tend to be more interested in emotional overtones.[24]

1.5 The Components of Public Communication

The process of public communication is highly complex and involves the interrelationship of a number of basic components. These are the source, the code, perceptions and attitudes, the message, the channel, the receiver, feedback, noise, and the environment. A model of this process is represented in Figure 1.1.

Figure 1.1 A Model of Public Communication

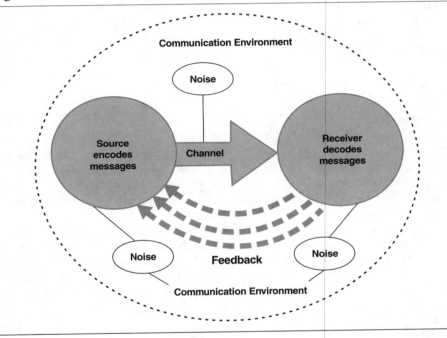

The Source and the Code

The process of public communication originates with a **source**, the speaker, who consciously or unconsciously is stimulated to communicate by some event, object, or idea. The speaker's need to send a message results in the search for a **code**—the appropriate verbal and/or nonverbal language with which to symbolize the message. The speaker **encodes** the message; the listener **decodes**.

Perceptions and Attitudes

As the source of communication, a speaker is influenced by a number of factors. **Perceptions**—the way a person views the world—affect a speaker's choice of topic and style of composing the message. Likewise, speakers are influenced by their own as well as the **listener's attitudes**—predispositions to respond—which usually are positive or negative expectations. These personal perceptions and attitudes affect the choices we make as communicators. A speaker's mental and physical state also may have a bearing on decisions about communicating. For a speaker who does not feel well or is preoccupied, it will be much more difficult to focus on communicating the message.

The Message

The encoded **message**, the speech itself, is composed of verbal and/or nonverbal symbols and supplementary aids, such as visual aids, selected by the speaker to convey his or her ideas. The language is **symbolic** in that the words represent the ideas, objects, and events that the communicator is expressing. The word *chair*, for instance, is an arbitrary selection of sounds that represents a particular type of furniture. Semanticists—those who study the symbolic nature of language—stress that just as maps are not the actual terrain but rather representations of that terrain, so are words representations, not the actual objects or ideas.

The Channel

The encoded message is carried through a **channel**—such as speaking, hearing, seeing, smelling, tasting, and touching. As speakers and listeners, we rely primarily on the channels of sight and sound, but sometimes a speaker may have members of the audience also smell, touch, or taste objects in order to convey meaning.

An encoded message may be conveyed to listeners via a mechanical or electronic means of carrying a message, such as radio, television, overhead projector, tape recorder, videocassette playback unit, or laser disk. Selecting and using the appropriate channel is a matter for careful decision making for speakers. This is because different messages may very well require different modes of transmission. For example, the advent of television changed the nature of political communication. Presidential candidates once traveled throughout the country giving speeches from the rear of campaign trains. Because they had personal contact with individual audiences at each train stop, they could tailor-make their messages. Today, through the use of television, they can reach a larger number of people without traveling, but they need to code their messages differently. Thirty-second spots do not lend themselves to long, eloquent speeches adjusted to individual audiences.

The Receiver

Regardless of the channel used, the message must be decoded before communication is accomplished. The **receiver**, or listener, receives the verbal and nonverbal signals and translates them. The decoded message will not be identical to the one encoded by the speaker, for each listener's symbol system is based on a unique set of perceptions. Just as speakers are influenced by their own perceptions, attitudes, and physical and psychological states, so, too, are listeners affected by these factors at any given moment in the communication process. How the listener interprets a message will depend, to a great extent, on how these factors interact to shape his or her decoding of the message.

Feedback

Once the listener assigns meaning to the message received, he or she is in a position to respond. This response, called **feedback**, can be a verbal or a nonverbal reaction (or both) to the message, the speaker, the channel, or even the rest of the audience itself. The speaker should carefully observe feedback because it can indicate whether the listener understands (e.g., nodding), misunderstands (e.g., "I don't understand"), encourages the speaker to continue (e.g., attentive expression, leaning forward), or disagrees (e.g., "No way!"). The act of responding, by which the listener sends feedback to the speaker, actually *shifts the receiver's role* to that of the source.

Noise

The content of a message is influenced not only by the source's coding and the receiver's decoding but also by noise. **Noise** is any internal or external interference in the communication process.[25] It can be caused by environmental factors, physiological impairment, problems with semantics or syntax, organizational confusion, or social or psychological factors. Control of noise is an important consideration for both speaker and listener in any public communication situation.

Environmental noise is outside interference that prevents the listener from receiving the message. This type of noise can occur during a lecture when the students around you are talking so loudly that you cannot hear the instructor, when people are shuffling through their notebooks looking for a clean page on which to take notes, or when some aspect of the room, such as the air conditioning or the lighting, distracts you from the speaker. In each of these cases, some form of environmental noise is blocking clear reception of the message.

A **physiological impairment**, unless compensated for, also can block the effective sending or receiving of a message. For example, to receive an oral message, a person who is hearing impaired must use a mechanical device, such as a hearing aid, or read the speaker's lips. To send a message to a hearing audience, such a person might use sign language that an able translator would then deliver orally to the listeners. Similarly, an individual with a speech impediment may be difficult for some people to understand. Physiological impairments can cause frustrating communication experiences for both speakers and listeners.

Problems also may arise with semantics—the meaning of words. **Semantic problems** often result when speakers use language that is common only to one specific group of people—from a particular region or country, for instance, or from a particular field, profession, or organization. Listeners can experience semantic problems when speakers use words without defining them. College professors, physicists, computer technicians, and other experts sometimes forget that those who don't have as much knowledge of their field as they do may not be familiar with its vocabulary.

One semantic problem that is particularly widespread is the use of initials instead of full names to refer to organizations, equipment, or activities. For example, federal agencies often are referred to with initials, such as SEC (Securities and Exchange Commission) and NOAA (National Oceanic and Atmospheric Administration). Government officials become so accustomed to this usage that they forget that most lay people don't recognize the "alphabet soup." In order to avoid semantic problems, public speakers must be aware that although *they* know the meaning of a term or a phrase, the listener must have a similar background to understand it as well.

Each language has a syntax—a customary way of putting words together into sentences—and if a speaker uses an unfamiliar syntax, the receiver may be confused. Various types of **syntactical problems**, or flawed grammatical usage, can interfere with communication. For example, listeners may become confused if a public speaker changes tenses in the middle of a story being used to make a point ("She is walking down the street and then she said to him . . ."). Or they may be confused by the use of double negatives ("He doesn't have no intention of doing that") or by other incorrect grammar.

Non-English speaking people who are learning English sometimes put words in the wrong order. The usual sequence of a grammatically correct English sentence begins with the subject or doer of an action and is followed by the verb and object (or indirect object, as in this example): "I give him the book." But other languages—Spanish, for example—do not follow this pattern. In Spanish the same sentence would be "Le doy el libro," or literally "To him I give the book." Thus it is clear that someone who is learning a new language must master not only the vocabulary but an entirely different system of syntax as well. Until the speaker becomes more fluent, the language may be quite difficult both to encode and to decode. Public speakers whose native language is not English may have trouble communicating their ideas fully. Conversely, to communicate most clearly with a non-English speaking audience, English speakers might be wise to ask an interpreter to carry the burden of clarification. This holds true not only for syntactic noise but for semantic noise as well.

A common problem for listeners is being unable to follow the structure of a speech. When the source fails to realize that certain ideas are best grasped by presenting them in a structured order, **organizational confusion** may be the result. If, for example, a geography instructor presents ideas in a random fashion, starting by talking about India, then jumping to China, then Greece, and back to India, after a while his students may become confused as to which country his comments pertain. If the speaker presents material in a specific pattern, the listener can process the ideas and readily grasp the meaning. If the message is not so organized, the receiver must try to sort out the information. As we will see later in this book, the use of visual aids and other devices can avoid organizational confusion.

Cultural noise, a strong factor in communication, is the set of preconceived group attitudes that individuals from different nationalities, races, and genders have developed. (We explored some of these differences in section 1.4.) Attitudes often prevent a receiver from dealing objectively with a message. A prime example of cultural noise is the attitude that any action by a representative of one's own group is always right, whereas the same action by a member of another group is always wrong. Thus an individual who has always voted for one political party may well ignore the negative aspects of that party while easily accepting the negative aspects of an opposing party—for example, an Israeli who can not listen objectively to a message about Arabic home rule.

Cultural noise can also arise from the topic chosen for a speech. Certain controversial subjects might cause members of the audience to become negative listeners. Religiously conservative audiences, for instance, may not be able to listen with an open mind to a speech about homosexuality, and a predominantly homosexual audience might be incensed by a speech that proposes mandatory AIDS testing. This does not mean that controversial subjects are taboo. What it does mean is that a person who picks such a topic must be aware of the possibility of negative reactions, or must confront the issue in a way that will at least get the audience to give it a hearing. This adjustment takes careful audience analysis.

It also takes knowledge of speaking techniques that compensate for negative reactions. Some speakers use negative feedback to their advantage, as Barbara Bush did in her commencement address at Wellesley College in June of 1990. Mrs. Bush was aware that many members of the graduating class felt she was not an appropriate speaker because she was not a professional woman in her own right but had received her position in society only through her husband's political achievements. Rather than avoiding the issue, she confronted it directly. She spoke about her choice to concentrate on her family, thus diffusing the hostility.

Finally, **psychological noise** confronts both speakers and listeners. We sometimes find ourselves in situations where stress, frustration, or irritation causes us to send or receive messages ineffectively. Think about what happens when you are so angry that you "can't think straight." Or remember the time when you got such stage fright that you were unable to speak, or when you couldn't concentrate on listening to a speech because of some problem at home. In all these cases, psychological noise is getting in the way of effective communication.

The Setting

Communication does not occur in a vacuum; it always exists in some context, some **setting**. Where we are and who is with us affect the message we receive. Such factors as the size of the room, the color of the walls, the arrangement of the chairs, the lighting, the ventilation, and the size of the audience can all affect communication. Setting control—of the lighting, the sound, the room temperature—can especially determine whether a speech is effectively presented and received.

The occasion, or the context itself, is also significant. Just what is the purpose for the speech event? Both the speaker and the listener must understand the nature of the occasion—what it is that brings them together. To a great extent, this shapes the outcome or effect of the speech.

The setting combines with the other components of communication—the source, the code, perceptions and attitudes, the message, the channel, the receiver, feedback, and noise—to form a very complex process. Some public speakers assume that all they have to do is present material and the audience will automatically listen, but effective speakers realize that a speech often is dynamic and transactive.

Communication does not occur in a vacuum; it always exists in some context. Where we are and who is with us affect the message we receive.

Photo: Randall Reeder

Live communication is **dynamic** in the sense that it is continuous, ongoing. As the speaker presents the message to the audience, the feedback from listeners can be instantaneous. Suddenly, both speaker and listener are encoding and decoding messages at the same time. Just as the speaker is encoding and sending the speech, he or she is receiving and decoding feedback from the listeners; likewise, as the listeners receive the speaker's message, they encode and send their feedback. This simultaneous sending and receiving of messages represents the **communication transaction**.

Becoming a Better Speaker

If you're not accustomed to public speaking or you need to help someone improve his or her speaking efforts, these observations and suggestions might help:

- Most people should speak a bit louder than normal and use larger gestures than they originally feel comfortable with.

- Invest quite a bit of time in analyzing the audience. Be sure to tell that audience something it doesn't know.

- Avoid reading a speech with your eyes glued to the lectern. If you want to read to people, just remember your parents read to you to put you to sleep. Work from an outline and trust yourself.

- Move away from the lectern. Establishing rapport with the audience is vital.

- Spend five or six seconds looking at each person in the audience. Shorter times can make you look like a "scared rabbit."

- Pause instead of inflicting "ums" and "ahs" on the audience.

Source: *Communication Briefings*, as adapted from Karen Padley, writing in *Investor's Business Daily*.

Public communication is dynamic also in the sense that it is ever changing. In this age of information, what both speakers and listeners know is in continuous flux. We are constantly learning new information and adjusting our beliefs and attitudes. **Public speaking competency**, the ability to create and present appropriate and effective messages, is based on an understanding of the dynamic and transactional nature of communication. Successful communicators make a considerable effort to become skilled senders and receivers of messages. As you embark on your study of public speaking, remember that communicators throughout history have recognized that public speaking competency can be developed through careful attention to the details of speaking and listening. It is worth the effort to acquire the skills of an effective speaker: They can improve your academic work and aid you in social and job-related encounters.

Summary

This chapter investigated the historical roots and the basic components of public speaking. The major concepts discussed were:

♦ *Public speaking is the act of communication that takes place between one person and an audience.*

♦ *Skill in public speaking is important.*

♦ *Public communication depends upon skilled public listeners.*

♦ *No matter what your career choice, most college graduates enter occupations that require some form of speaking before groups.*

♦ *The study of public speaking has a rich tradition in the study of rhetoric.*

♦ *The history of public communication is the history of ideas and their expression by competent speakers living in the midst of important human events.*

♦ *Culture affects the way people use, present, and regard public speaking.*

♦ *The basic components of the public communication process are the source, the code, perceptions and attitudes, the message, the channel, the receiver, feedback, noise, and the setting.*

Key Terms

public speaking
rhetoric
eloquence
nationality
source
encoding
perceptions
message
channel
feedback
environmental noise
semantic problems
organizational confusion

participative communication
sophists
canons of rhetoric
culture
code
decoding
attitudes
symbolic
receiver
noise
physiological impairment
syntactical problems
cultural noise

❖ ❖ ❖ ❖   psychological noise   setting
            dynamic communication   communication transaction
            public speaking competency

Learn by Doing

1. Research a historical era of public speaking or the history of public speaking in a non-Western society (e.g., China or Japan) and prepare a report on the rhetoric of that country.

2. Research a specific type of rhetoric, such as the rhetoric of the women's movement, the rhetoric of the gay rights movement, or the rhetoric of sermons. Prepare a report on your findings.

3. Identify which type of noise is present in each of these public speaking situations:

    a. The people sitting behind you are talking so loudly that it is difficult for you to hear the speaker.

    b. The speaker uses numerous curses. You have been taught that intelligent people don't use profane language. You become angrier and angrier with the speaker and finally stop actively listening.

    c. In a lecture your theatre arts instructor uses terms such as "fly space," "wings," and "scrim," which you have never heard before. You cannot comprehend the major points of what she is saying.

    d. The speaker is supposed to be informing the audience about international trade restrictions. His native language is Japanese and he has difficulty forming grammatical sentences in English. You are having trouble interpreting his ideas.

    e. The speaker is explaining how to operate a new computer system. She describes the first operation, then the second, and then the third. She then says, "Oh, I forgot to tell you, between the first and second operation you should not turn off the machine." She begins to describe the fourth operation but then says, "Oh, also, before you start, be sure to use a new computer disk." She then jumps back to the fourth operation. By now, you are lost.

Endnotes

1. *Bruskin/Goldring Research Report*, Bruskin/Goldring Research, Inc., February, 1993, p. 4.

2. Kathleen Edgerton Kendall, "Do Real People Ever Give Speeches?" *Central States Speech Journal*, 25 (Fall 1974), pp. 233–235.

3. Ibid.

4. Lloyd E. Corder, "A Survey Report of Presentation Skills Training in *Fortune 500* Industrial Companies" (Unpublished report, Pittsburgh: University of Pittsburgh, 1989).

5. *Honeywell 1988 Corporate Communication Plan* (Minneapolis: Honeywell Corporation, 1988), p. 43.

6. Lee Iacocca with William Novak, *Iacocca* (New York: Bantam Books, 1984), p. 55.

7. Sharon Warren Walsh, "The Lucrative Business of Speaking," *The Washington Post* (March 14, 1988), pp. 1, 34.

8. Michael and Suzanne Osborn, "Alliance for a Better Public Voice" (Dayton, Ohio: National Issues Forum, 1991), pp. 14, 17.

9. James R. Andrews, *Essentials of Public Communication* (New York: Wiley, 1979), p. 34.

10. Bruce E. Gronbeck, Kathleen German, Douglas Ehninger, Alan H. Monroe, *Principles of Speech Communication* (New York: Longman, 1998), p. 41.

11. For a more detailed overview of the history of rhetorical theory, see Andrew Thomas Weaver, Gladys Louise Borchers, and Donald Kliese Smith, *The Teaching of Speech* (Englewood Cliffs, N.J.: Prentice-Hall, 1952), Chapter 2. See also Karl R. Wallace, ed., *History of Speech Education in America* (New York: Appleton-Century-Crofts, 1954). The history of public speaking is described in Lewis Copeland and Lawrence Lamm, eds., *The World's Great Speeches* (New York: Dover Publications, 1942).

12. Milt Thomas, "Cultural Self-Identification in the Basic Course" (Unpublished paper presented at the Central States Speech Association convention, Oklahoma City, 1994), p. 8. For a discussion of culture see: Roy Berko, Andrew Wolvin, and Darlyn Wolvin, *Communication: A Social and Career Focus*, 7th ed. (Boston: Houghton Mifflin, 1998), pp. 5–7.

13. Gerald Alred, "Teaching in Germany and the Rhetoric of Culture," *Journal of Business and Technical Communication* 11 (1997), p. 359.

14. Ulla Connor, *Contrastive Rhetoric: Cross-cultural Aspects of Second Language Writing* (New York: Cambridge University Press, 1996), p. 53.

15. Earl E. McDowell and Noriko Yotsuyanagi, "An Exploratory Study of Communication Apprehension, Willingness to Communicate, and Sense of Humor between College Students from the United States and Japan" (Unpublished paper, Educational Resources Information Center, 1996), p. 12.

16. Ibid., p. 13.

17. Gerry Philipsen, "Navajo World View and Cultural Patterns of Speech, A Case Study in Ethnorhetoric," *Speech Monographs*, 39.2 (1972), p. 135.

18. Ibid., p. 139.

19. Melbourne S. Cummings, "Teaching the Black Rhetoric Course" (Unpublished paper, Educational Resources Information Center, 1983), p. 7.

20. Ibid., p. 6.

21. Ibid., p. 7.

22. Based on research by H. G. Whittington, Jamesa P. Smith, Leonard Kriegel, Lillian Glass, and Hilary Lips as reported in Roy Berko, Andrew Wolvin, and Darlyn Wolvin, *Communication: A Social and Career Focus*, 7th ed. (Boston: Houghton Mifflin, 1998), p. 144.

23. Ibid.

24. Patrick Fanning and Mathew McKay, *Being a Man, Guide to the New Masculinity* (Oakland, Calif.: New Harbinger Publications, 1993), pp. 11–13.

25. Factors that cause communication difficulties are sometimes called interference. In this text they will be referred to as noise.

CHAPTER TWO

The Public Listener: A Perspective

Chapter Outline

❏ 2.1 The Importance of Public Listening

❏ 2.2 The Listening Process
   Reception
   Perception
   Attention
   The Assignment of Meaning
   Response
   Listening Influencers

❏ 2.3 The Purposes of Listening
   Discrimination Level
   Comprehension Level
   Therapeutic Level
   Critical Level
   Appreciation Level

❏ 2.4 Listening to Speeches

❏ 2.5 Improving Listening
   Techniques
   A Willingness to Listen

Learning Outcomes

After reading this chapter you should be able to:

- *Explain the difference between hearing and listening.*

- *Explain the listening process.*

- *Recognize what influences listening.*

- *Describe the levels of listening.*

- *Recognize how to listen to speeches.*

- *Understand the techniques for improving listening in the public speaking setting.*

❖ ❖ ❖ ❖

The process through which the listener receives, perceives, attends to, assigns meaning to, and responds to messages is complex. The listener must be actively involved throughout and work to overcome any barriers that may arise during the listening experience.

2.1 The Importance of Public Listening

The importance of listening has been well documented. In fact, listening may take up as much as 45 percent of our communication time.[1] Some studies show that listening is more critical to success in school than is either reading or academic aptitude.[2]

As one observer points out, educated people have an obligation to strive to become responsible listeners. Responsible here means responsive; instead of being passive we should treat listening as part of ongoing communication with the speaker. We make decisions about how to listen based on the nature of our relationship with the other person. In making those decisions, however, we need to take special care to listen to and appreciate points of view other than our own.[3]

In the process of public communication, this responsibility for listening is particularly significant. Communication will be successful only insofar as the listener remains an active participant throughout the speech.

2.2 The Listening Process

Many people assume that hearing and listening are the same. However, the two are not synonymous. **Hearing** is a biological activity that involves reception of a message through sensory channels. But hearing is only one part of listening. **Listening** also involves *influencers*: reception, perception, attention, the assignment of meaning, and response by the listener to the message that is presented.

The process of listening is illustrated in Figure 2.1. Since all the components of this process occur almost simultaneously, they are shown as overlapping. Throughout, each step in listening is affected by the listening influencers.

The Chinese character that translates as listening combines the symbols for ears, eyes, and heart.

Reception

The initial step in the listening process is the **reception** of the stimulus or message. This includes both the auditory, heard message and the visual, nonverbal message. The healthy human ear has the capacity to distinguish approximately 340,000 different tones. Obviously, proper care of the ears is important because auditory acuity enhances one's ability to listen efficiently. The National Institutes of Health estimates that approximately

Figure 2.1 The Listening Process

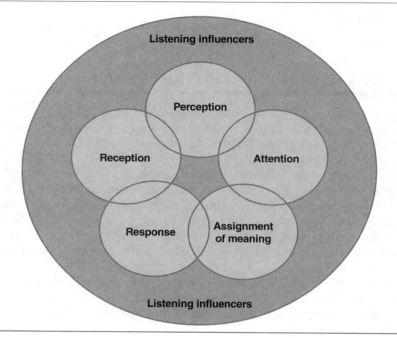

13 million Americans (almost 1 out of every 20 people) have some type of hearing impairment—ranging from hearing loss of tones to total deafness.[4] In order to keep these statistics from rising, people who work near loud machinery now are required to wear ear protectors. But the workplace is not the only source of potential danger. For example, individuals who expose themselves to loud music, especially by listening through earphones, also should be aware that they can damage their hearing mechanism. Indeed, the use of

Photo: Charles Kuo/ Daily Bruin

Attention represents the focus on a specific stimulus that is selected from all the stimuli we receive at any given moment.

earphones is considered to be the source of much of the ear damage suffered by Americans.[5]

In addition to using our ears, we also listen through our eyes. Barring physical defects, human eyes have the phenomenal capacity to discriminate 5 million images per second. Closely watching a speaker's facial expression, posture, and movement and noting his or her physical appearance provides us with important cues that may not be obvious merely by listening to the verbal part of the message. It has been estimated that about 90 percent of the total meaning of a message can emerge from nonverbal and visual cues.[6] Thus, sensitivity to these visual cues becomes a very important part of effective listening behavior.

Perception

As the stimulus or message is received, the listener's perceptions come into play. **Perception** is a screening process that filters the message according to the listener's background, experiences, mental and physical state, beliefs, attitudes, and values—in short, everything that makes up the listener's orientation to the world. Listeners cannot escape their perceptual filters. Studies on listening perception suggest that "the louder, the more relevant, the more novel the stimuli, the more likely they are to be perceived by the listener."[7] Good listeners, therefore, should recognize the influences of their own perceptions on what they hear and deal with these influences appropriately. For example, the listener who understands that, to many Americans, someone who speaks with a British accent sounds more authoritative may want to work harder to understand the content of such a person's public speech before drawing any conclusions about it.

Attention

Once the stimulus—the word and/or its visual cues—is received and sent through the perceptual filter, it finally reaches the listener's attention. **Attention** represents the focus on one stimulus which is selected from all the stimuli we receive at any given moment. At this point, all other stimuli recede in our consciousness so that we can concentrate on a specific word or visual symbol. Consider, for example, what happens when you are listening to a speech. Perhaps the person sitting next to you is wearing too much perfume, and perhaps the argument you had with a friend just before you arrived is still

---

Respect Attention Spans

Attention span—the sheer amount of time we willingly devote to an activity—varies with our personal interests, priorities, energy level, and time availability. A sensitive speaker introduced late in a seemingly endless program often elicits cheers of relief or respect when he voluntarily shreds his notes and bids his audience a good wish and a good night. Because the mind can absorb only what the seat can endure, most of us have a short tolerance for long-windedness. If all of us would respect this adage, none of us would ever endure the pain of verbal overkill.

Source: From *Tuning In: A Guide to Effective Listening* by Robert Maidment, © 1984, used by permission of the licenser, Pelican Publishing Company, Inc.

**A critical listener assesses the arguments and appeals in a message
and then decides whether to accept or to reject them.**

bothering you. In addition, the sound system is humming and you are worried because you left your car in a no-parking zone. Obviously, your attention is being pulled in several directions. But if the speech is well presented, with compelling information, you will focus on what is happening on the stage, and all the other factors will be relegated to the back of your consciousness.

The speaker, of course, is a major listening influencer. The **speaker's credibility** (the listener's perception of the speaker's trustworthiness, competence, and dynamism) can lead the listener to accept or to reject a message. If you feel you can't trust the speaker, you're not likely to trust his or her message. On the other hand, some listeners are so in awe of a particular speaker's outstanding credentials or reputation that they lose all objectivity in analyzing the message the speaker presents. The speaker's physical presentation, such as clothing and posture, can also have an instantaneous effect on whether or not you attend to the message.

Attention to a stimulus remains in an individual's short-term memory. The capacity of the short-term memory—our **attention span**—is about 60 seconds.[8] The ability of the listener to focus attention is therefore limited indeed. In fact, professional speakers have observed that their typical listeners cannot handle a speech that continues much beyond a 15-minute time frame. The reasons for this have not yet been traced, although some believe "it's entirely possible that our capacity for sustained attention and deliberate thought is being altered by television viewing."[9] Most of us who have been raised on television have come to expect a 7- to 10-minute viewing format, followed by a commercial break.

Paraphrasing—making a summary of the ideas you have just received—will provide you with a concise restatement of the speaker's message. It also will allow you to determine whether you understand the material or not. After all, if you cannot repeat or write down a summary of what was said, then you probably didn't receive the whole message or didn't understand it. Keep this in mind when you're in class listening to the instructor or any other speaker and taking notes. Instead of writing down direct quotes, try to mentally paraphrase the material. If you can't do it, that ought to be a clue that you should ask for clarification or make a note to read more about that particular material later on.

Human beings can think three to four times faster than the normal conversation rate of 125 to 150 words per minute.[10] And because we can receive messages much more quickly than a person can talk, we tend to tune in and out throughout a message. The mind can absorb only so much material. In addition, the brain operates much like a computer. It turns off, recycles itself, and turns back on in order to avoid information overload.[11] It's no wonder, then, that our attention fluctuates even when we're actively involved as listeners. Think back to the last class lecture or sermon you attended. Do you recall a slight gap in your listening at times? Were you conscious of the moment when your mind tuned out? This is a natural part of the listening process, but you must remember to make a conscious effort to tune back in so that you can concentrate on the message. When you turn off, the major danger is that you will begin to daydream rather than quickly turn back to the message. But by taking notes and forcing yourself to paraphrase you will avoid this pitfall.

Concentration on the message is an important key to effective listening. Developing the skills of concentration requires physical and mental effort. The listener must be thoroughly engaged in the communication and be able to focus his or her energies on the speech as it is presented. Concentrating on the delivery of a speech can be exhausting, but the reward of gaining the speaker's message is often well worth the effort.

The Assignment of Meaning

Once we have paid attention to the material a speaker has presented, the next step in the listening process is to assign meanings to the verbal and nonverbal stimuli. We are only now beginning to understand something about this cognitive structuring. Some researchers suggest that after we once receive a stimulus, we put it into some predetermined category.[12] Our ability to perform this process, the **assignment of meaning**, develops as we acquire our language system, which provides us with the mental categories for interpreting the messages we receive. For instance, our mental categories for the word *cheese* might include "food," "dairy product," "taste," and "nourishment"—all of which help us to relate the word *cheese* to the context in which it is used.

The categorical assignment of meaning that allows listeners to interpret a message is affected by the human cognitive process. This categorical context creates what psychologists have identified as **schema**—scripts for processing information. The cognitive process involves interpretation from all the schema that an individual develops throughout life, and it is these schema that provide the mental links for understanding and creating meaning from the stimuli that we receive.[13]

Research suggests that the two hemispheres of the human brain handle information differently and have different functions. The left hemisphere deals with verbal and numerical information in a linear form, providing an analytical function, while the right hemisphere specializes in processing shapes and images, performing a more spatial, intuitive function.[14] As researchers come to understand the implications of this division of function, we communicators probably will better understand why we respond as we do in assigning meanings to the messages we receive. This understanding could also allow us to become better listeners, because we may be able to learn to better use whichever part of the brain deals with particular materials presented in a speech.

A strategy useful to listeners in assigning meaning to messages is to differentiate factual statements (those based on observable phenomena or common acceptance) from opinions (inferences or judgments made by the speaker).[15] Speakers who have a strong, assertive style are likely to sound very authoritative and factual, but the message may be based more on their own opinions than on fact. The listener should be alert to such phrases as "In my opinion," "It seems to me," "I think," and "It would appear" as indicators that the content of the message is primarily based on the speaker's opinions. Likewise, it is helpful for the listener to be alert to the verbal obscurity of messages. Unclear terms and phrases and evasive language make interpretation difficult.

The assignment of meaning is a complex step in the listening process. Effective listeners are sensitive to how and why they are interpreting a message and use such self-monitoring to understand the influence of messages on their listening behavior.

Response

Once you, as a listener, have assigned meaning to a message, you continue your processing of the information with an internal or an external **response** (an intellectual or emotional reaction) to the message. In general, on a cognitive level, this response may be seen as a type of information storage; you recognize you have gained some idea by saying something like "Oh, I understand," either out loud or to yourself. In some cases this acquisition is below our level of awareness. In fact, some psychologists hypothesize that every stimulus we receive is stored somewhere in our brain, whether we recognize it or not.

How can you remember information you've heard? The authors of a study skills program for students recommend using the following techniques: (1) choose to remember, (2) visualize the material to remember, (3) associate the material with something familiar to assist in recalling it, and (4) practice with the material so that recalling it becomes easy.[16] For example, when you are introduced to a new idea during a speech, you must first decide that you want to remember that idea and get ready to remember it. You might then picture the idea in a particular context. Then try to tie the idea to something you are familiar with, such as finding a rhyme for a key word in the concept. Finally, repeat the idea several times or write it down. If you carry through with these techniques, the odds of your remembering the informa-tion increase greatly.

One response that can not only assist the listener in storing information into long-term memory but also provide meaningful feedback to the speaker is to ask questions. Asking questions provides listeners with the opportunity to ensure that the message they have received and interpreted is consistent with the original intent of the speaker. Questions offer the speaker a chance to clarify any points that seem confusing and demonstrate that listeners are in-deed involved in the communication transaction.

To be effective, however, questions must necessarily be relevant to the message the speaker has presented. Questions that are off the topic or beyond the scope of the speaker's message can disrupt the communication flow. Questions intended to increase the listener's understanding must be direct and to the point. Too frequently, listeners use the opportunity to ask ques-tions to take stands on issues and present their own messages rather than to probe for understanding of the speaker's intentions. This, of course, does lit-tle to help listeners comprehend the speaker's points. Question-and-answer sessions following speeches should concentrate on such requests as asking for clarification of the ideas presented or seeking more information, inquir-ing into the validity of sources the speaker refers to, or soliciting the speaker's in-depth views about ideas alluded to in the speech. Attention to feedback skills such as these is a critical part of being an effective listener. Good feed-back is appropriate to the speaker, the message, and the situation, and it should be clearly presented so that the speaker understands your feedback message.

Listening Influencers

In a public setting a listener may be influenced not only by the speaker but also by the other members of the audience, as illustrated in Figure 2.2. Research in listening has demonstrated that certain key influencers can facil-itate or deter the process at almost any point.[17]

Figure 2.2 Public Listening

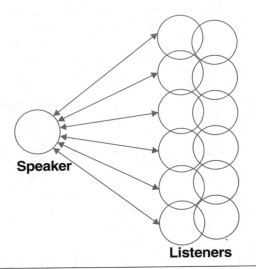

Speaker

Listeners

Another major influencer is the message itself. A critical factor in understanding oral messages is how well the message is structured. If the presentation is not clearly organized—if the arguments are not well ordered—it will be difficult for the listener to concentrate and stay tuned. Likewise, the tone and the treatment of the message can influence listening. If you don't agree with the point of view, or if the speaker is too strident or too ambivalent in the arguments presented, your listening comprehension will be affected. For example, speakers who make emotional appeals so strong that the audience is overwhelmed by the desperation of the predicament can turn listeners away from the message.

The communication channel, or means of delivery, also influences listening ability. Some people probably are more auditory and some are more visual in orientation, so channel preference can be a factor. The speaker who couples the message with some clear visual aids may assist listeners in comprehending the material.

Noise, any sort of interference in the communication channel, certainly diminishes the effectiveness of the listener. Static on the radio or distortions on the television screen can interrupt good listening. Noise in the environment also affects listeners. If the lighting is so poor that you can't see the speaker easily, or if the room temperature is too cold or too hot, you may have greater difficulty attending to the speaker's message.

Listeners are influenced not only by a vast array of external factors but also by internal variables, such as their physical state (general health, gender, age), experiences (background, life history, training, culture), attitudes (predispositions) and expectations, and memory. These internal factors are always with you and can enhance or detract from listening. A listener who feels ill, for example, will have difficulty focusing on the message. Some research illustrates that men and women listen differently, as do people of different ages.[18]

Life experiences likewise can be quite influential. People from different cultures have different ways of attending to each other in terms of eye contact, physical distance between speakers and listeners, and amount of patience afforded the speaker. Though there is little research on the effects of modeling on listening behavior, it appears safe to assume that we are influenced by how those around us listen. Good listeners among the teachers, parents, and other people with whom children come in contact on a regular basis can provide models for them to emulate as they build their listening skills.

The positive or negative attitude that one carries into a listening situation and the expectation one has for the listening experience is important. If you go to a speech convinced beforehand that it will be a waste of time, you probably will be unable to listen with comprehension. A person's attitude toward listening reflects his or her self-perception. Most of us have received very little praise or external reward for good listening, but we probably have heard lots of negative messages: "Sit down and listen" or "Keep quiet and listen" or "Why don't you ever listen to me?" These negative messages create a negative attitude about our own listening abilities. Most listeners who have received such negative messages expect to listen poorly, so they do.

Memory plays a significant role in listening. The listener must be willing and able to hold the message in short-term memory long enough to assign meaning to it. Sufficient auditory and visual memory is required to maintain this focus. As pointed out earlier, taking notes can serve as a useful aid to memory. It is also necessary for the listener to have the time—and to take the time—to listen with discrimination and comprehension in order to respond to the message.

2.3 The Purposes of Listening

We have seen that listeners may be influenced by a wide range of factors that can enhance or detract from the listening process. Reading specialists suggest that a person who establishes a clear goal before beginning to read some material will read more effectively.[19] The same principle applies to listeners.

We listen on a number of levels for a variety of purposes. Awareness of the purposes of listening sometimes aids a listener in selecting the listening techniques that best fit the desired outcome.[20]

Discrimination Level

At the **discrimination level**, we listen to distinguish or identify auditory and visual stimuli. Distinguishing the message stimuli is at the base of all listening we do, and experience and practice are our best strategies for improving discrimination. At first, we tend not to discern subtle shades of meaning and vocal nuances until we become accustomed to the communication style of a particular speaker. It takes some time to develop these skills. For example, during the first few class lectures, you may find yourself confused by your professor's way of speaking. Soon, however, you will probably find that there is a system to the way he or she organizes the lecture and stresses ideas, such as writing key terms on the chalkboard. Getting acquainted with a style of speaking helps you to listen more effectively.

Discrimination of both auditory and visual cues can enable listeners to be more sensitive perceivers of a message. Through discrimination we can come to understand differences in verbal sounds (dialects, pronunciation) and nonverbal behavior (gestures, facial expressions). We can then determine, for example, if a person is being sarcastic, evasive, or enthusiastic, realizing that the same set of words can be taken in a variety of ways. If we don't listen with discrimination to how something is said, we may miss the meaning of the message.

Comprehension Level

The objective of the **comprehension level** of listening is to recognize and retain information. Listening for comprehension is what you do most in college classes. Listening comprehension is a critical factor in the success or failure of college students. "Among the students who fail," one researcher commented, "deficient listening skills were a stronger factor than reading skills or academic aptitude."[21]

There are techniques that can enhance listening comprehension. One strategy is to concentrate on getting the main points of a message rather than remembering all of the supporting details. As you listen to a speaker discuss an idea, focus on the main point being made rather than on the elaboration and the details. When taking notes, it is wise to sort out the key points.

At the next class you attend, try this method for taking notes: Draw a vertical line down the middle of your paper from top to bottom, and put the main points in the left-hand column and the supporting ideas in the right-hand column. By abbreviating commonly used words, you save time in writing, which allows for more listening time. Many note takers like to provide examples to help clarify material. You will have to determine for yourself how much detail you will need in your notes. (See Figure 2.3.)

Figure 2.3 Note Taking Format

Lstng	Hearing-biological process
Lstng Process	Lstng—active processing of info heard
	Reception—get message
	Perception—screeen info
	Attention
	focus on ideas
	anticipate next point
	paraphrase—restate in own words
	get ready to lstn rapidly
	Assignment of meaning— categorize symbols
	Response-info storage
	choose to remember
	visualize what is to be remembered
	associate info
	practice material
	Listening Influencers
	speaker
	message
	channel
	noise
	internal variables
	attitude
	memory
	time
Levels of Lstng	Discrimination
	Comprehension

You also may need to develop a number of memory techniques in order to recall the main points at a later time. You can forget as much as 50 percent of any given information after the first day unless you take notes and review them.[22] Because it is so easy to forget information, good academic listeners

❖ ❖ ❖ ❖

Profile: James Scruggs, Lawyer, Legal Aid of Lynchburg, Virginia

Television, theater, and movies have given us an image of trial lawyers as great orators, moving judges and juries with their impassioned pleas for justice and mercy. History has also helped to fuel this image. Lawyers such as Daniel Webster and Clarence Darrow are noted for their powers of speech and their eloquence. Although the ability to speak persuasively is an important skill in a courtroom, a trial lawyer's most important skill is that of listening. Indeed, attorneys probably win more cases through the effective use of listening than by the impassioned closing arguments that we see on television shows.

Of course, direct listening is important. Attorneys listen to witnesses for inconsistencies in testimony, admissions of guilt, etc., and they listen to judges' questions to determine what elements of the case have most impressed them. But a lot of courtroom listening is in fact directed toward analyzing what is *not* said.

In normal conversation people often rely on assumption and inference. For example, someone may say, "My car was hit and I broke my arm." A typical response may be, "That must have been very painful," or "Does it still hurt?" We naturally presume that a car accident victim has experienced pain and suffering. But in a lawsuit, there is little presumption.

Each element of a claim must be proven. A plaintiff cannot recover money for pain and suffering simply because she has evidence that her car was hit and she broke her arm. A skilled attorney listens for what a witness doesn't say—for the elements of a case that are not proven—and lawsuits have been lost because a less-skilled attorney relied on presumption and inference and did not prove his case.

Conversely, skilled attorneys often use our natural tendency to rely on presumptions to protect their clients and themselves, which is one of the reasons attorneys are accused of "talking double-talk." For example, one of Bill Clinton's responses to allegations that he used marijuana was that he didn't break any of the laws of this country. The average listener may consider this a denial of the allegation. However, this statement does not deny drug use; it denies breaking any of the laws of the United States. It really does not even address marijuana laws. If a witness in a trial made this kind of statement, a good trial lawyer would immediately hear what was not said, and proceed to question the witness as to where he was living when he allegedly used marijuana, and what were the laws of that country regarding marijuana.

The ability to speak persuasively is certainly a useful tool in the courtroom. However, a good trial attorney must be able to listen carefully, to hear not only what is said, but what is not said, and to distinguish between statements of fact and statements that are conclusory and require the listener to make inferences to give them meaning.

have found that they retain ideas best if they review the information immediately after it is presented and then go over it daily rather than waiting to do a cram review session on the night before an examination.

Therapeutic Level

The **therapeutic level** of listening requires the listener to act as a sounding board so that a speaker can talk through a problem and, ideally, reach his or her own solution. This is important for those in such fields as psychology, social work, speech therapy, and counseling, and utilizes many of the techniques of a counseling interview. Therapeutic listening is not restricted to professional counselors, however; it also applies to public speaking.

> Listeners can't recall more than three compelling messages and remember best the first and last things they hear, research shows. *Moral*: Stick to three points and put your important points first and last and bury the least important point in the middle.
>
> ---
>
> Source: *Communication Briefings*, as adapted from *pr reporter*, Box 600, Exeter, NH 03833.

At times listeners may assume the role of sounding board for public speakers. Speakers often tell stories, and these personal anecdotes may reveal something about the speakers' emotions. Knowing this could be useful to a listener trying to understand the point a speaker is developing or to identify the speaker's perspective. Identification is an imperative of public speaking: "You persuade a person only insofar as you can talk his [her] language by speech, gesture, tonality, order, image, attitude, idea, *identifying* your ways with his [hers]."[23]

Therapeutic listening requires a willingness to suspend judgment and to listen with empathy—to understand where the speaker is coming from. A speaker who talks about his wartime service, for instance, might be telling "war stories" essentially to "purge" himself of the experience or to rationalize some of his behaviors while in uniform and thus needs a supportive, understanding audience.

Critical Level

At the **critical level** of listening, we evaluate the message that has been received. A critical listener assesses the arguments and the appeals in a message and then decides either to accept or to reject them. Ideally, this analysis should occur only after you have recognized, understood, and reflected on the entire message that the speaker has presented.

An understanding of both the tools of persuasion and the process of logic and reasoning will enable critical listeners to analyze the messages they receive. It is helpful to recognize the three components of a persuasive message—*ethos* (speaker credibility), *logos* (logical arguments and evidence), and *pathos* (psychological appeals—and how those three elements are used by the speaker to get you, the listener, to respond to the point of the message.[24]

To make an assessment of the persuasiveness of the speaker, you should consider what impact the speaker himself/herself is having on you. Is the speaker's reputation an influence on the presentation? Is the oral and physical presentation so positive or so negative that you are not responding to the message itself? And how is the speaker motivating you? What psychological appeals are being used to get you to respond? And is the argument acceptable? Is it based on solid evidence? Are you being manipulated by information that is not valid?

The critical listener analyzes information to assess the merits or demerits of a particular message. Campaign speeches, radio and television news reporting and commentary, and persuasive briefings are some examples of public speaking that require critical content analysis on the part of the listener.

Photo: Courtesy of University of Missouri —Kansas City, Communication Studies Department

Appreciation Level

At the **appreciation level**, we listen for enjoyment or for the sensory stimulation a message gives us. Listeners can appreciate a speaker's style, vocal tone, humor, approach to the audience, or any of the other elements in public communication—even the setting itself. A public speaker presenting an evening of poetry or describing a visit to a beautiful vacation spot may inspire appreciative listening. Appreciation is a highly individual matter—there are no rules on how to go about it. Some people believe that the more knowledge you have about a particular subject, the more you can appreciate it. Others feel that the more you know, the more critical you become, thus losing your ability to appreciate any speech on the subject that falls short of the very best. Public listening is appreciative when you have a pleasurable experience as a participant in the communication process.

2.4 Listening to Speeches

As a member of an audience, you are not the only one receiving the message and not the only one for whom the message is intended. As a result, your listening experience can be influenced by the speaker's efforts to target the audience as a group and by the responses of the various listeners within that group. Though in most public communication settings you will not have the opportunity to give direct verbal feedback throughout the speech, you will be sending nonverbal cues to the speaker through your attentive posture and facial expression. And you may be given the opportunity to ask questions or otherwise respond following the presentation.

Besides giving indirect feedback to the speaker, the public listener may be asked to make critical judgments about the speech and the speaker following the presentation. In public speaking classes, for instance, students will often be asked to comment on what they feel is effective and what might be improved in a speaker's presentation. Likewise, after presidential debates and speeches by diplomats and other politicians, listeners sometimes offer their views on the speaker's effectiveness. Some useful guidelines for evaluating speeches include:

1. *Did the speaker have a worthwhile purpose?*
2. *Has the speaker made an attempt to be objective and fair to himself or herself, to the audience, and to the subject?*
3. *Did the speaker know the subject?*
4. *Had the speaker analyzed the audience?*
5. *Was the speech structurally sound?*
6. *Did the speaker utilize effective language?*
7. *Did the speaker make use of factors of attention and interest in both the content and the delivery of the speech?*
8. *Did the speaker's supporting materials meet the tests of evidence?*
9. *How effectively did the speaker make use of the visual aspects of delivery?*
10. *How effectively did the speaker use his or her voice?*
11. *Was the speaker a credible spokesperson on the subject?*
12. *What was the total impression left by the speech?*

2.5 Improving Listening

You can do a great deal to improve your ability to listen. Improving listening skills starts with understanding the process so that you can monitor your own listening behavior at any given point. Taking the next step toward being a better listener may require you to break old habits and put new strategies in their place—and then to practice these new skills until they feel comfortable to you.

Techniques

These suggestions will help listeners develop greater skill as participants in communication.

1. *Recognize that both the sender and the receiver share the responsibility for effective communication.* As a receiver, you should ask questions and provide feedback if you cannot understand the speaker's point. If possible, restate the major ideas so that the speaker can check to be sure you have accurately grasped the meaning.

2. *Suspend judgments.* One of the greatest barriers to human communication is our tendency to form instant judgments about almost everything we encounter. As listeners, we are prone to making premature assessments of speakers even before comprehending their message. Statements such as "I don't like his

❖ ❖ ❖ ❖

Try to guess what a speaker's next word or point will be. *Reason*: You'll become a better listener because doing so will keep your mind from drifting.

Source: *Communication Briefings,* as adapted from *The Complete Guide to Performance Appraisal,* by Dick Grote, AMACOM, 1601 Broadway, New York, NY 10019.

voice," "This is a boring lecture," or "I disagree with her point" all set up barriers to effective listening. The good listener works to set aside these judgments and to listen for the message.

3. *Be a patient listener.* Avoid interrupting or tuning out while the speaker is communicating the message. We often find ourselves beginning to respond before we have completely understood what's being said. Think about how difficult it is to assemble an unfamiliar product until you have thoroughly comprehended the instructions. Or remember the times when you filled out a form only to realize later on that you had written your name when the directions said to print and that you had put your first name down when the last name should have come first. Patience in listening will help you avoid having to go back over messages you missed the first time around or didn't understand because you didn't let the whole message come through.

4. *Carefully note your emotional responses to words.* Some words can bring about instant reactions. **Inciting words** are words that trigger strong feelings within us, either positive or negative. How do you react to the words *child beater, rapist,* and *income tax?* Words like these often send us off on tangents, cause daydreaming, or break our concentration. You should be aware that we can be led astray through our emotional responses. There is no easy way to prevent yourself from reacting to inciting words. However, by monitoring your body you might catch yourself physically pulling in or daydreaming, or you might feel yourself flushing as you become upset.

5. *Be aware that your posture affects your listening.* When you listen to an exciting lecture, how do you sit? Usually you lean slightly forward, feet on the floor, and look directly at the presenter. On the other hand, if you slump down and stare out the window, it's very unlikely that you're actively participating in the communication act. What happens to you when you curl up in a comfortable chair, turn on soft music, and try to read? Most likely, instead of reading you fall asleep or do a lot of daydreaming.

Have you ever left a classroom feeling totally exhausted? It may well be that you were concentrating so hard that you became physically tired. After all, good listening is hard work. An effective listener learns when it is necessary to listen in a totally active way and when it is possible to relax. Consider this analogy: When you're driving a car with an automatic transmission, the car shifts gears when it needs more or less power. Unfortunately, people don't have automatic transmissions. We have to shift gears for ourselves. When you need to concentrate, you shift into

❖ ❖ ❖ ❖

your version of first gear (feet on the floor, posture erect, looking directly at the speaker in order to pick up any necessary nonverbal clues). Once you feel that you understand the point that's being made (a test for this would be the ability to paraphrase what has been said), then a shift of posture to a more comfortable position may be in order. When a new subject arises—or when you hear transitional words or phrases such as "therefore" or "in summary"—then you shift back into your active listening position.

6. *Make a conscious effort to listen*. If it is important for you to listen carefully to a message, then you must tune in to that message. As discussed earlier, hearing and listening are not synonymous. Listening requires a concerted effort on your part to receive, perceive, attend to, assign meaning to, and respond to the message. This does not happen automatically. If you are going to take notes, take out the paper and a writing instrument. If you know you are easily distracted, move away from the window or from friends who might prevent you from concentrating.

7. *Control distractions*. All of us are surrounded by noise. Sometimes the sound of other audience members talking, or even the hum of an air conditioner, can interfere with efficient listening. If the message is important to you, you should try to adjust the interference or control it. If possible, move to a different seat or ask someone to please be quiet. There is little point to being a participant in communication if you can't hear or see the speaker.

8. *Concentrate*. Focus your attention energy on the message. An effective speaker will provide listeners with verbal and nonverbal cues to assist concentration. You should recognize **transitions** (words indicating a change of idea or topic, such as "therefore," "another idea is," "finally"); **forecasts of ideas** (statements that indicate a series of ideas will follow, such as "there are three ideas," "the next point is"); and **internal summaries** (restatements of ideas that have just been explained, such as "and so we have seen that"). All these are vehicles for furthering your grasp of the major points that the speaker is presenting. The vocal dynamics, or **paralanguage**—the rate, volume, and pitch of speech and the length of pauses—used by the speaker can also help you understand the points being developed. By stressing words, pausing before an idea, or increasing the volume of a phrase, the speaker is telling you that something is important, unusual, or significant.

   The speaker's physical movements can carry meaning that might reinforce or even contradict the verbal message. Be aware of a speaker's use of forceful gesture or enumeration of ideas with the pointing finger. We often have to listen with our eyes as well as our ears in order to pick up all the cues that will help us understand the real message. It is important to look beyond the words themselves for the full intent of the message.

A Willingness to Listen

Once the listener develops a clear understanding of the complexities of the listening process, recognizes how she or he is functioning within that process, and builds some new skills to perform more effectively in listening, it still requires considerable commitment to be an effective listener. The good public receiver is one who is willing to listen.

Unfortunately, listening has been the most underrated of the communication modes. Many people have come to perceive listening as a passive act, assuming that the speaker can and should bear almost the total responsibility for the outcome of the communication. This, of course, is not true. The key to effective listening is caring to be a good listener—learning the skills to be effective, practicing these skills, and putting them into effect.

Summary

Listening is an important part of the communication process. This chapter developed these points about effective listening:

- *A great deal of our communication time is devoted to listening.*
- *Hearing is a biological process that involves the reception of a message through sensory channels; it may be affected by all of our senses.*
- *Listening is the active processing of the information we receive.*
- *Listening involves reception, perception, attention, the assignment of meaning, and response by the listener to the message that has been presented.*
- *Auditory acuity enhances an individual's ability to listen efficiently.*
- *Listeners use the visual system as well as the hearing mechanism.*
- *Attention represents the focus on a specific stimulus selected from all the stimuli we receive at any given moment.*
- *Making a summary of the ideas presented, or paraphrasing, can be a helpful technique for sharpening concentration.*
- *Both the interest level and the difficulty of the message affect our listening concentration.*
- *Studies indicate that we can comprehend at a much faster rate than people normally speak.*
- *Putting a stimulus into some predetermined category enables a listener to assign meaning to a message.*
- *Schema are scripts for processing information.*
- *The two hemispheres of the human brain process information differently.*
- *Once we have assigned meaning to a message, we continue the listening process with an internal or an external response (feedback) to that message.*
- *Memory capacity can be increased by choosing to remember, visualizing what is to be remembered, associating the information with something familiar, and practicing with the material.*
- *Listening influencers include the speaker, the message, the channel, noise, internal variables, attitude, memory, and time.*

- ◆ *The effective listener receives, perceives, attends to, assigns meaning to, and responds to messages while being influenced by a wide range of factors that enhance or detract from the process at any given time.*

- ◆ *There are five levels at which we listen: the discrimination level, the comprehension level, the therapeutic level, the critical level, and the appreciation level.*

- ◆ *Inciting words can interrupt good listening.*

- ◆ *Listening to speeches requires an understanding of your own response to the public communication and your adaptation of that response to the communication purpose.*

Key Terms

hearing	listening
reception	perception
attention	speaker's credibility
paraphrasing	attention span
schema	assignment of meaning
speaker's credibility	response
comprehension level	discrimination level
critical level	therapeutic level
inciting words	appreciation level
forecasts of ideas	transitions
paralanguage	internal summaries

Learn by Doing

1. Contrast hearing and listening. Draw an analogy between listening and reading.

2. Analyzing your own listening. Name one listening behavior that you have that does not match the characteristics of a good listener as described in this chapter. Consider how you could change this behavior so that you can be more effective as a listener.

3. Now that you are aware of some of the principles of effective listening, put them into practice. At the next speech or class lecture you attend, sit up, concentrate on what the speaker is saying, and focus all of your attention energy on comprehending the material. Work out strategies to provide internal summaries and paraphrases to assist you in concentrating and comprehending. After the session is over, analyze your listening behavior and determine what else you can do to improve your listening comprehension.

4. Make a list of terms that stimulate a strong emotional response in you. Go back and review those terms. Why do you think they are inciting for you? If time is available your instructor will divide the class into groups of four to six students. Discuss your

terms and what implications they have for your habits of communication.

5. Attend a speech presentation and listen on an appreciative or on a therapeutic level to the speaker's style and use of stories. What does the speaker do to enhance your appreciative or therapeutic response to the presentation?

Endnotes

1. Paul Tory Rankin, "Listening Ability: Its Importance, Measurement, and Development," *Chicago School Journal*, 12 (January 1930), pp. 177–179. Other studies support Rankin's findings: Donald E. Bird, "Teaching Listening Comprehension," *Journal of Communication*, 3 (November 1953), pp. 127–130; Lila R. Breiter, "Research in Listening and Its Importance to Literature," M.A. thesis, Brooklyn College, 1957; and Elyse K. Werner, "A Study of Communication Time," M.A. thesis, University of Maryland, 1975.

2. Margaret Conaway, "Listening: Learning Tool and Retention Agent," in A. S. Algier and K. W. Algier, eds., *Improving Reading and Study Skills* (San Francisco: Jossey-Bass, 1982), pp. 51–63. For a comprehensive review of information on listening, see the 1990 issue of the *Journal of the International Listening Association*.

3. William F. Eadie, "Hearing What We Ought to Hear," *Journal of the International Listening Association*, 4 (1990), p. 4.

4. "Hearing Loss: Ways to Avoid, New Ways to Treat," *U.S. News & World Report*, October 18, 1982, pp. 85–86.

5. Ibid.

6. Albert Mehrabian, *Silent Messages* (Belmont, Calif.: Wadsworth, 1971), p. 41.

7. Larry L. Barker, *Listening Behavior* (Englewood Cliffs, N.J.: Prentice-Hall, 1971), p. 31.

8. D. A. Norman, "Memory While Shadowing," *Quarterly Journal of Experimental Psychology*, 21 (February 1969), pp. 85–93.

9. Dorothy Singer and Jerome Singer, "Is Human Imagination Going Down the Tube?" *Chronicle of Higher Education*, April 29, 1979, p. 56.

10. Ralph G. Nichols and Leonard A. Stevens, *Are You Listening?* (New York: McGraw-Hill, 1957), p. 107.

11. Norbert Wiener, *Cybernetics* (Cambridge, Mass.: M.I.T. Press, 1961), and *The Human Use of Human Beings* (Garden City, N.Y.: Doubleday, 1964).

12. See Carl H. Weaver, *Human Listening* (Indianapolis: Bobbs-Merrill, 1972), pp. 42–59.

13. Jack C. Richard, "Listening Comprehension: Approach, Design, Procedure," *Tesol Quarterly*, 17 (June 1983), pp. 219–240.

14. See Sally P. Springer and George Deutsch, *Left Brain, Right Brain* (San Francisco: W. H. Freeman, 1981).

15. William V. Haney, *Communication Patterns and Incidents* (Homewood, Ill.: Richard D. Irwin, 1960).

16. *Harvard Milton College Study Skills Program Level HI* (Reston, Va.: National Association of Secondary School Principals, 1983).

17. Andrew D. Wolvin and Carolyn Gwynn Coakley, *Listening*, 5th ed. (Dubuque, Iowa: William C. Brown, 1996). Chapter 3 includes an analysis of the major variables that affect the listening process.

18. Ibid.

19. Ivan Quandt, *Self-Concept and Reading* (Newark, Del.: International Reading Association, n.d.), p. 31.

20. See Wolvin and Coakley, *Listening*, Part 2, for a detailed description of this listening taxonomy.

21. Conaway, p. 57.

22. H. F. Spitzer, "Studies in Retention," *Journal of Experimental Psychology*, 30 (1939), pp. 641–656.

23. Kenneth Burke, *A Rhetoric of Motives* (New York: World Publishing Company, 1962), p. 579.

24. For a discussion of ethos, logos and pathos see section 13.3 in this text.

CHAPTER THREE

The Responsible Public Communicator

Chapter Outline

❑ 3.1 Freedom of Expression

❑ 3.2 Reaching Conclusions

   Critical Thinking

   Theological Reasoning

   Philosophical Thought

   Conflicts Between Systems for Reaching Conclusions

❑ 3.3 Ethics

   Ethics and Society

   Ethics and You

   A Code of Ethics

   Differing Ethical Views

   The Ethical Responsibilities of a Public Speaker

      Plagiarism

      Fabrication

   The Ethical Responsibilities of a Public Listener

Learning Outcomes

After reading this chapter you should be able to:

- *Define freedom of expression and explain how it relates to the public forum.*

- *Explain how people reach conclusions through critical thinking, theological reasoning, and philosophical thought.*

- *Explain the role of evidence in critical thinking.*

- *Define ethics and explain the role of ethics in our society.*

- *Contrast differing ethical views.*

- *Explain the role of ethics in public speaking and listening.*

- *Be aware of the unethical nature of plagiarism and fabrication.*

Where do you stand on prayer in schools, animal rights, the environment, abortion, homosexual rights, racial intolerance, smoking in public places? Do you feel you have the right to speak out about it? Would you protest if a speaker whose views you opposed was scheduled to speak on your campus? Would you join a public march to get attention for your causes?

During the Vietnam conflict of the 60s and 70s there was prolonged civic unrest. When in 1970 four students were shot and killed by the National Guard during its efforts to quell a peace demonstration at Kent State University, Americans were divided over the extent to which people should be allowed freedom of expression. In 1991 during Operation Desert Storm, peace activists protested the United Nation's war actions against Iraq's invasion of Kuwait. In 1997 intervention in the Bosnian War brought protesters forth. How far can or should people be allowed to go in order to express their ideas?

3.1 Freedom of Expression

The legal guarantee of **freedom of expression**—the right to present one's views in a public forum—extends not only to protest speeches but also to speeches by hatemongers. It protects members of the audience who harass

The Supreme Court has determined that some speech has no value under the First Amendment.

invited speakers, and it protects speakers who use language that listeners might find offensive. Scholars, students, the national press, and the courts continue to face the question of what is really meant by freedom of expression, often in the highly charged, emotional context of recent events.

Many universities, often considered to be the last bastions of open speech, have or are developing policies on freedom of expression. These are important to public speakers, as they often set the guidelines for what can and cannot be said in university settings, including individual classrooms.

One university's policy, fairly representative of those of many public institutions, states, "This policy statement . . . recognizes the particular importance that the university, as an institution of learning, places on the free exchange of ideas."[1] It goes on to indicate the university's commitment to open, vigorous debate and speech. It places each member of the campus community on notice of his or her obligation to promote free expression and prohibits interference with such expression. It further encourages the members of the campus community to "consider the hurt which may result from the use of [discriminatory] slurs or epithets."[2] The policy sets forth guidelines for the protection of free speech in areas of campus designated as "public forums." It also acknowledges the right to dissent.[3]

Policies of this nature are important to public speakers. The fact that the First Amendment to the U.S. Constitution protects speech seems clear; however, speech is such a broad concept that the Constitution's implications are subject to an array of interpretations. The Supreme Court has determined that some speech has no value under the First Amendment. Categories of speech excluded from protection include defamation, invasion of privacy, fraudulent misrepresentation, obscenity, advocacy of imminent lawless behavior, and fighting words.[4]

First Amendment advocates contend that it is impossible to know specifically what the original intent was of any of the items in the Constitution or the Bill of Rights.[5] They believe that concepts change with time and that a document has to be interpreted according to the times. Since the framers of the Constitution were white male Protestant landowners, and they represented similar people, what they wrote is not necessarily applicable today, given the dramatic changes our nation has undergone in terms of expanded voting rights and representation. What was "politically correct" in the late 1700s may not pertain to today. The disenfranchised, such as urban African Americans and Mexican Americans, have seized new powers. They want to be heard and to demonstrate their power, as was evidenced during the Los Angeles riots in 1992.[6] These conditions were not present and did not have to be considered by our nation's forefathers.

As a public communicator you will constantly be making judgments concerning what you communicate, to whom you communicate, and how you listen to speakers. You will make decisions about who has the right to speak, about what, and under what conditions. You will, as both a speaker and a listener, be continually challenged to think, to reason to conclusions, and to act on those conclusions. Rhetoric itself is neither moral nor immoral. Public speaking itself is neither good nor bad. What we can make judgments about, however, is what people do with their communication skills as speakers and as listeners.

3.2 Reaching Conclusions

Because of their differing backgrounds and experiences, people process information differently; therefore, we reach conclusions and solve problems in a wide variety of ways. To be an effective public speaker, you must understand how you tend to reach conclusions and present your ideas. In addition, you might want to consider whether the way in which you develop your ideas, as well as the process you use to listen to others' ideas, needs some evaluation. You should recognize that other people may be using a different means of developing their message to you and of listening to your message. This section explores the different ways people reason and reach conclusions.

Critical Thinking

Some people reach conclusions through the process of **critical thinking**, reasonable, reflective thinking that is focused on deciding what to believe and do.[7] Proponents of critical thinking emphasize that it is essential for competent problem solving, clear understanding, and efficient processing of information, and as a tool to evaluate information received.

Critical thinking can be likened to the legal process in which the presentation of evidence substantiates claims and allegations. **Evidence** in critical thinking is all the means by which any alleged matter of facts is established or disproved. It includes testimony, records, documents, and objects that assist in building a logical case. The purpose of this information is not to decorate but to prove. A vast amount of information (quotes, for example) doesn't in and of itself prove that the information is either valid or leads to a particular conclusion. The relevant issue is whether the information is valid, is presented in a reliable way, and helps develop the specific contention.

Because of different backgrounds and experiences, people process information differently; therefore, we reach conclusions and solve problems in a wide variety of ways.

There are some common elements of critical thinking that communicators should incorporate into the sending and receiving of messages. Some may sound theoretical, but together they form a practical basis for applying the principles of critical thinking:[8]

1. *Seek a clear statement of the thesis or questions.*

2. *Seek reasons.*

3. *Try to be well informed on the topic or issue.*

4. *Use and mention credible sources.*

5. *Take into account the total situation.*

6. *Try to remain relevant to the main point.*

7. *Keep in mind the original or basic concern, issue, or topic.*

8. *Look for alternatives.*

9. *Be open minded.*

10. *Take a position (or change a position) when the evidence and reasons are sufficient to do so.*

11. *Seek as much precision as the subject permits.*

12. *Deal in an orderly manner with the parts of a complex whole.*

13. *Be sensitive to the feelings, knowledge, and degree of sophistication of others.*

14. *Be aware of other speakers' attempts to manipulate you with the use of doublespeak, false facts, partial information, biased stands, and emotional appeals disguised as logical ideas.*

Applying critical thinking to information you receive helps you diagnose the information (identify how reasonable it is in terms of personal experience, expert opinion, and factuality) and evaluate the information (determine how appropriate it is to the goal you want to attain or concept you want to understand). Critical thinking also enables you to implement a plan or idea because it gives you a clear sense of how and why the plan or idea was derived. Critical thinking, however, is only one way in which individuals reach conclusions.

Theological Reasoning

Some individuals claim that one should reach conclusions by acknowledging "the belief in the existence of a supreme personal being as the necessary foundation of the entire scheme of thought."[9] Public speakers and listeners who use **theological reasoning** determine whether an action is right or wrong by relying on a rule, a law, or the outcome of a moral debate that presupposes the existence of a prime mover, such as God, a natural force, or some other supernatural instigator.[10]

Most of the world's established religions have a tradition of revelation that usually is incorporated into sacred scriptures such as the Old and New Testaments, the Torah, and the Koran. Believers of these revelations turn to them as the basis for a theological defense of a particular argument. For example, a speech based on a theologically reasoned stand against the use of birth-control devices might characterize the procreative nature of the sexual act as God-given. Following this reasoning, any form of contraception would be wrong because it inhibits procreation.

Profile: Howard Stecker, Rabbi

A congregation member at the Jewish Community Center of West Hempstead in West Hempstead, New York, never knows what to expect when Rabbi Howard Stecker steps up to the pulpit for his weekly sermon. It might be a song by Simon and Garfunkel or possibly a story about one of his escapades at the Jewish Theological Seminary, where he received his training. What is certain though, is that week after week, Rabbi Stecker provides his congregation with an engaging, thought provoking, and entertaining sermon.

The preparation that goes into each sermon varies from week to week. Sometimes Rabbi Stecker reads the Torah portion to see what jumps out at him and relates it to a contemporary event, while other times he works in reverse by going back to the text with a pressing issue of the day. Unvarying, though, is Rabbi Stecker's attempt to "connect people to religious teaching and religious life." He works to ensure that the material is not remote and that it applies to people's lives. Yet Rabbi Stecker's strength as a speaker lies in more than the substance of his sermons; his strength comes from his dynamic style as well.

Because he never speaks from more than an outline, Rabbi Stecker is able to live in the moment and formulate new thoughts as they arise. This is critical because it frees him to gauge the congregation and make decisions about whether he should expand on a point that the congregation is connecting with. He is able to connect with the congregation often because he only speaks about subjects that have spiritual resonance for him and that he finds inherently compelling. But more than anything, Rabbi Stecker makes connections through his use of humor.

"I am consistently engaged by the Rabbi's sermons because of the way that he injects humor," says Kerry Weintraub, a congregation member at the Jewish Community Center of West Hempstead. "It draws me in and allows me to relate to what he is saying."

Rabbi Stecker adds that he "uses humor as a point of entry to connect people to a subject that might be dry. It is a way of bringing the Torah to life."

Even with a great sense of humor, not everyone finds it easy to address the same audience week after week. Rabbi Stecker approaches this challenge with a positive attitude and sees the advantages of speaking to the same people every Saturday. "At a certain point," he says, "having the same people there becomes an asset because people begin to get a sense of who you are. You are no longer just a conveyer of words but a real person sharing a part of yourself. Your message becomes cumulative and you have the opportunity to build on things that you have said earlier."

"And remember," he adds as a bit of advice, "when you speak, the audience has only one chance to hear the message. The only way that the people are getting the information is through you."

Philosophical Thought

There are those who have reservations about using a formal system of reason as the principal guide to life. "Those who express such reservations," explains one source, "would point to the positive value of certain levels of human existence that lie beyond the province of conceptual analysis and the practical uses of intelligence altogether, and yet that should also be given their due weight in an adequate philosophy of life."[11] This group of thinkers makes use of **philosophical thought**. As public speakers and listeners, they would, of course, reach conclusions in yet another way.

Some philosophers present alternative ways of thinking about life that are similar to those espoused by some Eastern religions, most notably Hinduism and Buddhism, that are found in countries such as India, China, and Japan. These traditions have always stressed certain insights or "modes of awareness" not normally found in the dominant religious traditions of the West—including, for example, transcendentalism, metaphysical speculation, intuition, and the transmigration of souls. The enlightenment sought by such Eastern sages as the Buddha or Lao-tse was the redemption of the individual, a redemption that was not believed attainable through solely intellectual and logical means. Over the last few decades, more people in the West have become interested in systems of thought originating in the East. Nevertheless, listening to a speaker who reaches conclusions primarily by nonintellectual means can be a frustrating experience for someone who is used to critical thinking or theological reasoning.

Conflicts Between Systems for Reaching Conclusions

Which reasoning system or systems do you use? How do you react to the type of reasoning used by others? It is important to note that each individual's reasoning process is probably not so neatly categorized as the previous discussion might imply. We often approach different problems in different ways. This makes it difficult sometimes for you not only to know exactly how you came to a conclusion but also to follow someone else's line of reasoning.

If we fail to recognize that not all people use the same type of reasoning, conflicts and misunderstandings can result. Let's say that, following a speech you've attended, you become involved in a disagreement concerning the validity of what the speaker has said. Did you stop to consider that you and the speaker might have different but equally defensible ideas about what constitutes valid evidence? Efforts to change the opinion of a devout religious believer by use of scientific proof may be futile, for example. Similarly, quotations from religious scholars and the Bible will probably not convince someone who thinks scientifically.

It is important to recognize that different individuals may select different solutions to a problem because they use different reasoning processes. Consider, for example, two speeches actually given by individuals who confronted the same problem: how to handle the birth of a child to parents with incompatible blood types. One speaker explained that he and his wife were aware of the possibility that their child might die or have a birth defect. They were told by their doctor that the baby might have to fight off the blood incompatibility and undergo transfusions because of AB-O blood incompatibility between his wife and the fetus. The speaker went on to state that on the advice of their physician, they had arranged for the birth to take place in a hospital noted for its excellent pediatric care, even though it was a considerable distance from their home.

The other speaker was a woman who also was aware that she and her husband faced the same problem with their pregnancy. These parents-to-be were practicing Christian Scientists. She explained that because their religion taught them to consider a human being as a God-created spiritual entity and not a material being, they believed that their baby would be made not of material elements like blood, brain, and bones but rather of spiritual qualities like intelligence, love, kindness, and health. Their solution to the problem, she explained, was to contact their Christian Science teacher, who helped them do prayerful work for their unborn child.[12]

Heckling on Campus: Freedom of Speech Depends on Teaching Students to Listen

By Andrew D. Wolvin

A coalition of organizations in higher education has issued a statement deploring the recent heckling incidents involving controversial public figures invited to speak on various campuses. The list of notables who have been heckled by members of campus audiences is growing; it includes Jeane Kirkpatrick, U.S. Ambassador to the United Nations; the social activist Eldridge Cleaver; and Sheik Ahmed Zaki Yamani, the Saudi Arabian oil minister.

The possibility that the demonstrations have political overtones has alarmed some people, but whether or not that is the case, the heckling should be of concern to all educators as a problem of basic communication.

One of the objectives of American education should be the development of effective communication skills and attitudes in students. Ours is a communication society, and speaking and listening play a prominent role in our careers and in maintaining our social relationships.

Studies have revealed that a major part of the time that people spend in communication each day is spent listening. Yet we're doing very little in our colleges to train students to listen.

That our students lack the requisite skills to be effective listeners came to light recently in a study conducted by New York's Center for Public Resources. In addition to decrying the decline in basic mathematics and science skills in the work force, the corporate executives and labor-union officials who were questioned in the study complained of a decline in their employees' speaking and listening skills. At the same time, the educators who were questioned observed that they were satisfied with their students' preparation in communication skills. Clearly, there is a gap between the employers' and educators' perceptions about how students are being prepared for the realities of the workplace. The heckling issue reflects that gap.

The students today who are not willing to give controversial speakers a fair hearing are short-circuiting the listening process in communication. The first step in listening is to receive and comprehend a message *before* forming judgments about its merits or its source.

Carl Rogers, the well-known psychotherapist, argues that the greatest barrier to human communication is the tendency to form snap judgments about a person or what he or she is saying and then "tune out." That tendency must be recognized and overcome—we must hear people out before deciding whether to accept or reject their message.

The listener shares equally with the speaker the responsibility to uphold the right to freedom of speech. Just as speakers who take that freedom seriously must strive to preserve it by not abusing it, so, too, should their hearers preserve it by listening.

The coalition of higher-education organizations summed up the issue in a "Call to Action":

"Unless there is freedom to speak and to teach, even for those with whom we differ on fundamentals," it said, "and unless there is freedom for all to listen and to learn, there can be no true college or university no matter how fine the buildings or modern the equipment."

Source: From "Heckling on Campus: Freedom of Speech Depends on Teaching Students to Listen," by Andrew D. Wolvin from *The Chronicle of Higher Education*, July 20, 1983, p. 20.

The speeches clearly showed the audience that each of these couples used a different reasoning process to arrive at a solution. Each couple was satisfied with the solution they had chosen, and neither would have chosen the other's solution. A major breakthrough in communication takes place when we accept the concept that it is possible to respect others' beliefs even if we do not share those beliefs. This does not mean, however, that a listener should blindly accept a speaker's contentions; the speaker must earn the listener's respect by developing ideas clearly and consistently.

3.3 Ethics

As you communicate with others in your daily and professional lives, you are influenced both as a sender and a receiver by your ethics. In fact, your ethical system is the underlying core of everything you say and everything you do. Your ethics are the values that have been instilled in you, which you have knowingly or unknowingly accepted. Your ethics tell you right from wrong.

Your **ethical value system** forms the basis for your decision making and for your personal understanding of why you will or will not behave in a certain way. You must also realize that other people have their own systems of ethics.

Ethics and Society

Ethics are action-oriented. A personal ethics system that enables you to make considered decisions and to explain and defend your actions calls for consistency among your beliefs, your words, and your actions. Unfortunately, what some people believe and what they do are not necessarily parallel. Recently there has arisen a strong emphasis on ethics in communication, in professional responsibilities, and in decision making. The reasons for this new emphasis are complex; perhaps it has come about because "large sections of the nation's ethical roofing have been sagging badly, from the White House to churches, schools, industries, medical centers, law firms and stock brokerages."[13]

There are many examples of questionable ethical conduct among those in American public life. Political candidates are often subject to ethical questioning, such as when Democratic presidential candidate Bill Clinton was accused of being involved in a sexual liaison while Governor of Arkansas and during his presidency, the investigation of Clinton and Vice President Al Gore regarding campaign financing, and when Republican Pat Buchanan was discovered hypocritically exhorting the nation to "Buy American" while owning a German-built Mercedes-Benz.

The upshot is that "Watergate-style revelations and reports of corporate bribery and white-collar crime have contributed to a sense of uneasiness within the country about the state of professional and private virtue in American life."[14] If we combine this sense of uneasiness with recent technological advances—in reproduction and organ-replacement techniques, in computer use, in machinery for prolonging life, in space exploration—additional moral dilemmas arise. An individual's system of ethics must be firmly enough established to serve as a guide to consistent behavior, yet flexible enough to adapt to a rapidly changing reality. This is a tall order indeed.

Ethics and You

❖ ❖ ❖ ❖

Your ethical system underlies the way you resolve conflicts that arise in your personal life and in your work. Your communication ethics are based on such matters as your selection of words, your style of presentation, and the manner in which you defend and develop your ideas.

To be an effective communicator, it is helpful for you to understand your own ethical system. Such an understanding has several benefits: making sense of your life; fulfilling personal, professional, and social responsibilities; making informed political judgments; and guarding against social or political excesses that promote bigotry and repression.

Making sense of your life. To have consistent and coherent beliefs and actions you need to understand that your ethics are the basis for what you do and what you refrain from doing, what you communicate about and what you refrain from communicating about. Have you ever asked yourself precisely why you believe or don't believe in the death penalty? How would you react if a friend of yours told you he had AIDS? Why would you react that way?

Fulfilling personal, professional, and social responsibilities. Life is a pattern of setting goals and then carrying them out. In order to do this, you must understand how these goals affect your daily life, your work environment, and your interaction with others. Why have you chosen your college major? Why do you want to do that type of work? If you have chosen a career that involves helping other people, such as psychology or counseling, do you really want the responsibility for assisting others to make life decisions? How would you react if your intervention did not prevent a person from committing suicide or a violent crime? It is difficult to say precisely what constitutes a "moral life," but consistent principles that govern one's words and deeds and that are applied uniformly in all areas of human responsibility—personal, professional, and social—would seem to be a significant part of such a life.

Making informed political judgments. As a member of a democratic society, you have an obligation to realize your role as a voter and a citizen. How do you select the candidate you will vote for in an election? How much of that decision is yours, based on an understanding of your ethical system, and how much is influenced by well-contrived advertisements emphasizing such extraneous factors as the candidate's physical appearance? Do you select a candidate according to factors that have little to do with the duties of the office, such as whether the candidate has the same religion as you? Carefully analyzing your ethical system will help you to understand why you make the political decisions you do and help preserve your integrity and autonomy as a member of a democratic society.

Guarding against social or political excesses that promote bigotry and repression. Other people's ethics will not always be similar to yours. Hatred of those who are different and the desire for power over others are prevalent trends in human history. In order to guard against unknowingly participating in acts based on these ethics, you must be aware of your own value system. What are your prejudices? Would you be willing to put your career or even your life on the line to support civil rights for all? Why or why not?

 **A Code of Ethics**

Because there seems to be no universal code of ethics that is true for all people at all times and in all places, we sometimes become confused about what is right and what is wrong. We are forced to think about what price we are willing to pay for decency, compassion, and sensitivity in our dealings with others. We must ask ourselves whether words such as honesty and integrity form the basis for the way we want to live. There seem to be five driving forces behind the way individuals apply ethics.[15]

Stimulating the moral imagination. Each moral choice we make has repercussions for ourselves as well as for others. This is true regardless of our occupation or role in society. Questions such as these lead to moral decisions: How would I decide whether extraordinary means should be used to keep someone alive? What effect does the grading system my instructor uses have on my entrance into graduate school? Why shouldn't I adjust my tax return in my benefit if I need the money more than the government does? If I behave according to the adage "Spare the rod and spoil the child," what effect will this have on my children's lives? As a businessperson, do I believe that pollution control should take a back seat to profits?

Recognizing ethical issues. Ethical issues are by their very nature overriding—that is, once we recognize an issue as an ethical matter, we attach more significance to it than we did previously. When we are aware that we are making an ethical decision, we may attempt to identify hidden assumptions and to determine whether there is a reasonable ground for making a judgment or for reaching a conclusion. We might ask ourselves: Do I have enough evidence to reach a decision? Is the person giving me advice or counsel a credible source? Is this a decision I should be making?

Developing analytical skills. Words such as *justice, dignity, privacy,* and *virtue* are not always used with clarity and consistency. People have a need to examine and make distinctions among concepts that center on ethical principles and moral rules. We must be aware of the need to challenge and think hard about ethical concepts so that we apply them consistently. We need to understand the logical and practical consequences of these applications and the extent to which such consequences are worth considering.

Eliciting a sense of moral responsibility. Part of the process of adopting an ethical system is that our ethical values will be reflected in our personal conduct. When we attempt to act consistently with our values, some basic questions about reaching conclusions arise: Do I have the freedom to make moral choices? If so, how should I go about making decisions? What is the connection between thinking about my ethics and my personal conduct? What would I do, for example, if faced with deciding for myself whether to get an abortion? How would I advise someone I am involved in a relationship with who is facing that question? Why would I make that decision? Do I have the right to make that decision? How would I feel about this decision if I were a doctor or nurse? Questions about moral responsibility cannot be set aside easily, since they concern matters that affect us daily.

Tolerating—and resisting—disagreement and ambiguity. Even if ethical certainty is impossible, ethical reasoning about choice can be precise. In other words, even though there may not always be "right" answers, we can reason clearly about the issues. If we know how we reached a conclusion we can explain how the decision was made, thus bringing some consistency and coherence to our decision-making process.

To understand your own ethical system and that of others, you should ask yourself some basic questions regarding the choices you make and the choices others make that affect you: Do I understand that it is possible to tolerate differences of choice and to refrain from labeling opposite choices as immoral?

As you think over ethical ideas and then communicate with others, you will encounter **dilemmas of principles**—situations in which you are torn between conflicting moral obligations that cannot be fulfilled at the same time. You probably will be faced with situations in which what you want to do may not be what you believe you should do. You probably will encounter situations in which you must choose between deception and telling the truth. Is the "little white lie" that protects you from punishment at home or at work really a harmless action? Is the answer to "Will I get caught?" your bottom line in deciding whether or not to tell the truth?

Differing Ethical Views

Defining "being moral" as "having a tendency to be concerned about happiness in general" has a long history in Western cultures. This viewpoint is epitomized by the golden rule: "Do unto others as you would have them do unto you." In contrast, certain Eastern philosophies (Buddhism and Confucianism, for example) understand morality less as doing unto others and more as *not* doing unto others. The essence of this morality, sometimes referred to as the "silver rule," is thus "What you do not want done to yourself, do not do unto others." According to these philosophies, the purpose of morality is the achievement of personal peace, contentment, and tranquility—not a concern for others.[16]

What is ethical or moral for one person or group of people might not be the same as for others. Navajo ethics, for example, relies on the principle, "Whatever one is told to do or not to do can be justified by some reason."[17] This belief leads Navajo speakers to reveal all of the reasons for and against a proposal. They believe not to do so is an unethical act: the listener is denied the opportunity to make a valid decision based on all the evidence. This is in stark contrast to most traditional Western public speaking in which only the point of view of the speaker is revealed because of the fear that exposing the opposing views allows the listener to have information that might be used against the proposal.

The "Japanese find their identities through membership in groups to which they belong and subordinate individualism to group identity and goals."[18] Thus, when the Japanese investigate what is right and wrong, they do so from the standpoint of how it will affect the group, not how it will affect the individual. Western speakers often center their arguments on swaying the listener by explaining how an action will aid the person directly. This approach is against the Japanese ethical code.

The Ethical Responsibilities of the Public Speaker

Ethical public speakers are generally defined as those who conform to the moral standards the society establishes for its communicators.

Ethical public speakers are generally defined as those who conform to the moral standards the society establishes for its communicators.

Over the decades, speech communication instructors have stressed that competent public speakers should, by necessity, be ethical speakers—that a speaker should give the listener assistance in making wise decisions, and should consider moral principles when planning what to say. Speech instructors also would stress that although propagandists (such as Hitler) are certainly persuasive and compelling speakers, they bring about much human destruction because of their skewed ethical values.

It is a generally accepted principle that the spoken word can have a significant effect on a listener.

We are aware that the use of language develops, enlarges, and enhances human personalities. Furthermore, we would all acknowledge that a speaker who uses language that degrades or injures human personality by exaggeration, pseudotruths, twisting words, and name calling is clearly acting unethically.[19]

Two important taboos regarding ethical speaking are plagiarism and fabrication.

Plagiarism

Plagiarism consists of a speaker using the ideas and words of others, while offering them as her or his own without giving credit to the originator of the material.

Plagiarism can be as seemingly innocent as overhearing someone's idea on a solution to a problem, presenting that idea in a speech, and not giving credit to the originator of the idea, but also means copying someone else's entire essay and presenting it as a speech with no reference to the source.

The extent of plagiarism may spread from using an idea to replicating an entire speech. There are unscrupulous people who encourage plagiarism by supplying opportunities to participate in the act. Theme and speech sales organizations allow for the purchase of a prepackaged presentation. Be aware that using one of these in a classroom, for example, can result in your failing a course or even being expelled.

Also be aware that there are federal laws regarding the illegal use of someone else's materials, especially if the ideas are copyrighted. Materials published in a book or magazine are almost always protected by copyright.

One of your authors found himself in a situation where, at a national convention, a graduate student presented a teaching activity which she credited as being her own. She supplemented her speech with a drawing. During the question-and-answer session, your author asked if this was the speaker's own material. He was assured that it was original and developed specifically for this presentation. However, your author had a copy of an Instructor's Manual, published several years previously, which he had written and which contained the exact exercise, complete with the exact drawing. Needless to say, the public apology was traumatic for the plagiarist.

Every idea you present in a speech does not have to be original; however, if the concept comes from another source, as an ethical speaker, you are obligated to give credit to that source.

Whether intentional or unintentional, plagiarism is stealing! Someone else has done the work, and you are taking credit for it. That is not ethical.

Fabrication

Fabrication is making up information or guessing at information and presenting it as fact.

If research doesn't reveal the desired statistics needed to prove a point in a speech, you can just make them up, right? Wrong!

Don't assume that listeners are naive. They read, they watch television, and they may even be experts on the particular topic you are addressing. How would you feel if you had fabricated statistics and, during the question-and-answer session following your presentation, an audience member indicated that the information was inaccurate and had proof to back it up? What would you do if, during a business briefing, your employer was made aware by a meeting member that the material you were using was made up, not accurate, had no substantiation?

Telling half-truths, because work has not been completed or time was not available for proper research, is still lying. Lying is not an ethical act.

Research in the field of speech has isolated additional traits identified with an ethical speaker. According to this research, an ethical public communicator:

- *Speaks with sincerity.*

- *Does not knowingly expose an audience to falsehoods or half-truths that cause significant harm.*

- *Does not premeditatedly alter the truth.*

- *Presents the truth as he or she understands it.*

- *Raises the listeners' level of expertise by supplying the necessary facts, definitions, descriptions, and substantiating information.*

- *Employs a message that is free from mental as well as physical coercion, by not compelling someone to take an action against his or her will.*

Campus Speech Codes

"Speech that wounds or insults or demeans by reason of race, gender, religion, or sexual preference has no place on a university campus. In fact, such expression seems least tolerable in an academic setting, where the values of rational discourse and the quest for truth are paramount. Universities also have a special need to establish an environment hospitable to persons who have felt unwelcome there for far too long, and whose very ability to learn may depend on civility and respect.

"Yet it is also in this setting—and for the most central educational reasons—that, in the words of the recent American Association of University Professors statement, 'no viewpoint or message may be deemed so hateful or disturbing that it may not be expressed.' And, as the statement adds, 'by proscribing any ideas, a university sets an example that profoundly disserves its academic mission.' Thus penalties or policies that might be found acceptable in the industrial workplace simply do not belong in the classroom or the laboratory, or even the dormitory or the locker room.

"What, then, are the options? Strong condemnation of racist and sexist epithets and slurs is surely appropriate, indeed essential. But many institutions rightly feel that they need to do more than simply make strong statements or even promote educational programs designed to increase sensitivity and enhance the campus climate. Such steps are well and good, they say, but may be—or may be seen as—less than an unpleasant or hurtful situation requires or the campus community expects.

"Several more tangible options do exist. We have never fully exhausted the potential of rules aimed at conduct and not at speech. Most of the inflammatory incidents of recent years have, in fact, involved some punishable conduct—whether it be defacing property, disrupting scheduled university events, or physically intimidating or harassing a fellow student.

"To take an example that is not hypothetical: You do not need a speech code to deal forcefully with a drunken student who awakens his dormitory mates at 3 in the morning—whether his words are racist or profane or simply nonsense or lyric poetry, for that matter. Such disruption of the essential life and tranquility of the academic community can and should be punished without reference to the content of the words, or the thought—hateful or benign—that may have impelled the disrupter."

Source: From "A Time to Re-evaluate Campus Speech Codes," by Robert M. O'Neil from *The Chronicle of Higher Education*, July 8, 1992, p. A40.

- *Does not invent or fabricate statistics or other information intended to serve as a basis for proof of a contention or belief.*

- *Gives credit to the source of information and does not pretend that the information is original when it is not.*

The basic concept of ethical speaking might be stated as: "You must understand that you are a moral agent and when you communicate with others and make decisions that affect you and others, you have a moral responsibility because there are human consequences based on your actions."[20]

The Ethical Responsibilities of a Public Listener

Speakers have the right to free speech in our democratic society, and so, too, do listeners have the right to free listening. With this freedom of communication, however, comes responsibility. Just as the speaker has a personal responsibility to communicate ethically and honestly, so, too, does the listener. You learned in the previous chapter that listening is far from a passive act; it requires a full commitment from the listener to be at least an equal partner in the communication. "To be an effective communicator, a listener should assume at least 51 percent of the burden of the communication. Such a responsibility requires that the listener be committed to active, involved, dynamic listening and engage constantly in the communication."[21]

The first responsibility of the listener is making the decision to listen to the speaker. In many instances, we voluntarily have taken our places as part of an audience; however, at other times, such as in required classes or business meetings, your attendance is not elective.

If you do decide to engage in public communication as a listener, then you should recognize your responsibility to be an active participant. Listening ethics require that the listener truly communicate, to be open and tolerant of the communicator and his/her views.[22]

The ethical listener must be willing to provide the speaker with a fair hearing and to receive and comprehend the message before making a decision to agree or disagree with the speaker's views. This can be difficult, for most of us have a very natural human inclination to form instant judgments and to tune in or tune out a speaker based on that fleeting first impression. This tendency to quick evaluation is considered by some to be the greatest barrier to human communication.[23]

It is your responsibility to yourself to listen constructively and objectively.[24] To listen constructively, you should determine the speaker's purpose, evaluate the message, and relate the message to your own frame of reference. Listening objectively requires that you identify your own predispositions on the topic, avoid jumping to conclusions, avoid emotional reactions, and avoid becoming too influenced by the responses of other audience members. "Responsible listening," observes a public communication specialist, "requires concentration, critical examination of ideas and arguments, careful thought, and judicious decision making."[25]

An ancient Greek philosopher characterized the responsible listener. His words are as relevant today as when they were written:

> There are others who think that the speaker has a function to perform, and the hearer none. They think it only right that the speaker shall come with his discourse carefully thought out and prepared, while they, without consideration or thought of their obligations, rush in and take their seats exactly as though they had come to dinner, to have a good time while others toil. And yet even a well-bred guest at dinner has a function to perform, much more a hearer; for he is a participant in the discourse and a fellow-worker with the speaker.[26]

Summary

This chapter investigated reasoning to conclusion, ethics, and freedom of expression. The major ideas presented include:

♦ *Freedom of expression is the right to present one's views in a public forum.*

♦ *The First Amendment to the U.S. Constitution protects speech.*

♦ *As a public communicator you will constantly be making judgments concerning what you communicate, to whom you communicate, and how you listen to speakers.*

♦ *People process information and reach conclusions in a wide variety of ways, such as through critical thinking, theological reasoning, and philosophical thought.*

♦ *Critical thinking is reasonable, reflective thinking that is focused on deciding what to believe and do.*

♦ *Theological reasoning is based on the concept that there is a prime mover that causes things to happen in a prescribed manner.*

♦ *Philosophical thought recognizes that some areas of human existence "lie beyond the province of conceptual analysis and the practical uses of intelligence" and involves alternative, nonintellectual ways of reaching conclusions.*

♦ *It is possible to respect others' beliefs without actually believing as they do.*

♦ *Ethics are the values that have been instilled in you, which you have knowingly or unknowingly accepted, and which influence how you act.*

♦ *It is helpful for you as a communicator to understand your own ethical system in order to be a responsible public speaker and listener.*

♦ *You experience a dilemma of principle when you are torn between conflicting moral obligations that cannot be fulfilled at the same time.*

♦ *Ethical communicators are those who conform to the moral standards the society establishes for its communicators.*

♦ *Public speaking itself is neither good nor bad. It is what you do with your public communication skills that can be ethically judged.*

♦ *In listening to a speech, it is your responsibility to yourself to listen constructively and objectively.*

Key Terms

freedom of expression	critical thinking
evidence	theological reasoning
philosophical thought	ethics
ethical value system	dilemmas of principles
utilitarianism	ethical public speakers
plagiarism	fabrication

Learn by Doing

1. As a homework assignment, determine what you would do in each of these situations. Write a brief answer for each. At the next class session, you will be divided into groups of four to six students to discuss your answers. After this session write a short paper examining what you learned about your ethical values.

a. You are taking a public speaking course. The instructor requires three quoted references in the speech that you are to present in about five minutes, but you didn't have time to do the necessary research. Would you (1) make up three references, (2) not give the speech and get a failing grade, (3) give the speech without the references and hope for the best, or (4) take some other action? If you would take another action, what would it be?

b. The business you work for is illegally storing chemical waste. You have just given a speech to the local chamber of commerce on the topic of your company's role in building community values. You are asked, during a question-and-answer session, about the rumor of the stored chemical waste. If the practice was discovered, the legal fine against the business would bankrupt it. Do you tell the truth?

c. You are a politician who is giving a speech one day before the election. It is a very close race. Whatever you say will probably not get into the newspaper because it is past the news deadline. Your opponent indicates that she has knowledge of your election committee having committed fund-raising manipulation, as well as indiscretions among your staff. What would you say?

d. A friend has asked you to introduce his speech at your school's honors day assembly. You know he plagiarized much of the material he is going to present. You have been announced as the introducer. What do you do?

2. How free is your speech? The student government association on your campus has announced its speaker series for the semester. There will be five guests: a member of the Ku Klux Klan, a known anti–African American racist, a neo-Nazi who has given anti-Semitic speeches, a minister who believes all homosexuals should be banned from public academic institutions, and an atheist who condemns all members of organized religious groups. The speakers' fees will be paid out of the student activity fund to which all students are required to contribute. Do you feel that these speakers should be allowed to make their presentations on your campus? Be prepared to defend your answers.

3. Recall the experience of listening to a speech in which the speaker used a reasoning system different from yours. What were your feelings? Did you verbally react in some way? How did you feel about the speaker? Did you listen intently to the speech or stop listening because you disagreed?

4. Each class member should bring in a letter to the editor from a local paper or your school newspaper in which the writer takes a stand. The class will be divided into groups. Group members are to read the letters, assuming that they are speeches that were given by the writers. Discuss the method or methods the writers of these letters used to develop their conclusions.

❖ ❖ ❖ ❖   **Endnotes**

1. Susan L. Bayly, *Freedom of Expression: Policy and the Law* (College Park, Md.: Office of Legal Affairs, 1991), p. 2.

2. Ibid.

3. Ibid.

4. Ibid, p. 3.

5. "Imprisonment of Ideas: What Is the First Amendment," a speech presented by Melvin Dershowitz, Eisenhower Symposium, Johns Hopkins University, Baltimore, Md., October 20, 1991.

6. Ibid.

7. Lorenz Boehm, *Critical Thinking/Critical Literacy: Teaching—As If It Matters* (Des Plaines, Ill.: Critical Literacy Project, Oakton Community College, 1990).

8. Based in part on Robert Ennis, "A Taxonomy of Critical Thinking Dispositions and Abilities," in J. Baron and R. Sternberg, eds., *Teaching for Thinking* (New York: D. H. Freeman, 1987).

9. William P. Alston, *Religious Belief and Philosophical Thought* (New York: Harcourt Brace Jovanovich, 1963), p. 15.

10. For more information on theological reasoning, see Father R. W. Mulligan, S.J., "St. Thomas Aquinas," *Encyclopedia International* (New York: Grolier, 1966), pp. 500–501.

11. Milton K. Munitz, *The Ways of Philosophy* (New York: Macmillan, 1979), p. 323.

12. A true story with the Christian Science explanation given by Mary Mona Fisher, the mother, in a class presentation at Lorain County Community College, Elyria, Ohio, where she served as an Adjunct Instructor of Communication. The critical thinking presentation was given by Roy Berko, Professor of Communication, to the same class.

13. Ezra Bowen, "Ethics—Looking to Its Roots," *Time*, May 25, 1987, p. 26.

14. "Applied Ethics: A Strategy for Fostering Professional Responsibility," *Carnegie Quarterly*, 28 (Spring/Summer 1980), p. 2.

15. Ibid., pp. 3–4.

16. Based on the concepts and writings of Charles Buckalew, Professor of Philosophy, Lorain County Community College, Elyria, Ohio.

17. Gerry Philipsen, "Navajo World View and Cultural Patterns of Speech, A Case Study in Ethnorhetoric," *Speech Monographs*, 39.2 (1972), p. 135.

18. Earl E. McDowell and Noriko Yotsuyanagi, "An Exploratory Study of Communication Apprehension, Willingness to Communicate, and Sense of Humor between College Students from the United States and Japan," an unpublished paper, Educational Resources Information Center, 1996, p. 12.

19. Synthesized from an unpublished paper entitled "Ethics and Effectiveness," which refers generally to J. W. Gibson et al., "The Basic Course in Speech at U.S. Colleges and Universities," *Communication Education*, 29 (1980), pp. 1–9.

20. Thomas Nelsen, *Ethics in Speech Communication* (Indianapolis: Bobbs-Merrill, 1966), p. 139.

21. Andrew D. Wolvin and Carolyn Gwynn Coakley, *Listening* (Madison, Wisc: Brown/Benchmark, 1996), p. 111.

22. Michael Purdy, "Ethics in Listening What's to Say?" Paper presented at the Speech Communication Association convention, San Antonio, Texas, November, 1995.

23. Carol R. Rogers and F. J. Roethlisberger, "Barriers and Gateways to Communication," *Harvard Business Review*, 30 (July 1952), pp. 46–52.

24. Robert N. Bostrom, *Communicating in Public* (Santa Rosa, Calif.: Burgess Publishing, 1988), pp. 46–47.

25. Thomas L. Tedford, *Public Speaking in a Free Society* (New York: McGraw-Hill, 1991), p. 62.

26. Plutarch, *Plutarch's Moralia*, trans. Frank Cole Babbitt (Cambridge, Mass.: Harvard University Press, 1927), p. 245.

❖ ❖ ❖ ❖

CHAPTER FOUR

The Listenable
Speech

Chapter Outline

❏ 4.1 The Foundations of Listenability

❏ 4.2 The Listenable Speaker

❏ 4.3 Listener Limits

❏ 4.4 Creating Listenable Messages

Learning Outcomes

After reading this chapter you should be able to:

- *Understand the concept of listenability.*

- *Recognize the need to develop listenable messages.*

- *Appreciate the limitations that listeners bring to speech events.*

- *Create listenable messages through strategy, support, structure, and style.*

❖ ❖ ❖ ❖

For decades, writers have been concerned about the readability of their texts. Reading specialists have devised formulae that help writers and readers alike to understand what it takes to write text that is comprehensible to the reading eye. **Readability** has been described as the ease of comprehension as measured by the number of words per sentence.

Just as writers must be concerned for the readability of their messages, so, too, should speakers be concerned for the **listenability**—the ease of comprehension—of their presentations.

4.1 The Foundations of Listenability

Are you aware that what is often referred to as your language really consists of four different languages? You speak one language, listen in another, read another, and write still another. To demonstrate this, read aloud an essay or term paper you wrote. You will find that the words do not flow the same way they do when you speak the information. This is one of the reasons that

---

Improve Presentations

You have a . . . presentation to make. . . .

- Let people know how the message applies to them. *One way*: Pepper your talk with statements such as:
  —"What this means to you is . . ."
  —"As a result, you'll enjoy . . ."
  —"You will find this especially useful for . . ."

- Encourage people to listen by using positive language. *Examples*:
  —Don't say, "I see no alternative but . . ." Instead say, "Clearly, our plan of action is . . ."
  —Don't say, "We can't possibly . . ." Instead say, "We can . . ." or "We will . . ."

- Use expressions that will elicit an emotional response. *Examples*: Use "ablaze" instead of "on fire." Use "delighted" instead of "happy."

- Stay away from "I" language. *Example*: Don't say "I want to tell you about . . ." Instead say, "We'll focus on . . ." or "Let's consider . . ."

- Let the listeners know you care about them. *How*: Treat them as peers and friends. Never lecture to them or display a condescending attitude. *Also*: Refrain from making comments that disparage another group or person.

- Reveal something personal about yourself. *Example*: "As a teen-ager, I was the skinniest kid in my class." This communicates to your listeners that you trust them. And it encourages them to trust you.

- Learn to pace your talk so it moves along at a lively clip. *Some ways*: Avoid belaboring any one point. Move to different positions on the platform. Inject some humor from time to time.

- When speaking to people of different ethnic backgrounds, refrain from using language that conveys bias. *Example*: Use "Asian" instead of "Oriental."

- Avoid using superlatives, such as "amazing" and "terrific." These exaggerated expressions may distract from your credibility.

Source: *Communication Briefings*, as adapted from *The McGraw-Hill 36-Hour Course: Business Presentations*, by Lani Arrendondo, McGraw-Hill, Inc., 1221 Avenue of the Americas, New York, NY 10020.

manuscript speeches often sound so formal and lack vividness. Oral language tends to be more informal, uses contractions (e.g., *didn't* and *can't* rather than *did not* and *cannot*). In addition, written language uses phrases that are not applicable in oral settings. It might be appropriate to write "as shown above," but saying that phrase orally can cause the listener to look to the ceiling for the information.

One of the major studies of listenability determined that an effective message requires an oral-based language, a structure that identifies **sign posts** for the listeners, phrases that tell a listener what is coming next (e.g., "First, I would like to point out . . ." or "A familiar story can illustrate . . ."). In addition, the text is easy to listen to because the information flows with cohesiveness and consistency.[1]

An analysis of listener responses indicates that speaker confidence and appropriateness, nonverbal behavior, logical structure, clarity and conciseness of style, and the encouragement of listener involvement are key elements of a listenable presentation.[2]

4.2 The Listenable Speaker

The listenable speaker is one whose presentation is readily received and understood by the listeners. The qualities that constitute you as a speaker—your verbal and nonverbal communications—represent your **speaking style**. Every individual's speaking style is distinctive and communicates much about the speaker as a person. Think of someone you know who is a public speaker—a politician, a religious leader, a teacher or professor. What is it that allows you to identify this person's distinctive speaking style? Usually it is the sound of the voice, the words chosen, the gestures and body positions. A **listenable speaker style**—a way of presenting material that

Photo: Randall Reeder

Every individual's speaking style is distinctive and communicates much about the speaker as a person.

Gender-Linked Language Effect

commands audience attention—has three important qualities: clarity, conciseness, and colorfulness.

Clarity characterizes how clear your presentation is to your audience. Your selection of words and phrases should communicate your intent and be understood by listeners. Sometimes it is easy to get wrapped up in technical jargon, slang, and imprecise wording that confuses audience members if they do not have the same background as you. Remember, if the message is important enough for you to be taking the time to give it, then you need to select wording that enables the listener to receive it. Speakers who use abstract, unclear, undefined terms are practically asking the audience not to listen, and intentionally or unintentionally ensuring that the message will not be understood. For example, a speaker who presents an informative briefing on future campus development and refers to traffic jams as "pedestrian-vehicular conflict" is not being clear. A business major who gives a speech about "MBOs" and never defines the term could lose the audience's attention.

It is important to explain unusual terms, especially if your audience analysis shows that your listeners may not be familiar with the vocabulary. For example, in a persuasive presentation about the role individuals could play in saving our nation's forests, one speaker realized that his audience had little background in forestry. He offered a definition of the term *duff* in his intro-

❖ ❖ ❖ ❖   ductory or orienting material, since the term would appear several times during the presentation. It helped the audience to know that *duff* is the layer of decaying pine needles, leaves, and branches that fall and collect on the ground in the forest.

Likewise, a speaker should strive for nonverbal clarity. Gestures, facial expression, and vocal inflections should enhance the presentation and reinforce the verbal message. A speaker trying to persuade listeners to attend a rally in favor of university tuition reform will fail to get the audience involved if the material is presented in an orally flat manner, with little facial enthusiasm, and few gestures. How we say something has a great deal of effect on how the listener receives the message.

Language that has **conciseness** is specific and to the point. Historically, speakers went on for hours. This is not the case today. Partially because of the influence of television, which presents and solves problems in half-hour time slots, including commercials, many listeners have become conditioned to brief, tightly organized messages. It is important, therefore, to get to the issues and make your points quickly. This lesson has been well learned by political speakers, who boil down their messages in an effort to create **sound bites**, 8- or 15-second messages that communicate the theme or main point of an entire speech. In his 1988 presidential campaign, George Bush's "No new taxes" was a tiny sound bite that became the major message of his campaign.

Photo: Jon Ferrey/ Daily Bruin

In his oft-quoted "Rainbow Coalition" speech, the Reverend Jesse Jackson used vivid language to make his point.

Colorfulness is language that helps the listener visualize the speaker's message. A good speaker tries to create word pictures that enhance the listening experience. Martin Luther King, Jr.'s, "I Have a Dream" speech has become a lasting example of an effective speech because of the color of the language selected. This speech is also memorable for the gesture and vocal in-flection style of the speaker. The Reverend Jesse Jackson, in his oft-quoted "Rainbow Coalition" speech, used vivid language to make his point:

> Young America, dream. Choose the human race over the nuclear race. Bury the weapons and don't burn the people. Dream of a new value system. . . . Dream of lawyers more concerned about justice than a judgeship. Dream of doctors more concerned about public health than personal wealth. Dream of preachers and priests who will prophesy and not just profiteer. . . .[3]

How much more colorful this wording is than "We have to change our ways, get a new value system, and be responsible."

Now you might be thinking, "I'll never have to give that kind of speech." No, your words may never become national treasures, but the way in which you present your class speech, or a speech to coworkers or the local city council, can have as much effect, in its own way, as any national or international speech. If a speech is worth giving, every effort should be made to make it as effective and meaningful for the listener as possible. A listenable speaking style will help you do this and is a valuable skill for all communicators to work to develop.

Getting Around the 18-Minute Wall

Listeners lose concentration after 18 minutes of a speech, according to a Navy study reported in *The Articulate Executive*, by Granville N. Toogood. To get around the 18-minute wall:

- Give them the basics in 15 minutes. Then, devote half an hour to Q&A to expand your main points.

- Alternate 18-minute segments with an associate speaking for two minutes to amplify a point in your speech.

- Speak for 18 minutes, show a 10-minute video, and then restart your 18-minute clock.

Source: *Communication Briefings*, as adapted from Across the Board, 845 3rd Ave., New York, NY 10022.

4.3 Listener Limits

There are a series of listening limit factors that should be taken into consideration in creating a listenable presentation.

Listeners are limited by the time dimension. The typical listener can receive and comprehend information about four times faster than the normal person speaks. The listener can grasp ideas at about 500 words per minute, while an average speaker sends messages between 125 and 175 words per minute. This differential between speech speed and listening/thought speed is a major trap in the listening system. Listeners have so much lag time that they may mentally drift off, day dream, or think of other things with their extra listening time.

Lack of time limits listeners. We have been conditioned to get the information quickly through media reports that are concise, specific, and limited. The average news story is presented in about 30 seconds. Therefore, it is quite difficult for many people to maintain a focus on a message for very long.

Our physiological capacity for attention is limited. Cognitive psychologists suggest that we can focus on any stimulus for no more than about 60 seconds. Therefore, our attention span fluctuates. We tune in and out on messages—it's a natural part of our cognition.

Our attention capacity has been tempered by television viewing. Educators used to believe that it was possible to keep a group attention span for about 20 minutes. Thus, classroom teachers were advised to lecture for 20 minutes, engage in a discussion or an activity for 20 minutes, and then change presentation modes again, as a way to segment a class to adapt to the attention limits. Listeners today, however, are products of television programming, so a more realistic time frame for an attention segment is probably about seven or eight minutes. We're accustomed to the typical network television format, which provides commercial breaks every few minutes!

There are limits to our retention abilities. Once the message has been received and interpreted in the short-term memory, the listener needs to store it in the long-term memory. Listening educators speculate that no more than about 20 to 25 percent of what you listen to can ever be recalled at a later time. Imagine! As much as 75 percent of what we listen to gets lost.

The 25 percent retention rate is based on listening as an auditory process. As the visual channel is added, the percentage of recall rises. Adding additional channels, such as touching, smelling, and tasting, increases the potential for memory.

How to Involve Your Audience

Get your audience involved in your speech with these "spur of the moment" adaptations:

- Refer to people in the audience by name: "Suppose Fred Jones wants to conduct a PR campaign for his shoe store."

- Mention other speakers for the occasion: "Those of us on this platform, such as Mayor Jones and the Reverend Smith, know these problems firsthand."

- Note something about the place where the speech is taking place: "I remember visiting the Los Alamos Laboratories back in the early fifties. The computers in those labs were housed in a building the size of this lodge. Today those same computers could rest in the palm of your hand."

- Mention something about common experiences: "How many of you have personal computers at home? How many would like to learn more about operating your computer?"

- Invite the audience to ask questions during your speech. Or if you want to control the situation (mainly because of time constraints), get your audience mentally involved through rhetorical questions: "Do you sometimes wish you had more time for exercise? Would you be interested in a program that lets you exercise on the job?"

- Talk directly to your listeners. Use the word "you" liberally: "When you read your daily paper . . ." "You must have seen the TV commercial . . ."

Source: *Communication Briefings*, as adapted from Denys J. Gary, 944 Campbell St., Williamsport, PA 17701.

The limitations of our sensory channels affect listening behavior. It is widely believed that humans process information primarily through the auditory channels for the early part of their lives. When one enters school, however, most learning is accomplished through reading texts. Consequently, much of what is retained, of necessity, comes through the visual channel. "The least developed learning channel for most students is the auditory, yet approximately 80 percent of secondary instruction is conveyed via the lecture format."[3]

Speakers need to be aware of how we function as receivers and adapt to them. It is necessary for speakers to create listenable messages—messages that are designed to reach listeners despite their limitations.

4.4 Creating Listenable Messages

Listenable messages require the speaker be concerned with four factors in his/her preparation and presentation: *strategy, support, structure*, and *style*.

Strategically, a speaker needs to know himself/herself as a communicator. What is your style? What makes you comfortable as a speaker? What makes you uncomfortable? How will you be perceived by this audience? What can you do to adapt yourself to the needs and expectations of these listeners?

The speaker's strategy also extends to the determination of the communication goal. Why have you been asked to address this group? What is their goal? What is *your* purpose? How does your goal match the objectives of your listeners? Do you wish to leave your listeners with information? A new understanding? A persuasive acceptance of your plan or point of view? An appreciation for your presentation as part of a ceremony?

Strategically, you need to know your listeners. Your analysis of your intended listeners should include an understanding of key demographic characteristics that may define who they are: their culture (geographic, national, or organizational); experience level; interests and background relevant to your topic; and physical characteristics (age, gender, race). Consider, too, the psychological characteristics of your listeners. They will have positive or negative attitudes (predispositions) toward your subject, toward the occasion, and toward you as their speaker. It is important to predetermine who are your listeners and what are their likely responses so that your message can be adapted accordingly.

A listenable message is also characterized by *support*. Because listeners have such limitations of attention, it is important to engage them in the message. Good speakers rely on a variety of visual and verbal supporting materials to get the listeners' attention and keep that attention throughout the presentation. Listeners like stories; we connect as people through the stories we tell. Consequently, verbal support (statistics, examples, quotes, explanations) should be selected to help the listener stay engrossed in the message.

Visual support also engages the listener. Because the impact of visual messages is so great ("a picture is worth a thousand words"), the use of slides, video clips, overhead projections, and computer graphics can enhance considerably the listener's retention of the material.

In addition to support and strategy, the listenable message is characterized by clear *structure*. Since the listener's attention span fluctuates, it is important to provide the necessary structural sign posts to help the listener get

Profile: Tony Snow, Presidential Speechwriter

Often, the eloquent words we hear uttered by our great orators have flowed first from the pens of speechwriters. Speechwriters are wordsmiths who craft language to communicate clearly and artists who give color and life to spoken messages.

No special set of background experiences or education is a definitive one for people preparing careers in speechwriting. For example, Tony Snow began as a high school debater, majored in philosophy in college, and had a long career in print journalism before becoming White House Director of Speechwriting for the Bush Administration. Though the path to a speechwriting career may be varied, Snow (now of Fox TV) offers some suggestions for people interested in entering this field:

1. *Study speechwriting.* As with many disciplines, we can learn the craft from those who have gone before us. Scrutinize their techniques and successes. Explore their styles. Learn from their mistakes.

2. *Learn some other discipline well.* In other words, have some other body of knowledge upon which you can draw. For example, study history, philosophy, science, or even mathematics. Furthermore, never underestimate the value of trivia. If you come out from behind your desk and participate in life, your speeches will reflect the depth of your experience.

3. *Learn how to write well.* Even the people who have the most profound ideas are rendered ineffective without the ability to communicate those ideas. In particular, know the basics, such as using the active voice and creating smooth transitions between points.

In public discourse, speechwriters often play an influential role; however, with that role comes responsibility. First and foremost, according to Snow, a speechwriter ought not to use a speaker as his or her own "mouthpiece." In Snow's eyes, a speech is composed specifically to communicate the sensibilities, ideas, emotions, arguments, or policies of the speaker. Once that speech is completed and given to a speaker, it becomes that speaker's property. Snow says, "Those writers who rely on speakers' utterances for their own reputations and places in history will be disappointed. The words will go down in history as the speaker's and that is as it should be."

One special feature of speechwriting and speaking in the information age is the need to build "sound bites" into the text. Because sound bites generally summarize arguments, Snow asserts that a good sound bite cannot exist without being preceded by a clear, strong argument. Therefore, if a writer composes an argument well, a sound bite can easily be plucked from it.

Speechwriters strive to write engaging, effective speeches. However, their written words can be either glorified or ruined by the speaker who vocalizes them. For Snow, there exists one particular quality of a good speaker which cannot be written into a speech's text. "A good speaker," he points out, "gives the audience the impression that this person is sharing a part of his or her soul with them, not merely condescending to spend a few minutes standing before them."

Based on telephone interview with Tony Snow, March 26, 1992, updated 1998.

back on track when he/she tunes back in. These sign posts establish the framework for the flow of the material.

Most listeners who have been versed in Western logic find a four-part structure to be the most listenable:

1. *Present an opening introduction that gets the attention of the listeners and then hooks them to the topic with orienting material.*

2. *Then present the main point, the thesis, of the speech.*

❖ ❖ ❖ ❖

3. *Follow this with the body of the presentation, where the main point of the speech is developed and discussed with points and supporting materials.*

4. *Conclude the speech with a recap of the points and a final clincher.*

The structural format serves to keep listeners on track *if* the speaker makes use of frequent transitions—verbal "bridges"—from one point to the next.

The fourth dimension of a listenable message is *style*. A good speaker will work for a verbal style that is clear and memorable. Given the limits of time and attention in our "sound bite" society, listeners need messages that are instantly comprehensible.

The listenable style extends to the nonverbal style as well. The speaker's vocal presentation can enhance the comprehension of the message through proper emphasis and phrasing. And the speaker's visual presentation through attention to gestures, posture, and appearance also makes a difference.

Thus, the listenable message is a comprehensible message if the speaker establishes strategy, support, structure, and style as the guiding principles for shaping the presentation. The listener needs all the help he/she can get. The goal of listenability must be paramount.

Chapters 5 through 10 will assist you, as a speaker, in learning how to develop a listenable speech, and will expose you, as a listener, as to how to evaluate the listenability of a speech.

Summary

This chapter described the concept of public speech listenability. The major concepts discussed were:

♦ *Listenability is the ease of listening comprehension of a presentation.*

♦ *Listenable speaker style is characterized by clarity, conciseness, and colorfulness of verbal and nonverbal elements.*

♦ *Listenability research has focused attention on the need for creating listening messages.*

♦ *Listeners bring limitations of time, attention, retention, and audition to speech events.*

♦ *Speakers should create listenable messages through attention to strategy, support, structure, and style.*

Key Terms

readability
sign posts
listenable speaker style
conciseness
colorfulness

listenability
speaking style
clarity
sound bites

❖ ❖ ❖ ❖   ## Learn by Doing

1. Using a recent issue of *Vital Speeches of the Day* (available in most college libraries), select a speech. Read the speech aloud. Using the concepts explained in this chapter evaluate whether the speech has high, medium, or low listenability. Be prepared to discuss this with your class.

2. Select a letter to the editor in a magazine or newspaper. Read the editorial aloud as if it were a speech. Using the concepts explained in this chapter evaluate whether the speech has high, medium, or low listenability. Be prepared to discuss this with your class.

3. Your instructor will play a videotape of a speech for you. Using the concepts explained in this chapter evaluate whether the speech has high, medium, or low listenability. Be prepared to discuss this with your class.

Endnotes

1. Donald L. Rubin, "Listenability = Oral-based Discourse + Considerateness," in Andrew D. Wolvin and Carolyn Gwynn Coakley (eds.), *Perspectives on Listening* (Norwood, N.J.: Ablex, 1993), pp. 261–281.

2. Ethel C. Glenn, Philip Emmert, and Victoria Emmert. "A Scale for Measuring Listenability: The Factors that Determine Listening Ease and Difficulty," *International Journal of Listening*, 9, (1995), pp. 44–61.

3. Jesse Jackson, "The Rainbow Coalition" (speech presented at the Democratic National Convention, San Francisco, July 17, 1984), transcript reprinted in Lloyd Rohler and Roger Cook, eds., *Great Speeches for Criticism and Analysis* (Greenwood, Ind.: Alistair Press, 1988), p. 111.

4. Lynn O'Brien, "The Learning Channel Preference Checklist," (Philadephia, Pa.: Research for Better Schools, 1990), p. 2.

CHAPTER FIVE

Getting Started

Chapter Outline

Learning Outcomes

After reading this chapter, you should be able to:

- *List and explain the components and process of communication analysis.*

- *Define and explain prior speech analysis.*

- *Prepare a personal speaker inventory.*

- *Conduct an audience analysis by investigating the prospective listeners' demographics, psychographics, and rhetorographics.*

- *Understand why and how to conduct process analysis.*

- *Understand why and how to conduct postspeech analysis.*

T he first questions usually asked by someone who is going to present a speech are "How do I get started?" and "Then what do I do?" When preparing a speech, many people first decide on a topic. Next, they do any necessary research to collect material for the content of their speech. After this preliminary work, they construct an introduction that will get the audience's attention and give listeners the necessary background material so they will be ready to hear the details of the subject. After providing these details, many speakers move on to the statement of the central idea, which tells the audience what the speech is all about. The main part of the presentation then fulfills the purpose of the speech. The conclusion summarizes the major points and wraps up the presentation. Though not all speakers follow this exact order, such a structure will ensure the presenter of a well-constructed speech.

But that structure requires a solid foundation. In order to prepare an effective speech, it is helpful for you to understand how to analyze yourself, the audience, the setting, and your purpose for speaking.

5.1 Elements of Analysis

Any act of communication involves the interaction of three elements:

- The *participants*—the persons engaged in the communication event, the speaker, and the members of the audience.

- The *setting*—the place, time, and emotional climate of the speech.

- The *purpose*—what the communicator is trying to accomplish (e.g., answer a question, change a point of view, influence others to take an action).

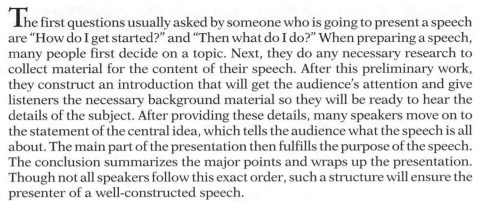

Profile: Sharon Pratt Kelly, Former Mayor of Washington, D.C.

For the mayor of the nation's capital, public speaking situations were part of the daily routine. As with most political figures, Mayor Sharon Pratt Kelly's statements, activities, and innumerable public messages were carefully recorded and reported. Therefore, she had to strive for flawless presentations.

Audience analysis and careful preparation helped Mayor Kelly deal wisely and effectively with the great variety of contexts in which she was called upon to appear. She had to be at ease whether she was speaking before a council meeting, at a parade, or with a group of concerned citizens. Her presentations encompassed both good news and difficult topics and were viewed by schoolchildren, reporters, or the entire nation. She had to be prepared to speak in almost any environment to almost any audience.

Says Kelly, "I would encourage those aspiring to become effective speakers to prepare their speeches thoroughly. In preparation for speaking in front of any group, regardless of its size, one should know the demographics of the audience. Researching the group or area to be addressed will enable the speaker to comment on those issues which are of concern to the audience."

She realizes that her style of delivery contributes to the effectiveness of the presentation as well as to her public image. She recommends that a speaker "take time before his or her scheduled speech to relax and release all tension from the body. Tension, the public speaker's worst enemy, causes nervousness, loss of thought, and shaky speech."

She maintains that staunch belief in the message is what contributes most to a speaker's potency. According to Sharon Pratt Kelly, "Perhaps the most important elements a speaker should exhibit are confidence and conviction."

Keep Your Audience Awake

Consider these techniques for making sure your audience doesn't nod off during your next presentation:

- Answer these questions before you prepare your presentation: "What's my core message and how does it benefit my audience?" "What barriers will keep them from accepting that message?" "What common ground do I share with the audience?" "When I finish, what do I want them to do?"

- Put on mini, one-on-one presentations by mingling with audience members as they arrive. State your core message, listen for objections, and find out what else people want to hear.

- Clarify your argument and keep people focused on your message by writing headlines, not labels, for overheads or slides. *Example*: A label might say "Frequency of Returns." A headline would read "Value Engineering Reduces Product Returns."

- Realize that your first and last impressions mean everything. *Reason*: People decide in the first 30 seconds if they'll listen to you. And you'll be "forgettable" if your closing doesn't relate to your opener and doesn't leave the audience with something of value.

Source: *Communication Briefings*, as adapted from *Fast Company*, 745 Boylston St., Boston, MA 02116.

In public speaking, each of these elements affects the topic selected, the language used, the types of supporting materials (such as examples and illustrations) chosen, and the supplementary aids needed to reinforce and clarify ideas.

To prepare effective speeches, you need to be able to analyze these elements and use what you learn. Determining the purpose of your speech (see Chapter 6) depends on your thorough analysis of the participants and the setting. This investigation is done in three stages: prior analysis, process analysis, and postspeech analysis. Though the majority of the work takes place during **prior analysis**, which you do before you give the speech, watching the audience for feedback (**process analysis**) and paying attention to the reactions after the speech (**postspeech analysis**) are also vital.

5.2 Prior Analysis

In some instances, you are given a topic and told who is going to be in attendance and how long you are to speak. At other times, you may be left on your own to figure out what you are going to do with the time you have before the audience. You must also eventually decide on the appropriate presentation style, the language, and the supporting materials to be used. Taking personal and audience inventories can help you make those decisions.

Personal Inventory

If you are given total freedom to choose a topic, spend some time examining yourself. What are you interested in speaking about? What do you know about that would be of interest to the audience to whom you will speak? What

We all have an inventory of possible ideas to share.

subject would you feel most comfortable with and most knowledgeable about? Do you think you could develop an interesting and successful presentation on this subject that will hold the audience's attention?

In searching for a topic, consider your **personal speaking inventory—** your life experiences and interests. Consider such areas as your hobbies and special skills, your work, places you have traveled, things you know how to do (sports, machinery you can operate, cooking skills), jobs you have held, your experiences (accidents, special events), funny things that have happened to you, books you have read, movies you have seen, interesting people you know, people you admire, your college major, class topics that you found interesting, social and political views you hold, or your religious or ethnic background. We all have an inventory of possible ideas to share. Do not assume that because you are not the world's greatest authority on something, or because you have had limited experiences in certain areas, you have nothing to

❖ ❖ ❖ ❖ talk about. If necessary, you can supplement your knowledge with research and interviews.

To discover your personal speaking inventory, complete activity 1 in the *Learn by Doing* section at the end of this chapter. If you are giving the speech for a class assignment, you may want to see which of the areas in your speaking inventory fit the assignment.

Audience Inventory

Individual listeners who make up a speaker's audience play a critical role in the communication process and should always be the center of focus for the speaker. They come to a speech event with a variety of individual objectives, but in general they tend to focus on themselves and their needs and wants. In order to gain and hold their attention, you must often center on satisfying a very basic, self-centered human question: "What's in it for me?"[1] One listener may have come to gain information he or she feels is important, another to critically analyze the speaker's arguments, and still another out of vague curiosity, with no specific set expectations. In all cases, they will tend to listen actively only if they feel that their needs are being met. Remember, physical limitations allow a person to focus on a single stimulus for no more than about 60 seconds at best. Therefore, even when someone is interested in a topic or in a speaker, concentrating on a speaker's message requires considerable energy as well as the desire to want to listen.[2]

Besides having individual needs, people begin to exhibit group dynamics as they assemble to become an audience. They develop into a group with its own specific characteristics, which the speaker must address in some way. **Polarization** takes place as the members of an audience begin to center their attention on the speaker and the message.[3] In order to get the audience to polarize, the speaker must find a way to grab and hold their attention.

How do you find out what will gain the audience's attention? How can you match that information with what you learned in your personal speaking inventory and choose an effective topic? The act of collecting the necessary information about listeners is called **audience analysis**. It is based on analysis of the listeners' **demographics** (characteristics such as age, gender, and interests), **psychographics** (attitudes, such as positive or negative predispositions toward the speaker, the speech, and the occasion), and **rhetorographics** (the setting, including the situational and environmental aspects of the speech event).

A Speaking Tip

If you've agreed to speak to an audience that you're not familiar with, ask for the names of a half dozen people who will be in the audience.

Contact them and determine their backgrounds and expectations for the presentation. Thank them when you start your speech. Doing this homework will impress the audience.

Source: *Communication Briefings*, as adapted from *The Write Source*, 2380 E. Birchfield St., Simi Valley, CA 93065.

Demographic analysis allows you to profile the features that distinguish your intended group of listeners. This will assist you in choosing a topic, appropriate language, and the types of aids that will help the audience grasp the meaning of the speech and motivate them to listen. You are looking for the common bonds among audience members—their uniqueness and differences.

Psychographic analysis enables you to determine whether the listeners are accepting of or hostile to your point of view, and perhaps to find out why they hold this attitude. This knowledge can assist you in developing the psychological strategies necessary to help alter their attitude. It may also lead you to decide on the overall method of organization to use for the speech.

Rhetorographic analysis has to do with such factors as where the speech will be given, the time allowed, and the characteristics of the place that might require you to use special equipment or restrict your topic choice. Seating arrangements, acoustics, style of lectern, and light are important rhetorographic findings.

Knowing generally what you are looking for is the first step in prior analysis. The process continues by knowing specifically how to probe for and find the demographics, psychographics, and rhetorographics.

Demographics

If you are preparing a speech for a class or work situation, look around at the people in the room. Try to figure out who they are. If you are going to speak to a group of strangers, ask the person who engaged you for some information about the group: "Why are these people gathered together?" "What types of presentations have they liked in the past?" "Are there special considerations I will need to make about the topic I pick, the approach I take, or the language I will be using?"

Some of your questions and observations can center on audience factors: age, gender, religion, cultural and ethnic uniqueness, intellectual level, and occupation. By finding out this demographic information, you can decide which topic from your personal inventory may fit this particular group. In addition, it should help guide you in developing the speech and eventually in selecting the language and supporting materials to use.

Age. The general age of the audience can have an effect on the topic and the approach you will take. A person near the age of retirement may be interested in hearing a speech about the present structure and payoff of the Social Security system, but an 18-year-old college student will probably be more interested in the financial implications of this system for young people. This does not mean that if you are knowledgeable in and wish to talk about Social Security you should avoid the topic. It simply means that you may have to adjust your approach if this is your topic choice.

Gender. Sometimes speakers should take the gender of an audience into consideration. A group of pregnant women who are deciding whether to breast-feed will have particular listener interests that a male audience might not have. Similarly, a group of single fathers will have their own particular interests and concerns. This does not mean that the topic of breast feeding or single fatherhood cannot be presented to audiences of the opposite gender, but a speaker who addresses a mixed audience on such a topic may need to make some adjustments.

Be aware that making statements based on stereotypes about gender can bring problems. For example, former president Ronald Reagan found himself in trouble when he addressed a female group by saying, " 'If it wasn't for women, us men would still be walking around in skin suits carrying clubs!' "[4] This statement was intended to acknowledge the contributions of women to American society, but it came just after the resignation of a member of his staff who had accused him of not offering equal opportunities for women in his administration. Because of the way in which the statement was worded, it was taken as demeaning and as encouraging the stereotyped view that a woman's primary role is to nurture others.

Religion. The way a speaker handles a topic can establish or destroy a bond with specific religious groups represented in the audience. It seems unwise, for example, to propose before a Catholic audience that Catholicism has been responsible for the decline of many civilizations, such as the Mayans and the Incas. Politicians especially can get into difficulty by making comments that alienate the audience. Jesse Jackson, a candidate for the presidential nomination in 1988, discovered this during a primary campaign when he referred to Jewish people as "Hymies" and New York as "Hymietown."[5] That slip of the tongue cost him many votes. Treating your audience with as much respect as you can will help you avoid this type of grave mistake.

Cultural and Ethnic Uniqueness. Effective speakers study the cultural and ethnic background of their audience and are open to new ideas, values, and ways of looking at the world. Considering what makes your audience unique and what topics its members might enjoy hearing about is time well spent. For example, a film producer planning a presentation for the members of an African American cultural center might speak on "The Changing Role of African Americans in Motion Pictures." A speaker asked to address a cooking club might want to find out about the ethnic backgrounds of its members and

Taking into consideration the cultural and ethnic uniqueness of the audience is increasingly important in both academic and business settings.

give a talk on the origins of foods from those areas of the world. This sort of audience analysis is necessary if you want to gain your listeners' attention and accomplish your public speaking goal.

Culture is the sum total of a group's social behavior, beliefs, and traditions. One of the most pervasive elements of a culture is its language system. Both the verbal and the nonverbal language symbols, developed by and agreed upon over time by the group of people within the culture, serve to unify individuals and to provide a common basis for communication. People from the same ethnic background usually have a shared language and national origin. **Cultural values**, what people of a specific culture hold to be of importance and worth, are the basis for understanding and preparing speeches for diverse audiences.

Cultural misunderstandings can create difficulties for public speakers. For example, in 1996 many Japanese people were offended by accusations made by a group of American business leaders about trade restrictions placed by Japan on the import of U.S. products. Concurrently, Americans were offended by comments made by a Japanese diplomat, who suggested that the U.S. economy was declining because American workers were lazy. Though speakers on both sides later indicated that they were misunderstood due to translation problems and different values and customs, the strong negative response of both Japanese and American publics to those speeches well illustrates the result of poor audience analysis.

Taking into consideration the cultural and ethnic uniqueness of the audience is increasingly important in all settings. College classrooms are rapidly growing more ethnically and racially diverse. As a student of public speaking, you should bear in mind the unique backgrounds of your classmates when choosing your topic, approach, supporting materials, and language.

More and more, speakers in business, industry, and the social sciences are being called upon to communicate with diverse audiences. American organizations are experiencing great changes in their work force. For example, white males no longer constitute the majority in American business; women and minorities make up at least 52 percent of the workers in organizations.[6] By the year 2000, approximately 46 percent of the U.S. work force will be female. In addition, African Americans, Hispanics, and other minorities will comprise 29 percent of new additions to the U.S. work force, and will make up more than 15 percent of the work force in the year 2000.[7] The number of Asian, Eastern European, Central American, and South American immigrants has increased as those areas of the globe continue to experience political and economic upheaval. The new workers bring with them their own cultural values and customs and are often confused by American ways.

Such demographic changes demand public speakers who understand how to analyze and adapt to different audiences. Gender is an especially significant factor in audience analysis. Since males and females often have culturally different ways of communicating and acting, the inclusion of more females in the work force has required some male speakers to confront their use of verbal sexism, sexually harassing language, and sexually inappropriate topics.

Be aware that making statements based on generalizations about groups of people can cause problems. Many of the generalizations we hold are based on our experiences and information which has been passed on to us by others. Neither our own experiences or the experiences of others may be accurate. This is not to say that you should not generalize. Indeed, much of the research reported in this book, and which you read in academic courses, is based on limited information which then allows for limited stereotyping. However, don't assume that all generalizations are true and can be applied to everyone from a particular group.

Intellectual Level. An analysis of the audience's intellectual level, educational background, and training in a particular area can help you select a topic. Remember that people may feel threatened if what you are talking about is beyond their understanding. Some people may be put off, for example, by a communication expert who begins a speech by saying, "There appears to be a definite anthropological basis, as developed through the works of [Edward] Hall, for the proxemic behavior of all people." Instead, for an audience that does not include specialists in the field, the speaker might be better off discussing an elementary aspect of nonverbal communication. At the same time, it is important not to make audience members feel as though you are talking down to them. Most people are intelligent enough to understand technical terms if they are clearly defined.

Occupation. It is an excellent idea to form a bond with an audience by using occupational interests and experiences as the basis for your communication. This is a comparatively common practice we all engage in daily: Students discuss their school activities with each other, factory workers discuss production problems, doctors and nurses discuss hospital procedures. Problems arise when speakers fail to realize that their occupational concerns may be of little or no interest to their audience, or are of interest to only a select group, and may not be appropriate to a public speech.

Psychographics

Psychographics allows you to discover how the audience feels about the topic you want to discuss. Such audience factors as political affiliation, conservative or liberal disposition, social and economic levels, and listening/learning style can help you make decisions about the topic, language, and supporting materials.

Again, be aware that making statements based on generalizations about groups of people can be dangerous. Don't assume that all generalizations are true and can be applied to everyone from a particular group. Yes, conservatives will generally be opposed to abortion and in favor of the death penalty, and liberals will oppose these actions, but this does not mean every conservative and every liberal will share these views.

Political Affiliation. Your political views do not have to parallel those of your audience, but you would be wise to tailor your speech to suit your listeners. Here are two examples of how this awareness can affect a speaker's reception.

The speaker rose from his seat, crossed to a position behind the lectern, looked at his audience, and said, "The changing role of politics in America indicates that the Democratic Party is out of touch with the mainstream and should be considered a dead institution." He then went on to develop the reasons for his stand, ending his presentation with the statement, "There will be no Democratic Party beyond the next five years." When he was finished, there was a stony silence in the room. After a few moments, the members of the audience rose from their seats and began to talk, ignoring him and his topic completely. The setting? A Democratic women's club meeting in a small midwestern town. The speaker obviously did not consider the audience's political beliefs and the fact that they had raised a great deal of money for the party of their choice.

Another speaker, realizing that she would be a Democrat speaking to a predominantly Republican group, started her presentation by explaining those views she held that were most like those of her audience. She wisely built a bridge to show that she was not completely out of touch with the audience. Her effort to build goodwill helped reduce the antagonism she might have created by focusing only on topics of disagreement.

Conservative or Liberal Disposition. When you speak on such controversial issues as abortion, the death penalty, homosexuality, biological engineering, law enforcement, individual rights, feminism, protection of the environment, universal health care, and prayer in school, you are taking on topics in which the listeners may well have an emotional investment according to their conservative or liberal dispositions. In attempting to persuade an audience to believe the way you do or to take some action such as vote for a candidate, give money, or sign a petition, you are well advised to know the disposition of your listeners. If the majority are on your side from the outset, your task will be very different from what it would be if they are opposed to your views or solutions. Chapter 13 presents some of the methods speakers use to work toward change of opinion. Knowing the predispositions of your listeners is a valuable tool to aid you in this process.

Social and Economic Levels. In selecting a topic, you might want to determine the social and economic levels of the audience members so that your approach fits their needs, interests, and attitudes. Different socioeconomic groups hold radically different beliefs, biases, and prejudices. For example, in addressing a gathering of wealthy patrons of the arts, it may be appropriate to comment on the strong financial support for a recent symphony performance. The same comment made to a group of less affluent people may elicit hostility. Keep in mind that different groups will enter the public speaking environment with preconceived ideas about certain topics.

Listening/Learning Style. People listen and learn in different ways. Think back to some of the classes you had in which you learned the material rather easily. Now recall those classes in which you had difficulty tuning into the material. The reason for your difficulty may be tied to your left- or right-brain dominance and your listening/learning style. Public speakers who want to help the audience understand and act on the message presented must adapt to people's various listening/learning styles. Ignoring this important psychographic consideration can limit the possibility of a speech's success.

The human brain is divided into right and left hemispheres. In most cases a person has a dominance that allows for learning and listening in a patterned

---

How to Sell Left and Right

When you sell to left-brain, analytical types, realize that they want facts and proof. So make your presentation as though you were a lawyer with creative flair proving a case.

For prospects who are right-brained and more creatively inclined, tell an entertaining, "feel-good" story but with enough facts to back up your claims.

Source: *Communication Briefings*, as adapted from Mark Lusky, writing in *The Denver Business Journal*, 1700 Broadway, Ste. 515, Denver, CO 80290.

way. For example, "the left hemisphere of the brain is most responsible for rational, logical, sequential, linear, and abstract thinking."[8] Among other things, the left side of the brain is the "word" side. As you listen, as you speak, you are pulling the words out of the left side of the brain. The right hemisphere of the brain is responsible for intuitive, spatial, visual, and concrete matters. "It is from the right side of the brain that we are able to visualize."[9] The right side interprets the printed word, creating characters, places, and things in our mind's eye.

It is important to analyze your brain dominance so you understand the way in which you function as a speaker and a listener. If you have a very strong **left-brain dominance**, you will probably desire to listen to a lecture rather than be an active participant, require handouts and other written material to review the presentation, and favor serious and logical ideas. As a speaker you will tend to be specific, use few examples, use few metaphors and analogies, and present logic-based arguments.

A listener with strong **right-brain dominance** tends to desire examples rather than technical explanations, needs word pictures to remember ideas, likes to explore ideas individually rather than be lectured to, prefers metaphors and analogies to facts, likes humor, and wants to know how information can be specifically useful or applied. As a speaker, the person with right-brain dominance tends to present materials in a creative rather than a structured format, relies on intuitive thinking, will present visual images, will give visually oriented instructions rather than word-oriented instructions, will explore possibilities without always coming to a conclusion, enjoys interaction rather than straight lecturing, and favors humor.

Complete activity 5 in the *Learn by Doing* section at the end of this chapter to determine your brain dominance. It may be impractical to give your audience such a survey, but the occupational and educational backgrounds of the audience members may indicate their general brain dominance. For example, persons with left-brain dominance tend to enter scientific, mathematical, legal, engineering, research, and computing fields; while persons with right-brain dominance may be found to favor writing, the arts, the social sciences, advertising, and media.

Understanding that audience members do not all listen and learn in the same way allows you to plan your speech so that all segments of the audience can gain information. You should be structured (*left-brained*) but give an overall view of the ideas (*right-brained*); use allusions, metaphors, analogies, and examples (*right-brained*) while presenting concrete information (*left-brained*); have visual aids that both illustrate (*right-brained*) and list facts and statistics (*left-brained*); draw relational concepts (*right-brained*) while verifying information (*left-brained*).[10]

Another factor that affects listening/learning style is how people use the information they receive. Some people receive information and act on it quickly; others must let the ideas sit for a while and think about them before reaching any conclusions. In preparing your speech, give both types of listeners a chance to use their style. If you want a decision by the conclusion of the speech, give the information early and let the "thinkers" ponder it as you expand on the ideas. If the decision does not have to be made immediately, conclude by reinforcing the need eventually to make a decision, thus giving the thinkers a chance to do their pondering with a guideline for action. **Feeling-doers**, those who act on information impulsively, respond well to emotional

Photo: Peggy Harrison (Courtesy of Elaine Lundberg)

Such factors as the size of a room, the temperature, the lighting, the arrangement of the furniture, and the physical comfort or discomfort of the audience all affect your communication.

appeals. **Watcher-thinkers**, those who need to ponder decisions, respond best to facts and logical appeals. Again, keeping in mind that you normally have both types in the audience, use both approaches as you plan your speech.

Rhetorographics

Important rhetorographic factors, which together comprise the setting, are the place, time limit, time of day, and emotional climate for the speech.

Place. The effect of place on the tone and topic of a speech is sometimes fairly obvious. For example, a detailed dissection lecture is more suitable for a biology class than a banquet hall. A speaker who wants to convey the beauty of the Hawaiian Islands by means of a slide show will not be able to communicate fully unless the lights can be dimmed and a screen set up.

The angle you take on a topic also varies with the setting. Suppose, for example, the subject is "Changing Sex Roles in American Society." In a sociology class, a speaker may consider the history of male and female roles in the United States, the differences in sex roles in various cultures, and the factors that have brought about changing attitudes toward male and female roles. In contrast, a speaker at an assembly of liberal female legislators, realizing the audience has already accepted the idea that society discriminates against women, may focus on a particular aspect of this issue by discussing a strategy for obtaining new legislation to ensure equal opportunities for women.

Such factors as the size of a room, the temperature, the lighting, the arrangement of the furniture, and the physical comfort or discomfort of the audience all affect your communication. For example, we tend to speak in proportion to the size of a room; a large, crowded room leads to larger gestures and louder speech, and close, intimate conditions lend themselves to quiet speech. Physical proximity cuts down the broadness of gestures. A brightly lit

When Speaking
If you need notes to refer to during a presentation, retain eye contact with your audience by using "hidden notes."
Place your brief notes in the frame of a transparency or below your main headings on the flip chart. A quick glance will prompt you to get to the next key point.
Source: *Communication Briefings*, as adapted from Norman B. Sigband, 3109 Dona Susana Drive, Studio City, CA 91604.

room fosters louder sounds than a dimly lit one, and a furniture arrangement that encourages people to sit in clusters produces more intimate transactions than one that allows audience members to spread out.

Time. Both the time limit and the time of day affect a speaker's performance. Time limits are set for various reasons. For example, the room may have to be vacated by a particular hour, or audience members may have other commitments. The time limit may also be dictated by radio or television coverage. The speaker may impose certain restrictions. For example, the length of a speech may be planned on the basis of past observations of how long a particular group was capable of paying attention. Or a speaker may set a time limit because audience members can dedicate only a particular segment of their meeting to the presentation. Whatever the reason for the time limit, a speaker has an obligation to stay within the prescribed boundaries. This requires careful narrowing of a topic and careful structuring of the presentation.

Speakers also should be aware that the time of day can affect an audience. Early morning and late evening hours often are difficult times to hold people's attention. An audience may have difficulty paying attention to presentations immediately after lunches and dinners because of the drowsiness that typically follows a meal. In these cases, special care should be taken to select unusual, dramatic, or humorous material to hold the audience's attention.

Emotional Climate. The setting for public communication also may be affected by its emotional climate—the overriding psychological state of the participants. A community recently devastated by a tornado, for example, certainly would have a special emotional climate. Thus a speaker called on to present a speech in such a setting would have to adapt the message to the tragedy and deal with the fears, bitterness, and trauma experienced by the audience. Similarly, a speaker invited to address a civic organization in a town that had just been named "outstanding community of the year" would want to adjust the message to reflect the pride and satisfaction felt by the participants. Special occasions like this often create an emotional climate and provide a framework for selection of both materials and language.

5.3 Process Analysis

From the information obtained in the prior analysis you should be able to reach a reasonable conclusion about a topic that will fit you and the audience, and make judgments about the language and supporting materials

❖ ❖ ❖ ❖

Getting Audience Participation

Try these techniques to guarantee maximum audience participation when you speak:

- Send audience members a case study to think about before they hear you speak.

- Arrange seating in tight rounds of six to eight chairs instead of auditorium or classroom style. This works especially well if you plan to have small-group discussions.

- Speak for only 10 minutes and then ask participants to form small groups and discuss what you've said with one another for about 10 minutes. Then have the entire group exchange ideas for about 10 minutes. Repeat this process two or three times.

- Hold a half-hour workshop at the end of your presentation so participants can prepare a personal plan to use the information or ideas you've given them.

Source: *Communications Briefings*, as adapted from Dr. Tom McDonald, writing in *Successful Meetings*, 355 Park Ave. S., New York, NY 10010.

---

needed to develop the speech. But your audience analysis should not stop there. It is important for you to analyze the listeners' responses during the speech—to perform process analysis—so you can make adaptations as you present the message.

The audience can convey verbal and nonverbal cues of attentiveness, boredom, agreement, and hostility through posture and facial expression. Some speakers and theater performers are sensitive to what they term a **cough meter**. If you have lost your audience, you will hear the results as the people clear their throats, cough, and become restless. Effective process analysis requires that you interpret these cues accurately and then adapt to them. Be careful not to assume, for instance, that a hostile response from one or two people represents the response of most of your listeners. The more experience you have in reading and adapting to feedback, the more accurate your process analysis will be.

There are various ways to adapt to the feedback you receive. For example, if you feel the audience does not understand a point, add an illustration, clarify your terms, or restate the idea. If you sense that the audience is not attentive, change the volume of your voice, use a pause, move forward, ask a direct question, or insert an interesting or humorous anecdote.

5.4 Postspeech Analysis

Postspeech analysis enables you to determine how the speech affected the audience. This information can be useful in preparing and presenting future speeches. One very direct way to conduct the postspeech analysis is to have a question-and-answer session. The questions your audience asks may reveal just how clear your presentation really was. The tone of the questions may also reflect the general mood of the listeners, telling you how positively or negatively they have received you and your message.

Informal conversations with members of the audience after the speech will also reveal a good deal.

Other postspeech techniques include opinion ballots, tests, questionnaires, and follow-up interviews. Some researchers even use electronic devices to measure such physical characteristics as pupil dilation, heart rate, and perspiration on the listeners' palms. These electronic techniques are usually appropriate only in laboratory settings and are of little practical value to public speakers.

One technique for postspeech analysis available to classroom speakers is the audience reaction sheet. Many instructors devise a form for student listeners to use in providing positive and constructive responses to their classmates' speeches. In some instances the instructor also fills out an evaluation sheet for the speaker. In other cases, instructors and students give constructive criticism verbally. Still another technique is to videotape or audiotape the speech and then the teacher critiques it. All of these procedures allow speakers to get feedback from the audience.

5.5 Getting Ready to Listen to a Speech

To be an effective listener in a group situation, it is wise to know some general principles of listening to public speeches. This knowledge aids you both to prepare for the experience and to understand how difficult it often is to act as an individual in a group setting.

A group of individual listeners becomes an audience by way of some important psychological phenomena. As you take your place with others in a speaker/audience format, you will focus your attention on the speaker (live or mediated). This creates the speaker as one stimulus and the audience as the other.

The audience's part of the experience is accomplished through **social facilitation**. As individual listeners become part of an audience, they lose some of their individual identity in the process of picking up on reactions and responses from those other listeners in that audience. Thus, you may find yourself laughing at the speaker's joke which you might not find particularly funny, but collectively, the audience does. You have become part of a group, acting like a group. This social facilitation results from listeners getting verbal, vocal, and even visual cues from the other listeners and then responding as they do. Savvy organizers will make sure that listeners are in close physical proximity if they want the participants to take on group social facilitation. Seats at a comedy club, for instance, are always set close to each other so that when one person laughs, the others will be swallowed up in the "we are in this together" attitude.

Another characteristic of audience behavior is the **circular response**. The feedback responses that you and your fellow audience members provide back to the speaker set up a chain reaction. For example, if you are sitting in the front of the audience and nod your head in agreement with the speaker, others will tend to pick up that motion. The smart speaker, in turn, will adapt and adjust to your responses, putting in motion a circular, interactive communication process. This circular motion is often the basis for getting an audience to react to the speaker's message.

One communication researcher summarized the important implications for the public communicator as listener when he noted:

Those who perceive audiences as shapeless masses subject merely to the ability of speakers of any ethical stripe to influence must put this concept aside. We are dealing with those partners who most influence the outcomes of any speech communications; we are dealing with listeners. Listening . . . is an active and influential process. Listening, when it takes place, is *directed* at speakers and speaking. . . . Our language permits us to conceive of listeners listening but never of audiences *audiencing*. . . . The speaker who can improve his [her] understanding of the fascinating interplay between listeners and speakers—the complexities of motivation, perception, and behavior that comprise the communication process—will become a more effective communicator in the day-to-day role of listener-speaker.[11]

Summary

This chapter examined important elements in the planning of a public communication. The major ideas presented were:

♦ *Three factors should be considered when planning a public communication: the participants, the setting, and the purpose of the communication.*

♦ *Prior analysis of the audience takes place before the speech is given.*

♦ *Process analysis is the act of responding to the feedback a speaker receives during a speech.*

♦ *After the presentation, postspeech analysis helps to determine the effectiveness of the speaker's efforts and allows for adjustments in future speeches.*

♦ *A personal speaking inventory can aid a public speaker in selecting a topic.*

♦ *Listeners act not only as individuals but as members of a group that responds dynamically to the speech setting.*

♦ *The audience inventory encompasses demographics, psychographics, and rhetorographics.*

♦ *Demographic factors include the age, gender, religion, cultural and ethnic uniqueness, intellectual level, and occupation of the audience.*

♦ *Psychographic factors include political affiliation, conservative or liberal disposition, social and economic levels, and listening/learning style.*

♦ *Rhetorographic factors include the place, time limit, time of day, and emotional climate for the speech.*

♦ *People listen and learn in different ways.*

Key Terms

participants
purpose
process analysis
personal speaking inventory
audience analysis
psychographics
culture
left-brain dominance
feeling-doers
cough meter
circular response

setting
prior analysis
postspeech analysis
polarization
demographics
rhetorographics
cultural values
right-brain dominance
watcher-thinkers
social facilitation

❖ ❖ ❖ ❖   ## Learn by Doing

1. One of the keys to giving an effective oral presentation is to choose a subject you are interested in and about which you have some knowledge. To learn about your interests, complete the following.

   My Speaking Inventory

   a. Hobbies and special interests

   b. Places traveled

   c. Things I know how to do (sports I can play, skills I have)

   d. Jobs I have had

   e. Experiences (accidents, special events)

   f. Funny things that have happened to me

   g. Books I have read and liked

   h. Movies and plays I have seen and liked

   i. Interesting people I have known

   j. People I admire

   k. Religious and ethnic customs of my family

2. A student volunteer is blindfolded, handed 10 pennies, and told that a wastebasket (preferably a metal one) is placed somewhere in the room. It is the student's task to throw the pennies, one at a time, into the wastebasket. The student is spun around several times to become disoriented. The class is not to make any sounds while the experiment is going on. After the student tosses all the pennies, he or she is given the opportunity to repeat the activity, but this time everyone in the class is to give directions simultaneously. Then the experiment is run a third time, but now the student is to select one person who will give directions. After the three attempts, the class will discuss the value of audience feedback, what happens when there is too much or not enough feedback, and how feedback can be used during public communication. This is an excellent way to gain an appreciation of process analysis during a speech.

3. What questions would you ask the guidance counselor at a local high school if she asked you to speak to the senior class about life as a college student?

4. Imagine a specific situation in which you would alter a speech because of the differing attitudes of two audiences. What is your topic? Who are the audiences to which you are going to speak? What adjustments would you make for the second audience that you did not make for the first audience?

5. Answer all of these questions quickly and do not stop to analyze them. When there is no clear preference, choose the one that most closely represents your attitudes or behavior.

Left/Right Brain Dominance   ❖ ❖ ❖ ❖

1. When I buy a new product, I

   A. —— usually read the directions and carefully follow them.

   B. —— refer to the directions, but really try and figure out how the thing operates or is put together on my own.

2. Which of these words best describes the way I perceive myself in dealing with others.

   A. —— Structured/Rigid

   B. —— Flexible/Open-minded

3. Concerning hunches.

   A. —— I would not rely on hunches to help me make decisions.

   B. —— I have hunches and follow many of them.

4. I make decisions mainly based on

   A. —— what experts say will work.

   B. —— a willingness to try things that I think might work.

5. In traveling or going to a destination, I prefer to

   A. —— read and follow a map.

   B. —— get directions and map things out "my" way.

6. In school, I preferred

   A. —— geometry.

   B. —— algebra.

7. When I read a play or novel I

   A. —— see the play or novel in my head as if it were a movie/tv show.

   B. —— read the words to obtain information.

8. When I want to remember directions, a name, or a news item, I

   A. —— visualize the information, or write notes that help me create a picture, maybe even draw the directions.

   B. —— write structured and detailed notes.

9. I prefer to be in the class of a teacher who

   A. —— has the class do activities and encourages class participation and discussions.

   B. —— primarily lectures.

10. In writing, speaking, and problem solving, I am

    A. —— usually creative, preferring to try new things.

    B. —— seldom creative, preferring traditional solutions.

❖ ❖ ❖ ❖   *Scoring and Interpretation*
    Give yourself one point for each question you answered "B" on numbers 1–5 and "A" on 6–10. This total is your score. To assess your degree of left- or right-brain preference, locate your final score on this continuum:

Left_____**Right**
    1 2 3 4 5 6 7 8 9 10

    The lower the score, the more left-brained tendency you have. People with scores of 1 and 2 are considered to be highly left-brained. The higher the score, the more right-brained tendency you have. People with scores of 9 and 10 are considered to be highly right-brained. Please bear in mind that neither hemisphere preference is superior to the other. If you are extremely left or right dominant, it is possible to develop some traits associated with the other hemisphere, or you may already have them.

Endnotes

1. Concepts developed and presented by Jean Berns, MJSolutions, "Small Group Presentation Effectiveness," Lincoln Assurance Company, Ft. Wayne, Ind., April 14, 1992.

2. Ralph G. Nichols, "Factors in Listening Comprehension," *Speech Monographs*, XV, 2 (1948), pp. 154–163.

3. One of the first to describe this phenomenon was F. H. Allport, *Social Psychology* (Boston: Houghton Mifflin, 1924).

4. *Time*, September 12, 1983, p. 53.

5. Bill Peterson, "Jackson's Strong Showing Brings Respect to His Candidacy," *Washington Post*, April 4, 1984, p. A8.

6. *America's Workforce Is Changing Dramatically* (San Francisco: Copeland Griggs Productions, 1989).

7. William B. Johnston and Arnold E. Packer, *Workforce 2000* (Indianapolis: Hudson Institute, 1987), pp. 85, 89.

8. Based on the information of Dr. Paul Torrance and Dr. Bernice McCarthy, 1979.

9. Ibid.

10. For an in-depth discussion of linear and global listening/learning see: Betty Edwards, *Drawing on the Right Side of the Brain* (Los Angeles: Jeremy Tracher, 1989); Constance Perchura and Joseph Martin, eds., *Mapping the Brain and Its Function* (Washington, D.C.: Institute of Medicine National Academy Press, 1991), and Rebecca Cutter, *When Opposites Attract: Right Brain/Left Brain Relationships and How to Make Them Work* (New York: Dutton, 1994).

11. Paul D. Holtzman, *The Psychology of Speakers' Audiences* (Glenview, Ill.: Scott, Foresman, 1970), pp. 1–2.

The Speech Purpose

Chapter Outline

Learning Outcomes

After reading this chapter you should be able to:

- *Explain the importance of having a purpose for a speech.*

- *Write a purpose statement by stating the goal and topic for a speech and specifying the method to be used in developing the speech.*

- *Explain the importance of establishing goals for listening to a public speech.*

S peakers should know specifically what they want to communicate. Thus, before they even start to develop their presentations, many public speakers write a **purpose statement** in which they define their subject and develop the criteria by which they will evaluate material that may be included in the speech.

6.1 The Purpose Statement

Writing a purpose statement ensures that you will have a clear idea of what you are trying to accomplish, determines the way in which the speech will be developed, and aids you in selecting the materials to include in the speech.

Taking the time to develop the purpose statement will save you time later on, as it will actually make it easier for you to prepare your speech. It will help you avoid the tendency of many novice speakers to rush through the steps of preparing a speech, only to have to redo it because the ideas are disorganized and the materials are not coherent. Clearly knowing where you are going also focuses your research, because you are aware of exactly what kinds of materials you will need. In addition, the development of a purpose statement allows you to use the information from your prior analysis of the participants and the setting of the speech.

Speakers who have difficulty writing a purpose statement that states exactly what the expected outcome of the speech will be often do not have a clear idea of what they are trying to say. They usually make a broad statement such as "I'm going to talk *about* income taxes." Unfortunately, this statement is so vague that it allows the speaker to wander in both preparation and presentation. The word *about* is unclear and nondirective. In this case, the speaker should be asking *what specifically about* income tax the speech will address: Tax history? Tax regulations? Tax penalties? Though developing a clear purpose statement may take time, it will save you the frustration of not being able to stick to a focused specific topic.

The purpose statement typically consists of three parts: the goal of the speech, the statement of the topic, and the method or process to be used to develop the speech.

When preparing a presentation, conduct a "so why?" test. Pretend you're a member of the audience and ask, "So why do I need to know this?" If you don't have a clear answer, your audience won't either.

Source: *Communication Briefings*, as adapted from *Simple Steps to a Powerful Presentation*, Quill, 100 Schelter Road, Lincolnshire, IL 60069.

6.2 The Speech Goal

The **goal** of a speech is expressed in terms of the expected outcome: **to inform** (imparting new information or reinforcing information and understandings that the listener already has) or **to persuade** (getting the listener to take some action, accept a belief, or change a point of view). By knowing how

Kathleen Kennedy Townsend, in her campaign for the Lt. Governorship of Maryland, needed to persuade listeners to vote for her.

you want to affect your listeners, you can develop a plan to accomplish the goal. For example, if your purpose statement is "To inform the audience of the psychological effects of child abuse by examining research studies," the goal is to inform. This means that you will be giving information. You will include only material that illustrates the psychological effects of child abuse. Let's say, however, that your purpose statement is "To persuade the audience to appeal to governmental officials for changes in child protection and child custody laws by showing how current laws are inadequate to prevent child abuse." In this case you would need not only to illustrate the effects of child abuse but also to suggest ways in which audience members could influence lawmakers.

6.3 The Speech Topic

State your **topic**, the subject of your speech, as specifically as possible. If you are not specific, you may find yourself mentally wandering around, unable to settle on your material. There is a difference between talking about "my trip to New Zealand" and "the art of natural wool weaving as done by New Zealand artists." There is a difference between talking about "education" and discussing "why I believe that assessment tests should be given for placement of all college freshmen into communication classes." If you are not specific in your topic choice, your listeners may never grasp your point.

Make sure you keep your audience analysis in mind when selecting the focus of the topic. A topic that fits you quite well may not fit your intended audience. The way you approach a subject will determine whether an audience becomes interested. Examine the topic from the audience's standpoint. If you were listening to someone else speak on the topic, what approach would interest you? For example, if you are knowledgeable about word processing,

A Speech Tip
When preparing a speech, begin at the end. Write down what you will want the audience to do as a result of having heard your speech. Keep this in perspective as you're preparing the rest of your speech.

Source: *Communication Briefings,* as adapted from *Speechwriter's Newsletter,* 212 W. Superior St., Ste. 200, Chicago, IL 60610.

simply telling the audience what you do as a word processor may not be very fascinating. However, if you are speaking to college students, describing how they can use a word processor to improve their grades would be a better approach. On the other hand, if the audience consists of other word-processing professionals, you might share with them "five tricks I've learned that have made it easier for me to save time while operating a word-processing program."

Remember, you are only one of the participants in communication. You must also take the audience into consideration. People tend to listen to topics that they perceive have some effect on them, some benefit for them. If given the opportunity to speak about a topic you've chosen, rather than one that has been assigned to you, select one that gives you a fighting chance to grab and hold the audience's attention. Consider the time you are allotted, the best way to structure the presentation, and the needs of your audience.

Time Allotted

You have only a certain amount of time. Make sure you can adequately cover your topic in the time allowed. Do not deceive yourself by thinking that the audience will listen merely because you are speaking. Recall the times you have mentally picked up your books and left class the instant the class period was supposed to be over, no matter how much the instructor believed

Speakers should be aware of the time frame.

❖ ❖ ❖ ❖   there was time for "just one more idea." Audiences react the same way to a long-winded speaker.

Time limits sometimes are set for you; sometimes you determine them on your own. In most speech classes, for example, instructors set time limits out of necessity and for educational reasons. Usually there is a fixed number of class members who have to give speeches, and specific limits ensure that all will get a chance to speak. If you go over your time limit, someone else will get less time. In addition, most instructors are aware that some speakers need to be taught to discipline themselves not to ramble, and that some speakers must be pushed to fully develop a presentation. Setting maximum and minimum time limits addresses both of these educational goals.

In the world outside the classroom, speakers almost always face time limits. If you are given 10 minutes to speak about your company's new products to a group of potential purchasers, they expect you to speak for approximately 10 minutes. They have taken time out of their workday to listen to you for that period. Going on for 20 minutes or so can almost guarantee negative perceptions. Likewise, religious leaders, politicians, and other prominent public speakers will fail to fulfill their speaking purposes if they ramble on and on. Think of the time limit for your speech in the same way advertisers think of a television commercial. If they have 30 seconds to get their message across, they must be clear, effective, and stick to the time parameters. If they go too long, the end of the commercial will be cut off the air. If they go too short, they will have dead air left over that they could have used to include more appeals for the product. Plan your speech so that it fits into the time span.

Structure of the Speech

Decide how best to approach the presentation. If the topic requires an in-depth study of one factor, then use a **narrow development** to look at a single issue in great detail. If, however, the topic requires a general survey of several ideas, use a **broad development**. Either approach can be successful, depending on the subject and your purpose. Say, for example, you want to speak on the subject of how a play is produced. You may narrow the topic so that you cover only the specifics of how a play is cast and go into detail about each phase of choosing the actors and actresses (narrow development). In contrast, you can use the same amount of time to discuss the overall process of staging a play. In this case, you would tell just a little about casting, blocking stage movements, and conducting rehearsals (broad development). In the narrowly developed speech, the audience becomes very knowledgeable about one phase of staging a play, whereas in the broadly developed speech the audience has a general idea of the entire process. If you choose a broad approach, be careful not to spread the ideas so thin that there is little idea development.

Figure 6.1 presents outlines for two speeches about phobias. The vertically developed speech discusses one subject: agoraphobia. Listeners gain an in-depth understanding of a narrow topic. The horizontally developed speech is an overview of several phobias. Listeners will gain a broad understanding of what a phobia is and general information about four phobias.

Figure 6.1 Narrow and Broad Approaches to Speeches

A Speech with a Narrow Development

Purpose statement: To inform the audience about the disease of agoraphobia by defining it, identifying its causes, listing the physical symptoms of an attack, explaining the agoraphobic personality, describing its consequences, and explaining treatment for the illness.

Topics covered in speech:

A. Definition of agoraphobia

B. The causes of agoraphobia

C. The physical symptoms of an agoraphobia attack

D. The agoraphobic personality

E. The consequences of agoraphobia

F. The treatment for agoraphobia

A Speech with a Broad Development

Purpose statement: To inform the audience about phobic diseases by listing, defining, and giving examples of agoraphobia, speechophobia, xenophobia, and claustrophobia.

Topics covered in speech:

A. Definition of phobia

B. Representative types of phobias

    1. Agoraphobia
       a. Definition
       b. Examples of

    2. Speechophobia
       a. Definition
       b. Examples of

    3. Xenophobia
       a. Definition
       b. Examples of

    4. Claustrophobia
       a. Definition
       b. Examples of

Audience Needs

Analyze your audience and satisfy its needs. You would be wise to ask yourself what phase of your topic the audience will be most interested in hearing about and how to get the idea or ideas across. Narrow your topic from broad to specific by deciding how to best approach your listeners. How much background will they need? If the topic is complex, devote time to providing definitions and explanatory material.

The more complex your subject, and the less experience or knowledge your audience has, the more specific you have to be. For example, in lecturing about nonverbal communication to a freshman speech class, an instructor who realizes that most students are unfamiliar with the vocabulary and the history of this field of study will lay the foundations and be alert to defining terms as she speaks. Your audience analysis should help you determine the necessary background material. Also, repeating your major concepts in various ways will help ensure that the audience understands. Break the topic into segments and approach each segment from several perspectives, so that if listeners do not grasp the material one way, they will another way.

Keeping the needs of your audience in mind will prevent you from trying to cover too much. For instance, a media major has decided to share with a class of nonmajors his knowledge about how a television show is produced, assuming that as media consumers they should be curious about how their favorite TV shows get from script to screen. After analyzing the audience, the speaker realizes that the vocabulary of TV production is too complex for his listeners. A typical vocabulary list for a beginning class in TV production contains about 250 terms, and an understanding of many of these terms is neces-

---

Profile: Robert Jamieson, President, RCA Records Label

The music industry is a young, fast paced business where formally educated, exacting people mix with emotionally driven creative artists. Changes occur overnight and to be successful one must be able to react quickly to the short shelf life that exists. Addressing the wide range of people in the industry, then, involves the ability to understand a complex audience and find a common ground.

As president of the RCA Records Label, Robert Jamieson has seen first hand the importance of effective public speaking in the music industry. In a position of leadership, he often addresses the company, one that includes executives as well as artists. He knows that a speech begins the moment you step in front of the audience.

"People form impressions of you when you are in front of them," he says. "You set a tone and an attitude by the way you look and act in addition to what you say. The audience receives and reacts to the message, in part, based on their opinion of the conveyor of the message."

The only way to form the correct impression, though, is to know your audience and prepare accordingly. It is important to be able to relate to the audience and communicate in a way that they are open to receive. In the music industry, formal speeches are not the norm. A rigid speech is seen as suspect, which means that Jamieson must prepare more diligently so that his words seem natural.

"It is important for a speech to appear impromptu," he says, " but this requires more organization so that the speech becomes very familiar. A major downfall is to memorize the speech verbatim. Instead you should have the general ideas and points set in your mind. This will make you less flustered if things go wrong. You are also able to ad lib more easily this way. The better prepared you are, the better you are going to come across and the more effectively you will be able to communicate your message. In a business like the music industry, it is important that what you say is from your heart. There is a passion in the music business that must be transmitted even if the subject is dry."

"And try to look at each public speaking experience as a challenge. Your message has the ability to create positive change and set the tone for your audience's future as well as your own."

❖ ❖ ❖ ❖

sary to grasp even the most elementary phases of TV production. Obviously, the speaker cannot impart all these terms and cover all the phases of TV production. If he narrows the subject to the role of the director, and then narrows it further to the steps a director takes for getting the shots on the TV screen, the task becomes manageable. By explaining the basic role of the director, which necessitates defining what a "storyboard," "script," and "calls" are, the speaker has laid the necessary foundation. Then he can go into an explanation of the steps a director takes in getting the shots on the TV screen. The speaker might even use visual displays and accompany the explanation with a videotape of a show in production.

6.4 The Method of Developing the Speech

When you write out a purpose statement, use key words to indicate the **method**, or process, you are going to employ in developing your goal. In an informative speech, for example, key words can include:

"by analyzing"

"by demonstrating"

"by explaining"

"by summarizing"

"by comparing"

"by contrasting"

"by describing"

"by discussing"

"by listing"

"by showing"

Here are some examples of informative purpose statements using these key words:

- *To inform the audience why competency testing is being used as a determination for high school graduation by discussing the three major reasons for its use.*

- *To inform the audience how to make a cut-glass sun hanger by listing the supplies needed and the step-by-step construction procedure.*

- *To inform the audience that vitamin C protects against the common cold by examining four scientific studies that provide evidence for this viewpoint.*

- *To inform the audience why I believe that the Beatles had an important effect on modern music by showing the changes in music before and after the Beatles' era.*

- *To inform the audience why I believe that the theory of color therapy is valid by examining the research and findings by color therapy investigators.*

In a persuasive speech, you can use these key words in your purpose statements:

"to accept that"

"to attend"

"to join"

❖ ❖ ❖ ❖

"to participate in"

"to support"

"to agree with"

"to contribute to"

"to lend"

"to serve"

"to volunteer to"

"to aid in"

"to defend"

"to offer to"

"to share"

"to vote for"

Examples of persuasive purpose statements are:

- *To persuade the audience to accept the belief that Columbus discovered America by investigating four different viewpoints concerning the discovery and showing why the Columbus version is the most plausible.*

- *To persuade the audience that video games have no adverse physical and psychological effects on children by presenting the research that proves this conclusion.*

- *To persuade the audience to fill out and sign living wills by listing five reasons for them to do so.*

- *To persuade the audience to accept the concept that getting help from a mental health professional can be a positive act by examining the five most common reasons people seek help and the statistics showing the success rate of treatment for those problems.*

Photo: Justin Warren *Daily Bruin*

By formulating a purpose statement that includes these three factors—goal, topic, and method—you can avoid some of the major pitfalls of speakers.

By formulating a purpose statement that includes these three factors—goal, topic, and method—you can avoid some of the major pitfalls of neophyte speakers. The purpose statement helps you finish your speech in the time limit, accomplish your speaking goal, and communicate effectively with the audience.

Speech Preparation Questions

Here's a list of questions to help you prepare a speech:

- Part I questions help you identify objectives: Why am I speaking? What's in it for the audience? What's my purpose—inform, instruct, persuade, entertain, all four? What do I want the audience to say, believe or do after I speak?

- Part II questions help you write your objectives: What will the actual content be? How much detail will I include? How long will the presentation last? Why will audience members wish to act after they hear my presentation?

- Part III questions help you test your objectives: Are the objectives clear? Do I know what I want to do, how I'll do it and why I want to do it? Have I used action words to describe what I'll do? Do the objectives give participants a good reason to listen?

Source: *Communication Briefings*, as adapted from *Inspire Any Audience: Proven Secrets of the Pros for Powerful Presentations*, by Tony Jeary, High Performance Resources, Inc., 3001 LBJ Freeway, Ste. 240, Dallas, TX 75234.

6.5 Establishing Listening Goals

Not only do speakers have to set goals; listeners who establish clear goals as they enter into a listening act will probably function more effectively and efficiently as listening communicators. Goals specify what we want to accomplish and serve to shape our behaviors as we work to achieve them.

Listeners who attend a presentation with little idea of what they want from the presentation often will not gain much, and if they perceive that there is nothing to be gained from the experience they will in fact learn little. Think back to a time when you went to a class with no motivation to learn anything, or had already decided that there was nothing to gain. You probably listened on a surface level, if at all.

"If you're unsure about what our listening goals should be in a particular situation," some listening experts advise, "you might ask yourself the question, 'What will I be expected to do when I have finished listening?'"[1] The answer to that question can be a useful guide to determining what your listening outcome ought to be.

Another way of accomplishing a listening goal to is be aware of what the speaker is trying to accomplish. To do so requires that you, the listener, carefully identify what it is the speaker is trying to accomplish in the presentation. Sometimes a speaker lets you know this in advance. The publicity for the presentation may alert you to the topic. An instructor or a person giving a business briefing or technical report may, at a previous session, let you know what the topic will be. If not, a good speaker will establish a clear communication goal early in the presentation so that there will be no question as to what he or she wants you to take from the speech. For example, at a meeting of the National Association of Elementary School Principals the organization's Executive Director was specific in his speaking goals when he stated, "We must figure out why computers have, so far, made so small a contribution to math and science achievement at the K-8 level."[2]

Establishing your listening goals can be linked to identifying your purpose for listening. The listener who is listening for *discrimination* has the goal of identifying and distinguishing the auditory and/or the visual message that the speaker is presenting. Such a goal might be appropriate to making determinations as to who is speaking, what language the speaker might be using, or how emotionally connected the speaker is to his or her verbal message.

Listening *comprehension* is most familiar to listeners. It is what we do when our goal is to understand the speaker's message, usually with the need to recall and/or to use the information at a later time. Informative briefings, reports, and lectures all require listeners to listen for comprehension in order to understand the material. This goal shapes listener behaviors as he or she is intent on gaining and remembering the material being presented so that he or she can feed it back on a test, be aware of how to operate a piece of machinery or computer program, or challenge the ideas of the listener.

Therapeutic listening asks the listener to serve as a sounding board, allowing the speaker to express emotions or talk through problems. If you determine that the presenter is using personal stories to "vent" his/her frustration, you may decide that your best strategy is to listen, not give any evaluative feedback or empathize with the speaker. For example, in 1997, as the U.S. Congress was taking more and more authority away from the District of Columbia's elected government and putting it in the hands of an appointed Control Board, D.C. Mayor Marion Barry's speeches asked his listeners to share his frustration at the loss of self-governance.

Critical listening is appropriate to persuasive messages. The listener should establish a goal of critically evaluating a speaker's message if the speaker's goal is to persuade the listener to agree, to think, or take an action. The assessment as to the validity of the message should occur *after* the person has listened to the entire presentation, comprehended it, and thought about the message. Critical listeners who make judgments while listening to the message run the risk of missing important material which might affect the analysis and close down the communication with the speaker. They also often fall victim to acting as the group acts without thinking about the ramifications for each of them as individuals. They might jump to a conclusion, act, and later regret having taken that course.

There are times when it is appropriate to establish as your listening goal to listen *appreciatively* to the speaker's presentation. If the speaker is a wonderful wordsmith, for example, you may want to listen to the beauty of his or her style, enjoying the response that the style provides you. Effective ministers, for example, offer eloquent language in their sermons.

Establishing your listening goal and matching that goal to the purpose of the speaker is a crucial step in successful public listening. Once you identify your purpose, you will need to apply your listening skills in order to accomplish that goal. You may find that you are listening for more than one purpose (to discriminate the speaker's vocal and visual cues while listening to comprehend his/her message, for example). It is helpful to keep your goal in mind as you listen, for it can provide you with direction, focus, and purpose as a public listener.

Summary

This chapter investigated the importance of having a purpose for a speech. The concepts developed were:

♦ *In developing a message, speakers should know specifically what they want to communicate.*

♦ *A purpose statement defines the subject of a speech and develops the criteria by which material will be evaluated for inclusion in the speech.*

♦ *Though developing a clear purpose statement may take time, in the long run it usually saves time by making the speaker select a narrow, specific topic and stick to it.*

♦ *The purpose statement typically consists of three parts: the goal of the speech, the statement of the topic, and the method or process to be used to develop the speech.*

♦ *The goal of a speech is expressed in terms of the expected outcome.*

♦ *The topic is the subject of a speech and should be stated as specifically as possible.*

♦ *Make sure the topic can be adequately covered in the time allowed.*

♦ *In narrow, or vertical, speech development the speaker presents a single issue in great detail.*

♦ *In broad, or horizontal, speech development the speaker presents a survey of general ideas.*

♦ *Narrow your topic from broad to specific by deciding how best to approach your listeners.*

♦ *The method is the process employed in developing the speech's goal.*

Key Terms

purpose statement	goal
to inform	to persuade
topic	narrow development
broad development	method

Learn by Doing

1. Your class will be divided into pairs. Each pair is to locate a copy of a speech that has been presented—for example, one reproduced in *Vital Speeches of the Day*. Each of you is to read the speech separately and write the purpose statement that the speaker intended. Compare your purpose statements. If they do not agree, discuss your different perceptions of the speech purpose.

2. Select a general topic (e.g., cubist painting, the U.S. presidency, date rape). Prepare purpose statements for a speech of 30 min-

utes, 15 minutes, and 5 minutes. Go back and analyze each of the purpose statements you wrote. How do they differ? Why did you make the changes you did?

3. Using the speaking inventory you completed at the end of Chapter 5, write five purpose statements that would be appropriate for an informative speech of five minutes, on a topic of interest to your class. Your instructor will divide the class into groups and you will evaluate each other's purpose statements. You may then be assigned to give a speech using that purpose statement.

4. Select three controversial issues about which you have strong feelings (e.g., abortion, prayer in schools, congressional reform, term limits for members of Congress, forced busing, required minimum racial hiring standards, mandatory AIDS testing, sexual harassment). Write a persuasive purpose statement for each of those topics. Your instructor will divide the class into groups and you will evaluate each other's purpose statements.

Endnotes

1. Carol A. Roach and Nancy J. Wyatt, *Successful Listening* (New York: Harper and Row, 1988), p. 44.

2. Samuel G. Sava, "Electronic Genie," *Vital Speeches of the Day*, 64 (November 1, 1997), p. 56.

CHAPTER SEVEN

Developing the Speech: Supporting Materials

Chapter Outline

❏ **7.1** Types of Supporting Materials
   Illustrations
   Specific Instances
   Exposition
   Statistics
   Analogies
   Testimony
   Visualizations
   Humor

❏ **7.2** Vehicles for Presenting Supporting Materials
   Attention Devices
   Restatement
   Forecasting

❏ **7.3** Supporting Materials—Accuracy, Currency, Presentation
   Accuracy of Materials
   Statistical Surveying
   Currency of Data
   Presentation of Data

❏ **7.4** Supplementary Aids
   Visual Aids
      Real Objects
      Models
      Photographs, Pictures, Diagrams, and Maps
      Charts
      Cutaways
      Mockups
      Presentation Graphics
   Audio Aids
   Audiovisual Aids
   Listening to Supporting Material

Learning Outcomes

After reading this chapter, you should be able to:

- *Identify the types of supporting materials and explain their role in the development of a speech.*

- *Describe the vehicles for support used in public speeches.*

- *Explain why it is important to consider the accuracy, currency, and presentation of supporting materials.*

- *Identify the different types of visual, audio, and audiovisual aids that speakers use.*

- *As a listener, evaluate supporting material.*

❖ ❖ ❖ ❖

It is important to remember that a good relationship between the speaker and the listener is best achieved when the listener clearly understands the intent of the message. The speaker develops the message by defining terms, offering clarifying examples, explaining abstract concepts, presenting proven statistics, and restating ideas. This development is done through the use of supporting materials.

When gathering information to develop a speech, be aware that you can use **supporting materials** to back up your major and subordinate points. Supporting materials should clarify your point or offer proof—that is, they should demonstrate that your claim has some probability of being true. Some forms of support are more useful for clarity, whereas others are more useful for proof.

7.1 Types of Supporting Materials

The most commonly used supporting materials are verbal illustrations, specific instances, expositions, statistics, analogies, testimony, and humor.

A Tip for You When Speaking

For every major point you make, try to do the following:

- Tell a story.
- Use a quote.
- Give an example.
- Use appropriate humor.

Not everyone is capable of doing all four of these. Pick those that work for you and try to support each major point with one of them.

Source: *Communication Briefings*, as adapted from *Presentations Plus*, by David A. Peoples, John Wiley and Sons Inc., 605 3rd Ave., New York, NY 10158.

Illustrations

Examples that explain a subject through the use of detailed stories constitute **verbal illustrations**. They are intended to clarify a point, not offer proof. They may be hypothetical or factual.

Hypothetical illustrations ask the listener to imagine a situation or a series of events. The speaker usually begins by saying something like "Suppose you were. . ." or "Let us all imagine that. . ." Hypothetical illustrations might be used, for instance, by a medical technician to take listeners on a theoretical trip through the circulatory system. This passage from a speech uses a hypothetical illustration to support the point that laws are necessary:

> *Suppose that America was a land without laws. People would then have no restraints. They would be free to murder their neighbors, steal from shopping centers, drive as they wished, and destroy the property of others. Chaos would reign, and human beings would soon be forced to return to a situation in which only the fittest would survive. This might lead to the establishment of laws so that individuals could live in harmony with their neighbors.*

Profile: Angela Guillory, National Vice President for Programming, Sigma Kappa Sorority

As national vice president for programming for Sigma Kappa Sorority, Angela Guillory has had more than her share of public speaking experience. She currently speaks to groups ranging from 15 to 200 in size at least three times a month and larger groups of 200 to 500 no less than six times a year. Her speeches cover a broad scope of topics from the risk of alcohol abuse and hazing to eating disorders and date rape. Because the nature of her speeches and the audience that she speaks to vary often, Guillory has come to recognize the importance of being adequately prepared for each new speech.

She says, "First and foremost, I research my audience. Who are they? What do they have in common? What brought them together? How old are they? What is their educational background? What do they care about? What are their fears? What are their stress points? What motivates them? Who are their leaders? What are their needs?

"After I do my research, I think of three points I want to make that I want them to come away from the speech with. I want them to walk away saying, 'That speech taught me three things, 1, 2, 3.'"

"I then weave in stories, personal application, humor, and interactive exercises. I type it out and practice. Then I place the main points of the paragraphs on notecards and practice and memorize. I then get it down to two index cards and practice again. My best speeches are those in which I have practiced delivering in front of a full-length mirror at least three times."

Guillory's strength as a speaker does not come from her preparation alone. Her detailed attention to the audience extends into the delivery of her speeches. She prefers to act as a "facilitator speaker" rather than "presenter speaker," which entails involving the audience in the topic and engaging them in the material through participation. By being warm and accepting, as well as attempting to relate to the audience, Guillory fosters trust, which in turn creates a more responsive audience. "I enjoy learning about them, asking them to share, getting them to participate, and making them laugh, ponder and question," she notes. She can then challenge the status quo and begin to make a difference in the cause at hand. For this reason, Guillory's audiences tend to "walk away motivated and begin working on whatever the cause may be."

Guillory offers a final point of advice to those who wish to develop their public speaking skills. "Seek out public speaking opportunities as often as possible," she says. "The more comfortable you are in front of audiences, the better you will become. . . . I am very comfortable in front of an audience which allows me to be more free with my thoughts during the cognitive process, especially when the task is problem solving or issue examining. I've grown more confident in my ability to speak in public which is very empowering."

In contrast, **factual illustrations** refer to real situations or events. They might be introduced by a statement such as "When I came to school this morning. . ." or "As the president recalls. . . ." A factual illustration might be used by a woman describing her experience during childbirth or by an earthquake survivor who tells the story of his rescue.

The retired Chief Operating Officer of Coca-Cola used a personal story in his speech to the Pepperdine Youth Leadership Seminar:

> . . . when passing through Warsaw, Poland, on my way home from Russia five years ago, I met by chance Christian Olziewski, and I was invited to his home for dinner. While talking with him, I noticed numbers on his forearm, and he explained this was his identification number while a prisoner at Auschwitz and

several other Nazi death camps. He had been captured as a member of the Polish underground and sentenced to death. For some reason the sentence was never carried out. Instead, he was assigned a daily task during the course of which he witnessed the slaughter of countless Jews. As we became better acquainted, I was thrilled to hear not a shred of bitterness or hate, for to indulge himself with these emotions, he said, would be to cede victory to his captors.[1]

A speaker must select illustrations carefully so they will be relevant to listeners. For example, a funny story about Uncle Henry that does not relate directly to the point is best saved for another time. To be interesting, illustrations should be presented concisely. If the story goes on and on, listeners will have difficulty following or remembering the point the speaker is trying to develop.

Think back to some of the more memorable speakers you have heard. They probably used a number of relevant, interesting stories to support their points. This technique offers listeners a chance to identify with and respond to the speaker's perspective. As a result, they can better understand the points being made.

Specific Instances

Condensed examples that are used to clarify or to prove a point are called **specific instances**. Because they are not developed in depth, they can help you say a great deal quickly. These instances can provide listeners with evidence they can relate to your point.

If you want to develop the idea that speech communication is an interesting major for college students, for example, you could support your point with specific instances of careers that employ communication majors: speechwriting, teaching, research and training in business and industrial communication, political campaigning, health communication, and public relations. These are all careers that should be familiar to your listeners. If you add an unfamiliar example, such as human cybernetic processing, without explaining it, you run the risk of losing your listeners while they try to figure out what you mean. Be sure to use specific instances that your listeners will understand.

Exposition

Exposition means giving the necessary background information to listeners so they can understand the material being presented. Sometimes speakers will need to define specific terms, give historical information, explain how they themselves relate to the topic, or explain the form the presentation will take.

For example, a speaker who wants to explain the advertising campaign for marketing a particular product may find it necessary—during introductory remarks or within the speech itself—to clarify such terms and phrases as "bandwagoning," "plus-and-minus factor of surveying," and "Nielsen average rating." An audience may need historical information as well. For listeners to understand the outcome of the Watergate investigation, for instance, they may need to know the specific events that led to the decision to launch the investigation. Similarly, in discussing the plays of Tennessee Williams,

❖ ❖ ❖ ❖   the speaker is wise to give a biographical history because many of Williams's plays draw on his personal life.

Listeners also may need a bridge between the speaker and the topic to understand why the speaker is discussing the subject or to establish the speaker's expertise. For example, a student nurse who is explaining the nursing program she recently completed should share her educational background with the audience. A woman who has undergone surgery for breast cancer will want to make that fact clear to a group of radiation technicians when explaining the emotional impact that treatment can have on a patient. A basketball coach who has worked with a star player would be an excellent source of information about the player's talents and dedication to the sport and the team.

Explaining the process that the presentation will follow, or the results the speaker wants to achieve, also may he helpful to listeners. The speaker might distribute or display an outline of the major points to be made, or verbally explain what he will be doing and will want the audience to do as the speech proceeds.

A speaker discussing the organizational structure of the U.S. Information Agency might provide this exposition:

> *The United States Information Agency is designed to tell America's story to people in other countries. The agency is made up of special offices that serve this purpose through their work in film, production, radio and television support, publications, and Voice of America broadcasting. Their effort is reinforced through the Overseas U.S. Information Services posts in prime locations throughout the world. The effectiveness of these services is assessed through an office of research. The key to the success of the various branches of the agency rests with the people who work in the services. They are committed to telling America's story professionally.*

Statistics

Any collection of numerical information arranged to indicate representations, trends, or theories is an example of statistics. Communicators use statistics to compare amounts ("The normal intelligible outdoor range of the male human voice in still air is 200 yards. Female screams register higher readings on decibel meters than male screams")[2] and to provide data ("The 1996 population of Italy was 57.8 million people, with the lowest birth rate in Europe.").[3]

A member of the World Future Society used statistics to make his point about the changing role of social responsibility in this country, when he stated: ". . . abortion in the U.S. increased from 605,000 in 1972 to 1,700,000 in 1991. . . children born outside wedlock, a growing proportion of them among teenage girls, increased nearly eight-fold between 1950 and 1991 from 146,000 to 1,151,000."[4]

You will read more on the use of statistics in public communication a little later in this chapter.

Analogies

A speaker often uses an **analogy** to clarify a concept for listeners—that is, the speaker explains an unfamiliar concept in terms of a familiar one. Analogies often take the form of a comparison or a contrast. A comparison attempts to show the specific similarity between two things, whereas a contrast highlights specific differences between things. For example, in discussing the human cortex, an analogy could be drawn between human information processing and a computer process. This comparison is not intended to indicate that the cortex and the computer are one and the same but to show that if a reader understands the functioning of a computer, he or she may also understand the basic operation of the cortex. Or a company manager, for example, may compare the firm's employees to the members of an athletic team. Each group has important members who function in specific capacities; each member wishes to contribute to the final product—success.

For an analogy to be effective the speaker must demonstrate a connection between the two items compared. In addition, if the listeners are not familiar with the object, idea, or theory being used as the basis for the analogy, they may be confused. Comparing one unfamiliar idea to another unfamiliar idea may do little to clarify the concept. President Bush confused some individuals when, during the 1988 election, he made references to a "thousand points of light." Some people did not see the connection between lights and his idea of an active citizenry. In fact, the phrase was so bewildering to some that many comedians included it in their routines.

Speakers should also be careful not to overextend an analogy. A college president once developed an inaugural speech by comparing the school to a football team. The analogy compared faculty members to team players, students to spectators, the president to the coach, and on and on. After a while, the listeners lost track of the initial comparison and stopped paying attention, and the intended effect was lost.

Exercise care in selecting analogies, since comparisons that do not really hold up may weaken your speech. Historians, for instance, are reluctant to draw historical analogies because the social, political, and economic forces of one era may not be comparable to those of another. Thus, despite the claims of many doomsayers, the crises and upheavals in the world today and those during the decline and fall of Rome may not be truly analogous.

Testimony

A direct quotation (an actual statement) or a paraphrase (a reworded idea) from an authority constitutes **testimony**. Speakers provide testimony in communication to clarify ideas, back up contentions, and reinforce concepts. Thus a speaker may use testimony if he or she believes that the opinion of an authority will make listeners more receptive to a particular idea.

An **expert** is a person who through knowledge or skill in a specific field gains respect for his or her opinions or expertise. We turn to lawyers, mechanics, economists, architects, and scholars to answer questions and give advice about their areas of expertise. We trust their opinions because they have acquired knowledge through personal experience, education, training, research, and observation. We also respect people who have academic degrees or licenses, who have received accreditation, or who are recognized by peers as leaders in their fields. For example, Dr. Michael Gottlieb, the noted AIDS virus researcher, would be regarded as an expert on the effects of AIDS on the immune system.

In presenting the views of experts, a speaker should be careful to quote accurately, indicate the time and circumstances under which the information

Locate and use expert testimony to supplement your own knowledge.

was supplied, and provide the source of the material. The testimony should be relevant and no longer than necessary. Listeners have difficulty handling lengthy readings of testimony and tend to tune them out rather quickly.

The direct quotations you select should be true to the source's original intention. Testimony taken out of context is not only misleading and confusing but also a dishonest way of using support. Before you accept testimony as support, assess it by asking the following questions:

1. *Is the material quoted accurately*? Advertisers for plays or movies are sometimes guilty of using only those quotes or parts of quotes that contain praise. For example, a statement that originally read, "The movie was effective if you like a weakly developed plot, poor acting, and confusing dialogue" could in a movie ad become "The movie was effective. . . ." Those little dots, ellipses, make all the difference; they indicate that something has been omitted, and in this case the omission totally changes the meaning. For the same reason, be alert to phrases such as "in part," "seemed to indicate," and "implied." These, too, are signs that not all the evidence is being presented.

2. *Is the source biased because of position, employment, or affiliation*? A quotation by the chairperson of the board of directors of a major tobacco company that cigarette smoking may not lead to cancer should be suspect because of the speaker's biased position. Listeners must be careful not to blindly accept sources that serve the speaker's points of view. Unfortunately, debaters, politi-

cians, researchers, speakers, and journalists sometimes manipulate listeners through this practice.

3. *Is the information relevant to the issue being discussed*? For example, in attempting to prove that vitamin C is not beneficial in protecting against the common cold, a speaker might say, "Vitamin C, as contained in oranges, can cause more harm than good. Take a dozen oranges, peel them, and crush them into a pulp. They will be in exactly the same state as they would be if you swallowed them. Pour the juice into a goldfish bowl, and place the fish in the bowl. Within minutes the acid in the juice may cause the goldfish to die." This statement has no relevance to the issue being discussed.

4. *Is the source competent in the field being discussed*? For example, what qualifies an actor to recommend changes in college administration procedures? What makes an athlete competent to recommend cars, insurance, credit cards, or soft drinks? Unless the speaker can show that these people are qualified experts in these areas, quotations from them should not be accepted as authoritative.

5. *Is the information current, if timeliness is important*? An advertisement for a musical production at a university theater raved: "*Chorus Line*, the best damn musical I've seen in years." Yes, a drama critic in a major newspaper did write that in reviewing the play. Unfortunately, unsuspecting readers may not realize that the statement described the original New York production of *Chorus Line*, not the performance being staged by the university students.

Visualizations

Visualizations allow the audience to see a relationship between things by creating pictures or images in the mind's eye of the listener. One managerial listening specialist used a visualization when he stressed that "communication occurs only when both the sender and the receiver have the same picture in their minds."[5]

The speaker who helps us visualize facilitates listening. In a 1997 speech, Secretary of State Madeleine Albright used a visual image in a speech about peace in the Middle East when she stated: "Prime Minister Netanyahu said recently that leading Israel was like a 'bed of roses' but with a 'lot of thorns'."[6]

Humor

Humor, the quality of being funny or witty, is useful strategy for gaining and holding the audience's attention. Humor has often been the key that unlocks an audience's receptivity. The apt, well-timed, and confidently executed opening puts listeners at their ease.[7] For instance, humor was creatively used by a speaker who knew that his audience had already sat through an evening of speeches. He started out his presentation by saying, "I realize that I'm the fourth speaker you've listened to tonight, so I'd like you to know I use one rule for giving speeches. The mind can only absorb what the seat can endure, and your seats have been enduring for a long time."

Research shows that:[8]

- *Relevant humor in informative discourse will probably produce a favorable audience reaction toward the speaker.*

- *Humor that is self-disparaging may further enhance speaker image. Laughing at oneself publicly shows that you have a good sense of humor, do not take yourself too seriously, and are warm and human. However, overdoing it might harm your speaker credibility.*

- *Relevant humor in a speech can enhance the interest of the speech. This is especially true if the speech does not contain many other factors of interest, such as suspense, animated delivery, concreteness, and specificity.*

- *Relevant humor seems not to influence the effectiveness of persuasive speeches either negatively or positively.*

- *Humor may or may not make a speech more memorable. Humor may increase the interest, but evidence suggests that it does not necessarily increase immediate recall of the subject matter.*

- *The use of satire as a persuasive device may have unpredictable results. Research shows that satire, under certain conditions, can be persuasive, but inconsistently so. This is especially true when it is used by amateur speakers, since they may tend to use it at inappropriate times. In the hands of a professional satirist, satire may be an effective tool. Research showed, for example, that satire by humorist and newspaper columnist Art Buchwald "changed attitudes toward labor unions and our policy of nonrecognition of China."[9]*

What are you looking for in using humor? Ask yourself:

1. *Is the item funny?*
2. *Would you feel comfortable saying it?*
3. *Is it performable humor?*
4. *Will it offend the audience, if offense is not your purpose?*
5. *Is it appropriate to the tone of the speech?*
6. *Is it appropriate for the topic and purpose of the speech?*

A person who effectively uses humor during a speech "never loses sight of his or her reason for being there. The laughs are supportive or illustrative of the occasion, the audience or the speaker. They show a speaker involved with his/her listeners and in tune with them."[10] In addition, care is taken not to offend the audience, unless offense is intentional and has a purpose. The 1992 Democratic presidential hopeful Senator Bob Kerrey found himself in hot water because of a joke he made about lesbians in a conversation before a speech that was recorded by C-Span and made public. The results were protests and demonstrations; Kerrey apologized, but many believe that he lost a number of followers because of his untimely use of humor. Ironically, the very next evening at a Bush/Quayle campaign fund-raiser, Vice President Dan Quayle's press secretary, David Beckwith, referred to Kerrey's joke and said, "The good news is that the lesbians are upset with Kerrey. The bad news is

❖ ❖ ❖ ❖

Putting Humor in Its Place

Humor has a place in your presentations and your work with others. Even if you feel you can't tell a joke, you can still make humor work for you.

Humor should be relevant to the message you are giving. Link it to a point you are making, and make it the type of humor that is in good taste.

- Analogies are one way to use humor. Linking your present situation or problem to something else often provides an opportunity for humor. The link can be either logical or illogical and could even be a personal anecdote.

- Another way to use humor—and an easy one for the person who falls into the "can-not-tell-jokes" category—is to use funny quotes. Get a book of humorous quotations.

    Also: Have you seen an amusing cartoon in the paper or in a magazine? Describe it. Show it on a screen.

Some specifics on using humor:

- When you are telling jokes or quips, don't pre-announce them. Just insert them here and there.

- Avoid anything offensive or sarcastic. If in doubt, leave it out.

- Remember that sometimes things occur—such as power failures, dead mikes, etc.—during presentations. Have a joke or comment ready for emergencies.

Source: *Communication Briefings*, as adapted from Dr. Stephanie Slahor, P.O. Box 2625, Palm Springs, CA 92263.

---

that they'll be coming our way to support us." Again, a poor choice of humor, and more negative reactions.[11]

Where does apt humorous material come from? Sometimes it is professionally written by a speechwriter or humorist specifically for the occasion. The problem with such material is that it is expensive. The best sources for most public speakers are humor books.[12] The speaker, too, is a fruitful source of humor. Humorous observations or experiences can be clever inclusions, and since they are personal, the audience can relate to the speaker's use of them.

Here are some hints for effectively using humor in a speech:

- *Practice your humorous lines as you do the rest of your speech.*

- *Don't announce that you have a joke or a humorous story to tell. The worst thing you can do is say, "That reminds me of a funny story," because then you are challenging the audience. You're saying, in effect, "I'm going to make you laugh," and your listeners are likely to fold their arms across their chests in an attitude of "Oh yeah?"*

- *Don't attempt humor unless you are comfortable telling funny stories. If you thoroughly believe that you can't tell a joke, don't. You won't fool the audience, you will be uncomfortable, and it will show.*

- *Don't use puns, unless for some reason you want to elicit groans from your audience. Puns are the antithesis of what you are striving to achieve. A pun says, "Look how clever I am." It separates you from your audience.*

An effective use of humor was demonstrated by the vice president of a paper company, when he told this humorous story at the International Pulp Paper Conference:

> *There once lived a king loved by his subjects. He ruled a little kingdom tucked away in a pleasant corner of Europe.*
>
> *One day an army came and overran the castle, making off with half the treasury. The king decided he had to tell his people he had to increase taxes to make up for the loss. He called in one of his court wise men.*
>
> *"How can I break the news without inciting a revolt?" he asked.*
>
> *The wise man pondered and then suggested that the king explain the theft as a tragedy for the entire kingdom, imploring the people for their support. That worked pretty well. And, believe it or not, it worked once more after a second invasion—though with some grumbling from the populace.*
>
> *But then, after the neighboring army raided the kingdom a third time, taking all the food and the queen's jewels, the king wailed: "What can I do this time?"*
>
> *The wise man hesitated and then said, "I think it's time for your highness to put the water back in the moat."*
>
> *The moral of the story for us in the pulp and paper industry is this: "We need to quit explaining our poor performance and take action to end it."*[13]

It was effective because it was appropriate to the audience, the setting, and the purpose of the speech—and it was funny.

Because we can attend to any one stimulus for onlty a short period of time, a speech must be sufficiently compelling to ensure that listeners will tune back in to it.

Photo: SMART Technologies, Inc.

7.2 Vehicles for Presenting Supporting Materials ❖ ❖ ❖ ❖

Speakers often use attention devices, restatement, and forecasting as a means of presenting and focusing supporting materials.

Attention Devices

Attention devices focus the listener's concentration on one stimulus over all others in the environment. When you consider the amount of stimuli that are continually bombarding us, it is no wonder that speakers have difficulty gaining and maintaining the attention of their listeners. This task is made even more difficult by the fact that listening involves a process of tuning in and tuning out throughout the message. Some research suggests that a person can concentrate for no more than 60 seconds.[14]

Because we can attend to any one stimulus for only a short period of time, a speech must be sufficiently compelling to ensure that listeners will tune back in to it. To accomplish this, try to choose **concrete supporting materials**, which are specific rather than general or abstract. Abstractions are usually not interesting to listeners. The speaker who explains the process of lunar landings to a nontechnical audience will probably find that an abstract discussion of the principles of velocity and stress will not hold the audience's attention. Instead, the speaker should use concrete illustrations from past Apollo landings.

You also should choose **familiar supporting materials**, which refer to ideas or objects about which the audience already has some knowledge. For example, a speaker who wants to describe a new economic program might refer to the daily effects inflation has on a household budget. Familiar examples help enable listeners to comprehend concepts that may be new to them.

To be a compelling speaker, you must work to be vivid—distinct and graphic—in your presentation. Lively descriptions, a colorful choice of language, and a vigorous style can all encourage listeners to pay attention to

---

Help Listeners Get the Picture

To capture the attention of today's visually oriented readers, speeches need to:

- **Be descriptive**. Paint a picture with sentences that allow for visual cues. *Examples*: "Let's examine this closely," "To illustrate my point . . ." or "Imagine this scene."

- **Be brief**. Pretend you must get across your point in seven seconds or less, an eternity in television. Don't say, "It is our intention to have a new and efficient method of operation in place in 30 days." Instead, say, "We'll upgrade operations in a month."

- **Be a storyteller**. Entice readers with a clever beginning. Entertain them with an absorbing middle. And reward them with an unforgettable ending.

- **Be plain**. Use language geared for junior high school rather than high school comprehension levels. Instead of, "The experience left me enervated," say, "The experience left me tired."

Source: *Communications Briefings* as adapted from Allen Stahl, NCM International Inc., 3000 Malmo Drive, Arlington Heights, IL 60005.

your message. A speaker addressing a group of potential airline flight attendants might stress the importance of cabin safety with some vivid descriptions of past accidents. You also may wish to use **novelty** by treating the subject in a unique or surprising fashion. One speaker chose a novel opening for his speech by saying, "I'm much like you in many ways. I have two arms, two legs, two hands, two eyes, and two ears. I wear clothes, go to school, and enjoy good food. I'm different from you, however, because I'm on methadone. You see, I'm a heroin addict."

Another device is **suspense**, whereby you develop expectation and uncertainty in your audience. A series of questions might create suspense: "What has three professional theaters under one roof? What is endowed with expensive Italian marble, Scandinavian crystal chandeliers, and other gifts from all over the world? What is designed to be a living memorial to a great American president? The Kennedy Center in Washington, D.C."

Material that demonstrates **conflict**—strife and confrontation—is another effective attention device. A speaker might use conflict to interest listeners in a local political issue: "We have to decide today whether we are going to use our tax revenues to hire more teachers or more police officers. Both alternatives have advantages and disadvantages. Let me explain them to you."

Above all, speakers should be careful to use a variety of devices that are relevant to the subject of the speech and to the listeners. Effective speakers seek out materials that contain such devices to capture and maintain the attention of their audience.

Restatement

Have you ever been on the receiving end of a message and found yourself totally confused because of the amount of material it involved? Speakers often forget that listeners may not be able to sift through the information as it is presented. Therefore, to avoid confusion, summarize each segment of a presentation by **restatement** before proceeding to the next one. Effective restatement is accomplished by rewording key points so that major ideas stand out for the listeners without becoming boring or repetitious. Internal summaries are not always necessary; but if material is complicated, a speaker is wise to use this method of clarification. For example, a speaker might restate the sentence "The United States should adopt a more aggressive foreign policy" with "Our nation, then, needs to pursue a more vigorous, definitive approach to its international relations." Care should be taken, however, not to use too many restatements because they can easily lose their impact.

Forecasting

To get the audience ready to focus on the next idea to be presented, speakers use forecasts. A **forecast** is a statement that alerts the audience to ideas that are coming. A sample forecast statement is "Let's now examine three ways in which bulimics purge food." The speaker would then proceed to develop the forecasted idea.

7.3 Supporting Materials—Accuracy, Currency, Presentation

No matter what supporting materials you select to use, make sure they are accurate, current, and presented in a way that effectively and ethically develops the speech.

Accuracy of Materials

To make a statement and develop it with accurate support, begin with a **statement of declaration**, which presents the major contentions or assertions of the speech. Then give the necessary exposition to clarify necessary terms, and develop the idea with illustrations, specific instances, statistics, analogies, and testimony. Without such clarification and development, the audience often will not understand the idea and will have little reason to accept your contentions. For example, a well-developed speech on bulimia included these statements and supporting materials:

- *Statement of declaration*: "Bulimia is an eating disorder that involves binging and purging."

- *Exposition (definition of term)*: "Binging is the act of taking in as much food as possible, as much as 20,000 calories at a time."

- *Statistics*: "This would be like eating 210 brownies or 5 1/2 layer cakes or 18 dozen cookies."

- *Exposition (definition of term)*: "Purging is the evacuation of the food."

- *Specific instances*: "The ways bulimics purge are by self-induced vomiting, use of laxatives (as many as 100 at a time), or ingestion of diet pills."

Before accepting statistics or any other information as truth and using them in your speech, ask yourself:

1. *Who says so?*
2. *How does he or she know?*
3. *Is any information missing?*
4. *Did somebody change the subject?*
5. *Does it make sense?*[15]

When information is accurately discovered, researched, or developed, has been properly interpreted, and is not out of date, it is a valid aid in reaching conclusions. Unfortunately, not all information and research, especially statistical studies, are accurately done, properly interpreted, or current. If you are going to refer to scientific studies in your speech, you need to be aware of the process of statistical surveying.

Statistical Surveying

Researchers and statisticians have developed methods for collecting data, called **statistical surveying**, that provide some degree of assurance that the resulting information will be correct.[16] Ideally, to find out everyone's opinion on a particular issue, everyone should be asked, but of course this is impossible for large populations. Thus, to make educated guesses about what people generally think about a subject, statisticians have devised methods of random sampling, which allow them to survey less than the entire population. These methods recognize the probability of error, so a speaker should indicate the possible margin for error when reporting the statistical results of a survey.

Be wary of studies in which people are allowed to call in their response to a radio or television station. In this sort of survey, the population cannot be controlled—that is, the same people may call in over and over, or they may not be representative of the entire population. Also be suspicious if the number of people questioned is very small. Asking 10 people at your college or university a question and then publishing the results as representing the entire school does not constitute a valid survey. Sometimes, too, a surveyor might be trying to get a specific result and may keep testing until the desired conclusion is reached, or may ignore results that do not agree with the goal. For this reason, be wary of statistics that are taken out of context, that are incomplete, or that do not specify the method used to collect the data.

Currency of Data

Studies and surveys done in the past may have been perfectly accurate at the time they were conducted. This does not mean, however, that they are accurate now. It is important that you use the latest data and not allow yourself to be influenced by information that is not up to date. When you give statistical information, always note when it was collected. When you receive it, be sure to ask for such information if you have any doubts. Some material, such as the generally accepted year of 1492 as the date for Columbus's arrival in the

---

When Analyzing That Data

How you analyze marketing data that you've collected is just as important as deciding to collect the data. Here are some suggestions:

- Use the data correctly. Don't try to adjust the information to produce the results you were hoping for. Don't give prominence to favorable evidence and lose negative data in the shuffle.

- Make solid and reliable deductions. Don't try to read big news into commonplace results.

- Keep the results as simple as possible. Don't let any analysis develop into a mass of statistics that few can understand. Remember, the goal is to produce summary information out of raw bulk details.

- Be sure the sample size is big enough to project comfortably. If you want to use the results based on a small sample, flag them with a warning that they are based on an insufficient sample.

- Don't equate opinions with facts. Point out the difference in the data presented. When looking for cause-and-effect relationships, be thorough. Misreading the relationships can severely damage the validity of an analysis.

Source: *Communication Briefings,* as adapted from *Marketing for Nonmarketers,* by Houston G. Elan and Norton Paley, AMACOM, 135 W. 50th St., New York, NY 10020.

Americas, doesn't have to be from a current source. However, if you are tracing the development of the AIDS epidemic, having current information from this year is imperative. As a public speaker, it is your responsibility to make sure that your conclusion is based on accurate and current information.

Presentation of Data

In using information in a speech, especially statistics, remember that a listener can retain only a limited amount of material. Long lists and complex numbers may go right over your listeners' heads if you do not help them visualize the information. For example, a long list—such as the figures representing the cost of each material used to produce a piece of machinery—can be written on a chalkboard or poster or can be projected on a screen. In this way, listeners view as well as hear, and they can refer to the numbers as needed.

Complicated numbers can be treated in the same manner. Consider, for example, the difficulty of learning geometry, algebra, or accounting without supplemental visual aids that assist the oral presentation. A number such as $1,243,724,863 is difficult to comprehend even if it is written down, but the phrase "approximately $1.25 billion" is within the grasp of an audience.

If statistics are important enough to be included in a presentation, they are important enough to be clarified. Technical subjects in particular require visualization. Speakers are responsible for determining the best way to convey the message to listeners. Here is an example of one way to use statistics effectively to support the thesis that there is a great deal of illegal immigration into the United States from Mexico: "The Immigration and Naturalization Service reported more than 1 million arrests for illegal crossings of the Mexican border in the fiscal year that began last October 1—a 40 percent rise over the same period a year earlier."[17] The fact that there were 1 million arrests means little to the audience. But the interpretation of this data—that this was 40 percent more than last year—conveys the message that illegal immigration is rising.

Be careful not to misuse information, either accidentally or intentionally. This can happen when only part of the information is present, the information is misinterpreted, or the information is used to prove something it was not intended to prove. Consider the following statements: "There were 51,000 rapes in the United States in a given year." "Two children die each day in the United States as a result of child beating." "College expenses will rise around 8 percent for resident students and 6 percent for commuting students next year." These are all numbers, statistics. But are they valid? How should we interpret these statistics?

There may have been 51,000 rapes reported to the police departments in the United States in a year, but was that the total number of rapes committed? Were all rape cases reported to the police? Who determined the number of children's deaths? On what basis can we predict rising college expenses? If you do not quote the sources of the statistics you include and explain how they were compiled, an audience may feel there is good reason to question their accuracy and therefore their value.

❖ ❖ ❖ ❖   ## 7.4 Supplementary Aids

Many speakers find the use of **supplementary aids**—visual, audio, and audiovisual—valuable in reinforcing the oral segments of their presentations. Nevertheless, a speaker should ask three questions before deciding to use such aids: Is the aid relevant to the presentation? Will listeners better understand the material through the use of an aid? Will the aid create potential problems for me? Aids are intended to facilitate listener understanding, not function as decorative touches; they are to help, not hinder.

The supplementary aid is relevant if the speech cannot be given effectively without it. Listeners need to see the brushwork of Vincent van Gogh in order to appreciate how he achieved his visual effects. The audience needs to hear examples of country and western music in order to compare it with rock and roll. Watching a demonstration of how a particular piece of machinery works makes it easier for listeners to understand its application.

A supplemtary aid that is not carefully chosen can be a drawback. The speaker who brought his pet puppy to class in order to illustrate how animals can be trained did not expect the dog to become frightened by the crowd and proceed to bite a student. Even if the puppy performed exceedingly well, where do you keep him after the speech if you are one of the first speakers?

In the classroom, supplementary aids often are used to teach particular techniques. For example, nurses sometimes learn how to give shots by insert-

Photo: SMART Technologies, Inc.

Computerized presentation graphics offer ways to develop images which can be projected directly from a computer and allow for varying the visuals through a variety of media and media techniques.

ing needles into grapefruits; firefighters study methods of ladder placement on film; and law-enforcement students listen to recorded interrogations as a supplement to discussions of methodology. All these aids are intended to supplement the speaker's voice.

Visual Aids

Visual aids appeal to our sense of sight. They can include real objects, models, photographs, pictures, diagrams, charts, cutaways, and mockups.

Real Objects

To demonstrate the process of swinging a hammer, why not use a real hammer? Why not use an actual form to show how a traffic ticket is filled out, or bring in samples of the chemicals that are mixed to produce a particular product? All these are examples of using **real objects**—the actual thing—as visual aids.

Models

At times, it is impossible to use real objects. In such cases, a **scale model** (in exact proportion to the dimensions of the real object) or a **synthetic model** (not in proportion but nevertheless representational) may be used. For example, although a Boeing 747 jet cannot be brought into an aviation classroom, a scale model certainly can be.

Photographs, Pictures, Diagrams, and Maps

Visual representations such as photos, pictures, or diagrams can be effective in reinforcing a message or even in providing new information to listeners. A photograph of a crime scene might be shown to a jury if the members of the jury cannot visit the scene themselves. General Norman Schwarzkopf, who led the American effort in Operation Desert Storm, made extensive use of photos and maps in his press briefings about the military maneuvers in the Persian Gulf War.

Charts

A **chart** is a visual representation of statistical data that gives information in tabular or diagrammatic form. For example, by visually displaying increases and decreases in sales, a speaker can more easily discuss the general sales trend as a whole. By the same token, a pair of columns comparing the number of doctors available to a hospital with the number of doctors needed presents a visual image of the problem.

When preparing presentations, don't place red and green side by side.

Why: One in 10 people cannot clearly distinguish between them.[21]

Source: *Communication Briefings*, as adapted from *Business Presentations*, by Lani Arredondo, McGraw-Hill Inc., 11 W. 19th St., New York, NY 10011.

Cutaways

A **cutaway** is a model that shows the inside of an object, which an audience would otherwise have to imagine. To show the seating plan of an airplane, for instance, a segment of the body is peeled away to reveal the interior. To show the layers of materials used to construct a house, a wall is cut in half so that we see a cross section of the aluminum siding, the insulation, the studding, the wallboard, and the wallpaper.

Mockups

A **mockup** is a model constructed in sections. It is typically used to show how an object is put together. For example, in a speech explaining the plans for the new student activities building on your campus, you might use a mockup to demonstrate the process of construction. One room of the model might come off, revealing what will be on the second floor of the building; the second floor might be removed to reveal the layout of the first floor, and the first floor might be removed to reveal the basement. You would show the various segments of the building as your speech progresses.

You could use the same principle in a step-by-step speech on how to do something. Let's say you want to illustrate outlining techniques. On an overhead projector, place a transparent sheet on which is written the Roman numeral I and the first major heading. Now explain the use of the Roman numeral. Then place another sheet on top of the original that shows points A and B under this heading. Now discuss the secondary level of an outline. Continue to add sheets and discuss the remaining levels of the outline. Use of this mockup visually illustrates the outlining procedure as you describe it orally.

Presentation Graphics

Many speakers turn to **computerized presentation graphics** for preparing and displaying their visual aids. Presentation graphics packages such as *PowerPoint*, *Astound*, and *Action* incorporate word processing, outlining, graphs, tables, logos, clip art, illustrations, photography, video images, audio clips, and Internet connectivity. They offer ways to develop images that can be projected directly from a computer, printed on transparencies for use on an overhead projector, made into hard copy for use with an opaque project, or used to produce slides.

Computer graphics allow people who are not artists to prepare attractive visual aids. In addition, apprehensive speakers may feel less fear since they perceive that the audience members are looking at the visuals, not at the speaker.

A computerized presentation allows you to vary the visuals through a variety of media and media techniques. Using colored backgrounds, inserting cartoons and illustrations, and varying fonts and font sizes, add interest to the graphics, and, therefore, to the speech. It has been observed that "a true multimedia experience keeps a person's attention longer and gives you the ability to leave a visual impression in their mind."[18]

To realize the full advantage of a presentation program, you need to understand not only how to input the information (Figures 7.1 and 7.2), but also how to use the process during a presentation. Many colleges offer classes on how to prepare and use the programs, while some packages have video or computer tutorials. The *PowerPoint* package, for example, comes with *PowerPoint Wizard*, a program that directs you through each step of creating

Figure 7.1 PowerPoint® Presentation Graphics as Seen on Computer Screen

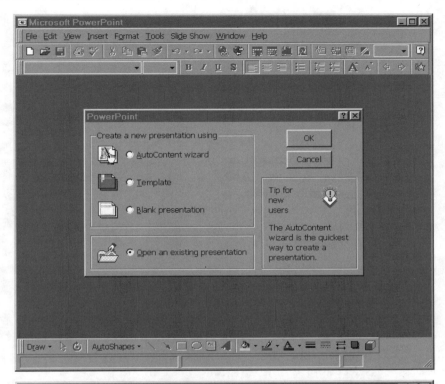

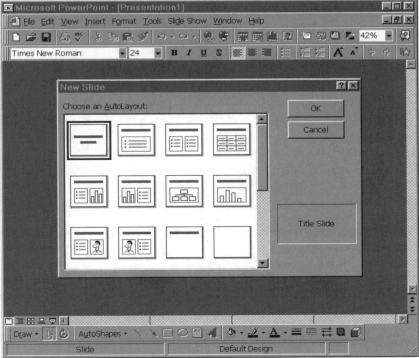

Source: Screen shots reprinted with permission from Microsoft Corporation.

❖ ❖ ❖ ❖

Figure 7.2 Creating a PowerPoint® Presentation

Using an Existing Outline
- Open an existing outline in your favorite word processor
- Save as text file
- Open Powerpoint
  - Select *blank presentation,* click *ok*
  - Click *ok* through default slide screen
- *Insert* menu, *Slides from Outline* option
  - Select appropriate file then insert
- Go to *View* Menu, *Outline* option
- Adjust hierarchy as needed, edit text as needed
- Go to *View* menu, select *Slides* to see content in slide format
- New slide can be added in this view:
  - *Insert* menu, *New Slide* option,
  - choose an appropriate *Autolayout*
  - enter text right on the slide

Add Some Zip
- *Format* menu, *presentation template* option
  - You might have to find the PowerPoint directory (folder) then Templates directory
  - Select appropriate directory for your output
  - Select desired look

Adjust Format
- *View* menu, *Master, Slide Master* options
  - drag and select text then change color, font, size, etc. Changes will be reflected in all slides when you return to slide view (*View* menu, *Slides* option)

Insert Graphics
- *Insert* menu, select *picture, clipart* or *movie* options
- Point to appropriate directory (folder) to find files

To Create a Powerpoint Presentation from Scratch
- *File* menu, *New* option
  - select *blank* or *template* for presentation
  - select appropriate *autolayout* style
- Select preferred view for entering text into slides, *View* menu, *Slides* or *Outline* option

go to it . . .

Catherine Hays, Electronic Media Center, University of Maryland. Reprinted by permission.

the visuals. For those who prefer to read instructions, books specifically written for the presentational packages are available.[19]

Like any communication strategy, using a computer presentation program probably will not be comfortable at first. However, some tips for the use of the technique may make it easier. These include:

1. *Plan systematically.* You should remember that presentation graphics, like any visual aids, are designed to aid your oral presentation, not replace it. As a result, you will want to plan carefully how best to incorporate the graphics so they reinforce or clarify your verbal points. Recognize that some speakers rely far too extensively on visuals, putting their entire presentation on the screen. Remember that "audiences are expected to comprehend word slides at a glance, without breaking concentration on the speaker. . . . [B]ombarded by word slides, audiences can only pretend that they're taking in the visuals and the voice."[20] Also be aware that the audience must sit in the dark during the use of the mechanical equipment. Darkness can be depressing, lead to sleepiness, and make it difficult to take notes.

2. *Keep in mind the purpose of supplementary aids.* If you can say something without any visual assistance, do so. Do not use visuals as decoration. Make sure that the materials aid your speech, not detract from it. After a while the novelty of graphics wears off and audience members find themselves bored, or they pay attention to the process rather than to what you are saying.

3. *The materials should be easy to read, visible by all, and simple to understand.* Some basic concepts for development of materials include:

   • *A slide presentation should utilize one main font, typically one that is easy to read when projected, perhaps Chicago or New York style fonts.*

   • *Limit color use to three or four different colors. Contrasting colors are more distinct and easier to see. Use of dark backgrounds and light text is easier on the eyes when projected.*

   • *Limit the amount of information presented on any one slide. A good rule of thumb is to apply the 4 by 6 rule. Slides should have no more than four lines with approximately six words per line or six lines with four words per line.*

   • *Each slide or visual should focus on a single idea and convey that information effectively.*

   • *Punctuation and capitalization should be consistent throughout.*

   • *Spelling and punctuation should be correct.*

   • *Prepare a neutral color ending slide. This avoids a glaring white screen after your last visual.*

4. *Practice thoroughly.* One of the questions often asked is, "How much should I practice?" A valuable rule here is to spend at least as much time in practicing delivery as you spend on preparing

You think presenting with visuals is more effective than just talk alone, but you'd like some hard evidence. Here it is from a test of both methods done at the Wharton School of Business:

- Audience members perceived presenters who used visuals as more effective than those who did not. *Some audience comments*: clearer, more concise, better prepared, more professional, credible and interesting.

- 79% of the audience that saw the visual presentation reached consensus, compared to 58% in the non-visuals group.

- 67% of the visuals group members found the presenter convincing, versus 50% in the other group.

- 64% of those in the visuals group were able to make decisions right after the presentation. Those in the non-visuals group lagged in decision making.

And if that's not enough evidence for you, consider this time-saving point: Using visuals cut meeting time by 24%.

Source: *Communication Briefings,* as adapted from *pr reporter,* P.O. Box 600, Exeter, NH 03833.

the visuals. If it takes an hour to pull together visuals, then the speaker should plan to spend an hour with those slides in actual delivery practice. Because of differences in equipment, practice with the actual equipment to be used during the presentation is preferred. Once you get your materials developed, work with the computer and/or the projector so that you can use the equipment smoothly.

If you are using a computer, learn how to use the mouse so that you can get to the right slide at the precise time in the sequence of your talk when it should appear. While practicing remember that listening to a speaker read word-for-word from a slide visible to all is both uncreative and boring. Look at the audience, not the visual.

5. *Maintain a clear focus with the graphics.* A speaker must be certain to connect the verbal discussion to whatever visual elements are presented. Listeners shouldn't have to struggle to comprehend the connection between the visual and verbal message.

6. *Maintain control of the presentation.* The speaker, not the technology, must maintain control. Just as you should cover your poster board visual aid until you want the audience to see it, an effective speaker controls the use of the projection equipment throughout the presentation. Be familiar with the equipment and be patient. Accidentally advancing two slides instead of one takes control away from the speaker. If something goes wrong, and with use of electronic equipment it well may, don't panic. Adjust to the place in the presentation you need to be at, apologize for the interruption or make a joke about it, and go on.

7. *Be prepared for the worst.* Have a contingency plan available in case of equipment failure. Ask yourself what you will do if, at the start or during the speech, the equipment malfunctions. Many

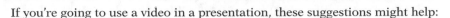

If you're going to use a video in a presentation, these suggestions might help:

- Preview the video at least twice. Decide which part of the video you will show. It's not always necessary to show the entire tape.

- Be prepared to show a clear link between the content of the video and the training program.

- Introduce the video in depth. Don't just turn it on and get out of the way.

- Prepare questions and discussion points related to the video.

Source: *Communication Briefings*, as adapted from Louise Brinie, cited in *Creative Training Techniques*, 50 S. 9th St., Minneapolis, MN 55402.

speakers print copies of the necessary graphics for distribution as a hedge against negative possibilities.

8. *When you get to the site of the presentation, check the facilities out.*

- *If you did not bring your own equipment, make sure any equipment that has been ordered is present, working, and has the right software loaded.*

- *Pull down the projection screen.*

- *Check the lighting to determine the appropriate light level for audience viewing.*

- *Check the power connections to be sure that they are operational.*

- *If you are using an overhead projector, check to ensure that the machine comes with a spare light bulb, just in case it burns out.*

Computer-based presentation tools offer powerful advantages to both speaker and listener. Corporate boardrooms, training seminars, college classrooms and lecture halls have seen the use of presentation tools move from a rarity to a requirement. Unfortunately, examples abound of speakers who fail to use the presentation tools effectively. Don't be one of those people.

Audio Aids

Audio aids such as tape recordings, CDs, and other sound duplication mechanisms may be the only way to demonstrate a point accurately to listeners. For example, a discussion of composer Andrew Lloyd Webber's music in the plays *The Phantom of the Opera, Evita, Jesus Christ Superstar*, and *Starlight Express* can be enhanced by allowing the audience to hear excerpts. Likewise, playing a recording of Martin Luther King, Jr.'s "I Have a Dream" speech is an excellent way to demonstrate King's style of oral presentation.

Audiovisual Aids

Audiovisual aids such as films, videotapes, and audiotapes combined with slide shows mix sight and sound. Thus a video of a senatorial candidate making a victory speech at party headquarters on election night allows the audience not only to hear the performance but also to see the reaction of the people who worked for the candidate's election. Showing a videotape of an executive's speech is an excellent way to illustrate that person's vocal and physical mannerisms. A presentation that combines audiotapes with slides, in which the pictures are synchronized with a prerecorded oral text, would make the step-by-step procedure used by a nurse to prepare a patient for surgery much more vivid.

Listening to Supporting Material

Because the listener's attention span is constantly fluctuating, speakers try to keep their listeners engaged throughout the presentation by selecting interesting supporting materials. As a listener, you need to be aware of the types of devices speakers are using and realize that they are intended for your benefit. You also should be aware, however, that you may get so involved in the supporting materials that you find yourself being taken in by the device and lose track of your personal responsibility to listen at the critical level, evaluating what is said and how conclusions are reached.

If you are a typical listener, you will find yourself positively influenced by personal stories; humor; unusual, startling, dramatic material; a shocking statistic; and visualizations.

The statistics, testimony, examples, and information should support the speaker's claims. The listener should examine evidence for clarity (how clear and intelligible it is), accuracy (how precise and factual it is), and reliability (how trustworthy and dependable it is).

Some basic questions can guide the listener in assessing the speaker's evidence:

1. *Is the evidence clear?*
2. *Is the evidence consistent with other known evidence?*
3. *Is the evidence consistent with the speaker?*
4. *Is the evidence timely?*
5. *Is the evidence applicable to the argument?*
6. *Is the evidence pertinent to the argument?*
7. *Is the source of the evidence reliable?*
8. *Is the source of the evidence competent in the area cited?*
9. *Is the source of the evidence free to report all findings?*
10. *Is the source of the evidence suppressing or distorting facts?*
11. *Is the source of the evidence sincere?*[22]

Summary

This chapter described the types of supporting materials to be used in developing a speech. The major ideas presented were:

♦ *Supporting material can be used to develop the major and subordinate points within the body of the speech. Supporting material should clarify the speaker's point or demonstrate that the point has some probability of being true.*

❖ ❖ ❖ ❖

♦ *Supporting material includes illustrations, specific instances, exposition, statistics, analogies, testimony, and humor.*

♦ *Three means for presenting and focusing supporting material are attention devices, restatement, and forecasting.*

♦ *Using visual, audio, and audiovisual aids is often a valuable way to help the listener understand the message.*

♦ *Types of visual aids include real objects, models, photographs, pictures, diagrams, charts, cutaways, and mockups.*

♦ *Listeners need to be aware of the types of devices speakers are using and realize that they are intended for the listener's benefit.*

Key Terms

supporting materials	audiovisual aids
hypothetical illustrations	verbal illustrations
specific instances	factual illustrations
statistics	exposition
testimony	analogy
visualizations	expert
humor	attention devices
concrete supporting materials	familiar supporting materials
novelty	suspense
conflict	restatement
forecast	statement of declaration
statistical surveying	random sampling
supplementary aids	visual aids
real objects	scale models
synthetic models	charts
cutaways	mockups
computerized presentation graphics	audio aids

Learn by Doing

1. Find a humorous story that you could use in a speech about the educational system of the United States, male-female communication differences, or sports.

2. What analogy could you use to explain each of the following?

   a. The growth cycle of a plant

   b. A tornado

   c. Living with a cat or a dog

   d. Attending a university or community college

3. Select one of the following purpose statements. Identify some supporting material that would be needed to develop the speech.

   a. To inform the audience why competency testing is being used as a determination for high school graduation by discussing the three major reasons for its use

b. To inform the audience why I believe that the theory of color therapy is valid by examining the research and findings by color therapy investigators

c. To persuade the audience to fill out and sign living wills by listing five reasons for them to do so

4. What supplementary aid would be appropriate for a speech on these topics?

   a. A comparison between the population figures of the United States, Canada, China, India, and Brazil

   b. A demonstration of how to operate a Macintosh Power Book computer

   c. The western migration of the pioneers across North America

   d. The interior and exterior design of Oriole Stadium at Camden Yards in Baltimore

   e. An explanation of the step-by-step construction of Jacobs Field, the home baseball park of the Cleveland Indians, which will allow the audience to understand the stages of the construction

   f. An explanation of the physical parts of the brain so the audience can see its three-dimensional structure

   g. The difference between the vocalizations of a dolphin and a whale

   h. The performance of the Washington Ballet's production of *The Nutcracker*

5. Select a newspaper or magazine article that bases its conclusions on the use of statistical surveying. Evaluate the statistics by using the information on statistical surveying in this chapter.

6. Select a topic with which you are familiar. List the type of support you would most like to hear in a speech given by someone on this topic. Your instructor will break you into groups of four or five. Share the topic and the types of support with your group members. Have a general discussion on whether the members agree with each speaker's assessment of the support you selected.

Endnotes

1. Thomas P. Kemp Sr., "Progress Is Providential," *Vital Speeches of the Day*, 63 (September 1, 1997), p. 696.

2. Norris McWhirter, *Guinness 1984 Book of World Records* (New York: Sterling, 1984), p. 28.

3. Helen Gillman and Damien Simonis, *Italy, A Lonely Planet Travel Survival Kit* (Hawthorn, Vic, Australia, 1996), p. 37.

4. Graham T. Molitor, "What Prompts Criminal Behavior?" *Vital Speeches of the Day*, 64 (November 1, 1997), p. 45.

5. Ernest Parker Mills, *Listening: Key to Communication* (New York: Petrocelli Books, 1974), p. 36.

6. Madeline K. Albright, "The Israeli-Palestinian Peace Process," *Vital Speeches of the Day*, 63 (September 1, 1997), p. 675.

7. Bob Orben, "How to Spruce Up Those Dull Speeches," *Enterprise, the Journal of the National Association of Manufacturers* (April 1978).

8. A summary of Charles R. Gruner, "Advice to the Beginning Speaker on Using Humor—What the Research Tells Us," *Communication Education*, 34 (April 1985), pp. 142–145.

9. Ibid., p. 145.

10. Orben, p. 1.

11. Cheryl L. Coward, "Gays Angered by Lesbian Jokes Told by Politicians," *Washington Blade*, November 22, 1991, p. 1.

12. Sources include: Bob Orben, *2500 Jokes to Start 'Em Laughing* (Comedy Center, Inc., 700 Orange Street, Wilmington, Del. 1981), *Reader's Digest Treasury of American Humor; Encyclopedia of Humor, The Comic Encyclopedia, The Speaker's Handbook of Humor, Podium Humor, Treasury of Humor, Jokes and How to Tell Them, How Speakers Make People Laugh,* and *Stories for Speakers*.

13. Carl Geist, "The Pulp and Paper Industry," *Vital Speeches of the Day*, 63 (September 1, 1997), p. 685.

14. D. A. Norman, "Memory While Shadowing," *Quarterly Journal of Experimental Psychology*, 21 (February 1969), pp. 85–93.

15. Darrell Huff, *How to Lie with Statistics* (New York: Norton, 1954), pp. 123–142.

16. Two excellent sources on statistics are Herbert Arkin and Henry Hill, *Sampling in Auditing: A Simplified Guide and Statistical Table* (Price Waterhouse and Company, n.d.); and D. A. Johnson and W. H. Glenn, *The World of Statistics* (St. Louis: Webster, 1961).

17. "Haul of Illegals Hits All-Time High," *U.S. News & World Report*, October 3, 1983, p. 11.

18. Russell Shaw, "When the Presentation Went Up in Smoke," *Sky* (November, 1996), p. 39.

19. Doug Lowe, *PowerPoint for Dummies* (Foster City, Calif.: IDG Books, 1994) is a useful guide for using *PowerPoint*.

20. Steve Zousmer, ". . . And, in Conclusion, Just Look at the Screen," *New York Times* (December 28, 1997), p. BU12.

21. Lani Arredondo, *Business Presentations* (New York: McGraw Hill, 1994.)

22. Andrew D. Wolvin and Carolyn Gwynn Coakley, *Listening* (Dubuque, Iowa: Brown/Benchmark, 1996), pp. 335–336.

CHAPTER EIGHT

Sources of
Supporting Materials

Chapter Outline

❑ 8.1 Print Sources of Information
   Books
   Magazines
   Newspapers
   Journals
   Indexes
   Government Pamphlets
   Publications From Special-Interest Groups

❑ 8.2 Nonprint Sources of Information
   Audiovisual Materials
   Interviews

❑ 8.3 Computer Searches
   Computer-Based Retrieval Systems
   The Internet

❑ 8.4 Recording Your Research

❑ 8.5 Listening to Sources

Learning Outcomes

After reading this chapter you should be able to:

- *List and describe the research sources available for use in developing public speaking messages.*

- *Identify and evaluate basic reference sources used for obtaining overviews, concepts, data, and other types of information necessary to develop public speeches.*

- *Explain the value of using, and the method for finding, research sources such as books, magazines, newspapers, journals, indexes, government publications, publications from special-interest groups, and nonprint media.*

- *Record research information.*

❖ ❖ ❖ ❖

Some of the information we use to develop messages is based on **personal knowledge**—personal experiences, observations, or learning acquired through sources such as school, the media, and reading. As we are exposed to information, we retain a certain amount of it. This knowledge forms the core of our basis for communication. We select words and examples from this storehouse, and we use it to organize messages.

Many times, however, to develop a message fully, we need information that is not part of our personal core of knowledge. In such cases, we must find **outside knowledge**—information from sources outside of our own experiences and direct observations. A research chemist, for example, could probably give a speech describing the company's major products. But what if she were asked to give a detailed presentation on the company's budget or to tell the complete history of the organization? Most speakers would find such topics difficult to handle without more knowledge. Sources of outside knowledge include books, magazines, newspapers, special journals, indexes, government publications, and the publications of special-interest groups. (See Figure 8.1.) Additional sources include nonprint materials such as tape recordings, CDs, films, videotapes, charts, and models, as well as interviews or correspondence with knowledgeable people in a particular field. You can find this information by going to the library, searching on the Internet, and doing interviews.

Figure 8.1 Quick Guide to Basic Reference Tools

For Overviews and Conceptual Information

♦ *Encyclopedias*. Use for historical, conceptual, and factual information written by experts, and for bibliographies (at the ends of articles) of works by important authors.

♦ *Handbooks*. Use for more detailed overviews of subjects, usually in single volumes devoted to narrow fields, with articles written by experts, often with bibliographies at the ends of sections. (To locate in the card catalogue or computer index, look under *handbooks, manuals*, or the specific title of the handbook or manual.)

♦ *Dictionaries*. Use for definitions of terms you do not understand and for synonyms of key words. Many dictionaries specialize in one subject only. (To locate in the card catalogue or computer index, look under *dictionaries*, then a specific title such as "Education.")

♦ *Annual Reviews*. Use for recent overviews of significant developments in a subject field, and for bibliographic information. (To locate in the card catalogue or computer index, look under *yearbooks*.)

For Data

♦ *Fact Books*. Use for hard information on names, places, and dates in a concise format. (Listed under *almanacs* in the card catalogue and computer index. Examples: *Facts on File, Information Please Almanac*.)

♦ *Statistical Sources*. Use for statistical support and documentation of your ideas. (Listed in the card catalogue and computer index under *statistics* and then the subject heading, for example, "Statistics—Labor Supply.")

♦ *Biographical Sources*. Use to verify the credentials of authors and to get information about people. (To locate in the card catalogue or computer index, consult personal names under subject headings or the name of the occupational group of the person.)

Springboards to More Information

♦ *Bibliographies*. Use to identify other books, parts of books, films, and magazine articles on a subject. (To locate in the card catalogue or computer index, consult the subject heading followed by the words *bibliography, biobibliography, discography*, or *film catalogue*.)

♦ *Indexes*. Use to locate more information, usually but not always limited to periodicals. Indexing is done for research reports, government publications, and parts of books, plays, poetry, or songs. (To locate in the card catalogue or computer index, consult the subject heading followed by the words *indexes, abstracts*, or *bibliography*.)

Be aware that there is a difference between gathering information about a topic and doing research for a specific speech. In gathering information, you are looking for general material that might lead you toward a speech goal, specific topic, or method of delivery. By contrast, in doing specific, purposeful research, you know exactly what you are looking for based on the speech goal, topic, and method, and you selectively pick material that will help develop the specific outcomes of the speech. For example, if you knew you wanted to give a speech about phobias, you would start gathering information about anything that had to do with phobias. From this accumulated information you should then be able to develop a purpose statement. However, if you already had developed a purpose statement, the search would be different. Let's assume your purpose statement is "To inform the audience about phobic diseases by listing, defining, and giving examples of agoraphobia, speechophobia, xenophobia, and claustrophobia." You would specifically restrict your search to finding a definition of phobic diseases and definitions and examples of agoraphobia, speechophobia, xenophobia, and claustrophobia.

Speakers also must assess the validity of the information they locate. All sources of information reflect certain perceptions and biases. Consequently, it is wise to try to determine the bias of a source and to interpret its information accordingly.[1] When doing research for a presentation, it is a good idea to find several agreeing authoritative sources so that your supporting details will be credible to your listeners.

8.1 Print Sources of Information

Books

Personal, academic, and public libraries are the font of much information; nevertheless, you must know how to find the materials you need. In academic and public libraries, books are shelved according to a numerical system and can be located by looking through the **computer output microfiche (COM),** card catalogue, or the library's electronic computer catalogue, under the title, the author's name, or the general subject. The code number indicates where the volume is shelved.

Unfortunately, not all subjects are easy to locate. For example, an average library's card catalogue or computer search system would probably reveal no information if you looked under the title "Arapesh." To learn which books contain material about this subject, you would need some additional information. By looking in the encyclopedia, you would discover that the Arapesh are a primitive mountain-dwelling people of New Guinea whose society was investigated by anthropologist Margaret Mead and discussed in her book *Sex and Temperament in Three Primitive Societies*. Based on this information, you could look in the COM under such subjects as anthropology, Margaret Mead, New Guinea, and *Sex and Temperament in Three Primitive Societies*. You could then check the indexes of the books you find or do a computer search for references to needed facts.

Books are of great value in supplying information, but they quickly can become out of date. It generally takes at least a year for the average book to move from the author's final draft through the printing process and onto the shelves of a library. This is in addition to the time the author has taken to write the book. Some subjects change little, and in these areas books are a good research source. But for quickly changing subjects, more up-to-date sources are needed for a thorough investigation.

Be aware that just because someone wrote a book does not mean the person is an expert. Books get published because the author has been able to convince a publisher that the material should be put into print, or because the publisher has determined that there is a need for such material. Also realize that some authors may be biased and unethical. This often necessitates your ascertaining such factors as the author's political, social, or religious views.

Magazines

Most magazines are designed to print recent information quickly. Sources such as *Time, Newsweek*, and *U.S. News & World Report* are published weekly, so their information is current. Researchers must be aware, however, that because these sources gather their data so quickly, some inaccuracies may occur. In addition, the editorial staffs of magazines—like the authors of books—have political and ideological biases, such as being politically conservative or liberal, that may temper what they write or influence what subjects they cover.

To find information in magazines, start with the *Readers' Guide to Periodical Literature*, a publication that indexes magazine articles by subject, title, and author. Remember, however, that not all magazines are listed in this guide. Check inside the cover of the bound volumes to see which magazines are listed. Many libraries also indicate which magazines they subscribe to so that researchers can narrow their choices to those publications. Besides using this index, you may undertake a computer search of magazine sources.

Further periodical listings may also be found in the *International Index* or in indexes to special magazines that report on particular areas, such as computers, nursing, or dental care. Business information can be found in the *Business Periodicals Index*, and educational concepts in the *Education Index*; the arts are covered in the *Humanities Index*, and psychology and sociology are in the *Social Sciences Index*.

❖ ❖ ❖ ❖   **Newspapers**

Newspapers, like magazines, contain current information that is published daily, weekly, or biweekly. Again, as is the case with magazines, because of the speed with which newspapers are written and printed, you must be aware of the possibility of error. In addition, understand as you read that not all parts of newspapers play the same role. News stories report events that have happened or are happening. Editorials reflect the beliefs of individual writers. News stories, it may be assumed, are based on research and facts; editorials are the opinions of the writers.

Many libraries do not keep past issues of newspapers, but some store newspaper information on microfilm. Some newspapers, such as the *New York Times*, have indexes which may be available in a library or revealed through computer searches. Or, if you know specifically what newspaper you are looking for, you can go to the home page of the newspaper and search from there.

Journals

Professional organizations often publish journals reporting research and theories in their specific fields. The National Communication Association, for example, publishes such journals as *Communication Education*, the *Quarterly Journal of Speech*, *Communication Monographs*, and *Critical Studies in Mass Communication*. Thus, students interested in finding out about some area of speech communication can refer to these journals. These can be accessed by finding the journal in the library or locating it on the Internet through the publishing organization. The NCA, for example, has a home page which you can use to access the journal information. In addition, the association offers a CD ROM that lists journal articles in the field and contains the articles themselves. Similarly, students of law enforcement can find topics directly related to their field in such publications as *The Training Key*, a brochure circulated by the International Association of Chiefs of Police, and the *Journal of Law and Criminology*.

You can locate professional journals in various ways. Libraries have catalogues that list organizations and their publications. Checking the footnotes in a textbook on the subject of interest will often give you clues to professional journals related to that field. Writing to or calling a professional organization is another way to find out about such publications, as is, of course, searching the Web.

Indexes

Encyclopedias, atlases, and bibliographical guides are all indexes that provide descriptive information in certain categories. In trying to find bibliographical material about the American poet Carl Sandburg, for instance, you are wise to consult *Who's Who Among North American Authors*. *Who's Who in America*, another index, is also a possible source for this information.

Remember that an index gives you a minimal amount of information. Thus, if you want in-depth material about Carl Sandburg, a more fruitful approach is to search the subject index of the card catalogue or the electronic catalogue to locate such sources as *Carl Sandburg*, by G. W. Allen, and *Carl Sandburg, Lincoln of Our Literature*, by N. Callahan.

When using bound encyclopedias, you do well to recognize that many of them are expensive to produce and therefore are not completely reprinted each year. As a result, some material in encyclopedias may be out of date as well as limited.

Be aware that some encyclopedias are available on CD ROM, and these are often updated. In addition, the information may be accessed through the Internet if your driver can locate the source.

Government Pamphlets

The U.S. government publishes pamphlets, available at minimal cost, on a variety of subjects. These can be found at bookstores inside federal buildings in many major cities of the United States. If there are no such outlets in your area, write to the Superintendent of Documents, U.S. Government Printing Office, in Washington, D.C., and ask for information about the specific topics you wish to research. Because it takes time for the information to be processed, plan ahead if you want to use this source. Also be aware that many libraries have government pamphlets in their research sections. Many government pamphlets can be accessed through the Internet.

Publications From Special-Interest Groups

Special-interest groups such as the American Cancer Society, the Coalition for Rural Development, the American Chemical Society, and the American Society for Training and Development publish information regarding their research and programs. A telephone call or a letter to such an organization often brings a prompt response with the requested materials. Information about these groups can be located in the telephone book or in *Gale's Encyclopedia of Associations*.

If you use information from a special-interest group, remember that the organization has probably been founded to put forth a particular philosophy, or may have a bias because of its sponsorship or mission. For example, Planned Parenthood is an organization that provides people with birth control and abortion counseling. If you are looking for information about those topics, Planned Parenthood would be a good source; however, if you are looking for an unbiased, objective viewpoint on abortion, it probably would not be a valid source. Similarly, publications produced by Jewish organizations such as B'nai B'rith, while being good sources of information about the realities of contemporary Jewish life, would not necessarily be helpful if you were seeking unbiased information about the Arab-Jewish conflicts in Israel.

8.2 Nonprint Sources of Information

Audiovisual Materials

Much information is also available from nonprint media. In fact, libraries and audiovisual departments of colleges and universities often have tape recordings, records, CDs, films, filmstrips, and videotapes from commercially and noncommercially prepared sources covering a variety of topics. These sources usually are catalogued in a manner similar to that used for books and periodicals. Some nonprint materials are available for general circulation, but others must be used on the premises.

Interviews

Researchers use interviews to find information that is not available from written or audiovisual sources or to supplement other types of research. What better way is there to find out how the budget of your college is developed, for example, than by talking to the treasurer or the budget director? Interviews can be conducted in a variety of ways. If the person you wish to interview is not available for a face-to-face or a telephone session, you can submit a series of questions to be answered either through writing or tape recording.

Here are some specific suggestions for conducting an informational interview:

1. *Prepare for the interview.* Determine what information you need. Select someone who is an expert on the topic. You can find the names of people by asking friends, instructors, or relatives about anyone they know or know about who is knowledgeable in the specific field. Consult such sources as professional directories, which are available in many libraries, and refer to the yellow pages of the telephone book. Call resource lines such as doctors' and counselors' services, governmental offices, or members of a college faculty. Call the local newspaper and talk to reporters or editorialists who may be able to lead you to an expert in the field.

   Prepare questions that will give you specific information that relates to your topic. Frame the questions so you get the exact material you desire. If, for example, you are interviewing a human resource manager for your speech about the nonverbal aspects of employment interviewing, you could ask, "What specific clothing should a male college graduate wear when interviewing with a Fortune 500 company?" This question would be more likely to yield usable information than the question, "What can you tell me about job interviewing?"

2. *Make the initial contact recognizing that many people lead busy lives.* Realize that people usually can't and won't drop everything because you have a speech due tomorrow. Few people will see you on the spur of the moment. Give yourself enough lead time to call or write and set up the appointment. Depending on the person and the position he or she holds, you may need to work through a secretary, an agent, or some other source to make the contact. Do not be discouraged if your first choice is not available; keep trying until you locate a viable source. Be sure when you do locate a source that you set an exact date, time, and location for the meeting.

   Even if the person agrees to supply information, he or she may not want to do an in-person interview. Some people prefer that you submit the questions you will be asking in advance, or might want to write their answers for you rather than be interviewed in person. If the person is going to respond in written form, include a self-addressed, stamped envelope with your questions. If you are planning on video taping, using an audio recorder or camera, ask in advance for permission. You may also find that some people will be open to telephone or e-mail interviews.

3. *Much of the success of an interview is often based on the initial contact.* Be prompt, dress appropriately, have the necessary equipment you need (writing tool, paper, tape recorder with active batteries, and/or a camera). When you enter the office, or wherever the interview is to take place, identify yourself by name and follow the greeting by introducing the topic.

4. *Give any necessary background information.* Explain to the person you are interviewing what your topic is, why you are interviewing her or him, what you expect to find out, and what you will do with the information. Even if you have already discussed these issues when making the initial contact, you might consider going over them again to remind the interviewee.

5. *Ask purposeful questions.* You are interviewing this person because he or she has information you want. Don't waste time. Ask direct questions that elicit the specific information you are seeking. Follow up any unclear or incomplete answers by asking for specifics and examples. Ask a single question at a time, not a whole series, because multiple questions are confusing. If the interviewee gives short answers, ask for an explanation. For example, as you are interviewing an academic department chairperson about why there are fewer classes offered this semester than last, she answers, "The budget." You might follow up by asking, "Specifically, what about the budget brought the need for the change?" Ask for examples, clarifiers, details, statistics, and illustrations so you have material to develop your speech.

6. *Listen to what is said and how it is said.* Take notes or ask if you can tape-record the interview. If you are taking notes, be sure they are accurate. To make sure you have recorded the material correctly, you may want to repeat major ideas back to the interviewee by stating, "Therefore, what you are saying is . . ." Ask for any written material that might be available about the topic. Organizations can often provide materials such as pamphlets, press releases, books, or directories which will make your search for information easier.

7. *End the interview by thanking the person.* Besides the personal expression of appreciation, it also is customary to send a thank-you letter to the interviewee.

8.3 Computer Searches

Traditionally, a researcher would obtain information by going to a library and looking in the card catalogue or asking the reference librarian what sources were available. Recently, however, there has been a marked change in the nature of information gathering in libraries and on college campuses. In most libraries, computer output microfiche (COM) or **electronic catalogues** accessed through on-line computers have replaced the card catalogues. Besides COM, some libraries have their catalogues on magnetic tape that requires a special computer terminal for access. When going to a library, ask which system is in operation.

Computer-Based Retrieval Systems

The computer search is the use of a **computer-based retrieval system** that allows the researcher to compile a bibliography or a set of facts relevant to a specific topic. Searches may be used for a variety of purposes, including gathering research or references, compiling a reading list, acquiring statistical information, or simply keeping abreast of developments in a field. Naturally, a major advantage to this method is the time saved, as a computer retrieves in minutes information that otherwise takes much longer to compile. The search is also quite comprehensive and can locate references that the most careful conventional searches may not. Another feature is the timeliness of the material, since these data bases are frequently updated. Some services charge for access to their information.[2]

The Internet

The Internet can be a valuable information exploration tool. It is possible to search in places which were inaccessible to most people in the recent past. The speech researcher is not restricted to what is available at local libraries, but can use the entire world as a potential source of information. Valuable information can be gleaned from government agencies or organizations who do research and publishing on specific topical areas (e.g., health, business, social service, political science).

However, researchers should realize that the Internet is not always a perfect search source. As one Internet expert states, "The Internet makes readily available so much information that students think research is far easier than it really is. Students are producing superficial research papers [and speeches], full of data—some of it suspect—and with little thought."[3]

An investigation concerning the use of the Internet as a means of finding material reveals potential problems for speech researchers:

It is difficult for the uninitiated to find their way around the Internet. Few people have sufficient expertise to unlock the code to finding all of the potential sources of information on the Internet. Most researchers simply tinker around until they think they have found the information and stop. One of the major things that is missing is a reference librarian.

"The Internet is commonly thought of as a library, although a poorly catalogued one, given limitations of the search engines available."[4] "Search engines are imprecise."[5] The quality of equipment available and the format design of the software can greatly limit the depth of the search for information.

"Because information is so accessible, students stop far too quickly."[6] Assuming that everything about a particular topic will be revealed through an Internet exploration, researchers often stop short in looking for information elsewhere. Don't overlook the fact that many books, professional journals,

and organizational pamphlets are not available to webmasters. In addition, using only the Internet eliminates one of the best research sources—the interview. The best advice is to use the Internet as a part of, not as the whole, in researching a topic.

Many sites are not kept up-to-date.[7] Don't assume that because something appears on the Internet it is up-to-date and accurate. Lots of information is entered and then forgotten about. Also, some information may be fabricated and sent out. People with biases or prejudices may manipulate information for their own means and then post inaccurate material on the web. Anyone can enter anything he or she wants. Just because you find some information, doesn't mean it is true, well researched, and up-to-date. There are no editors, evaluators, or research scholars screening much of what appears.

An expert on research gave some excellent advice on using the Internet for research when he stated:

> Academic research is a three-step process: finding the relevant information, assessing the quality of that information and then using that information either to try to conclude something, to uncover something, to provide something or to argue something. At its best the Internet, like a library, provides only data. The Internet mainly is only useful for that first part, and also a little bit for the second. It is not useful at all in the third.[8]

With these warnings in mind, follow these suggestions to locating the best possible Internet sources:

Find valid sources. Look for sources recognized as generally doing accurate research, such as universities, scholarly organizations, and the government. If you are looking for statistics for a speech about rape, for example, you may be able to find information from your local police department or the FBI. In addition, associations like the American Psychological Association and the American Counseling Association have home pages which can lead you to information that has been published after being reviewed by experts in the field.

Use the data bases available through college libraries. Your university or college is probably part of a library consortium. This means it pays a fee to get a site license so that you have full access to the sources available in all of the libraries that are part of the consortium. These data bases give citation information and abstracts so you can find the article you need, sometimes telling you whether or not it is available at your local library. Since these are academically based, you are likely to get more accurate material than from a generic data base.

8.4 Recording Your Research

As you do your research, keep a record of where all the information comes from so you can refer to the source to find additional information, answer questions about the source, or give oral footnotes during a speech. When you write a term paper, you footnote **quotations** (material written or spoken by a person in the exact words in which it was presented) or **paraphrases** (someone else's ideas put into your own words). Do the same in public speaking, except orally. For example, in a speech concerning male-female communication, you might make the following **oral footnote** to present information from a source:

As you do your research, keep a record of where all the information comes from so you can refer to the source to find additional information, answer questions about the source, or give oral footnotes during a speech.

> *Deborah Tannen, in her book,* You Just Don't Understand, *stated, "Habitual ways of talking are hard to change. Learning to respect others' ways of talking may be a bit easier. Men should accept that many women regard exchanging details about personal lives as a basic ingredient of intimacy, and women should accept that many men do not share this view."* [9]

In some instances, you may also feel that it is necessary to establish the quoted author as an authority. In this case, you might preface your oral footnote by saying,

> *Deborah Tannen, an internationally recognized scholar, has received grants from the National Endowment for the Humanities and the National Science Foundation, and is a professor of linguistics at Georgetown University.*

There are many ways to record both the bibliographical information and the notes that result from your research. As Figure 8.2 shows, one method is to use a running bibliography that lists the names of the authors, the titles of sources used, and the places, publishers, and dates of publication. The list is numbered so that you can easily refer to it when taking notes.

Figure 8.2 Recording Bibliographical Information and Notes

---

1. Tannen, Deborah. <u>You Just Don't Understand.</u> New York: William Morrow, 1990.

2. Bate, Barbara. <u>Communication and the Sexes.</u> New York: Harper & Row, 1988.

3. Pearson, Judy Cornelia. <u>Gender and Communication,</u> 2nd ed. Dubuque, Iowa: William C. Brown, 1992.

As you do your research and record your information, label your notes with the number of the source instead of repeatedly writing out the bibliographical material. Many researchers like to take notes on three-by-five-inch or four-by-six-inch cards, others on sheets of paper, and still others enter the material into their computers.

Figure 8.3 shows how a typical footnote reference to the passage quoted from Tannen's book would appear on a card. The source of the quote is labeled as 1–122 (source 1 on the bibliography, page 122). Because the material is directly quoted, it has quotation marks around it. If you paraphrase material, quotation marks are not used, but it should be made clear that the material is from another source and not original to you.

Figure 8.3 Footnote and Bibliographic Reference on Notecard

Topic: Change Male-Female Communication Patterns

Source: 1-122

Information: "Habitual ways of talking are hard to change. Learning to respect others' ways of talking may be a bit easier. Men should accept that many women regard exchanging details about personal lives as a basic ingredient of intimacy, and women should accept that many men do not share this view."

If you use sheets of paper or do keyboarding into a computer, identify the source in the left-hand margin. Later, cut the paper into strips, or print out the pages, cut them, and arrange them as you organize your speech.

8.5 Listening to Sources

As a listener, you should be aware of potential positive and negative uses of information which the speaker presents. Ideally, researchers search out facts and other sources which precisely back up their ideas, record that information accurately, and relate it to you, the listener, with the original intent of the developer of the ideas. However, speakers may distort evidence, intentionally or unintentionally.

As prospective speakers search for materials to back up their ideas, he/she may find information that generally fits, that can be manipulated to fit, or that can be altered to create the desired meaning. Your job as an efficient listener of speeches is to ascertain whether the ideas seem reasonable, are parallel to what you know to be true, and are used in a manner that allows you to believe that the speaker is using the materials in an ethical manner.

Furthermore, many information sources—the press, government agencies, pressure groups, and professional scholars—have biases that can limit the credibility of the information they produce. Good listeners make every effort to assess the biases of the information sources a speaker uses. Realize that "ideology, national or other group interest, individual self-interest, career involvement, unconscious partisanship, exile mentality, reaction against one's past, and desire for power are some of the biases which distort perception."[10]

"Consider the source."

Knowing, for example, that the National Rifle Association is opposed to gun control, any quote of NRA arguments against gun control should be viewed with suspicion. The same is true for support of school prayer by fundamentalist religious groups, or pro-women stances proposed by the National Association of Women.

Also realize that as a listener you enter into any public communication with your own biases and prejudices. Many of these are the results of your personal cultural background including your race, age, religion, ethic origin, and gender. You have been influenced by the communication sources which surround you. Most people, for example, are heavily influenced by the popular media. If you are typical, your primary source of world information is television: 69 percent of Americans turn to television for their information. 43 percent rely on newspapers, 16 percent use the radio, 6 percent learn from other people, and 4 percent rely on magazines as their major news source.[11] You may have to set aside your learned biases in order to give the speaker a chance to convince you that what is being said is valid. Again, let your common sense set in as you listen. Ask yourself questions. Does the idea, whether I agree with it or not, have some creditability? Is this view, though different from mine, valid? If so, you might want to adjust your vision, accept a different stance.

You may have heard the comment "Consider the source." Such advice is good warning for all of us as public listeners. In addition, be aware of how the information is used, as well as realizing that you come into a listening experi-

Photo: Justin Warren/ Daily Bruin

As a listener, you should be aware of potential positive and negative uses of information which the speaker presents.

ence with points of view that may deter your being an open and receptive listener.

Summary

This chapter discussed the sources of supporting materials for a speech. The major concepts discussed were:

♦ *The sources of information available to a speaker are personal experiences, personal observations, and accumulated learning, plus information derived from research and interviews.*

♦ *Research information may be found in books, magazines, newspapers, journals, indexes, government publications, and publications from special-interest groups. Additional information can be found in nonprint media and interviews.*

♦ *A computer-based retrieval system allows a researcher to compile a bibliography or information about a topic from a computer data base.*

♦ *The Internet can be a valuable research and exploration tool; however, researchers should realize that information found on the Internet is not always accurate.*

♦ *When doing research, you should keep a record of where your information comes from.*

♦ *An oral footnote indicates the source of the information included in a speech.*

♦ *A quotation is material written or spoken by a person in the exact words in which it was originally presented.*

♦ *To paraphrase is to put someone else's ideas into your own words.*

♦ *Listeners should be aware of potential positive and negative uses of information which the speaker presents.*

Profile: Brendan Sullivan, Attorney

"Every moment of glory in the courtroom is the product of hundreds of hours of hard work."

For trial lawyer Brendan Sullivan, as this comment suggests, there is absolutely no substitute for painstakingly thorough preparation. Unlike speakers who simply preach "practice, practice, practice," Sullivan unwaveringly preaches "first, prepare, prepare, prepare!" In other words, practice is useless—particularly in the courtroom—until you have mastered your material.

For speakers, hard work and uncompromising preparation will likely be read by an audience as confidence—and confident speakers are convincing speakers. Sullivan, a graduate of Georgetown University Law Center and a familiar TV face during Oliver North's Iran-Contra trial, rigorously follows his own advice, spending hours—often at night and on weekends—readying his cases. The result of his dedication? Not one of his clients since 1973 has gone to jail. Not one.

Sullivan's outwardly mild-mannered appearance belies the impassioned eruptions he sometimes allows to surface in the courtroom. The intensity of his words and delivery helps show judges and jurors his sincere, steadfast belief in the arguments he presents. Though Sullivan is convinced that preparation is of the utmost importance, he would never sacrifice skillful delivery. In court, he seeks a delicate balance in which he can sway his audience's emotions while maintaining his credibility.

"Do not read to your audience," Sullivan advises. A flat, lifeless recitation of text prevents you from connecting and relating to your listeners. It's also boring. (Besides, speakers should be so well prepared that a simple outline provides all of the prompting they need.)

The seemingly basic ability to deliver a spoken message effectively is, in fact, a skill to be honed in oneself and respected in others. This fact Brendan Sullivan understands.

An important point about listening is that we shouldn't always think in terms of "listen to." "Listen with" is also a significant part of the experience.

A speaker's listeners interact with one another as well as with the speaker. The listeners' interactions should be a meaningful part of the communication process and a source of satisfaction and growth. Couples, or groups of friends, often enjoy attending speech events together and then discussing their individual responses. Indeed, "listening with" other people can be a true growing experience as you come to understand more about yourself and how you respond and more about your listening partners.

Recognize that each individual has a different listening style, just as each speaker has a different speaking style. It is interesting to consider why your listening style and, indeed, listening preferences may be so different from those of your listening partners.

Key Terms

personal knowledge   outside knowledge
computer output microfiche (COM)   electronic catalogues
computer-based retrieval system   Internet
quotations   paraphrases
oral footnote

Learn by Doing

1. Select a controversial subject (e.g., abortion, mercy killing, legalization of marijuana) and identify a person who is an authority on it. Interview this person using the interviewing suggestions presented in this chapter, and then give an oral presentation to the class on the result of the interview. You should clearly state the interviewed person's stance concerning the issue and the reasons for the stance. After all the presentations have been made, a class discussion will be held on the value of the interview as a means of collecting relevant data for a speech.

2. Use the information collected from the interview in activity 1 to research the same topic. Look for the views of other authorities on the subject.

3. Find this information:

   a. The name of one book in your college library that contains information about the life of Harriet Tubman, and some information from the book using the bibliographical form explained in this chapter.

   b. A magazine article about nuclear-waste disposal.

   c. The longitude and latitude of Hempstead, New York.

   d. Three encyclopedia notations about the White House.

   e. The definition of the word *cacophony*, citing a dictionary.

   f. The name of one of the journals published by the National Communication Association.

   g. The population of the United States according to the 1990 census.

   h. The birthplace of Carl Sandburg.

   i. The name of a U.S. government pamphlet about the space program.

   j. The gross national product of the United States in 1998.

   k. The name of the person who wrote the musical *Rent*.

   l. The subject matter of the play *As Is*.

4. Use the format explained in the chapter to record three note cards for a speech with the purpose statement "To inform the class about the effects of the Salk polio vaccine." Two cards should have quotations, and one a paraphrase. No more than one card can come from a book.

5. Locate and footnote three sources of testimony concerning the effects of smoking on human beings.

6. Select one of these topics and do an Internet search to identify 15 sources relating to the subject. Go to the library, find three of these sources, and ascertain whether you think the information they provide should be included in an ethically developed, well-documented speech. Write a short paper, which may be given as a speech, which indicates your findings and reasons.

❖ ❖ ❖ ❖   **Endnotes**

1. See Robert Newman and Dale Newman, *Evidence* (Boston: Houghton Mifflin, 1969), for insight into the types of bias present in many different sources of information.

2. For a discussion of computer searches, see Carolyn Wolfe and Richard Wolfe, *Basic Library Skills*, 2nd ed. (Jefferson, N.C.: McFarland, 1986), pp. 113–118.

3. Knowlton, Steven R., "How Students Get Lost in Cyberspace," *New York Times*, November 2, 1997, p. 21.

4. Ibid.

5. Ibid.

6. Ibid.

7. Ibid.

8. Ibid., p. 21

9. Deborah Tannen, *You Just Don't Understand* (New York: William Morrow, 1990), p. 122.

10. Newman and Newman, p. 72.

11. Network Television Association, National Association of Broadcasters, and the Roper Organization, *America's Watching: Public Attitudes Toward Television*, 1993 (New York: NTA, NAB, and the Roper Organization, 1993).

Structuring the Speech

Chapter Outline

Learning Outcomes

After reading this chapter, you should be able to:

- *Explain why it is important to structure a speech carefully to meet the needs of the listeners.*

- *Explain what makes an effective introduction, central idea, body, and conclusion for a speech.*

- *Give examples of attention getters for the introduction of a speech.*

- *Identify the purpose and the various types of orienting materials.*

- *Explain the purpose of the central idea of a speech.*

- *Describe several different methods of arranging issues in the body of a speech.*

- *Describe the different ways to conclude a speech.*

- *Identify and illustrate the various types of overall speech organization.*

- *Recognize that culture has an effect on organizational methods and language choices.*

- *Understand the role of the organization of a speech as an aid to listeners.*

There is a long rhetorical tradition in Euro-American history, going back to the time of Aristotle, which recognizes that structure is important in audience understanding. This tradition dictates that a speaker is probably wise to present an organized speech.

However, we all don't speak and listen in the same way. Our cultural backgrounds influence how we speak, listen, and organize ideas. We'll examine some of the variances in cultural idea development later in the chapter. But, since the majority of users of this book are American English speakers, and you will be presenting the bulk of your ideas to speakers from that culture, this chapter will center primarily on the traditional Western logical approach of organizing and developing a speech.

Keep in mind, however, that, as you learned in Chapter 5, audience analysis is an important consideration in preparing and presenting a speech. If you present a speech to an audience consisting mainly of listeners from another culture, it may be necessary for you to alter your organizational approach. Even within the parameters of an American English-speaking audience there are of course countless distinct audiences. Attention to the demographics of your particular audience will be rewarded.

9.1 Structuring the Speech: The Rationale

Listeners have limited attention spans, and they are always tuning in and tuning out on speakers' messages. Consequently, it is important to present a consistently structured message so that listeners will easily get back "on track" when they again tune in to the speech. In addition, most listeners have difficulty following the idea flow of a speech that does not have a clear step-by-step structure. If a speech is well ordered, the traditional view of Euro-American public communication rhetoric indicates that the chance of the presentation being successful increases.

In structuring your speech, you must make decisions about the type of introduction, the statement of your central idea, the method of arranging the is-

Most listeners have difficulty following the idea flow of a speech that does not have a clear step-by-step structure.

sues in the body of your speech, and the type of conclusion to use. A well-structured speech ties together four elements—introduction, central idea, body, and conclusion—in a unified overall organization. The three basic approaches to overall speech organization are the partitioning, unfolding, and case methods, which are discussed in detail later in this chapter.

9.2 The Introduction

The purpose of the **introduction** is to gain the listeners' attention and orient them to the material that will be presented.

> Avoid starting a presentation by saying "What I want to talk to you about today is . . ." *Reason*: Putting "I" first stresses what the speaker wants, not what the audience needs. *Better*: "Today, *you'll* learn . . ."
>
> ---
>
> Source: *Communication Briefings*, as adapted from *Gower Handbook of Internal Communication*, edited by Eileen Scholes of The ITEM Group, Gower Publishing Ltd., Gower House, Croft Road, Aldershot, Hampshire, GU11 3HR, UK.

Profile: Patricia Fripp, Professional Motivational Speaker

"Come out punching!" Counsel from an enthusiastic boxing trainer? No, this is sound public speaking advice from Patricia Fripp, a popular motivational speaker. Although her informational brochures quietly promote her as "A Speaker for All Reasons," she has been hailed as "electrifying," "highly energetic," and "a forceful presence."

In 1966, at age 20, Fripp left her native England and set foot in the United States armed only with a positive attitude, $500, and her skill as a hair stylist. She had no job, nowhere to live, and no contacts. But, she says wryly, she "knew everyone in America was rich, and movie stars flocked through the streets!" Fripp worked as a hair stylist in San Francisco and eventually began traveling as a demonstrator of various beauty products and techniques. Because her stories and chats about her business experience added noticeable flair to her demonstrations, audience members soon began inviting her to speak at their Rotary Clubs, Kiwanis Clubs, and other civic organizations.

In 1977 Fripp attended her first National Speakers Association Convention. Seven years later, she became the National Speakers Association's first woman president. She is a Certified Speaking Professional (CSP) and has received the Council of Peers Award of Excellence (CPAE), the highest recognition for professionalism in speaking. In general, her work ranges from 25-minute keynote speeches to all-day seminars. She has spoken to government agencies, at independent rallies, and at meetings for such corporate giants as IBM, AT&T, and General Electric. Her presentations have titles such as "Creative Thinking for Better Business" and "Adapting to Change." Fripp states that her job is to present a message that is "in harmony with, and reflects the philosophy of" the company or organization that hires her.

Fripp's list of "Basics on Speaking for Your First or Fiftieth Talk" includes 21 noteworthy recommendations, such as:

Come out punching! Because people tend to remember a speech's beginning and end, make them worth remembering. Use startling statements or other attention grabbers rather than saying "Good evening ladies and gentlemen. It's a pleasure to be here."

Recognize that because television has helped shape today's audiences, they demand more powerful speakers and have shorter attention spans. Be unique and interesting.

People do not remember what you say as much as what they "see." Tell stories to illustrate your points and make them come alive. A story or vignette should be able to stand alone as a short talk.

Public speaking skill is important for almost all of us. "Your value in the marketplace depends very much upon how easy or difficult it is to replace you," Fripp says. "If you can learn to stand up and speak eloquently with confidence, you will be head and shoulders above your competition." The self-motivated young woman who arrived from England took her own advice and has forged a successful career for herself in the business of motivating others.

Attention Material

Speakers can use many types of introductory devices to gain the audience's attention, such as personal references, humorous stories, illustrations, references to the occasion or setting, rhetorical questions, action questions, unusual or dramatic devices, quotations related to the speech topic, and statements of the theme. We'll look more closely at some examples of these attention getters below.

Personal References

Introductions containing personal references provide the speaker's reasons for undertaking a presentation on a specific topic. For example, to introduce a fund-raising appeal, a speaker might describe his personal experience of receiving aid from the Muscular Dystrophy Association. Or a heart specialist might share her medical background and training with the audience before making comments about the health hazards associated with being overweight.

If you're looking for a way to get an audience's attention when you start a speech, try this:

"I'm going to make this talk short because I read the other day that the No. 1 fear of many people is having to make a speech. The No. 2 fear might be having to listen to one."

Source: *Communication Briefings*, as adapted from IdeaBank ® online database, 11 Joan Drive, Chappaqua, NY 10514, cited in *The Executive Speaker*, P.O. Box 292437, Dayton, OH 45429.

Humorous Stories

Humorous stories are often an effective way to start a presentation. Make sure, though, that the humor fits the audience and the occasion, is relevant to the material that follows, and sets the desired tone. Realize that a story or joke that is quite funny in one speaking situation may be totally inappropriate in another. For example, a slightly off-color joke may be received positively in an informal speech setting but negatively in a formal setting.

Try to imagine how your listeners will receive humor. The purpose of the introduction is to gain an audience's attention and provide a bridge into the body of the speech. An audience is likely to believe that a humorous story told in the introduction has something to do with the topic of the speech and may become confused if the rest of the speech is not related to the story. Say, for example, a speaker begins a presentation with the following anecdote:

> A railroad agent in Africa had been bawled out for doing things without orders from headquarters. One day headquarters received a telegram from the agent which read, "Tiger on platform eating conductor. Wire instructions."

From this story an audience might logically expect the speech to be about following directions, making creative decisions, or working as a railroad agent.

Remember that humor sets a light tone. Speakers who want to give a serious presentation may have difficulty attaining a somber tone if the introduction has led the audience to anticipate something lighter. Telling a series of jokes at the start of a speech may give an audience the impression that the presentation will contain only humor. (For a more in-depth discussion of humor, see Chapter 7.)

Illustrations

Illustrations in the form of stories, pictures, and physical objects help make ideas more vivid because they allow listeners to visualize the topic to be discussed. For example, a medical technician could clearly illustrate the success of a new skin-grafting process for burn victims by showing slides of patient results. Similarly, a speaker who is going to talk about the need for well-equipped police cars might begin a speech with the following illustration:

Picture yourself stuck on a dark road some night with car trouble. Suddenly you see the headlights of a car. It could be almost anyone. But wouldn't you feel better if it turned out to be a police officer with all the repair equipment you needed?

References to the Occasion or Setting

In referring to the special nature of the occasion or setting for the presentation, a speaker tries to build a strong bond, an alliance, and empathy with the audience. When this is accomplished, audience members will be responsive listeners because they will regard themselves as participants in the occasion. Speakers might refer to mutual experiences, common beliefs, or mutual needs. For example, in addressing an Independence Day company picnic, a speaker may refer to the founding of the nation and how both the speaker and the audience have benefitted from the acts of our forefathers.

Rhetorical Questions

A rhetorical question is a question the speaker does not expect the audience to answer directly. For example, a speaker might begin a speech on self-defense training by saying to the audience, "Have you ever asked yourself what you would do if someone tried to rob you?" In this case, the speaker does not intend to count how many audience members have or have not asked themselves this question. Instead, the speaker's purpose is to get the audience thinking about the topic and to build curiosity. Although they are sometimes overused, rhetorical questions can be an effective method of encouraging the audience to ponder a topic. Many times a speaker asks a second rhetorical question to further direct the audience's attention.

Action Questions

Speakers use action questions as a means of involving audience members in the presentation and stimulating them to think and respond. For example, a speaker once started a presentation by asking, "How many of you have ever been involved in an auto accident? Will you please raise your hands?" After the hands went up, the speaker said, "For those of you with your hands up, do you remember that instant when you knew the accident was going to happen and you couldn't do anything about it?" After a pause, the speaker went on. "For those of you who haven't experienced that feeling, it's one of total helplessness." In a few brief sentences the speaker had involved the audience in a constructive way and was able to move easily into the next segment of the speech.

Unusual or Dramatic Devices

Unusual or dramatic devices get the attention of the audience because of their unexpectedness or shock value. In one dramatic opening, a speaker trained as a lab technician set up equipment and drew blood from a student volunteer to show how blood is analyzed. Another speaker, in illustrating the influence of predetermined assumptions, asked for a volunteer who felt knowledgeable about rock music groups. The speaker wrote the names of three rock groups on the board and played short cuts from three songs. The volunteer identified which song was by which group. He was wrong in all three cases. The speaker stressed that she had selected pieces that were not typical of the groups, and therefore the "expert" was misled by his predetermined assumptions.

Quotations Related to the Speech Topic

Speakers sometimes begin by quoting the words of a famous person, reading an account of a specific event, reciting a section of a poem or play, or reading a newspaper editorial. To introduce a presentation on the differences between the ways males and females communicate, for example, a speaker might state:

> *Deborah Tannen is a sociolinguist on the faculty of Georgetown University. She is noted for her studies on male and female communication. In her book* You Just Don't Understand, *she states, "If women speak and hear a language of connection and intimacy, while men speak and hear a language of status and independence, then communication between men and women can be like cross-cultural communication. Instead of different dialects, it has been said they speak different genderlects."*[1]

Such an introduction gains the audience's attention and indicates the general trend of the speech to be presented.

Quotations must be relevant to the subject of the speech. But even when they are relevant, quoted ideas become meaningless if they are not presented effectively. The greatest mistake most speakers make in providing quotations is to read them too quickly, without stressing the appropriate words. Quotations are most effective when read meaningfully, slowly, and loudly enough to be heard. In addition, the speaker should establish the background and credibility of the source so that listeners understand the validity of the quotation.

Statements of the Theme

Many untrained speakers start out their presentations by saying, "Today I am going to tell you about . . ." Although this type of statement of theme is direct, it is not a particularly interesting or effective opener. A more creative theme statement will hold the audience's attention. For example, a mechanic started his presentation to a group of women at a YWCA by saying:

> *I don't like changing tires, and you probably don't either. However, if you get stuck some night on a lonely road and there's no way to call the auto club, and no one else around to change your tire, you'll probably thank me for spending the next couple of minutes telling you the five steps that can make tire changing easy.*

Orienting Material

Orienting material, the second part of an introduction, is designed to give the audience the background necessary to understand the basic material of the speech. It leads to the central idea, provides needed information, establishes personal credibility for the speaker, and demonstrates that the subject is important to the listeners. Orienting material might supply the historical background for an issue or a problem, define special terms, describe the speaker's relationship to the topic, or point out the audience's stake in the topic.

Historical Background

To present a topic fully, speakers often must explain what led up to present events. For example, a speech intended to persuade the audience to vote for a renewal of a school tax levy ought to include the pertinent facts about the history of the levy.

Definition of Terms

If special terms are going to be used during the entire speech or as the basis for the speech, the introduction is the place to define them. In a speech about agoraphobia, for example, the definition of this term (the fear of being out in public) should be given as orienting material so the audience understands it early in the presentation. This does not preclude defining other terms later. Only those terms that occur throughout the speech have to be included in the orienting material.

Speaker's Personal Relationship to the Topic

Speakers can sometimes gain credibility by describing their own personal tie to or experience with the topic. The fact that the speaker has a personal connection to the topic is of interest to most listeners. For example, a speaker intending to demonstrate the steps in mouth-to-mouth resuscitation could describe his Red Cross training and background as a lifeguard which included lifesaving techniques. Such documentation establishes the speaker's authority to speak about the subject. If the speaker is introduced by someone who mentions this personal connection, then it is probably not necessary for the speaker to repeat it.

Importance to the Listeners

The most critical role of orienting material is to tie the subject to the listeners in some way. Listeners pay attention to ideas and issues they feel are relevant to them, so it is imperative that the speaker make that link at the outset. One good strategy is to show the importance of the topic based on the interests of the audience: "Look around you—many of you have just filed your income tax forms and wonder whether you will be audited." It may also be useful to connect the topic to a larger segment of the population to illustrate the importance of the subject both to the immediate listeners and to the general public: "The Internal Revenue Service reported that 106,853,000 income tax forms were filed in 1997. Your tax form was one of them."

9.3 The Central Idea

The purpose statement, examined in Chapter 6, is designed to help the speaker prepare a speech by defining a topic. It can also can serve as the basis for developing a **central idea**—the overall point of the speech. The central idea explicitly gives the goal of the speech; at the same time, it implies the type of response the speaker wants from listeners.

If, for example, the purpose statement of a speech is "To inform the audience of the complex process employed in compiling information for *The Guinness Book of World Records*," then the central idea is "The process of collecting information for *The Guinness Book of World Records* is complex." If the purpose statement is "To persuade listeners that they should vote for the school-bond issue on November 2," then the central idea is "We should all vote for the school-bond issue on November 2." The importance of actually stating the central idea in a speech cannot be overemphasized. An audience that is not given the central idea may be frustrated and may never be sure what the exact point of the speech really is.

The central idea should be presented as a statement because a speaker who uses a question ("Should the federal government provide financial aid to private educational institutions?") is not indicating to the listeners what the main point really is. A speaker who presents the point as a statement ("The federal government should provide financial aid to private educational institutions") is clarifying which persuasive stand will be advocated. Notice also that the statement is concise and contains the overall idea.

9.4 The Body

The **body** of a message develops the major points of the speech and any subpoints that pertain to the speaker's central idea. When a speech lacks this sort of organization, listeners may become so confused that they simply give up trying to understand the message. Perhaps, for example, you had a history instructor who started a lecture by talking about the causes of World War I, then inexplicably wandered into a discussion of the marriage customs of Greece, and then commented on the Equal Rights Amendment. By the end of the class, you were no doubt confused and came away without a complete message or a well-defined idea.

To avoid confusing the audience, speakers can organize the major points and subpoints of a speech in a variety of ways. One of the most common methods of sequencing is **issue arrangement**. The issue arrangement of a speech depends on two factors. One is the method of development you have specified in your purpose statement. If, for example, the purpose statement indicates that you will be developing the speech by "listing and discussing the step-by-step process of . . .," you will probably want to use chronological issue arrangement. The second factor that determines the type of issue arrangement you use is the overall form of organization you choose for your speech. As discussed later in this chapter, the partitioning, unfolding, and case methods of organization each have patterns of issue arrangement that fit them best.

Issue arrangement can take a number of forms. The most commonly used are spatial arrangement, chronological or time arrangement, topical arrangement, causal arrangement, comparison-contrast arrangement, and problem-solution arrangement. Issue arrangement for major and subordinate points may be a mixture of these forms as long as they are consistently handled.

Spatial Arrangement

Many people organize information automatically, even though they are not aware of it. Suppose some friends of yours are visiting you at your college. They have never been on campus before, and they ask you to tell them about the institution. You start by describing the building located on the south end of the campus and then proceed to talk about all the other buildings, citing their locations from the south to the north. You have organized your presentation according to **spatial arrangement**. In other words, from a set point of reference (the southernmost building), you proceeded to explain each building in terms of its geographical location. This is a common method for giving directions, for routing merchandise in a store or factory, or for talking about where you went on your vacation.

In using spatial arrangement, a speaker sets a point of reference at some specific location and then proceeds to give directions starting from the established reference point.

In using spatial arrangement, a speaker sets a point of reference at some specific location and then proceeds from there. Thus the organization is based on keeping to a set order following a pattern: left to right, north to south, or from the center to the outside. For example, spatial arrangement might be used for the body of a speech with the purpose statement "To inform the audience of the financial tax base of Ohio by examining the state from north to south." Accordingly, the body of the outline for a speech may look something like this:

III. Body

    A. Northern Ohio
        1. Toledo
        2. Lorain/Elyria
        3. Cleveland
        4. Youngstown

    B. Central Ohio
        1. Mansfield
        2. Akron
        3. Canton

    C. Southern Ohio
        1. Cincinnati

2. Dayton
3. Columbus

The major headings in the body of this speech are developed spatially from north to south, and each of the subdivisions is developed from west to east.

Chronological or Time Arrangement

Chronological or **time arrangement** orders information from a beginning point to an ending one, with all the steps developed in time sequence. Recipes, for instance, are often given in time sequence, as are reports of chemistry experiments or the charts of patients in a hospital. By telling what happened—or what should happen—first, second, and so on, the speaker presents a pattern that allows the audience to understand the ideas.

For example, chronological arrangement can be used to develop the body of the speech with the purpose statement "To inform the audience of the major accomplishments of the Reagan administration by identifying those accomplishments from 1981 through 1988." The outline for the body of such a speech might read:

III. Body

    A. Accomplishments of the first term
        1. 1981
        2. 1982
        3. 1983
        4. 1984

    B. Accomplishments of the second term
        1. 1985
        2. 1986
        3. 1987
        4. 1988

Topical Arrangement

A speaker who uses **topical arrangement** explains an idea in terms of its component parts. For example, a speaker might organize a talk on dogs (*the general topic*) by discussing cocker spaniels, poodles, and then collies (*the component parts*), developing ideas about each breed completely before going on to the next one. The three parts of this speech could be further organized by covering each breed's temperament, size, and coloring. In this way, the speaker would organize the ideas by classifying dogs (*the general topic*) according to specific identifiable characteristics (the component parts) and by developing each subsection according to an identifiable pattern of information.

Topical arrangement lends itself to certain subjects. For example, if you wanted to explain to an operating-room technologist the instruments to be used, the procedures to be followed, and the responsibilities of each member of the medical team, you would discuss all aspects of one component before proceeding to the next.

Using this process of organization, an outline of the main headings and subheadings of the body of a speech whose purpose statement is "To inform the audience about Siamese cats by discussing their coloring, vocal characteristics, and behavior patterns" would be:

III. Body

    A. Coloring patterns
        1. Seal point
        2. Chocolate point
        3. Blue point
        4. Lilac point

    B. Vocal characteristics
        1. Does not meow
        2. Sounds like a baby crying
        3. Talks back

    C. Behavior patterns
        1. Crawls into any opening
        2. Plays with small objects
        3. Jumps onto high surfaces
        4. Likes warm surfaces
        5. Is extremely curious

Causal Arrangement

To write an accident report, a police officer uses a method called **causal arrangement**. This is the process of showing how one event made another event happen—in other words, how a cause (*the first event*) led to an effect (*the second event*). Thus, the officer would determine what series of events took place and then would demonstrate how these events caused an end result: "Car X was proceeding south on Main Street and failed to stop at the corner of Main and Canal streets for the red traffic light [*series of events—the cause*]. Car X proceeded into the intersection and was struck by Car Y [*end result—the effect*]." An alternative way to use causal arrangement is to begin with the effect (Car X was struck by Car Y) and then to explain what caused it (Car X was proceeding south on Main Street and failed to stop at the corner of Main and Canal streets for the red traffic light). This second method is a good one to use when there is a specific observable result that can be fully understood only by determining what brought it about.

In cause-to-effect organization, the body of a speech whose purpose statement was "To inform the audience that a series of identifiable events result in the disabling fear known as agoraphobia, by listing and discussing these events" would be:

III. Body

    A. Cause—Sequence of events
        1. First event
            a. Physical symptoms such as heart palpitations, trembling, sweating, breathlessness, dizziness
            b. No apparent cause for the physical symptoms

2.   Second event
     a.   Duplication of physical symptoms in a place similar to the site of the first event
     b.   Increasing awareness of fear of going to certain places
3.   Third event
     a.   Symptoms occurring when person thinks of going to a place similar to the site of the first event
     b.   Feeling of being out of control when thinking of leaving the safety site (usually the person's home)

B.   Effect—Agoraphobia
1.   Personality changes
     a.   Frequent anxiety
     b.   Depression
     c.   Loss of individual character
2.   Emotional changes
     a.   Impassiveness
     b.   High degree of dependence on others
     c.   Constant alertness

Note that this outline lists the events leading up to the final result and discusses the final result last. The alternative arrangement, called effect-from-cause organization, would give the final result first and then list the events leading up to it.

Comparison-Contrast Arrangement

Suppose a friend asks you to explain the similarities between a community college and a four-year college. Your explanation will probably follow the **comparison method** of organization, in which you describe how two or more things are alike. You would probably talk about the similarities in curriculum, staff, facilities, activity programs, and costs. If, however, your friend asks you about the differences between the two types of colleges, you would use the **contrast method**, developing your ideas by giving specific examples of how these institutions differ. By combining these two methods into the **comparison-contrast arrangement**, you could discuss both the similarities and the differences. You might set up the body of a speech with the purpose statement "To inform the audience of some of the similarities and differences between state-sponsored two- and four-year colleges in Ohio" as:

III. Body

A.   Similarities
1.   Are governed by the Board of Regents
2.   Receive state funding
3.   Offer general studies courses
4.   Must receive permission to add new curricula
5.   Are governed by a board of trustees appointed in part by the governor

B. Differences
1. Two-year colleges: funded in part by their local communities; four-year colleges: not funded by communities
2. Two-year colleges: offer associate degrees; four-year colleges: offer bachelor's and advanced degrees
3. Two-year colleges: have certificate and two-year terminal programs; four-year schools: no certificate or two-year terminal programs
4. Two-year colleges: less expensive

Problem-Solution Arrangement

Speakers use the **problem-solution arrangement** when they are attempting to identify what is wrong and to determine how to cure it or make a recommendation for its cure. This method can be used to think through a problem and then structure a speech. A speaker discussing the problem of child abuse, for instance, may wish to begin by analyzing the problem: the influence of family history, the lack of parental control and/or knowledge, and the different types of child abuse—physical, sexual, mental, and emotional. Such an analysis may then lead to a consideration of various solutions, such as stricter legislation mandating penalties for child abuse, stronger enforcement of child abuse laws, improved reporting procedures, and greater availability of social services to parents and children alike. The key to effective problem-solution arrangement is to come up with solutions that will be workable, desirable, and practical for the people who will implement them.

An alternative form of the problem-solution method is the **see-blame-cure-cost method**. In this four-step organizing technique, the evil or problem that exists is examined (*see*), what has caused the problem is determined (*blame*), solutions are investigated (*cure*), and the most practical solution is selected (*cost*).

When you develop a message using problem-solution arrangement, always clearly state the problem, its cause, the possible solutions, and the selected solution. This allows your listeners to share a complete picture of your reasoning process. If the message is well developed, listeners will understand why the selected solution is best, how it will work to solve the problem, what it will or will not do, what the costs will be, how long it will take to work, and what is needed to implement it.

This method of organization is particularly useful for speeches that seek to confront and solve the problems of life, business, industry, and government. It can be used to decide among treatments or procedures to follow, products to buy, or machines to use. Consider, for example, this outline for the body of a speech with the purpose statement "To inform the audience why I believe that the solution to the acid rain problem is to require coal-burning companies and smelting plants to build taller smokestacks, use scrubbers, and wash their coal before using it":

III. Body

A. Problem
1. Acid rain is caused by substances such as sulfur oxides and nitrogen oxides.

2. Acid rain falls anywhere that is downwind of urban or industrial pollution.
3. Acid rain has significant negative effects.
   a. It decreases the fertility and productivity of soils.
   b. It causes freshwater lakes and streams to become barren of fish, amphibians, invertebrates, and plankton.
   c. It deteriorates such materials as stone, marble, and copper.
   d. It affects human health through the contamination of the water we drink and the fish and wildlife we eat.

B. Solution
   1. Coal-burning companies and smelting plants should be required to build taller smokestacks to disperse the pollution.
   2. Scrubbers, traps in smokestacks that can catch 90 percent or more of the sulfur oxides emitted, should be required for all industrial users of smokestacks.
   3. All coal burned by industrial users should be washed before it is used.

A more detailed outline of this speech might include subdivisions under each of the statements of solution to explore whether it is *workable* (developing why the suggestion will solve or help solve the problem), *desirable* (explaining why the suggestion will not cause greater problems), and *practical* (indicating how the suggestion can be put into practice).

Here is an outline to a problem-solving speech with the purpose statement "To inform why, by listing my reasons, I believe the use of a waterbed can aid in overcoming common sleeping problems":

III. Body

A. Problems
   1. Insomnia (difficulty in falling asleep)
   2. Chronic backaches
   3. Sleeping discomforts caused by pregnancy
   4. Concerns for unborn child
   5. Bedsores caused by confinement to bed

B. Solution—Use of a waterbed
   1. It increases ease in falling asleep because of flotation feeling.
   2. It has the same soothing effect as sleep-inducing drugs without the medicinal side effects.
   3. It provides longer periods of sleep with less movement.
   4. It eliminates sore muscles and swollen joints, thus reducing stiffness.
   5. Its heat reduces tension, which reduces stress.
   6. It increases comfort during pregnancy by allowing the user to lie in a stomach-down position.

7. Its flotation and heat act like a second uterus for the unborn child.
8. Even body distribution on the surface of the mattress reduces bedsores.

Arrangement for Major and Subordinate Points

Speakers typically use one method of issue arrangement for the major points, always keeping in mind that other methods may be used as necessary to present the subordinate points. For instance, in a presentation on the causes of World War II, a speaker may decide to organize the major points with a chronological arrangement and use a spatial arrangement for the subordinate points.

The outline would be:

III. Body
   A. Events in 1935
      1. England
      2. France
      3. Germany
      4. Russia
      5. Japan
   B. Events in 1936
      1. England
      2. France
      3. Germany
      4. Russia
      5. Japan
   C. Events in 1937
      1. England
      2. France
      3. Germany
      4. Russia
      5. Japan

No matter which pattern you select to develop the major points of your message, use that pattern consistently for each major heading. Likewise, be consistent in your handling of the subordinate points. Otherwise, your audience will be confused by sudden changes or shifts in sequence and will fail to follow the presentation.

9.5 The Conclusion

Whatever the purpose of the speech, the presentation should end with a **conclusion**, which is usually a summary and a clincher. A summary should restate the major points of the speech so that the listener can recap what has been covered. A clincher should leave a final message of intent.

The Summary

The **summary** of a speech restates the main points of the body of the speech. It is a redundancy device intended to allow the audience to hear the important issues once again, for the last time. The simplest way to accomplish the summary is to repeat the major points of the body in the order in which you presented them.

The Clincher

A **clincher** is a device used to make a final appeal to the audience and to ensure that they remember your message. Some common clincher techniques are personal references, humorous stories, illustrations, rhetorical questions, action questions, unusual or dramatic devices, and quotations.

A *personal reference* might be appropriate for a heart specialist who established his expertise at the start of the speech and wants to reestablish his authority in the conclusion. Another speaker may find it appropriate to end the presentation with a *humorous story* that summarizes the ideas. As mentioned earlier, humorous stories should always be appropriate to the central idea of the speech.

A young person who had become dependent on drugs might end a speech with an *illustration* of how difficult it was for her to turn away from the drug scene. A speaker who posed *rhetorical questions* or *action questions* at the beginning of a presentation can conclude by answering them. For example, the speaker who asked audience members what they would do if they were robbery victims might restate the major alternatives presented in the message. The speaker who asked the audience members to raise their hands if they had ever been involved in an auto accident might summarize the experience of losing control of a car.

One speaker concluded a speech about the necessity for proper dental hygiene by passing out a small cup of disclosing solution and a small mirror to each member of the audience. She then asked them to rinse out their mouths

---

Closings to Impress Audiences

Try these closings to make sure your presentations don't end with a whimper:

- Challenge your audience to act on the information you've presented. *Example*: "I urge you to take the time to compare the systems I've explained so you can decide for yourself which will give you the speed you need."

- Recap your main ideas. *Examples*: "If a system fails, remember these steps . . ." "Let's review the four key steps necessary to . . ."

- Ask for agreement. *Examples*: "If you agree to start today, we can have the system running in 90 days." "Based on what you've heard, can we agree that we need a more aggressive marketing approach?"

  Additional tip: Avoid these poor closings: "I'm out of time." "That's all I have to say." "I've been told I have to stop now."

Source: *Communication Briefings*, as adapted from *Loud and Clear: How to Prepare and Deliver Effective Business and Technical Presentations*, by George L. Morrisey, Thomas L. Sechrest, and Wendy B. Warman, Addison-Wesley, One Jacob Way, Reading, MA 01867.

with the solution, which turns plaque and other substances on or between the teeth bright red. This activity effectively demonstrated the importance of proper brushing and the value of *unusual* or *dramatic devices* for concluding a speech. *Quotations* can also restate memorably the major theme of a presentation. For example, a speaker might summarize a speech against the death penalty by reading the vivid description of an execution presented in Truman Capote's book *In Cold Blood*.

9.6 The Overall Organization of a Speech

The three basic approaches to overall speech organization are the partitioning, unfolding, and case methods. Whichever type of overall organization you choose, you should realize that to remember a message, listeners require repetition of key points. They do not have a chance to run through the message a second time to grasp points that were not clear when presented. A reader can reread a passage, but a listener cannot relisten unless the speech has been recorded (and even then, it may not be played back immediately). Consequently, you need to be obvious in stating your main points—the central idea and the issues in the body—and in providing transitions and internal summaries that assist listeners in following the sequence of your speech.

Speakers who use **redundancy**, or repetition of their points, can foster listening comprehension of their messages. Television commercials use the technique of redundancy by extensively repeating material to reinforce the message in the viewer's mind. Politicians use redundancy in developing campaign slogans that can be repeated at many speaking occasions.

The Partitioning Method

The **partitioning method of organization** depends on a great deal of repetition and is the most direct ordering of ideas for listeners to follow. The sequence requires adherence to this outline:

I. Introduction
   A. Attention material
   B. Orienting material
II. Central idea
   A. Statement of central idea
   B. Restatement of central idea
   C. Division (listing of issues by some method of issue arrangement)
      1. First main issue
      2. Second main issue

3.   Third main issue (and so on)

III. Body

(Transition: forecast of the first issue)

    A. First main issue

       1. Discussion of first main issue through examples, illustrations, and explanations

       2. Discussion of first main issue through examples, illustrations, and explanations (and so on)

    (Transition: restatement of first main issue and forecast of second issue)

    B. Second main issue

       1. Discussion of second main issue

       2. Discussion of second main issue (and so on)

    (Transition: restatement of second main issue and forecast of third issue)

    C. Third main issue

       1. Discussion of third main issue

       2. Discussion of third main issue (and so on)

IV. Conclusion

    A. Summary (restatement of issues and central idea)

    B. Clincher

When using this type of organization for a speech, you start with the introduction and lead into your central idea. Then you state the central idea, restate it, and divide it by listing the main issues you will cover in the order in which you will cover them. This restatement and division constitute what is called the **partitioning step**. For example, a speaker whose central idea is "there are several problems with the use of radiation therapy" may use this partitioning step: "To understand these radiological difficulties, we will look at the harmful effects of radiation therapy and the poor quality of radiation facilities in hospitals."

From the partitioning step, you move into the first issue of the body of the speech with a transition that forecasts that first issue. For example, the speaker might say, "Turning, then, to our first point, let us consider the harmful effect that radiation therapy has had." If such a direct statement may be unacceptable to listeners because of opposition to the idea, the speaker can use an indirect forecast: "We can begin with a look at the effects of radiation therapy." This forecast should lead into a discussion of the main points of the issue. Restatement is also important. As new material is added, the speaker should hold the audience's attention and clarify the main points by repeating them in different words. This enables listeners to keep the main points in mind and not to get lost in the supporting details.

When moving from one issue to the next in the body of the speech, a speaker is wise to use clear bridges between ideas. These bridges, called **transitions**, provide the listener with a connection between the points. Thus, a good transition consists of two parts: the restatement of the previous issue and the forecast of the next one. For example, a speaker presenting a talk on marine biology provided a transition between two issues by stating, "From the evidence presented, it appears that the problems of water pollution are massive. How, then, can we tackle these problems?"

Use of the partitioning method requires careful transitions, each containing a summary and a forecast, from one issue to the next. There should be only a small number of issues in the body of the speech. The more issues developed, the longer the speech will be—and a long speech may strain the listening process. Once the last issue in a partitioned speech has been discussed, the presentation concludes with a summary that restates the central idea and the main issues. This summary gives listeners a chance to review the points that have been discussed.

Successful partitioning requires the repetition of major points. It follows this format: "I tell the audience what I'm going to tell them, then I tell them, and then I tell them what I've told them." If the purpose statement is: "To inform the audience of the alternatives an intake counselor has by listing and discussing the options," the partitioning method of organization would develop the speech according to this outline:

I. Introduction

    A. Attention material: Each of us probably makes hundreds of decisions every day. We decide what to eat, what to wear, what television program to watch, what time to go to bed.

    B. Orienting material: In my work as an intake counselor with the Department of Juvenile Services, I must make decisions that can seriously affect a child's life. An intake counselor gets the police report when a juvenile commits a crime, calls in the parents and the child to decide what actions should be taken, and counsels them. An investigation of such work can help you to understand some of the procedures that local governments use to combat the problems of juvenile delinquency.

II. Statement of central idea

    A. Let us consider the alternatives an intake counselor has.

    B. The counselor can make three major decisions.

    C. These decisions are:
        1. Send the case to court.
        2. Close the case at intake.
        3. Place the child on informal supervision for forty-five days.

III. Body (One decision that a counselor may make is to send the case to court.)

    A. The law states that you must send the case to court if:
        1. The charge is denied.
        2. The juvenile has a prior record.
        3. You notice signs of trouble with the family.
        4. The case is like Tommy's. Tommy had been picked up for breaking and entering . . .
        (Thus a case may be sent to court. A counselor may also decide to close a case at intake.)

B. There are several reasons for closing the case at intake:
1. The child admits guilt.
2. The incident was a first offense.
3. The parents are supportive and the home life is stable.
4. An example of a case closed at intake was Henrietta's . . .
(As a result, a case may be closed at intake. A counselor may also decide to put a juvenile under informal supervision.)

    C. Supervision for 45 days is warranted if:
1. The child or the family is in need of short-term counseling.
2. The procedure is not used often.
3. The court has never ordered this in the past.
4. The case is like Lynn's. Lynn . . .
(Through informal supervision, some children can be helped.)

IV. Conclusion

    A. Summary: The basic decision is to arrange court appearances, stop the action at the beginning, or supervise the client.

    B. Clincher: The goal of the whole intake process is to provide whatever is best for the child so that the child will have proper care, treatment, and supervision.

Even though partitioning organization can be used for a speech with any purpose, it is especially well suited to informative speaking and informative briefing. Because the aim of such a speech is to increase the listener's comprehension of a particular body of information, a clear structure and repetition of the major points are warranted.

The Unfolding Method

The **unfolding method of organization** can be used for a speech with any purpose, but if you want to persuade your listeners of something, you will find this format useful. An unfolding organization differs from a partitioned organization in one important way: It does not restate the central idea or include the division step. The unfolding method of organization is more flexible than the partitioning method because it lends itself to a variety of formats. For example, you can place the statement of the central idea anywhere in the speech as long as it comes before the conclusion. Your transitions do not have to restate and forecast issues; they simply have to establish clear connections. Furthermore, with this method you do not have to restate all the issues and the central idea in the conclusion. Remember, however, that a good conclusion should summarize your presentation in some way.

One possible sequence for an unfolding format is:

I. Introduction

    A. Attention material

    B. Orienting material

II. Statement of central idea

III. Body (organized by some method of issue arrangement)

  (Transition)

  A. First issue
    1. Discussion of first issue through examples, illustrations, and explanations
    2. Discussion of first issue through examples, illustrations, and explanations (and so on)

  (Transition)

  B. Second issue
    1. Discussion of second issue through examples, illustrations, and explanations
    2. Discussion of second issue through examples, illustrations, and explanation (and so on)

  (Transition)

IV. Conclusion

  A. Restatement
  B. Clincher

The unfolding format may be appropriate for an audience that initially agrees with the central idea and issue that the speaker plans to develop. At other times, however, a speaker may want to use variations of this format. For example, if prior analysis leads you to conclude that you are going to face a hostile audience, a group unsympathetic to your purpose statement, you will want to approach your listeners more subtly, moving from particular facts to a general conclusion. If members of the audience oppose your stand, it does not make sense to alienate them by stating your central idea early in the presentation. Instead, present the body of your speech first. Lead them through the main points, moving from areas of shared agreement into areas of controversy. If you arrange the main issues subtly and word them carefully, you may be able to establish acceptance of your purpose statement just before you reach the conclusion. This variation of the unfolding format would be:

I. Introduction

  A. Attention material
  B. Orienting material

  (Transition)

II. Body (organized by some method of issue arrangement)

  A. Discussion of first issue
    1. Examples and illustrations
    2. Examples and illustrations (and so on)

  B. Statement of first issue

  (Transition)

  C. Discussion of second issue
    1. Examples and illustrations
    2. Examples and illustrations (and so on)

❖ ❖ ❖ ❖   (Transition)

    III. Statement of central idea

          (Transition)

    IV. Conclusion

          A. Restatement

          B. Clincher

For instance, if you are trying to persuade a group of people to vote for a candidate, and you know the audience is not committed to that candidate, you are wise to develop your position by stating the issues, stands, and actions of the candidate; stressing the positive aspects of your candidate; and building strong support. After establishing this argument, then state the central idea by revealing the voting action you want from the audience.

As a speaker, you want to maintain a clear framework for your listeners so that the speech moves forward sequentially. Remember that the speech is of no value if at the conclusion the audience does not clearly understand your central idea. This outline develops a speech according to the unfolding method of organization, if the purpose statement is "To persuade each member of the audience to donate his or her body to science by listing and discussing the reasons for donation":

    I.   Introduction

          A. Attention material: Picture a three-year-old girl attached to a kidney machine once a week for the rest of her life. Picture a little blind boy whose world is blackness or a father who is confined to his bed because he has a weak heart.

          B. Orienting material: Such pictures are not very pleasant. But you can do something about them.

    II. Statement of central idea: You should donate your body to science.

    III. Body

          A. Scientists need organs so that others may live normally.
              1. List of organs that can be donated.
              2. The need for speed in transplanting organs. (Thus specific organs can be used.)

          B. Your body can be used as an instrument for medical education.
              1. Who can donate and how.
              2. The need to eliminate shortages.
                  (As a result, your entire body can continue to serve a useful purpose.)

    IV. Conclusion

          A. Summary
              1. Organs are needed so that others can live normally.
              2. Your body can be used for medical education.

B. Clincher
       1. I am a benevolent person who believes that everyone is born with a benevolent nature. I know that you and I will help those less fortunate than we are. I am a potential organ and cadaver donor through my will. A donor's card, like the one I carry, can be obtained through any medical foundation. I cannot overemphasize the need for body and organ donations.
       2. Don't, as the saying goes, wait "for George to do it." You do it! Take immediate action to become an organ and cadaver donor.

The Case Method

In some respects, the **case method of organization** is less complex than the partitioning and unfolding methods because here the speaker discusses the central idea without breaking it into subpoints. As a result, this format is especially suitable for speeches designed to amuse, entertain, or present a single issue. If, for example, your central idea is that "Kids say the funniest things," then the body of a speech organized using the case method would include a series of examples of children's clever sayings connected by clear transitions. Here is the format for a speech developed by case organization:

    I. Introduction
       A. Attention material
       B. Orienting material
          (Transition)
    II. Central idea
          (Transition)
    III. Body
          (Organized in a sequence)
       A. Example—a case
          (Transition)
       B. Example—a case
          (Transition)
       C. Example—a case (and so on)
          (Transition)
    IV. Conclusion
       A. Summary
       B. Clincher

When you use case organization, be careful not to develop subpoints in the body of the speech which become main points in themselves. The danger of subdividing is that you may not develop each subdivided point fully, and your listeners may become confused. If, for example, your central idea is that "Kids say the funniest things" and you say in one of the transitions, "Kids say

❖ ❖ ❖ ❖   funny things at school and at camp," you have subdivided your central idea into two issues.

This outline develops a speech according to the case method of organization for the purpose statement: "To inform the audience of some ways in which left-handers are discriminated against by listing some examples."

I.   Introduction

    A.   Attention material: Have you ever pondered the design of a butter knife or the structure of a gravy ladle?

    B.   Orienting material: These structural problems are important to all of us who are afflicted with a key social problem—left-handedness. (As a left-handed person I believe that . . .

II.   Statement of central idea

    A.   Left-handers are discriminated against.

    B.   Let's look at some examples.

III. Body

    A.   Example: Tell a story of the difficulties encountered when using scissors.

    (Transition: Another experience I've had . . .)

    B.   Example: Tell a story of the problems with school desks designed for right-handed people.

    (Transition: This experience points out another one . . .)

    C.   Example: Tell a story about the problems with words such as "gauche" and "southpaw."

    (Transition: So you see . . .)

IV. Conclusion

    A.   Summary: Left-handers are discriminated against all the way from the design of items to the names they are called.

    B.   Clincher: To add insult to injury, recent research suggests that left-handedness may result from brain damage at birth. But, then, we're in good company. Eleven presidents of the United States have been left-handed!

A consistently structured speech is an advantage to both the speaker and the listeners. The speaker is assured of developing a presentation that is clear and that accomplishes its goal. In addition, since the speaker has taken care to develop a sequential speech and to consider the audience and its needs, the listeners are able to easily follow the flow of ideas.

All of these speeches develop in a linear fashion, the English American tradition based on Western rhetorical theory, which leads a listener through the speech in a logical, step-by-step way. Some non-Western speakers use alternative methods for organizing their ideas. Don't be surprised if you are listening to someone from another culture who does not use a linear format. If you are ever in a situation where you are going to give a presentation to a non-rhetorically based audience, you may want to familiarize yourself with alternative methods that would better fit the listening mode of that audience.[2]

9.7 The Role of Culture in Speech Structure ❖ ❖ ❖ ❖

"Languages differ in the very assumption of how information should be organized, of what is to be or not to be described and expressed."[3] In other words, as we develop our language skills we hear ideas presented in certain patterns. If concepts are presented in an unfamiliar pattern it can cause listening problems. Korean presentations, for example, are characterized by indirectness and nonlinear development. Memory research shows that "Koreans have more difficulty recalling information when that information is presented in a linear rhetorical style."[4]

Other examples of how culture affects the organization of ideas:

- *"Black rhetoric depends on a unique style of language, for its effectiveness."[5] Thus, white U.S. listeners to African American speakers may get confused when the presenter fails to set a specific theme but strings together stories, anecdotes, and biblical quotations in a random order.*

- *Spanish writers and speakers use loose coordination of ideas, elaboration, and narrative in the form of stories.[6]*

- *Because discourse for the Navajo is designed to secure order, harmony, and balance, they are interested in dialogue, not a speaker expounding her or his point of view to silent listeners. Public speaking, Navajo style, is interactive, with no prescribed structure.[7] White Americans and Navajo speakers and listeners often get into conflict not over what is said, but how it is organized and presented.*

- *Americans have been schooled to emphasize a purpose early, to advance their argument linearly by connecting ideas with clear concise bridges, to omit any material that does not obviously contribute to their linear progression. By contrast, the German tradition promotes a logical progression but imposes fewer restrictions on the inclusion of material. Germans may appear to digress from the main point if they feel that the additions contribute to their purpose.[8]*

- *Most American Indian presentations start with homage to their forefathers.[9]*

- *English writers and speakers tend to follow either a deductive or inductive organization pattern: deductive if the thesis comes at the beginning of the argument, or inductive if the thesis comes after the argument. Japanese, Chinese, Thai, and Koreans follow an organizational pattern that is "quasi-inductive." In the Asian organization, the thesis is often buried in the materials, with the topic implied, not stated.[10]*

- *The Chinese tend to present ideas through a variety of indirectly related views. This may take the form of an eight-legged essay:[11] the opening-up, amplification, preliminary exposition, first argument, second argument, third argument, final argument, and conclusion. The most important part is the amplification, which consists of two or three sentences, in which the chosen topic is expressed. This is in contrast to the American tradition of the body being the most important part of the presentation because it amplifies the reason for taking specific actions.*

- *Arabs use "a completely different persuasive style"[12] from that set in Western logic. Arabic speakers value telling a story or a series of tales and letting the listener figure out the moral of the narrative, depending greatly on parables from the Koran, which are based on the concept "because Islam says so."[13] This indirect presentational style, with little structure, often confuses English-speaking Americans who are used to a direct format in which a statement is made and evidence is presented to clarify the proposition. Western listeners may disregard the information because it is not based on logic proofs, such as statistics and research findings.*

Thus, it is significant that culture plays a major role in the way in which speakers organize information. These differences can cause problems for comprehensive and critical listeners.

9.8 The Structure as a Listening Tool

As a public listener, you may have to adapt your listening patterns to fit the uniqueness of a speaker's culture. In a speech presented in a Western tradition, structure is often the major key to listener comprehension. If the speaker sets out the necessary "sign posts" to keep listeners on track and in focus, then it should be fairly easy for the receiver to follow the presentation. However, no matter how careful a speaker is, he or she must be aware that because attention is always fluctuating, the listener may not be tuned in at all times. Be aware that as a listener, your attention may waver. If it is important to gain the information being presented, it is important for you to tune into the speaker's cues to the structure of the speech. Listen for phrases such as, "There are three steps that you will need to follow in order to send messages via our e-mail system," or "What caused the drop in profits this year? It appears that we have not listened to business trend forecasts and analyzed our projected sales records." In both of these cases, the speaker is indicating the structure of the body of the speech and is alerting you as to how to listen for the ideas.

Unfortunately, not all speakers will give you clues as to how to listen. Most commonly, this is because the speaker is unaware of the necessity for aiding the listener to gain the message. Many speakers think that it is the job of the listener to just "figure out" what is being said and don't assume the necessary responsibility as message preparers. Accept that many speakers are not readily listenable. Consequently, you, the listener, must work at sorting through the speaker's verbal and nonverbal messages. One technique that many listeners find helpful is to identify the main points and keep a mental "flow chart" of these points as the speaker progresses. Since we listen so much faster than the normal conversation rate, we have plenty of time to recapitulate, to create mental summaries of what the speaker has said, and even to anticipate what he or she will say next.

Some listeners rely extensively on taking notes to structure their understanding of a speaker's presentation. This can assist you in focusing on the message. Others find that making mental notes works well. Still others, those who tend to remember things by pictures rather than words, watch the speaker carefully and make mental pictures of what is being said. No matter which method you use, do a quick follow-up after the presentation. When the speech is over, try to summarize the main points—even write them down if necessary. Review your mental summary to ensure that the speaker's points are in place in your long-term memory and that you can recall and use them as needed. Attendees at classroom lectures recount that if they immediately review their notes or their images of what took place during the presentation, studying for exams becomes an easier task.

Summarizing the research on listening to structure, one scholar concludes: "Listeners who understand principles of organization recall more details when they listen to messages. Knowledge and skill in organization can also help the listener to use details to form generalizations, use information to solve problems, and even comprehend more when reading as well as listening."[14]

❖ ❖ ❖ ❖

Summary

This chapter investigated the principles of structuring a message. The major ideas presented were:

♦ *A public communication message is usually divided into four parts: introduction, central idea, body, and conclusion.*

♦ *The introduction contains the attention material and the orienting material.*

♦ *The central idea describes the purpose of the presentation and specifically states its main theme.*

♦ *The body develops the major points of the presentation.*

♦ *The conclusion summarizes the presentation and may also contain a motivating statement.*

♦ *Attention material can include personal references, humorous stories, illustrations, references to the occasion or setting, rhetorical questions, action questions, unusual or dramatic devices, quotations related to the theme, and statements of the theme.*

♦ *Orienting material gives an audience the background necessary to understand the basic material of the speech. It may include historical background, definition of terms, the speaker's personal relationship to the topic, and the topic's importance to the listeners.*

♦ *The central idea should be presented as a statement.*

♦ *The method of ordering the points and subpoints in the body of a speech is called issue arrangement.*

♦ *Issue arrangement takes one of six forms: spatial arrangement, chronological or time arrangement, topical arrangement, causal arrangement, comparison-contrast arrangement, or problem-solution arrangement.*

♦ *A summary restates the major points of the speech.*

♦ *Clinchers can include personal references, humorous stories, illustrations, rhetorical questions, action questions, unusual or dramatic devices, and quotations.*

♦ *The basic approaches to overall speech organization are the partitioning, unfolding, and case methods.*

♦ *Listeners who understand principles of organization recall more details when they listen to messages.*

❖ ❖ ❖ ❖   ## Key Terms

introduction	orienting material
central idea	body
issue arrangement	spatial arrangement
chronological or time arrangement	topical arrangement
causal arrangement	comparison method
contrast method	comparison-contrast arrangement
problem-solution arrangement	see-blame-cure-cost method
conclusion	summary
clincher	redundancy
partitioning method of organization	partitioning step
transitions	unfolding method of organization
case method of organization	

Learn by Doing

1. Your instructor asks for a volunteer and gives him or her a card that has a picture drawn on it. Each member of the class has a sheet of paper and a pencil. The volunteer tells the class how to draw the picture exactly as it appears on the card. No one is allowed to ask any questions. When the volunteer has finished giving directions, the members of the class compare their drawings with the original. After the activity, the class discusses these questions:

   a. Would it have helped if the volunteer had given a general overview of what to draw before beginning to give directions? How does this question relate to what you have read in this chapter about the purpose of an introduction?

   b. Did the volunteer's instructions have a conclusion? How might a conclusion restating the major points have helped you?

   c. Were there any words used in the directions that caused noise to enter into the communication? What were they? How did they cause problems?

   d. Was the structure of the directions clear?

   e. Do you think a question-and-answer session following the instructions would have been valuable? Why or why not?

2. Do activity 1 again. This time, the next volunteer builds on the positive things the first volunteer did and makes improvements based on the discussion.

3. Each speaker informs the class about an unusual topic—something about which the class has no knowledge. Sample topics are the language of bees, the structure of a glacier, or organic architecture. Be sure the speech has a clear structure and lasts no more than five minutes. Be sure this presentation is a well-organized speech following the basic elements of speech development discussed in this chapter.

4. Select a subject on which you are an expert. Present a speech to your classmates in such a way that when you finish, they too will have a thorough understanding of the topic. Take no more than six minutes to deliver it. Be sure this presentation is a well-organized speech following the basic elements of speech development discussed in this chapter.

5. Prepare a speech of no more than five minutes informing the class about a controversial theory. Sample topics are: "The Loch Ness monster exists"; "Vitamin C prevents and cures the common cold"; "Rational emotive therapy can alter behavior"; "Homosexuality is neurological"; and "Alcoholism is an inherited disease." Explain the theory and the various arguments concerning the theory. Be sure this presentation is a well-organized speech following the basic elements of speech development discussed in this chapter.

6. You are going to give a speech about your education (elementary, high school, college). The speech is to be presented to your college speech class.

   a. Write a purpose statement for the speech.

   b. Prepare an attention-getting introduction for the presentation that uses each of these introductory devices:
       1. Personal reference
       2. Humorous story
       3. Rhetorical question
       4. Unusual or dramatic device

   c. What orienting material would be needed for this speech?

   d. Write the purpose statement as a central idea.

   e. What would be the major points for the body of the speech?

   f. What would be an appropriate clincher for the speech?

7. Select a cultural group (ethnic, racial, gender) and find at least two factors which relate to the rhetorical structure style of their public communication. An excellent source for this is George Kennedy, *Comparative Rhetoric: An Historical and Cross-cultural Introduction (New York: Oxford University Press, 1998)* or any of the footnoted sources from Section 9.7 of this chapter. Report back to the class on your findings.

Endnotes

1. Deborah Tannen, *You Just Don't Understand* (New York: William Morrow, 1990), p. 42.

2. For an extensive discussion of alternative methods of organizing a speech see Clella Jaffe, *Public Speaking: Concepts and Skills for a Diverse Society*, 2nd ed. (Belmont, Calif.: Wadsworth Publishing Company, 1998), pp. 156–162 and the works of C. Jorgensen-Earp.

3. Senko K. Maynard, "Contrastive Rhetoric: A Case of Nominalization in Japanese and English Discourse," *Language Sciences*, 18 (1996), p. 944.

4. Ulla Connor, *Contrastive Rhetoric: Cross-cultural Aspects of Second Language Writing* (New York: Cambridge University Press, 1996), p. 45.

5. Melbourne S. Cummings, "Teaching the Black Rhetoric Course," an unpublished paper, Educational Rources Information Center, 1983, p. 5.

6. Connor, p. 52.

7. Gerry Philipsen, "Navajo World View and Cultural Patterns of Speech, A Case Study in Ethnorhetoric," *Speech Monographs*, 39.2 (1972), p. 133.

8. Gerald J. Alred, "Teaching in Germany and the Rhetoric of Culture," *Journal of Business and Technical Communication*, 11 (1997), p. 363.

9. Richard Morris and Philip Wander, "Native American Rhetoric: Dancing in the Shadows of the Ghost Dance," *Quarterly Journal of Speech*, 76 (1990), p. 170.

10. Connor, p. 41.

11. Ibid., p. 37.

12. Ibid., p. 36.

13. Ibid.

14. Roberta Turnball-Ray, *The Power of Listening* (Dubuque, Iowa: Kendall/Hunt, 1994), p. 88.

CHAPTER TEN

Formats for the Speech

Chapter Outline

❑ 10.1 The Impromptu and Ad Lib Modes of Presentation

❑ 10.2 The Extemporaneous Mode of Presentation
Developing a Speech Outline
Mind Mapping
Practicing with the Outline/Mind Map

❑ 10.3 The Manuscript Mode of Presentation
Adjusting From a Written to an Oral Style
Preparing the Manuscript

❑ 10.4 The Memorized Mode of Presentation

❑ 10.5 Listening Channel Preferences

Learning Outcomes

After reading this chapter, you should be able to:

- *Identify the four modes of speech presentation.*

- *Explain how to develop an impromptu or an ad lib presentation.*

- *Describe the advantages and disadvantages of the extemporaneous mode.*

- *Describe the advantages and disadvantages of the manuscript mode.*

- *List some ways of preparing effective oral language.*

- *Describe the advantages and disadvantages of memorizing a speech.*

- *Explain channel preferences of listeners.*

❖ ❖ ❖ ❖

After analyzing the audience, developing a purpose statement, doing whatever research is necessary, and deciding on the supporting materials to use, speakers have to select the mode of presentation. There are four basic modes of presentation: impromptu and ad lib, extemporaneous, manuscript, and memorized.

10.1 The Impromptu and Ad Lib Modes of Presentation

In **impromptu speaking** there is very little time for preparation, so the speaker must organizes ideas while communicating. Some speech theorists distinguish this mode from **ad lib speaking**, in which a speaker has no time to organize ideas and responds immediately when answering a question, volunteering an opinion, or interacting during interpersonal communication.

The impromptu mode gives the speaker a short period of time to decide what to say, whereas the ad lib mode requires complete spontaneity. For example, when a teacher asks a question in class and gives the students a minute or so to think of the answer, the students are using the impromptu mode.

Profile: Sandy Linver, President, Speakeasy Inc.

"The most effective speakers—the ones you sit up and listen to—are those who take the risk of being themselves."

In 1973, with this idea as a foundation, Sandy Linver started Speakeasy Inc., a consulting firm with offices in Atlanta and San Francisco that teaches speaking skills to business and professional people. The company's mission reflects her strong belief that "effective speaking doesn't depend on magic formulas or mechanical techniques. It depends on each individual's willingness to reach inside for the best of himself or herself and to reach out to share that with the audience." Linver is the author of two books, *Speak Easy: How to Talk Your Way to the Top* and *Speak and Get Results*.

What does Speakeasy offer its clients? "Whether it's a seminar or a consulting project, a speech rehearsal or a workshop, our goal is to give each individual we work with the skills and support to make the most of a communication situation." With its tantalizing array of workshops, private coaching and consulting services, and seminars, Speakeasy attracts an impressive list of clients, including IBM, The Coca-Cola Company, Arthur Andersen, and Gannett Broadcasting. Speakeasy offers programs with such fascinating and practical titles as "Talk So People Listen," "How to Face an Audience Without a Tranquilizer," and "Take Charge of the Q & A."

Crucial issues in contemporary organizational communication leap from the pages of Speakeasy's promotional literature:

Data don't communicate. People do. You know you're better than your competition. But has your market got the message?

Leaders not only have a vision— they have the ability to communicate their vision to those who can help make it a reality.

Developing communication skills does more than grow your bottom line. It also grows your people.

This company does not mass-produce communicators. Its seminars and workshops are rigorous and intensely personal, and often are limited to as few as 10 people per class. Using a variety of tools such as videotaping, coaching, critiquing, discussion, and written feedback, Speakeasy earns high marks for improving business communication in the boardroom, among workers, with customers, and with the media.

Thus, the impromptu and the ad lib modes are both characterized by the short period of time used to prepare an answer and by the lack of or minimal use of notes. They allow the speaker to appear natural and spontaneous and thereby encourage listeners to believe that the speaker is revealing his or her real feelings. Spontaneity has its costs, however. The speaker has no chance to develop an organized and well-analyzed statement or to research statistics, examples, or illustrations to explain the ideas clearly. Still another liability is the speaker's tendency to ramble or use unnecessary phrases such as "you know" and "stuff like that" to gain thinking time or gloss over nonspecific information. The lack of preparation can also result in uncertainty.

Facing a Last-Minute Speech

If you have to present with little notice, follow these tips:

- Write down a single phrase describing what you need to communicate to your audience. Then, write three actions, reasons or qualities supporting that phrase. *Example*: If you want to communicate how to increase sales, three actions to do so could be: make more cold calls, ask for referrals and survey customers. Mention the points during your speech. *Tip*: Write them on the back of a business card for easy reference.

- Answer the questions *who, what, when, where, why* and *how*. *Example*: If you're talking about change that will occur in your organization, tell the audience *who* will be in charge of the change effort, *what* the change is, *why* it's necessary, *when* it will occur, *where* it will take place and *how* it will be achieved.

- Refer to a current event or personal story and link either to your main point. Audiences will remember these more easily than facts or figures.

- Use an analogy to help get your message across. *Example*: If speaking about a new product, say, "Our new widget is like a stealth fighter because it gets the job done and you don't even know it's there."

- Memorize four or five quotes about motivation, communication, teamwork, etc., and mention them in your talk.

Source: *Communication Briefings*, as adapted from *Smart Moves for People in Charge*, by Sam Deep and Lyle Sussman, Addison-Wesley Publishing Co., Reading, MA.

Putting together an impromptu speech requires quick work and immediate decisions. The process is the same as preparing for any other type of speech, except that there is less time to organize the material. Unless you know in advance that you are going to be asked to speak, you are not going to have the opportunity to do any research. Therefore, everything to be included must come from your own personal knowledge. As you try to organize your thoughts, keep the following in mind:

1. *Ask yourself what topic you wish to present.*

2. *Word a purpose statement that represents the topic.*

3. *List the major headings that develop the purpose statement.* If paper is available, jot them down. Write these in the middle of the sheet of paper so you have time to add the introduction and the statement of the central idea later. Skip spaces in between each

of the major headings so that if you have time available for developing subpoints, you will be able to write them in.

4. *Arrange the major headings according to one of the methods of organization (spatial, chronological, topical, causal, comparison-contrast, or problem-solution).* Use the list you developed for step 3 to jot down the order of each heading next to the item.

5. *Decide on an introduction.* Most ad lib speakers tend to use a rhetorical question or a reference to the theme, but often you can think of a story (an illustration), a dramatic device, or another introductory device. Because you probably will not have time to write out the whole introduction, jot down several key words so you will remember what you want to say.

6. *Formulate your central idea.* This should be no problem because it parallels your purpose statement.

7. *The easiest form of conclusion is simply to restate the major points you made.* If you can think of a clincher, all the better. (Below the list of major headings, write down several words that will remind you of the planned conclusion.)

8. *If you have time, go back to see if you can think of any examples that back up the major ideas you want to present.* If you have examples, write them in at the appropriate places. If not, try to think of some as you speak, making sure that you clarify or define any words that may be unfamiliar to your listeners.

10.2 The Extemporaneous Mode of Presentation

People who know in advance that they will be giving a presentation most often use the extemporaneous mode of speaking, developing a set of aids, such as notes or outlines, to assist them in presenting their ideas. In **extemporaneous speaking**, speakers take time to think about personal informa-

The extemporaneous mode usually results in a more spontaneous, natural oral presentation and physical presentation than are likely in the manuscript or memorized mode.

tion they have that would help develop a well-thought-out speech and, if necessary, do research. Teachers and clergy, for example, frequently are extemporaneous speakers.

The extemporaneous mode offers many significant advantages: enough time to structure the presentation and find the information needed to develop the central idea; the security of having notes or an outline to refer to throughout the speech; the use of quotations, illustrations, and statistics in written form for backing up ideas; the opportunity to develop solid analytical information; the opportunity to go over the materials before presenting them; and a more spontaneous and natural oral presentation and physical presentation than are likely in the manuscript or memorized mode.

Unfortunately, the extemporaneous mode has some disadvantages as well. For example, speakers who do not allow sufficient time for preparation and rehearsal may lose their train of thought during the presentation and have to grope for words. Speakers who refer to materials too frequently during the speech or have too many notes may fail to interact with the audience. Furthermore, because extemporaneous material is never written out word for word, a speaker will not have a permanent record of the speech.

To avoid having an excessive number of notes, you should limit the quantity to those needed for security without being overdependent on them. In determining just what is essential, you are wise to consider this analogy: The first time you drive to a particular site, you may need an in-depth set of directions, complete with route numbers, road markers, and indications of the exact mileage. On your second trip you need less information, and by the third trip you need almost none. So it is with your use of notes and outlines. You should have enough information to feel comfortable and free to navigate through the presentation with no fear of getting lost. The only way to discover the extent of your readiness is to take several oral test drives through your speech to ascertain how much prepared information you really need to have with you in the form of notes.

Developing a Speech Outline

As an extemporaneous speaker you need to determine if you wish to use an outline while presenting the speech. An outline helps you make sure your speech develops your purpose statement and gives you a presentational aid while you speak. Many speakers start out with a **planning outline**, a brief framework used to think through the process of the speech. It contains the major ideas of the speech, without elaboration. It is your means of thinking through the things you wish to say and putting them in a structural order. Here is a sample planning outline for a speech based on the purpose statement "To inform the audience about organ transplants by discussing the parts of the human body that are commonly donated, the need for donations, who can donate, and the process of becoming a donor."

   I. Introduction

      A. Attention getter—story of Debbi, who died in an accident

      B. Orienting material

         1. Definitions of organ donor, transplant

         2. History of donations

II. Statement of central idea—parts of the human body that are commonly donated, the need for donations, who can donate, and the process of becoming a donor

III. Body

    A. Parts of the human body that are commonly donated

    B. Need for donations

    C. Who can donate

    D. The process of becoming a donor

IV. Conclusion

    A. Restatement—parts of the human body that are commonly donated, the need for donations, who can donate, and the process of becoming a donor

    B. Clincher—contribution of Debbi and her family

At this point you will need to decide whether you are going to proceed with generating a **developing outline**, which expands the planning outline by adding the details that will flesh out the speech. If so, you will need to add the attention getter and orienting materials; expand the major topics of the body with examples, illustrations, and analogies; determine the internal summaries and forecasts; list the major ideas for restatement; and settle on the clincher. In order to do all this, it helps to know the form for constructing an outline and some general rules that relate to the format.

The purpose of the outline format is to interconnect the various parts of a speech. Traditionally the outline contains Roman numerals for major headings and letters and numbers for subordinate points.[1] The format is:

I. Major heading

    A. Major point(level 1)

        1. Subordinate point(level 2)

            a. Subordinate point(level 3)

                (1) Subordinate point(level 4)

                    (a) Subordinate point(level 5)

There is controversy over the general principles of outlining etiquette. Experts espouse "rules" that they feel must be followed. Others disagree with those regulations. If you are presenting the speech in an academic setting, the course instructor will probably give you specific rules for outlining. Here are some generally accepted, but not universally agreed on, suggestions for developing a speech outline:

1. *Block information on your paper for clarity of ideas.* One of the major fears speakers have is that they will get lost in the middle of the presentation. In order to avoid this possibility, use consistent indenting in your outline, so that each major head is flush with the left margin, each major point is indented five spaces, each level 2 subordinate point is indented 10 spaces, and so on. If you use this form, you should be able to find your place visually as you proceed through the speech. Note the consistent indenting used in the outlines presented in this text.

2. *On the outline, use sentences, phrases, words, or a combination of sentences, phrases, and words.* As a speaker you will need to determine what you desire to have in front of you while you speak. If you feel most comfortable writing whole sentences on your outline, then do so. Be careful, however, that you don't put down so much material that you read rather than speak to the audience, or get lost in the reams of material. Some speakers like to write out their introduction and conclusion in sentence form, include the text of quoted materials, and use phrases and words for the rest of the outline. Some speakers, wishing to ensure that they speak rather than read, use only short phrases or words on the outline to clue them to their next idea. Though some sources will advise you to use only sentences or only phrases, your comfort and the usability of the materials should dictate what form you decide on.

3. *Use parallel wording for the major points of the body of the speech.* One purpose of the outline is to allow you to be sure your ideas cover the topic sufficiently and are all given equal weight. Word your major points so the relationship among your ideas is clear. For example, using the planning outline for the speech about organ donations, parallel wording for the main points would be:

   A. The most commonly donated human organs

   B. The need for donations of human organs

   C. Who can donate human organs

   D. The process of becoming an organ donor

   All these major points clearly relate back to the purpose statement and develop the major theme of the speech.

4. *Use subordinate points to support the preceding major point.* The purpose of subordinate points, at any level, is to flesh out the preceding idea by adding clarifiers, examples, illustrations, analogies, or quotations. Some outlining purists contend that "for every A there should be a B and for every 1 there must be a 2." In general, this makes sense. If you are subdividing an idea, or breaking it into parts, then by definition you must have at least two subideas. This does not mean, however, that if you are supporting an idea with an example you must have two examples. Again, the important thing to remember is that the purpose of an outline is to help you develop a clear and organized speech.

5. *Decide whether to include speech structure labels.* The planning outline for the speech about organ donations indicates the formal segments of the speech (introduction, central idea, body, conclusion, and each subordinate heading). Many speakers prefer this, as it helps them keep track of where they are in the outline and make sure that all the necessary parts of the speech are present. If these headings are distracting to you, you may choose to omit them in the final outline you take before the audience as your presentational aid.

6. *Include internal summaries and forecasts.* Many speakers use an **internal summary**, which summarizes each major point before proceeding to the next major point, and make transitions in the form of **forecasts**, which tell the listener what is coming next. Speakers who wish to do this often write out their summaries and forecasts and place them on the outline in brackets between one major point and the next. For example, here is how the first major point of the speech on organ donation would appear with an internal summary and a transition:

III. Body
    A. The most commonly donated human organs
        1. Cornea
        2. Kidney
        3. Heart
        4. Lungs
        5. Pancreas
        6. Liver
        7. Bone
        8. Skin
           (Internal summary: The parts of the human body that are commonly donated are the cornea, kidney, heart, lungs, pancreas, liver, bone, and skin.)
           (Forecast: Let's now examine the need for these tissues and organs.)
    B. The need for donations of human organs
       Again, if you find the speech structure labels "internal summary" and "forecast" distracting, you may want to leave them out.

7. *Write notes in the margins to remind yourself of necessary information.* Some speakers like to alert themselves to things as they speak. For example, if you tend to speak rapidly, you might want to write "Slow Down!" in the margin in red ink. If during practice you keep forgetting to show the chart you want to use, indicate in the margin the point at which you want to display it. Though marginal notes are not an official part of the outline, they are yet another device to make the speech effective and to help you feel comfortable and gain confidence.

Mind Mapping

An alternative to using an outline for the extemporaneous mode of presentation is to use mind mapping. Mind mapping arranges the materials visually rather than in list form. This is a method often favored by right-brained people (see the section Psychographics, *Listening/Learning Style*, in Chapter 5), who are stimulated by pictures rather than words. Mind mappers can use the procedure either to develop the presentation or to develop and use the visual images for the presentation stage of speaking.

To use a mind map, the potential speaker makes a list of all the ideas to be included in the speech. Then major headings are selected, each major idea is placed in a circle, and then the subpoints are grouped around the major heading circles and connected to the circles with spokes. During the actual presentation, the speaker presents the major heading, then orally flows from one spoke to another, etc. When one circle and its spokes are finished, the speaker proceeds to the next circle and discusses its topical spokes. For example, you are planning on speaking about a visit to Washington, D.C., the nation's capital. You make a list of the things you want to do and the things you want to see (Figure 10.1). You then set the major theme ideas in circles and group the subhead ideas around those major themes (Figure 10.2). The speaker then uses this drawing as the basis for the extemporaneous speech.

Figure 10.1   Mindmapping Procedure

A. Listing of Topics	**B. Mapping visual outline**
Subject: Visiting Washington, D.C.	**Outdoor Things to Do**
Smithsonian Museums	Arlington Cemetery
Georgetown	National Zoo
Kennedy Center for Performing	Korean Memorial
Arts	Viet Nam Memorial
Tyson's Corner Center	Lincoln Monument
Korean Memorial	Jefferson Memorial
Metro	Roosevelt Memorial
*Outdoor things to do	Washington Monument
Viet Nam Memorial	Tidal Basin
Ford's Theater	The Mall
Jefferson Memorial	**Shopping**
Beltway	Old Town Alexandria
Bureau of Engraving and Printing	Mazza Gallery
The White House	Smithsonian Gift Shops
Capitol Building	Fashion Mall @ Pentagon City
Mazza Gallery	Georgetown
*Indoor things to do	Tyson's Corner Center
Holocaust Museum	**Indoor Things to Do**
Washington Monument	Smithsonian Museums
Arlington Cemetery	Kennedy Center for Performing
National Zoo	Arts
FBI Building	Bureau of Engraving and
Parking lots	Printing
*Transportation	The White House
Roosevelt Memorial	FBI Building
Corcoran Art Gallery	Corcoran Art Gallery
Lincoln Monument	Pentagon
The Mall	Capitol Building
*Shopping	Holocaust Museum
Tidal Basin	Ford's Theatre
Pentagon	**Transportation**
Old Town Alexandria	Beltway
Smithsonian Gift Shops	Parking Lots
Fashion Mall at Pentagon City	Metro
*Main topics	

Figure 10.2 Mind Map Diagram

Mind Maps

"If I'm concerned about having too much to say or what to cover in a speech, I organize it by mind mapping the material. I put the topic or theme in the middle of the page. Then I brainstorm everything I can think of about that topic. I write just a word or so that represents each of those thoughts. I put little squiggles around each word, just for fun. I then look at the thoughts and number each one in the way I might use them. I don't draw pictures or get elaborate in terms of colors—my wife, Marge, does like to organize her talk that way." Dr. Ken Blanchard

Yellow elephant As you read that phrase, did you think of letters Y-e-l-l-o-w-e-l-e-p-h-a-n-t? Or did you see an image? Of course, you saw the image. The mind thinks in images and pictures. Mind mapping was developed by Tony Buzan, author and brain researcher, as an alternative to outlining. He suggests you organize your material by drawing pictures. For example, you might draw a simple picture of a yellow elephant (assuming you were doing a talk that involved a yellow elephant), then a line with an arrow to the next thought you want to talk about.

When you try to force your mind to think in a traditional outline form—with words and sentences—you may wait around forever, staring at a blank paper, waiting for Roman numeral *I* to bounce into your head. But in mind mapping you draw each idea as it pops up, then connect the pictures later into a speech.

As you draw your mind map, you can more easily see when you've got too much stuff in one place and not enough in another. If you can't easily connect from one line to another, then you can see it may not belong in the presentation at all.

❖ ❖ ❖ ❖   Practicing with the Outline/Mind Map

Preparing your fully developed mind map, or the **presentational outline** (the material you will take before the audience as your presentational aid), is among the final steps in polishing your speech. After you have completed the developing outline or mind map, practice using it. You may find that there is too much material, or so much detail that you get lost in all the words. You may find that you know the material fairly well and don't need lengthy outline entries.

As you practice, cross out unneeded material and add necessary ideas. When you feel comfortable—when the speech is about the right length and you are speaking with ease—transcribe the presentational outline/mind map. Practice with it to make sure it is right and write down any marginal notes you need. At this point you are prepared to give an extemporaneous speech.

10.3 The Manuscript Mode of Presentation

Usually speakers adopt the extemporaneous mode because it allows them to interact freely with the audience and adapt to feedback. There are times, however, when a speaker finds it necessary to prepare an exact word-for-word presentation—for example, when the speaker will be quoted, must meet specific time requirements, or must have exact word selection. A business executive who makes a statement for the company, a police officer who reports an arrest of importance to the community, a nurse responsible for reporting the condition of a patient—all must be sure their statements are exact.

Some people find it necessary to hand out copies of their speeches to the newspaper, radio, and television media for reproduction after the oral presentation. This is true for political candidates as well as labor representatives and the officers of boards of education and corporations. In all these cases, the material these speakers present must be quoted word for word. Radio and television announcers write down their exact remarks so they can fit their presentation into precise time slots. Speakers who have been asked to talk for only a certain predetermined time at a meeting or conference also find it useful to script their presentations.

In the **manuscript mode** of delivery, the material is written out and delivered word for word. This mode of speaking has the advantage of providing accurate language, solid organization, and a permanent written record of the speech. But this mode also has some disadvantages. It is very difficult for a speaker who reads from a manuscript to adapt the speech during the presentation to suit the audience. As a result, the speaker is very dependent on prior audience analysis. Another problem with the manuscript mode of delivery is that it requires the ability to read effectively from the written page. A good manuscript speech should be conversational and animated, and the speaker should use extensive eye contact, vocal inflections, and physical actions to maintain rapport with listeners.

One method for establishing eye contact with the audience while following the manuscript in an unobtrusive way is called **eye span**. This involves training your eyes to glance down quickly, allowing you to pick out a meaningful phrase and deliver it to the audience as you look at the listeners. As you

The manuscript mode requires the ability to read effectively from the written page.

reach the end of the phrase but before you have finished saying it, glance down again and grasp the next phrase to say. It is helpful, in using eye span, to underline key words and mark off phrases. Television newscasters who do not have a Teleprompter available often use this method to maintain contact with viewers, looking into the camera as they speak.

Adjusting From a Written to an Oral Style

Effective manuscript presentation requires an effective oral style. Remember that writing a speech for the listening ear is quite different from writing an essay for the reading eye. Because your listeners will hear your words only once, your choice of language, materials, and structure must be designed to achieve instant understanding. To understand this, find an essay that you wrote for English class and read it aloud. You will probably discover that it sounds stilted because of its complex sentences and other features of

Photo: Courtesy of University of Missouri—Kansas City, Communication Studies Department

A good manuscipt speech should be conversational and animated, and the speaker should use extensive eye contact, vocal inflections, and physical actions to maintain rapport with listeners.

written language style. Written phrases such as, "therefore, by reviewing the presented ideas," and "by reviewing the ideas discussed on previous pages" should be avoided.

Even though written language and spoken language may be used to develop the same ideas and to accomplish similar communication objectives, there are some distinct differences of form. Therefore, in preparing a speech in which you are going to use a manuscript, you must be sure to prepare the material as spoken, rather than written, language.

Preparing the Manuscript

Effective oral language is designed for instant intelligibility by the listener. Unlike the reader, who has the opportunity to reread a passage, the listener has only one opportunity to receive, understand, and interpret the oral message unless he or she has used an audio- or videotape recorder and can replay passages for review. When composing something that will be heard, rather than read, you must write as though you are speaking. To do this, write the way you would talk, say the material aloud as you are writing, and practice reading the material aloud. In addition, be aware of these pointers:[2]

1. *Use the active voice, not the passive voice.* ("The manager wrote the report" rather than "The report was written by the manager.")

2. *Keep sentences short.* The reading eye cannot comprehend a sentence much more than 17 to 20 words long. The listening ear has an even shorter attention span.

3. *Amplify rather than describe.* Long descriptions are boring to listeners; instead, show them your point in a brief verbal or even a visual segment. Use supplementary aids if they are appropriate.

4. *Use short, simple words.* Remember that while readers have the privilege of going over your material again, listeners do not have that option.

5. *Use repetition.* Memorable speakers are those who repeat words and phrases in order to allow the listener to hear a major concept more than once. One theory is that major concepts should be repeated three times. They realize that it sometimes takes more than one hearing for the receiver to grasp their meaning and enhance remembering. Be careful, however, that restating over and over can bore an audience.

6. *Write to reflect your audience's personality.* Adapt your word choice and style of language to your listeners.

7. *Write for one member of the audience.* A good way to personalize your manuscript is to think about one person as you put it together.

8. *Avoid abstract language.* Keep your language concrete and clear. Avoid using vague or technical terms that the audience may not understand.

9. *Avoid referent problems.* Be careful not to use the pronoun "they" to refer to one person. Also, be very specific as to the referent for a pronoun. If you mention one man's name and then another man's name, do not use "he" to refer back to one of them. The audience may become confused about which person you are referring to.

10. *Watch the context of your sentence.* Planned humor is an excellent device to get and hold attention, but unplanned humor that emerges from the way sentences are worded can be embarrassing.

11. *When you are finished, stop.* A short, to-the-point presentation often has the greatest impact. The classic example of this is Lincoln's "Gettysburg Address," which was only three minutes long.

12. *Avoid using "you" when referring to yourself.* If audience members are expected to apply the material to themselves, then "you" is appropriate, but if the reference is to an experience you yourself had, or to something you are going to do, then use "I."

13. *The word* we *is more involving than the word* you. Because saying "we" gives the audience the idea that you are including yourself, it establishes a common bond between you and your listeners.

14. *Unless precision is absolutely necessary, round off any numbers you use.* It is difficult to comprehend a number such as $1,124,569.68. Rounding this off to "a little more than $1 million" makes it much easier to grasp.

15. *Avoid using words and phrases not intended for listening, including "phony fancies" and verbs turned into nouns.* Phony fancies are fuzzy words or expressions a speaker might use in order to sound important, impressive, or knowledgeable. A few examples include "for the purpose of finding" rather than "to find"; "in reference to," "of the order of magnitude," or "pertaining to" rather than "about"; "prior to" rather than "before"; and "procure"

rather than "get." Some expressions that start out as verbs end up as nouns if you add too many words. Examples include "he tends," which becomes "he exhibits a tendency to"; "I appreciate," which becomes "allow me to express my appreciation"; and "let us consider," which becomes "let us take into consideration."

16. *Be appropriate.* Language must be adapted to the components of communication—the speaker, audience, topic, and occasion. Build your speech with language you are comfortable using. The purpose of language is to convey a message, not impress the audience. The use of "big" words, technical terms, and acronyms to represent ideas may give the impression that you are well versed in the subject, but if the audience fails to understand the message, the end goal of the presentation—understanding—is lost. Your strategy in word selection centers on analyzing the components of the speaking situation and selecting words that best convey the message orally.

17. *Be clear.* Clarity is based on the selection of simple, specific expressions—words that allow for understanding because they are aimed at the audience's level of knowledge. To achieve clarity, do not speak down to the audience, but use language the audience understands. Compare these pairs of statements in terms of ease of understanding:

    a. A joyful feeling of contentment is not a commodity that can be obtained through the normal channels of currency exchange. *Money can't buy happiness.*

    b. A basic writing implement, used judiciously, has the potential for greater impact than an ancient, double-edged weapon. *The pen is mightier than the sword.*

    In addition, clarity is achieved through the use of a grammatical style that does not confuse. What is really meant by each of these church-pulpit announcements?

    > *This being Easter Sunday, we will ask Mrs. Johnson to come forward and lay an egg on the altar.*

    > *This afternoon there will be a meeting in the north and south ends of the church, and children will be baptized at both ends.*

18. *Use phrases that are easily remembered.* Many memorable phrases are clear ideas with profound meanings that were expressed with simplicity. Two examples of such messages are President Franklin Delano Roosevelt's appeal for national unity in the face of the Depression of the 1930s when he said, "We have nothing to fear but fear itself," and John F. Kennedy's inaugural call for a national referendum of dedication when he said, "Ask not what your country can do for you; ask what you can do for your country." Many bumper stickers and highway advertising signs express ideas in catchy phrases by employing a few well-chosen words: "Born to Shop," "Save the Whales," and "If You Can Read This, Thank a Teacher."

19. *Be vivid*. Vividness is the use of words that express forceful ideas and that create an emotional or sensory experience for the listener. Advertisements that stress "lemon scents," "fluffy softness," and "bone-chilling cold" create vivid sensory images. Vividness allows the audience to become involved in the ideas being expressed. Selecting words or images that incite strong emotions creates vividness. For example, a commercial against drug use showing a dead body in a morgue, an identification tag hanging from one toe, followed by a voice stating, "Drugs kill!" presents a vivid message.

It takes considerable experience to retrain your writing style so you can produce a speech that is appropriate for the listening ear. Just because you are a great writer does not mean you can prepare a great speech. Indeed, great prose writers often do not make great speech writers because, as one expert noted, "Public speaking must be recognized as a separate art.... The words may be the same, but the grammar, rhetoric and phrasing are different. It is a different mode of expression—a different language."[3]

10.4 The Memorized Mode of Presentation

In the **memorized mode**, a speech is written out word for word and is then committed to memory. Public speakers seldom use this mode of communication because it is potentially disastrous. After all, even if the speaker commits the information to memory, forgetting any one idea can lead to forgetting everything. Whereas speakers who use the extemporaneous or the manuscript mode can refer to information, those who memorize their speech have no notes available for reference. Furthermore, memorizers may be so concerned about getting the exact word in exactly the right place that the meaning of the words becomes secondary.

The few advantages of the memorized mode include the ability to select exact wording and examples, to look at the audience during the entire speaking process, and to time the presentation exactly. For this reason, some speakers like to memorize their openings and closings to ensure that they can comfortably get started and finished. But the manuscript mode provides these same advantages and is less fraught with danger. Thus the disadvantages of memorized speaking usually so overshadow its advantages that few people choose to use this mode.

Knowing the advantages and disadvantages, if you feel that you really will perform best using memorization, it is recommended that you memorize thoughts rather than word by word. This allows you to speak extemporaneously, but not be dependent upon notes or an outline. Write out the manuscript, underline key ideas, and memorize those ideas. Finally, rehearse using only your memory cues until you are comfortable and can easily recall your cues, and then speak from those memorized cues.

10.5 Listening Channel Preferences

Think back to classroom lectures, speeches, training briefings, and technical reports you have experienced. Did you seem to listen more attentively to material accompanied by a handout that detailed the concepts so you could follow them as the speaker presented the materials? Were you more interested when the speaker used a computer and projected a PowerPoint presentation for you to view? Were you most intrigued when the speaker spoke directly to you with no use of supplementary aids?

Just as speakers make decisions about what presentation mode will work best for their messages, so, too, do listeners make decisions about how they tend to receive information best. In this age of technology, most listeners probably are conditioned to rely on visual messages—video presentations, overhead projections, slides, film clips, or computer-generated graphics.

Most learners begin as listeners, progress to video watching, and then turn to reading. An interesting theory on preferences for receiving information states:

> Most people find it difficult to understand purely verbal concepts. They suspect the ear; they don't trust it. In general we feel more secure when things are *visible*, when we can "see for ourselves." We admonish children, for instance, to "believe only half of what they see, and nothing of what they *hear*." . . . We are so visually biased that we call our wisest men *visionaries*, or *seers*![4]

This theory may or may not parallel your experiences, but it does indicate that if you prefer to see information, you probably are in the majority.

Using what you know about your receiving preferences, try to select the format that best fits them. For example, many universities allow students to take large group lectures, or long-distance learning via television, or small activity-based classes. Some businesses offer their employees the opportunity to participate in hands-on training in a classroom lecture setting, or to select pre-recorded television programs that can be viewed and reviewed. When you have a choice, turn to your preferred style.

You must realize that the speaker's choice may not match your preferred listening style. It is important, therefore, to be able to adjust to a format if you are going to gain the most from the public communication experience.

Solutions to Speech Snafus

Here are some ways to salvage a speech if you run into one of these sticky situations:

- You realize the audience has already heard the story you're telling. *What to do*: Ask audience members to take 60 seconds to come up with a different ending.

- You strongly disagree with the speaker before you. *What to do*: Begin your speech with something such as, "Chris and I may have differing views, but one thing we do have in common is the privilege to speak to a terrific audience like you."

- You receive a poor introduction. *What to do*: Don't insult the introducer or you'll alienate your audience. Instead, write your own introduction for the next time you speak.

Source: *Communication Briefings*, as adapted from Nancy K. Austin, writing in *Working Woman*, 230 Park Ave., New York, NY 10169.

Summary

This chapter examined the formats for speeches. The major ideas presented were:

♦ *The speaker can use four basic modes of presentation: impromptu or ad lib, extemporaneous, manuscript, and memorized.*

♦ *Impromptu speaking requires you to present your ideas with little preparation.*

♦ *Ad lib speaking allows you no time to prepare.*

♦ *In the extemporaneous mode of speaking, you develop a set of speech aids, such as notes or an outline, to assist during the presentation.*

♦ *In the manuscript mode of delivery, you write the material out and deliver it word for word.*

♦ *In the memorized mode, you write the speech out word for word and then commit it to memory.*

♦ *Just as speakers make decisions about what presentation mode will work best for their messages, so, too, do listeners make decisions about how they tend to best receive information.*

Key Terms

impromptu speaking	ad lib speaking
extemporaneous speaking	planning outline
developing outline	internal summary
forecasts	presentational outline
manuscript mode	eye span
memorized mode	

Learn by Doing

1. The class sits in a circle. The instructor throws a ball to someone in the circle and then passes an envelope to the same person. The person selects one of the statements (see list below) from the envelope, takes several minutes to prepare, and gives a two-minute presentation on the topic. But before speaking, the first person tosses the ball to someone else, who will be the second speaker. While the first person is speaking, the second person selects a topic and prepares a speech. Each speaker, in turn, tosses the ball to the next speaker. This process continues until all members of the class have spoken. The envelope may contain these statements:

    a. "I did something that I was proud of."

    b. "I made a promise and I kept it."

    c. "I believe that college is necessary."

    d. "The thing I like best about my college job is . . ."

    e. "The thing I like least about my college job is . . ."

    f. "The person I respect most is . . ."

g. "The place I visited that I liked most was _____
_____ because . . ."

h. "If I had $1 million, I would . . ."

i. "If I had three wishes, they would be . . . and I would . . ."

2. Most of the time when you give impromptu speeches you know about the topic a little bit ahead of time. To practice impromptu speaking, list on a three- by five-inch card three topics you think you could speak about for a minimum of two minutes. Your instructor will collect the cards and select one of the topics for you to give an impromptu speech on. You will have two minutes to get ready. You may use any notes you can prepare within that time.

3. Prepare a speech of three to five minutes using the extemporaneous mode. Choose a subject you feel strongly about (a pet peeve, a belief that someone holds that you cannot accept, a political candidate you support, etc.). All students will present their speeches on the same day. On that day, the class is divided into groups of three to six. Present your speech to the other members of your group. After all the presentations, each listener makes two positive comments about the first speaker's presentation and suggests one improvement. The second speaker's presentation is then discussed, and so on. After this practice day, you will each present your speech to the class as a whole. Before the whole-class presentation, adjust your presentation according to the analysis your group members have given you.

4. The instructor brings to class a shopping bag filled with miscellaneous items (a comb, an eraser, a panda bear, a feather, a ball, a block, and so on). The class is seated in a circle. The bag is handed to one student, who reaches into it without looking and pulls out an item. The instructor reads one of these statements and gives the student about one minute to think, and the student gives a speech of at least two minutes.

a. "I would like to be a (name of the object) because . . ."

b. "I would not like to be a (name of the object) because . . ."

c. "(Name of the object) reminds me of a time in my life when I found myself . . ."

d. "The (name of the object) I removed from the bag is similar to (name of another object) because . . ." "It is different because . . ."

Alternatively, a student could choose an item and prepare a speech while the preceding person speaks. This will necessitate a delay while the first speaker prepares, but after that each person gets as long to prepare as the preceding speaker talks.

5. Memorize a short poem or speech you either wrote or took from another source. Present the material to a small group within your class. Then, tell about the material in your own words using notes or an outline. This should give you the experience of realiz-

ing the difference between the extemporaneous and memorized modes of presentation.

Endnotes

1. Andrew Wolvin, *Effective Speechmaking* (Washington, D.C.: Transemantics, Inc., 1977), p. 20. For an in-depth discussion of outlining formats, see Stephen D. Body and Mary Ann Renz, *Organization and Outlining: A Workbook for Students in a Basic Speech Course* (Indianapolis: Bobbs-Merrill, 1985).

2. Judson Smith, "Writing for the Eye and Ear," *Training* (March 1981), p. 67–68.

3. Louis P. Nizer, as quoted in Jerry Tarver, *Professional Speech Writing* (Richmond, Va.: Effective Speech Writing Institute, 1982), p. 100.

4. From *The Medium Is the Massage* by Marshall McLuhan and Quentin Fiore. Coordinated by Jerome Agel. Copyright 1967 by Bantam Books, Inc. Reprinted by permission of the publisher. All rights reserved.

CHAPTER ELEVEN

Oral and Physical Presentation

Chapter Outline

Learning Outcomes

After reading this chapter, you should be able to:

- *Identify some oral and physical factors that lead to an effective presentation.*

- *Use visual aids in a presentation.*

- *Define speechophobia and identify some ways of dealing with it.*

- *Explain the existence of listener anxiety and how to cope with it.*

❖ ❖ ❖ ❖

People who are able to capture their listeners' attention typically share certain qualities. These include confidence and ease, authority, conviction, credibility, sincerity, warmth, animation, enthusiasm, vitality, intensity, concern, and empathy. They also make effective use of eye contact, conversational tone, variety of pitch, pacing, projection, and phrasing.[1] Regardless of whether they approved of his politics, speech analysts generally agreed that early in his administration President Ronald Reagan established himself as an effective communicator, a skill that helped him get some of his programs passed against great odds. As one critic observed, "He has a style that doesn't interfere with the content, and he seems to be able to make his listeners sit up and take notice."[2] This chapter looks at the various techniques and skills practiced by successful communicators—and available to you.

11.1 Vocal Delivery

Audience members often have to be enticed to participate actively in a speech. They will tend to listen with attention when the speaker's delivery is dynamic and enthusiastic. The vocal elements of communication are **pitch**, the tone of sounds, ranging from high (or shrill) tones of soprano to low (or deep) tones of bass; **volume**, the fullness or power of the sound, ranging from loud to soft; **rate**, the speed at which words are spoken (most people speak about 150 words per minute, the equivalent of one-half to two-thirds of a double-spaced, typewritten page); **quality**, the characteristic tone of a speaking voice; **animation**, having to do with the liveliness of the presentation; and **pause**, a temporary stop or hesitation. All these elements set the vocal level of speech.

A well-prepared speech can be enhanced by effective vocal delivery, but it also can be diminished by poor delivery. Speaking in a monotone—a flat, boring sound resulting from constant pitch, volume, and rate—or with a shrill pitch (much like fingernails dragged across a blackboard) will eventually cause the audience to tune out. Another distracting vocal trait is speaking at so rapid a rate that listeners cannot follow the ideas. Speakers who have a nasal sound to their voice or who speak too softly or too loudly may also have trouble keeping their audiences interested. Some people have physical problems that prevent them from articulating words correctly; others have extremely high or low vocal pitches or unpleasant tonal qualities. These problems can all be addressed by a speech therapist. Most aspects of vocal delivery, however, involve skills that students in the communication classroom can develop on their own.

For example, if your vocal presentation lacks variation in pitch, try to raise and lower your voice as you speak. You can do this by tape-recording a presentation several times, trying different varieties of pitch. Follow the same procedure to correct speech that is too fast or too slow. Even if you do not think you have any vocal problems, tape-recording is an excellent way to observe your style of delivery. Remember, however, that sitting down with a tape recorder and speaking into it will not give you as accurate a tool for assessment as will using the recorder in a natural speaking setting. Once you have an accurate recording, ask yourself whether you would enjoy listening to you as a speaker. If the answer is yes, go right on fascinating people with your dynamic animation. If the answer is no, identify the vocal elements you have problems with and concentrate on making changes to correct them. If you

❖ ❖ ❖ ❖   feel incapable of adjusting your vocal delivery on your own, seek advice from your speech instructor.

Profile: Doug Capasso, Program Director of AIDS Family Support Services-Mid-Hudson Division, Volunteers of America, Greater New York

---

Starting his career as the owner of an employment agency, Doug Capasso never imagined the twists and turns his life would take to bring him where he is today. It is equally unlikely that he could have anticipated the wide varieties of exciting public speaking opportunities he has had along the way. Anyone who speaks with him, though, immediately knows why he has become so successful. Capasso is a dynamic and enthusiastic man whose incredible interpersonal skills easily carry over into the public speaking arena.

Capasso became involved in the fight against AIDS in the early 1980s when he saw numerous friends suffer from and die of AIDS. He volunteered his much needed time and energy and began providing home respite services. This was during a period when there was great social fear of AIDS, yet Capasso was an immediate leader, helping a community in need.

Eventually, Capasso found himself in Westchester County, New York, volunteering with HIV/AIDS programs. It was there that he read an article in a local newspaper about a Volunteers of America AIDS support program that was getting off the ground. He applied for a volunteer position and was one of the first seven volunteers trained. Capasso began moving up the ranks very quickly, admittedly not due to his qualifications, but because of his electric personality and knowledge of the disease. Now, in his position as program director, he is responsible for hiring and training volunteers as well as finding funding for Volunteers of America's AIDS Family Services–Mid-Hudson Division, a program which provides AIDS respite and permanency planning for parents dying of AIDS.

It is in his capacity as a fundraiser that Capasso does the majority of his public speaking. He has gone before Rotary clubs, women's clubs, and service provider organizations to present VOA programming throughout the community. In addition, he has had the opportunity to speak before the New York State Assembly and in Washington, D.C. at national AIDS conferences and to numerous senators.

Capasso believes it is his personality that makes his speeches so successful. While the agenda sets the tone, it is his candor and honesty that enable him to achieve his goals. "I tell you what I think," he says. "You know what's going on with me." He also makes a concerted effort to share a piece of Volunteers of America and himself with the audience. He believes it is that connection that will make a difference in the end.

"Most importantly," asserts Capasso, "It's important to have a passion about what you're doing. You need to believe in what you are going to talk about. The audience will be able to sense when you are just wording it. . . . You need to feel very positive about what it is you are doing."

"And finally," Capasso adds slyly, "show no fear. Even if they are intimidating or not particularly friendly, *never* be afraid of your audience."

11.2 Pronunciation

As one observer has written, "To **pronounce** means to form speech sounds by moving the articulators of speech—chiefly the jaw, tongue, and lips. There are many different and acceptable ways of pronouncing American English, because our language is spoken differently in various parts of the

United States and Canada."[3] **General American speech**, defined as that spoken by well-educated Americans and Canadians of the central, midwestern, and western regions of North America, has been perceived as the most acceptable of the regional dialects. Nevertheless,

> speech in general and pronunciation in particular are appropriate if they are consistent with the objectives of the speaker in his/her role of communicator of ideas. The listeners, the occasion, and the speaker as a personality are some of the factors that determine appropriateness. Speech becomes substandard if the pronunciations are such that they violate the judgments and tastes of the listeners.[4]

Because your audience will evaluate you not only on the basis of what you say but also on how you say it, you should be aware of some common pronunciation problems and their causes. Then you can work toward making your use of oral English representative of the type of image you would like to portray. There are several common types and causes of pronunciation problems.[5]

1. *Sloppy or incorrect articulation.* If you say "air" for "error" or "dint" for "didn't," you are being lazy in your use of articulators. As you practice a speech you have prepared, be aware of words you mispronounce. Be conscious of dropping the "g" sound at the end of words ending in "ing," such as "going," "doing," and "watching." Also be aware of slurring words together. "Alls-ya-godado" is not an understandable substitute for "all you have to do." "Ja-know?" is not as clear as "Did you know?"

2. *Affectation.* In New England and southern speech, saying "eye-thuh" for "either" is generally acceptable, but in the western or midwestern states this pronunciation may sound out of place. Some people pepper their speech with a "British" sound because they think it makes them appear more sophisticated. If used inconsistently, such overdone pronunciation comes off as affected and can be distracting. As you prepare to speak to an audience, avoid putting on an affected tone or overdoing the pronunciation of words such as "envelope," "tomato," and "ask."

3. *Ignorance of correct pronunciation.* Most of us have reading vocabularies that are far larger than our speaking vocabularies. Sometimes, when reading aloud, you might come across a word you understand the meaning of but that is not part of your speaking vocabulary. Or, you might encounter a technical term or a name with which you are totally unfamiliar. In preparing a public speech, you may want to use a dictionary to look up the pronunciation of words you are not in the habit of saying aloud. It is very difficult to fake your way through a word that is beyond your pronunciation abilities, and incorrect pronunciation tells the audience you have not prepared properly.

4. *Vowel distortion.* Some of us have grown up in oral language environments in which words are mispronounced because of vowel substitutions. Some examples of vowel distortion are "melk" for "milk," "sekatury" for "secretary," "minny" for "many," "jist" for "just," "Warshington" for "Washington,"

"punkin" for "pumpkin," and "git" for "get." In some cases, vowel distortion may be such a strong habit that the speaker needs the help of a speech pathologist to correct the problem. Being aware of these distortions allows some people to begin monitoring their own pronunciations and correcting themselves.

5. *Pronunciation outside the norm.* If we assume that general American speech is the norm, certain pronunciations are generally not considered acceptable in the communication marketplace of business, education, and the professions. "Asked" is not "axt," "something" is not "sumptin," and "picture" is not "pitcher."

11.3 The Physical Elements of Public Speaking

The physical aspects of communication include personal elements such as gestures, movement, posture, and eye contact.

Gestures

Gestures are hand and body motions and facial expressions. Interestingly, researchers have determined that people who use hand movements when they talk appear freer, more open, and more honest to an audience.[6]

Each person uses a distinctive pattern of gestures when speaking.

Photo: Peggy Harrison (Courtesy of Elaine Lundberg)

People who use hand movements when they talk appear freer, more open, and more honest to an audience.

Each person exhibits a distinctive pattern of gestures while communicating; some use a great number of gestures, whereas others use only a few. Gesture patterns result from environmental influences and are often tied to the emotional involvement we feel as we are speaking. Emotional involvement also affects the vocal elements of delivery—the pitch, volume, and rate of speech. Broad gestures are often accompanied by loud volume and strong changes in pitch. To an audience, speakers who use few gestures sometimes seem personally uninvolved with the topic. At the same time, speakers who overplan and use practiced gestures usually appear to be insincere, automatic, and lacking in natural presentational style.

Rest Your Hands When Speaking

Unsure of what to do with your hands while giving a speech? Rest them lightly on the corners of the lectern.

Don't drop them at your sides or touch your notes except when "absolutely necessary."

This will permit you to begin your speech without appearing unsure and use gestures naturally as you "get into" the substance of the speech.

Source: *Communication Briefings*, as adapted from Dr. Jim Vickrey, Professor of Speech Communication, Troy State University, Troy, AL 36082.

To be effective, gestures should be natural and complement the speaker's oral dynamics. As you begin to feel comfortable in presenting materials you will find yourself less conscious of what you are doing and simply doing it. Just recall how you talk on the telephone or get involved in an animated conversation. You don't worry about your hands in those situations, so you

❖ ❖ ❖ ❖   should not worry about them during a speech. Forget them and they will take care of themselves. Your hands will be active when your body calls for their movement—unless you are gripping the lectern so tightly that you cannot let go, or have your hands jammed inside your pockets, or are playing with keys, money, jewelry, or the buttons on your clothing.

Uncommon Presenting Advice

Some uncommon knowledge that many speakers should find worthy reading.

- Good body language, eye contact and vocal skills enhance any presentation. But speakers who are weak in those skills can still get their message across if they have lots of credibility and match their message to the audience's needs.

- You shouldn't try to impersonate a census taker when you set out to collect demographic data about your audience. Instead, zero in on one or two things about the audience that will make a real difference. The best way to do it: Interview some audience members.

- Writing a short speech is more difficult than writing a long speech. So if someone asks you to speak "for only 10 or 20 minutes," keep this in mind: How long you'll speak means less than how than how long it will take you to prepare.

- Videotaping your presentation and viewing it is great advice. But don't wait until the last minute to do so. *Reason*: You may get depressed when you see mistakes you're making. Then if you don't have time to practice and correct those mistakes, your depression can affect your presentation.

- If you feel more comfortable when you stay behind the lectern and nervous when you venture away from it, then stay behind it. You'll present much better.

- Persuasion can pack more power if you use the third-party approach. *Example*: Don't try to persuade people to stop smoking because they may kill themselves. Instead, tell them that if they don't stop, their children may lose a parent.

- If highlighting parts of your speech helps, avoid yellow. Use pink instead. *Reason*: Pink is much easier on the eyes.

- Visual aids can grab attention and help the audience remember key points. But using them won't always improve a presentation. In fact, they're essential only when you present complex material.

- Consider using a current copy of a newspaper as a prop. Chances are good you can find something to read that ties in to your talk. *The plus*: It helps make what you say seem fresh and timely.

Source: *Communication Briefings*, as adapted from *Successful Presentations for Dummies*, by Malcolm Kushner, IDG Books Worldwide Inc., 919 Hillsdale Blvd., Ste 400, Foster City, CA 94404.

Movement

Movement (such as walking back and forth in front of an audience) is influenced by the emotional distance a speaker wants to establish, the amount of emotional energy within the speaker, and the speaker's need to stay near the lectern to refer to notes or use a microphone. A person who wants intimate interaction with audience members will move or lean toward them. But if the desire is to create a more formal feeling, the speaker will remain stationed behind the lectern, using it as a barrier. To avoid distracting their listeners, some speakers consciously limit the area they cover so that their movements do not become more interesting than their speaking. Of course, if a microphone is anchored to the lectern, the speaker must remain there. In addition, the arrangement of the audience may confine the speaker's space.

It is usually a good idea for a speaker to employ opening and closing pauses in the presentation. Because it takes an audience a while to settle down to listening, a speaker is wise to assume a comfortable position before the audience and pause for several seconds before starting the presentation. At the end of the speech, the speaker usually presents the last sentence emphatically—by raising or lowering the voice—to indicate that the presentation is over. The speaker should then pause again for several seconds before leaving the lectern.

Posture

The effective speaker devotes some attention to **posture**, the way you stand can add or detract from a speech. Have you ever watched a speaker and said to yourself, "He doesn't look comfortable," or "Why is she leaning on the lectern?" or "Why is he swaying back and forth?" The speaker's posture should not distract the audience from the speech itself. Speakers must be careful not to lean to one side or to shift their weight back and forth, because this draws attention from what is being said to the manners of the presenter.

Eye Contact

Establishing **eye contact** by looking into the eyes of your listeners as you speak is another key to effective speaking. In fact, eye contact is considered by some public speaking theorists to be one of the most important aspects of speech. It is your way of establishing credibility, as you can "look the audience in the eye," and ties you directly to your listeners. Audience members are likely to feel more involved in the presentation if you look at them. Maintaining eye contact also helps you receive feedback so you can adjust the presentation accordingly.

To use eye contact effectively, look directly at your listeners, not over their heads. Be sure to shift your focus so that you are not maintaining contact with just one section of the audience, and be especially careful not to overlook those in the front or back rows. One technique, the Magic V (Figure 11.1), has been used successfully by speakers.

11.4 Reading From the Manuscript

Using a manuscript can be difficult because you must look at the audience at the same time that you are trying to read your material with animation and naturalness. To do this, you will have to work out some system of following the script unobtrusively so you can maintain eye contact with the audience without losing your place. Be careful not to move or flip the manuscript pages unnecessarily because this draws attention away from you and toward the manuscript. Also try to avoid falling into a monotone. Read according to the meaning by stressing important words and ideas, and vary your tone of voice so that you are speaking naturally. Some speakers run the index finger of their left hand down the side of the manuscript so they are

❖ ❖ ❖ ❖

Figure 11.1 The Magic V

Let's say there are 500 people in your audience. It's very difficult to make actual eye contact with 500 people. However, there's a trick to help called the Magic V (see the figure). When you look at someone, everyone in a V behind that person thinks you are looking at them.

Divide the room up into a tic-tac-toe board. Look at one of the "squares" and use the *V* and the mind touch to lift that section. Once you have them, move to another square.

When the crowd is large, use the Magic V. Draw a "tic-tac-toe" in your mind over the crowd. As you look at each square, you are actually looking at all the people in a "V" behind the person you are really looking at.

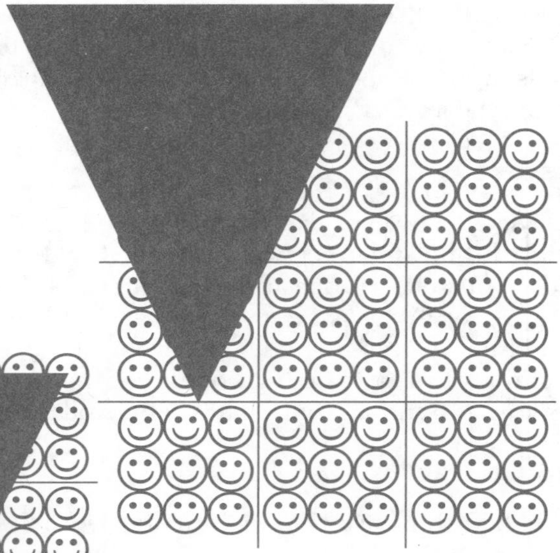

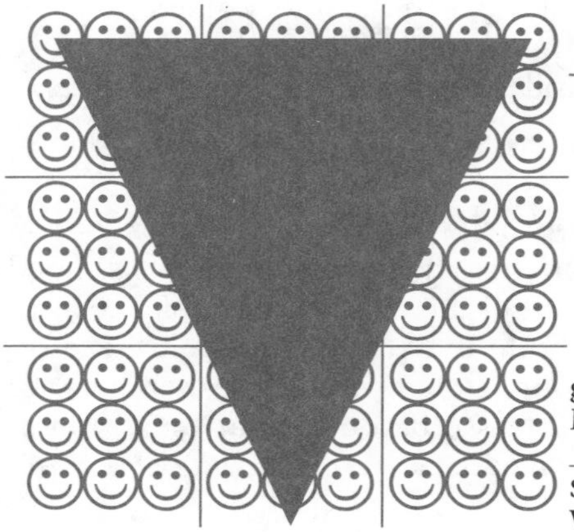

After you have made contact with that group emotionally, switch to another square. Make sure you work the squares at random.

Source: From *Secrets of Successful Speakers* by Lilly Walters, pp. 138–139. Copyright © 1993. Reproduced with permission of McGraw-Hill, Inc.

continually pointing to the start of the next printed line that they will be reading. This way, when they look up, they can find their place when they return to the manuscript.

It also helps to arrange the script in a format that keeps you from getting lost. Double- or triple-space the information; do not divide sentences by starting them on one page and finishing them on another; and do not write or type on the back of the pages. If useful, place diagonal lines and underscores in the script so that you remember when to pause and what words to stress.

Slash marks can be used to indicate a pause or a stop. Usually, / is used for a short pause, / / for a longer pause, and / / / for a full stop. Underscores are placed beneath a word or a phrase to indicate that it should be stressed. For example, the word *now* is to be stressed in the sentence: Do it now. Notice that the entire meaning of the sentence changes if the underscoring becomes: Do it now. If you feel that underscoring will help you to present the material in a meaningful way, be sure to use it. Usually a single underscore indicates a minor stress, and a double a stronger stress; a triple underscore represents the point at which you should increase the volume and the power of your vocal delivery.

11.5 Listening to Presentations

As you listen to a sermon or a class lecture, what holds your attention? One of the first scholars to study the behavior of listeners described the psychology of the listening audience:

> Signs of emotion, or interest and enthusiasm, or approval or resentment, of apathy or protest, of amusement, sorrow, or tenderness, on the part of a neighbor, tend reflexively to arouse similar feelings or attitudes in the observer. These signs are more likely to consist of facial changes, bodily attitudes, gestures, and other visible manifestations.[7]

As already discussed in this chapter, good public speakers know about the effect of oral and physical presentation on an audience. Public communication listeners also need to be aware that how and why they listen is affected by auditory and visual cues.

The auditory cues afford important points of reference. You hear a speaker's vocal emphasis, and emotionally respond to his or her message, the speaker's degree of involvement in communicating with us, and how comfortable he or she feels with that communication.

A speaker's visual cues also offer a basis for interpreting and responding to his or her message. Consider the impact of first impressions and how lasting those impressions are. A speaker communicates a great deal by what he or she chooses to wear and how he or she presents himself or herself before the audience. Does the speaker approach the lectern with assurance? Is the speaker enthusiastic and animated? What does his or her posture say to you? Does the speaker establish eye contact with the listeners? As a public communication listener you should be aware that you are affected by each of these factors.

The speaker's verbal and nonverbal style can turn you on to listening or turn you off to the message. Be aware that sometimes you need to put aside the oral and physical presentational attributes and realize that the real intent of the message is carried through what is being said. Realize that how the material is being presented is what captivates your attention and manipulates you to listen. Be aware of the tendency to pay attention to the packaging when, in reality, it is the contents that are the most important.

Have you ever seen a motivational speaker on television or been in an audience of someone who is trying to excite you to make changes in your life or to buy a product? Motivational speakers often receive positive immediate reaction from listeners or viewers. However, their long-term effect tends to be minimal. People get excited while listening, and they vow to make changes; yet few make long-term commitments. As soon as the excitement wears off, the reality of the message sets in. Purchasers often fall for the speaker's convincing mode of presentation; afterwards the buyer realizes that the product was not needed or wanted. In order to protect the vulnerable listener from such irrational or emotional acts, many states have passed laws that allow a person to cancel orders or return products as much as three days after they have taken the action. This gives time for rational logic to set in and the emotional presentational effects to wear off.

If you find yourself being captivated by the oral and physical presentation of a speaker, force yourself to look at the material being presented in as logical a mental framework as possible. Determine whether it is the oral and physical presentation that is being bought, or the message, itself.

It often is difficult to listen to a speaker who talks in boring monotone, doesn't use many gestures, and doesn't look at you directly as the presentation is being made. Good speakers will realize this and try to build the necessary emotion and logic into a speech. However, just because the presentation is not inspiring, does not mean the message should be ignored.

11.6 The Use of Supplementary Aids

Effective use of supplementary aids such as visual, audio, and audiovisual material is often critical to the impact of a speech.

Using Visual Aids

While Chapter 7 explored the selection and preparation of visual aids, here are some basic suggestions to keep in mind when using them in a speech:

1. *Do not stand between the visual aid and the audience because you will block the view*. If an aid is important enough to use, it is important that the audience see it.

2. *Speak toward the audience, not toward the visual aid*. Focus your attention on the aid only when you want the audience to look at it.

3. *Know the visual aid well enough so that you do not have to study it while you talk*.

4. *Point to the particular place on the aid that you are discussing*. If, for example, you are speaking about the Yucatan peninsula and you have displayed a map, point specifically to this area of Mexico with your finger, a pencil, or a pointer. You know where the Yucatan is, but your listeners may not.

5. *Use the aid at the point in your presentation where it will have the greatest impact*. Prepare the listeners for the aid by explaining what they are going to see (for example, "We are going to look at a chart that will demonstrate what has been happening to one business in this country during the last 5 years"). Then clarify what the aid is illustrating ("This chart shows the decline that has taken place in shoe production in the last 20 years. As you will note, production in 1973 was at this level, whereas the chart shows a decrease in 1998 to this level"). Finally, pull the ideas together ("Thus, a look at one industry, the shoe industry, can help us to see . . .").

6. *If you do not need the aid for other parts of the speech, put it down, cover it up, or turn it over*. An exposed visual aid can distract listeners. Indeed, it may become so interesting that they will stop paying attention to your presentation. If you are going to refer to

the visual aid throughout the presentation, keep it exposed; but once its purpose is completed, put it away.

Using Audio and Audiovisual Aids

Though not as commonly used as visual material, audio and audiovisual supplementary aids also must be carefully planned. Here are some suggestions for using them:

1. *Be sure you are familiar with the operation of the equipment.* Know how to turn on and adjust the television, video recorder, tape recorder, overhead or opaque projector, or other aid.

2. *Make arrangements for turning the lights on and off at the appropriate times.* It is extremely frustrating for an audience to be seated in the dark for long periods of time. Your credibility may suffer if you must pause in your presentation to ad lib a procedure for the lighting.

3. *If you are using slides, plan whether you yourself will run the equipment or whether an assistant is needed.* If you need assistance, make prior arrangements.

4. *Make prior arrangements for the equipment you need.* If you must have equipment, check to make sure that it is available and that it will be present when you arrive.

5. *Make sure the materials you are going to use are compatible with the equipment.* Not all audio, visual, and audiovisual equipment is compatible. Make sure that your materials will work with the available equipment.

When Preparing Audio-Visuals

When preparing slides or overheads, you should limit punctuation. Specifically, avoid using:

- Slashes. *Example:* "yes/no." *Why:* When seen from a distance, slashes can resemble letters. They will confuse your audience, which may think you are using longer words that don't make sense.

- Em-dashes, short dashes that serve to separate expressions. *Example:* ". . . is of course—hypothetically speaking—. . . ." *The problem:* When these expressions are knocked to the next line as a single word, you'll get awkward line breaks.

- Exclamation points. *The problem:* When projected, an "!" may resemble a "1."

Source: *Communication Briefings,* as adapted from Roger C. Parker, writing in *Technique,* Boston, MA.

11.7 Culture and Speaking Style

It is important to recognize that not all people are trained to speak and present ideas in the same way. Culture plays a major role in the way you use words and what your body does during a speech. To this point in the chapter

❖ ❖ ❖ ❖

Culture plays a major role in the way a person uses words and what the body does during a speech.

we have placed an emphasis on English American speakers. Because of the cultural hodge-podge of this nation, you undoubtedly will be listening to and speaking before people of various cultures. Let's consider a few of the cultural differences you may encounter.

African American audiences expect to be entertained, comforted, inspired, and given reason.[8] They come from traditions where storytelling, preaching, gospels, spirituals, secular music, dancing, and speaking are all part of the public speaking environment.[9] Listening to African American speakers is often a unique situation for those not used to the history of black speechmaking and preaching. "The rhetorical situation demands that the rhetoric be innovative and novel, for unlike the traditional public speaking situation where the speaker talks without interruption to a usually passive audience, a formal Black speaking situation show how the speaker, the message, and the audience are one."[10] Listeners shout out in agreement or to repeat the message of the speaker for emphasis.

Those not familiar with African American listeners need to understand that "The language and delivery components are necessary to capture audience, for many Black audiences are notoriously unresponsive to small voice, unimaginative and uncreative speakers."[11]

Do not be thrown off by the posture of African American audience members, especially the males'. Not looking directly at the speaker and slouching in their chairs is not unusual listening posture and has little to do with attention or agreement.

German listeners tend to display stoic facial expressions. Americans look for smiles and other expressions to confirm that listeners are or are not engaged. Germans, as a whole, are quite serious and are more reserved than Americans.[12] Therefore, an American speaker should not be discouraged if the Germanic audience members do not respond with great physical and visual enthusiasm.

On the other hand, do not be lulled into a false sense of security when speaking before a Chinese audience. Listeners will often shake their heads up and down as they listen, thus giving Americans the idea that the listeners are agreeing. This is not necessarily so. Chinese society is traditionally polite, and Chinese audience members may nod their heads vertically only to indicate that they are receiving the message. The Chinese seem to avoid free expression of personal views and feeling, so don't be concerned if they do not ask questions during the question-and-answer session, even when encouraged to do so.[13] The same is to be said for Japanese listeners who will seldom ask questions in public forums. The concept of "saving face" is so ingrained that they will not put speakers on the spot for fear that the speaker will be embarrassed in the eyes of others for not knowing the answer.

Cultural differences are even found in the fear of public speaking. Research shows that 50 percent of Japanese students are highly apprehensive

---

America's Number One Fear: Public Speaking

Things Americans Fear

Americans fear more than just things that go bump in the night. A lot more, like public speaking, financial problems, heights, and deep water. In a nationwide survey recently conducted among 1,000 adults, we asked about the things of which nightmares are made . . .

Speaking before a group is the top terror, frightening 45% of American adults; 40% are afraid of financial problems, 40% fear heights, and 33% get the shivers when they think of deep water. . . .

Fifty-four percent of women and 34% of men fear speaking before a group. Twenty years ago, this was the most common fear of both men and women. It is still the most dreaded among women, but has dropped to second place among men, who now fear financial problems most. More respondents from the North Central region (55%) than the Northeast (37%) say this is one of their fears.

Source: From *Bruskin/Goldring Research Report*, February, 1993, p. 4. Published by Bruskin/Goldring Research, Inc. Reprinted by permission.

Fear by Gender

	Total	Women	Men
Speaking before a group	45%	54%	34%
Financial problems	40%	42%	38%
Heights	40%	50%	29%
Deep water	33%	45%	19%
Death	31%	34%	28%
Sickness	28%	34%	21%
Insects and bugs	24%	34%	13%
Loneliness	23%	27%	18%
Flying	22%	30%	15%
Driving/riding in a car	10%	13%	7%
Dogs	10%	11%	8%
Darkness	9%	14%	4%
Elevators	8%	13%	4%
Escalators	8%	13%	4%

about giving speeches.[14] United States college students show less apprehension than Japanese college students.[15] This centers on the cultural norms in Japan, which do not value talkativeness; therefore, the Japanese tend not to be outspoken in contrast to Americans, who are encouraged to speak out for their rights.[16] This does not mean that Americans are not anxious about public speaking—just that they are less so than people from other cultures.

11.8 Speaker Anxiety

Very few speakers escape the "butterflies." A study of what Americans fear the most reveals that public speaking is the greatest fear.[17] Some people are so terrified by the prospect of giving a speech that the condition has been given a psychological term: **speechophobia**. It is so universal that even humorists refer to it. Mark Twain once comforted a fright-frozen friend about to give a speech by saying, "Just remember they don't expect much."[18]

U.S. astronaut Sally Ride, the first female crew member of a space shuttle mission, followed her historic accomplishment by "giving an average of one speech a day, traveling across the country and Europe. . . . In a question-and-answer period after her speech to the American Bar Association, a woman

Speechophobia

asked, 'Were you afraid?' 'I was a lot more scared getting up to give this speech,' she replied."[19]

Are all of these references to fear intended to scare you even more? No, they are just an attempt to get you to realize that you are not alone if you do have fears and say to yourself, "I don't want to get up. My knees knock, my stomach churns, my legs shake, and my mouth gets dry."

Let's be realistic. Sometime during your life you are almost certainly going to have to get up and give a speech. You may even be planning on entering a career field where speeches are necessary—such as teaching, selling, the law, marketing, or public relations. So, you are going to have to confront the fear and deal with it. There is no quick fix pill or liquid that will "cure" you. There are, however, some excellent plans of action that you can study and experiment with that can be of assistance.

First and foremost, if you are anxious, recognize that you can do yourself either a great deal of emotional harm or some good by the way you approach the anxiety.

Negative Dimensions of Speaker Anxiety

Speakers who perceive the public speaking situation to be traumatic often have some false assumptions about what they should do to help themselves. None of these actions, however, truly help people handle anxiety.

- *They avoid the experience of giving a presentation.* The more you speak, the more comfortable you will get. Though the nervousness may not go away completely, it should let up as you get more practice.

- *They fail to prepare, assuming that the longer they avoid confronting the situation, the less time there will be to build up anxiety.* If you are not prepared, your panic upon stepping up to speak will probably be greater than it would have been if you had given your presentation some practical thought.

- *They take drugs or alcohol because they think it will relax them.* All these substances will do is dull your reflexes, increase your likelihood of forgetting your material, and help you make a total fool of yourself.

Now that you know what *not* to do, let's examine what you can do.

Does Your Heart Flutter Before a Big Speech?

Psychologists have identified and recorded three stages of heart rate increase that occur before and during a speech. Keep in mind that the average resting heart rate is between 60–80 beats per minute.

Anticipation Stage: This is the time just before a speaker stands up to begin a presentation. The average heart rate is 90–140 beats per minute.

Confrontation Stage: This stage occurs during the first 30 seconds of a speech. The average heart rate is 110–190 beats per minute.

Drop-Off Stage: The average heart rate goes back down to 90–140 beats per minute after the first 30 seconds.

Source: "Speak with Impact," Communication Development Associates, Inc., 21550 Oxnard St., #880, Woodland Hills, CA 91367.

❖ ❖ ❖ ❖   ## Positive Ways of Handling Speaker Anxiety

Though no definitive research demonstrates that there are guaranteed ways to completely overcome public speaker anxiety, there are some concepts that you might consider.

We know that proper preparation is a huge factor. In addition, many seasoned speakers employ techniques that help them manage their nervousness. These include relaxation techniques, expectancy restructuring, visualization, rehearsing, videotaping, and stance.

Relaxation Techniques

When it comes to relaxation, speakers find it helpful before beginning to take several deep breaths and expel all the air from their lungs. Others like to shake their hands at the wrists to "get out the nervousness." Some people favor grabbing the seat of their chair with both hands, pushing down and holding the position for about five seconds, repeating this action about five times. This tightens and then loosens the muscles, which causes a decrease in physical tension.

Though traditionally many speakers try to shake off their anxiety, Gestalt psychology has suggested a different approach: that speakers get in touch with their feelings.[20] Rather than pushing your anxiety away, advocates recommend, you should let it go as far as it can. What will typically happen is that your anxiety will reach a peak and then subside. If you are dubious, try the following experiment: sit in a chair and place your hands one inside the other with the palm of one hand resting on the palm of the other hand and the fingers of one hand wrapped around the back of the other. Force your hands together and keep forcing them. Do not let them move. Even though the force will make your hands start to shake, keep on forcing them together. Soon your whole body will probably start to shake. You will then reach a point where the shaking will stop and relaxation will set in.

There are two ways you can use the above exercises in speaking. If you perform the hand-in-hand activity immediately before you get up to speak, you probably will be physically relaxed by the time you greet the audience. Alternatively, think of the experience of getting up before the audience and let yourself feel the anxiety. Let it stay in your mind and imagine that you are going through the experience. Let yourself be as nervous as you can; psychologically push it as far as you can. Some people report that by imagining the upcoming experience in its worst way, the actual experience becomes much easier.[21]

Expectancy Restructuring

Another way of managing anxiety is to change your expectations. We all tend to perform the way we expect to perform: **expectancy restructuring** is based on the idea that if you expect to do well, then you will do well. If you have negative expectations, you must change them to positive expectations. If you are afraid to get up and give a speech because you expect the experience to be negative, you may experience some or all of the negative side effects of that fear—sweating palms, quivering voice, and so forth.

To overcome this, first prepare a well-structured and well-supported speech so that you have confidence that the material will be well received. Then use **visualization** to picture yourself successfully delivering the speech. Visualize the actual setting in which you are going to give the speech. Picture yourself getting out of your chair, walking to the front of the room, arranging your materials on the lectern, looking at the audience, and giving the speech. As you see yourself presenting the material, look at various people. They are nodding their heads in agreement; they are interested and are listening attentively. You complete the speech and return to your chair, feeling good about yourself. The more you visualize this positive experience, the more you will expect to do well. Soon you will be expecting success, not failure.

Rehearsing

You practice keyboarding by sitting at a computer and entering information on the keyboard; you practice driving by sitting behind the wheel of a car; and you practice a sport by imitating the competitive setting. You learn these skills by practicing. The same thing is true for speaking: you need to learn the skill of presentation.

It cannot be stressed enough: one of the best ways to give a speech effectively is to know the skill of presenting. This means starting to prepare far enough in advance so that you have enough material, the speech is well structured and well organized, and you have a chance to practice it. Some speakers try to convince themselves that they will do better if they just get up and talk, with little or no thought as to what they will be saying. This is a fool's contention; it is usually proposed by a procrastinator or a person who is not properly aware of the speaker's responsibility to audience and self. Yes, some speakers can get up and "wing it," but the normal mortal cannot. So prepare and practice!

Rehearsing the Speech

Common sense can also dictate the forms your rehearsal might take. The following are some of the possibilities:

1. Read the speech over several times, silently.

2. Read the speech several times aloud.

3. Practice your delivery, including the entire address, standing in front of the mirror. This gives you the opportunity to observe not only your general attitude but also your gestures, posture, and facial expression.

4. Read the speech into a tape recorder and listen to the results. Then listen to them again. At this stage you will make an astounding discovery. Things begin to become apparent to you at a second listening (or, for that matter, a tenth) that had escaped your attention earlier.

5. If you have access to videotaping equipment, make a record of your performance in that way.

6. If you have cooperative family members, deliver the speech to them and ask for their honest comments. Don't make the mistake of welcoming only compliments and tuning out messages that are analytical or critical. If your spouse says something like "I think it's quite good but you were talking too fast," don't argue the point, whether or not your ego will permit you to agree at that moment. Just absorb the message and let it bounce around in your internal computer.

Source: From *How to Make a Speech* (McGraw-Hill) © 1986, material reproduced with permission of Steve Allen.

There is no one best way to rehearse. For most people, sitting at a desk and going over the material by mumbling through the outline or notes constitutes a starting point. This will alert you to ideas that do not seem to make sense, words you cannot pronounce, places where you go blank because you need more notes, and passages that need more or fewer examples. Make the changes, and continue to review your notes orally until you are satisfied with the material.

Once you are satisfied with the material, try to duplicate the setting in which you are going to speak. In most instances, you will probably be standing behind a lectern. If so, practice with a lectern, put a box on a desk, or place a piece of cardboard over the bathroom sink. Put a couple of chairs in front of you. Stand and speak. This will get you comfortable with moving pages and looking up from the notes or manuscript; you will also find out whether your typing or writing is going to cause you reading problems.

Rehearse as closely as possible what you are going to do. If you are going to use visual aids, use them. If you are going to demonstrate some object, demonstrate it. The more familiar you become with exactly what you are going to do, the more likely it is you will be comfortable doing it. Remember, you practice typing sitting at a typewriter, you practice driving sitting behind the wheel of a car, and you practice a sport by duplicating the competitive setting. Do the same thing with your speech.

Stop practicing when you are comfortable with your material and have worked out the problems related to using notes and supplementary aids. Do not overpractice. You can never become perfect. You are striving to become as comfortable as you can in what is a stressful situation for almost all of us.

Videotaping

An effective strategy for improving your presentation abilities and thus building your confidence is videotaping your speeches. The opportunity to see and hear how you come across in your presentations is a wonderful benefit. You can use the video tape during your rehearsal period or have your presentation taped for later viewing and personal critique.

If you have a personal videotape recorder, you can set it up, turn it on, and tape your rehearsal. You may want to have someone operate the camera for you so that you don't have to concentrate on anything other than giving your speech. If you don't have your own equipment, check out the college library; many communication departments that offer public speaking courses also have such equipment available.

Rehearse your presentation without the equipment. When you are comfortable, go before the camera in a "dress rehearsal." This will give you a look at how the speech comes across to your intended audience. After you have recorded the speech, play it back. You may want to take notes as you go along. Then go back into segments that you would like to study in greater detail, using the pause control, to determine what modifications might be appropriate.

Don't panic when you see yourself on tape for the first time. Cameras tend to make features larger, and the vocal quality of the tapings don't exactly duplicate your voice quality. Consequently, avoid being too critical of your style and your delivery. But do pick up on annoying distractions that you might unconsciously have (such as playing with your hair, saying "like," shoving your hands into your pockets, or hanging onto the podium so that you cut off gestures, over- or underusing gestures). Such self-analysis has been demonstrated to benefit student speakers to see and hear problems and to improve their performances.

The tape also can help you put your message into your long-term memory for access as you speak before your live audience. It is helpful to have heard yourself saying your speech; your points will be retrievable in your head.

It is very useful to be videotaped as you present each of your speeches in your public speaking classroom. This can provide you with an invaluable opportunity to develop a video portfolio. If your instructor does not video tape speeches, ask if you can bring in your own camera and tape your presentation so that you may review it in order to improve future presentations.

Keep your video tapes. Employers today are looking for college graduates who demonstrate effective oral communication skills. A video portfolio of your presentations gives prospective employees the competitive edge in the workplace.

Stance

The way you stand can affect your presentation. Place yourself in a balanced and comfortable stance during the speech. Do not lock your knees, as this makes the whole body rigid, causes difficulties in breathing, and often results in shaking, a dry mouth, and vocal quivering. Try not to lean on the podium because this will cut off your ability to make gestures and discourage natural movement.

When you begin, put into practice what many speakers have found to be an effective stress reliever—the **triangle stance**. In the triangle stance, as Figure 11.2 shows, you place foot A at a slight angle and foot B at about a 45-degree angle, with your heel placed roughly even with the arch of foot A. Keep your feet about six inches apart. Shuffle your feet slightly until you feel comfortable and balanced. Place your weight on foot A and let your hip extend a bit. You will feel your other leg relax. This process allows you to breathe and gesture more easily. As you proceed through the speech, you can alter the stance by switching the foot positions, always remembering to put your body weight on the foot placed in back.

Look at the people in the audience who are alert during the presentation, noddin g their heads as you speak. Concentrate on your material. Try to relax and do as well as you can . . . no one can ask for anything more! And if all else fails, remember that there have been no reported deaths from the shock of giving a speech!

Figure 11.2 Foot Placement to Relieve Speaker Anxiety

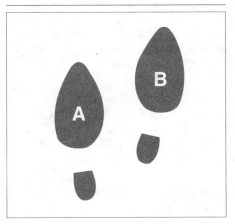

Organizing the Speaking Environment

Many speakers make the mistake of starting to talk before they are ready. Don't do this. Take time to get yourself organized. Arrange your papers on the lectern, check to make sure they are in the correct order. Check out any supplemental aids that you are going to use. Be sure the overhead projector, the computer, the other mechanical devices are working and are in focus. When you are comfortable, set yourself comfortably behind the lectern, look at the audience, and start.

11.9 Listener Anxiety

Just as speakers suffer from communication apprehension, so, too, do listeners experience such anxiety. Have you ever become nervous before going into a classroom lecture? There are students, for example, who are so fearful of going into some instructors' classes that they get stomachaches or headaches even when thinking about being subjected to that speaking experience.

Listening apprehension is "the fear of misinterpreting, inadequately processing, and/or not being able to adjust psychologically to messages sent by others."[22] Research suggests that such listening fear can interfere with listening efficiency.

Listeners can feel highly anxious about listening if:

- *The speaker's message is highly important.* If you are going to be examined on the information later, for example, you will be more apprehensive about listening to that information.

- *The speaker has high status.* The speaker may hold a position or have power to control you in some way. If she is the president of your company, for instance, and has the power to hire or fire you, this can lead to increased apprehension. You may be in awe of the person and fear making a fool of yourself if you feel inadequate because of the person's stardom, athletic abilities, or performance skills.

- *You perceive you lack the ability to listen effectively to the presentation.* If you don't have enough background to understand or the speaker assumes a higher level of technical expertise on your part, you may feel apprehensive. This is especially true if the presentation will include some interaction between you and the speaker, such as the speaker asking specific questions of the audience, as often happens in classrooms.

- *The outcome of the communication is highly important.* You are going to be more likely to feel nervous about your listening abilities as you enter into the speaking situation where you need to understand and comprehend the information, or there will be a penalty attached. Classroom and training lectures often hold this aura of pending doom.

Control, letting go, and realization are the keys to dealing with listening anxiety—control of yourself, letting go of centering on yourself, and realizing that fears seldom become realities.

Speakers are told to be well prepared and are taught techniques for bringing their natural state of apprehension under control. Listeners would do well to use the same strategies. If possible, come to the listening situation with sufficient background and information to process the message effectively. Be ready to listen. Review your listening goal, sit up straight, try and set aside other thoughts in your mind, focus your energy, and engage with the speaker. You might want to review the section "Positive Ways of Handling Speaker Anxiety" in this chapter, paying special attention to the breathing techniques and expectancy restructuring sections. Many of the same techniques work for listeners. Use these methods before and during the presentation to relieve your listening anxiety.

Most of our fears never actually come to fruition. Think back to the number of times you anticipated that bad things would happen to you. Remember the time you thought you would faint while giving a speech? It didn't happen. Fears are anticipation of what might happen. If you don't perceive they will happen, the odds are likely that they won't.

Summary

This chapter examined the oral and physical elements of delivering a speech. The major ideas presented were:

♦ *The vocal elements of communication are pitch, volume, rate, quality, animation, and pause.*

♦ *To pronounce means to form speech sounds by moving the articulators of speech. Speakers should be careful to pronounce words clearly.*

♦ *The physical elements of communication include gestures, physical movements, posture, eye contact, and the use of visual aids.*

♦ *Speechophobia is the fear associated with giving a speech.*

♦ *Speaker anxiety can be minimized through breathing techniques, expectancy restructuring, rehearsing, and stance.*

♦ *Just as speakers suffer from communication apprehension, so, too, do listeners experience such anxiety.*

Key Terms

speaking style	pitch
volume	rate
quality	animation
pause	pronounce
General American speech	gestures
movement	posture
eye contact	speechophobia
expectancy restructuring	visualization
triangle stance	

Learn by Doing

1. Some of the most commonly mispronounced words in General American speech are listed here. Look up each word in a dictionary or pronunciation guide. During a class session, you will be asked to pronounce these words and use them in sentences: *across, acts, actually, all, ambulance, any, asked, because, catch, doing, familiar, fifth, genuine, going, horror, hundred, introduce,*

just, library, next, nuclear, particular, picture, prescription, proba-bly, pumpkin, recognized, sandwich, secretary, Washington, with.

2. Below are six statements concerning feelings about speaking in public.[23] Please indicate the degree to which each statement applies to you by marking whether you (1) strongly agree, (2) agree, (3) are undecided, (4) disagree, or (5) strongly disagree. Work quickly; record your first impression.

_____ 1. I have no fear of giving a speech.

_____ 2. Certain parts of my body feel very tense and rigid while I am giving a speech.

_____ 3. I feel relaxed while giving a speech.

_____ 4. My thoughts become confused and jumbled when I am giving a speech.

_____ 5. I face the prospect of giving a speech with confidence.

_____ 6. While giving a speech, I get so nervous I forget facts I really know.

To obtain your score: Add 18 to your scores from items 1, 3, and 5, and then subtract your scores for items 2, 4, and 6. This is your final score.

Interpretation: Scores can range from a low of 6 to a high of 30. Any score above 18 indicates some degree of apprehension. If your score is above 18, you are like the overwhelming majority of Americans.

3. Your instructor has prepared a set of note cards for use in a speech. Each card contains an emotion (e.g, glad, mad, sad, uncertain). The cards will be placed blank side up on the lectern. You will draw a card. Your task is to convey that emotion to your classmates who will listen, but may not verbally react. You may not use any words except by counting from one to 25. You may use your voice, hands, face, or body to aid you. You may stop short of 25 if you think the class can identify the emotion. After you stop, your classmates will let you know what emotion they thought you were conveying.

Endnotes

1. Dorothy Sarnoff, "Self Esteem," *New Woman*, July 1983, p. 76.

2. "How to Speak Better in Public: An Interview with Sandy Livner," *U.S. News & World Report*, April 6, 1981, pp. 60–61.

3. Stuart W. Hyde, *Television and Radio Announcing*, 4th ed. (Boston: Houghton Mifflin 1983), p. 130.

4. John Eisenson, *Voice and Diction: A Program for Improvement* (New York: Macmillan, 1974), pp. 158–159.

5. Hyde, pp. 131–132.

6. M. L. Clark, E. A. Erway, and L. Beltzer, *The Learning Encounter* (New York: Random House, 1971), pp. 52–65.

7. H. L. Hollingsworth, *The Psychology of the Audience* (New York: New American Book Co., 1935), pp. 15–16.

8. Melbourne S. Cummings, "Teaching the Black Rhetoric Course," an unpublished paper, Educational Resources Information Center, 1983, p. 5.

9. Ibid., p. 13.

10. Ibid., p. 5.

11. Ibid.

12. Gerald Alred, "Teaching in Germany and the Rhetoric of Culture," *Journal of Business and Technological Communication,* 11 (1997), p. 361.

13. Ulla Connor, *Contrastive Rhetoric: Cross-cultural Aspects of Second Language Writing* (New York: Cambridge University Press, 1996), p. 39.

14. Earl E. McDowell and Noriko Yotsuyanagi, "An Exploratory Study of Communication Apprehension, Willingness to Communicate, and Sense of Humor between College Students from the United States and Japan," an unpublished paper, Educational Resources Information Center, 1996, p. 12.

15. Ibid.

16. Ibid.

17. Bruskin/Goldring Research Report, February, 1993, as published by Bruskin/Goldring Research, Inc.

18. George Plimpton, "How to Make a Speech," *Psychology Today,* October 1981, pp. 58–59.

19. "Ms. Ride Yearns for an End to Her Speaking Schedule," *Norfolk Virginian Pilot,* August 3, 1983, p. A-2.

20. This discussion is based on information shared by Les Wyman at a workshop entitled "Introductory Gestalt Workshop," at the Gestalt Institute, Cleveland, Ohio, February 1982.

21. Ibid.

22. Lawrence R. Wheeless, "An Investigation of the Effects of Receiver Apprehension and Social Context Dimensions of Communication Apprehension," *Speech Teacher,* 24 (September, 1975), p. 263.

23. This is a section of the Personal Report on Communication Apprehension (PRCA-24), from Virginia P. Richmond and James C. McCroskey, *Communication: Apprehension, Avoidance and Effectiveness*, 3rd ed. (Scottsdale, Ariz.: Gorsuch Scarisbrick, 1992), pp. 125–126. For a more comprehensive public speaking apprehension test, students should take the PRPSA (Personal Report on Public Speaking Anxiety), which is reprinted in the Instructor's Manual accompanying this text.

❖ ❖ ❖ ❖

Informative Speech

Chapter Outline

Learning Outcomes

After reading this chapter, you should be able to:

- *Define informative speaking.*

- *Discuss the need for informative speaking.*

- *List and explain the types of informative speeches.*

- *Describe the steps a successful informative speaker takes in developing a speech.*

- *Explain the role of listening for comprehension as an important aspect of being a public communication listener.*

$\mathbf{W}$e live in an information age: "Knowledge is doubling at the rate of 100 percent every 20 months."[1] One social observer has suggested that the need for people who can retrieve and explain information will greatly increase in the future.[2]

We rely on speakers in all sorts of settings to provide us with the information we need. We may attend lectures to learn about social and political issues and participate in seminars to learn new skills and upgrade others. Job training is based on a great deal of oral instruction, and the classroom lecturer delivers most of the material necessary to master the content of many college courses.

Businesses have recognized this need for information disseminators. For example, the Boeing Company employs an information specialist to help employees present information in the best way possible. According to one specialist, "A factor vital to the health of any corporation is the constant exchange of accurate information. Although traditional, written forms of business communication remain important, the oral exchange of information occupies an increasingly important role in the functioning of today's companies."[3] More and more organizations are hiring consultants to do information training as the quick upgrading and changing of equipment and job needs take place. These public speaking sessions are forms of informative speaking.

12.1 Characteristics of Informative Speaking

Traditionally, **informative speaking** has been defined as discourse that imparts new information, secures understanding, or reinforces accumulated information. However, controversies have developed among communication theorists with regard to this definition. For instance, some theorists propose that all speaking is persuasive in nature—that is, that the traditional distinction between informative speaking and persuasive speaking is simply a matter of degree.

This text assumes that all communication contains elements of persuasion. Any audience must be persuaded to accept the information a speaker presents. (Indeed, even the act of using materials to gain attention is a persuasive act because the speaker is asking listeners to dismiss other competing stimuli.) However, there is a distinction between informative and persuasive speaking that centers on the structure of the message and the particular appeals used in the persuasive speech. Persuasive speaking is covered in the next chapter.

As in any other type of presentation, effective informative speaking depends on audience analysis. The speaker must consider the audience's present knowledge about the subject, the background information the audience possesses, and the extent to which definitions, understandable analogies, examples, and clarifiers need to be used. The speaker must also determine the appropriate language level, the attention devices to be used, and the structure of the message that will best fit the group. Research suggests that speakers often may think their listeners lack the necessary information, whereas the listeners themselves may not feel the same way.[4] Mindful of this discrepancy, the astute speaker determines the listeners' real needs and uses that information to develop the speech.

In an informative presentation, the speaker must always keep the purpose of the presentation firmly in hand. A clear purpose statement is essential. Consider these three sample purpose statements:

- *To inform by defining what the drug Rho-Gam is and to explain the reasons it has eliminated the need to give blood transfusions to some newborn children who have a problematic factor in their blood composition.*

- *To inform the audience what the Heimlich maneuver is, how it was developed, and how this technique can prevent people from choking to death.*

- *To inform the audience of what the Heimlich maneuver is and to teach them how to do the maneuver by demonstrating each step.*

Note that the last two purpose statements have the same subject but different goals. The former explains the maneuver and its value. The latter explains the maneuver and then teaches the steps for performing it.

These purpose statements may sound rather formal, but they are stated in a manner that narrows the subject and indicates specifically what the speech will include. The purpose statement thus serves as a fence around the territory to be covered in a presentation and indicates how to "corral" the information. If you do not set up these sorts of boundaries, you may find yourself discussing many things but not achieving your desired outcome.

12.2 Types of Informative Speaking

There are many ways to classify the types of informative speaking. One classification scheme focuses on the subject matter, examining presentations about objects, processes, events, and concepts.[5] Informative speeches also can be identified by the setting in which they are typically used. Examples include informative briefings, technical reports, lectures, and question-and-answer sessions.

Speeches About Objects

Speeches about objects describe a particular thing in detail. The object may be a person, a place, an animal, a structure, a machine—anything that can be touched or observed. The speaker first identifies the object, and then discusses its specific attributes.

Here are two sample purpose statements for informative speeches about an object:

A good speech should be carefully adapted to the intended audience.

- *To inform the audience what a compact disc (CD) player is and to cite some specific factors to consider when purchasing one.*

- *To inform the audience why a dolphin is classified as a mammal and to describe some of the experimental work on identifying the language capabilities of this unique creature.*

Speeches About Processes

Speeches about processes instruct the audience about how something works, is made, or is done so that the listeners can then apply the knowledge themselves. The end purpose may be either to gain understanding of the process or to be able actually to do something. This type of speech would be used to train people to operate a piece of equipment or to perform a manufacturing process. Sample purpose statements for informative speeches about processes are:

- *To inform the audience of the step-by-step process of using the move feature of the WordPerfect word-processing program.*

- *To inform the audience of the step-by-step process employed by Chrysler Corporation in developing a design for an aerodynamic automobile.*

- *To inform the audience, through a demonstration, of the steps to follow when filling out the income tax short form.*

Speeches about processes often lend themselves to chronological arrangement. In this method of organization, the speaker describes the first step of the process, then the second, then the third, and so on.

Speeches About Events

Speeches about events inform the audience about something that has happened, is happening, or is expected to happen. This type of presentation can be developed in many ways, but it tends to work well in a chronological, comparison-contrast, or spatial arrangement (as explained in Chapter 9). Here are several purpose statements for informative speeches about events:

- *To inform the audience of the spread of the AIDS virus in the United States by examining the statistics for the years 1980 to 1998* (time sequence arrangement).

- *To inform the audience of the similarities and differences in the American and Russian revolutions based on their economic causes* (comparison-contrast arrangement).

- *To inform the audience of western migration in the United States by tracing the major stages of the pioneer movement from the East Coast to the West Coast* (spatial arrangement).

Speeches About Concepts

Speeches about concepts examine theories, beliefs, ideas, philosophies, or schools of thought. Much of the formal educational process consists of speeches about concepts. Possible topics for such speeches are explanations and investigations of business theories, philosophical movements, psychological concepts, and political theories.

Because many ideas about concepts tend to be abstract, a speaker must be sure to use precise language, define terms, give historical background, avoid undefined slang and jargon, and use appropriate clarifying support materials such as audio, visual, and audiovisual aids. Examples of purpose statements for informative speeches about concepts are:

- *To inform the audience of the existential movement in philosophy by stating Jean-Paul Sartre's definition and application of existentialism in the play* No Exit.

- *To inform the audience about the theory that abused children grow up to be child abusers through an examination of three classic research studies.*

- *To inform the audience of the theory that musical theater composers Alan Jay Lerner and Frederick Loewe used the theme of the search for a perfect time, a perfect place, and a perfect love story as the basis for their musicals.*

Informative Briefings

Most business, organizational, and technical communicators gain current knowledge in their fields as a result of **informative briefings**. The fundamental objective of an informative briefing is to share data and insights among people with common interests. The briefing usually involves delivery of information to the audience, followed by the exchange of data, ideas, and questions among participants.[6] This type of speech is used to explain organizational policies, procedures, and issues. For example, the sales manager of an automobile dealership might use an informative briefing to tell her staff about the new models, the head of a nursing unit might explain to his staff the procedures to follow when treating new patients, or a military commander might outline troop movements to the press.

As with any other kind of speech, preparation for an informative briefing requires careful audience analysis to determine what background and definitions are needed to ensure comprehension. It is not uncommon, given the nature of when and how briefings are used, for the audience to be quite knowledgeable about the subject. If the audience has considerable knowledge, the speaker does not have to cover the background material in as much depth as he or she would for uninformed listeners.

Technical Reports

Technical reports are concise, clear statements explaining a process, detailing a technique, or discussing new elements either to people within a business or industry or to people outside it. Unfortunately, a majority of executives in corporate America are convinced that recent college and university graduates cannot give technical reports effectively. Executives surveyed said that fewer than 20 percent of the people they worked with were capable of giving a concise, clear oral report and that they had far greater difficulty training people to do this than they did teaching them how to write a clear letter.[7]

One of the major factors in the development of a technical report is determining the proper format. The first rule of giving a report is to ask those who request the report what form they would like it to take. Find out how much time will be allowed and how much detail is required.[8]

Speakers who give technical reports must have a good sense of the audience. If the audience consists of nontechnical people, all technical words must be defined, and analogies familiar to the audience should be included to clarify the ideas presented. This does not mean the speaker has to water down the material so that it is no longer accurate. Instead, the speaker should be sure to define words, give examples, and present ideas in a variety of ways to make sure that listeners understand the concepts being set forth.

If your presentation includes technical drawings or a number of statistics, use handouts so that everyone can examine the materials. If the group is small, consider allowing audience members to ask questions as you develop your ideas so that they have the opportunity for immediate clarification where necessary. Be careful, however, to maintain control of the structure and the material as you answer questions.

When you structure a technical report that involves a recommendation, start with a statement of the proposal unless there is a compelling reason not to do so. (You may want to hold the recommendation until the end if you know the audience will be hostile to it or if you want to give complete background information before revealing your recommendation.) After you have made your proposal, explain how you arrived at it. Give just enough background to clarify but not so much as to make the presentation dull.[9]

❖ ❖ ❖ ❖   ## Lectures

Probably the most familiar type of informative speaking is the **lecture**, the formal presentation of material to facilitate learning. Lectures are an integral part of academic life, serving as the main vehicle for the presentation of information in almost all subject fields. Lectures also are used in many other settings—by guest speakers at Parent-Teacher Association, Kiwanis, fraternity, or sorority meetings; invited speakers at lunch or dinnertime seminars in corporate headquarters; or distinguished speakers at public arts, religious, or academic events.

To be effective, lectures should conform to the same characteristics we expect in other forms of informative speaking. A good lecture should be carefully adapted to the intended audience. It should be clearly organized with easy-to-follow transitions so that listeners can stay "on track." A memorable lecture is well developed, with supporting details to elaborate each major point. Like all informative speaking, lectures often tend to be heavy with explanations and consequently are considered to be dry. A variety of supporting materials (stories, statistics, analogies) enhance the explanatory details and involve the listeners more readily. Many lecturers also use humor to get and hold attention. The speaker also may involve the listeners by asking them questions, probing for information, and inviting inquiries during the presentation instead of waiting until the question-and-answer session.

Timing is an important consideration. Lecturers should be aware of the time frame. An audience usually expects a lecturer to stay within a certain framework (such as a class period) or within the boundaries of what the audience can comfortably absorb.

Question-and-Answer Sessions

Photo: Justin Warren/Daily Bruin

A question-and-answer session is an on-the-spot test of unrehearsed answers that measures the speaker's knowledge, alerts the speaker to areas in the speech that were unclear or needed more development, and gives the listeners a chance to probe for ideas.

The **question-and-answer session** that follows many speeches is a type of informative speech itself.[10] It is an on-the-spot test of unrehearsed answers that measures the speaker's knowledge, alerts the speaker to areas in the speech that were unclear or needed more development, and gives the listeners a chance to probe for ideas.

In some instances, the question-and-answer session allows receivers to point out the weakness of the speaker's arguments or present alternative views. This occurs more frequently after persuasive speeches than after informative presentations. Some communication analysts wonder whether it is acceptable for a question-and-answer session to serve as a forum for the proposal of alternative concepts. If confronted by a hostile questioner,

---

When You Answer Questions

If you've made a presentation and are fielding questions from the audience, here are some ways to build credibility:

- If you don't know the answer to a question, don't pretend to. Admit you don't know and offer to get the information to the person.

- Refer to your professional and personal experience when addressing questions. Just be careful not to sound as if you're bragging.

- Quote experts on the topic being discussed.

- Offer as many facts as possible.

- Establish a bond. *Example*: "I can certainly appreciate your concern."

- Recognize the importance of the question being asked. But be careful not to sound patronizing.

- When possible, dissociate yourself from a problem caused by a previous administration. *Example*: "That was the policy during the last administration. Our policy is . . ."

- Prepare one-liners that you'll be able to weave into the answers—key points you want the audience to remember.

Source: *Communication Briefings*, as adapted from *Power Communications*, by Valerie Wiener, New York University Press, Washington Square, New York, NY 10003.

---

speakers themselves will have to determine whether they want to deal with the issue or remind the prober that the purpose of the session is to ask questions, not to give a counter-speech or engage in debate.

12.3 Developing the Informative Speech

Every informative speaker has a challenge—to get the audience to understand and retain the information presented. When we consider that the typical listener remembers only about 10 percent of an oral presentation three days after hearing it, we recognize how great a challenge this is.[11]

Learning-theory specialists point out that the basis for retention and understanding is the establishment of relationships (associations and connections) between information and physical or mental activities. We learn through *repetition* (by hearing ideas over and over) and

Photo: Magic Management

Every informative speaker has a challenge—to get the audience to understand and retain the information presented.

Profile: Thomas W. Faranda, professional speaker and management consultant

Calling effective public speaking his "most visible and important skill," Thomas Faranda, president of Faranda and Associates, an international management training and development firm, acknowledges the value of developing and maintaining excellence as a speaker. When combined with effective listening and creative problem solving, public speaking serves as a powerful tool for expressing his ideas to corporations and having those ideas accepted. Fifteen years as a professional speaker on the lecture circuit have taught Faranda some important lessons. His advice? Do some serious work before you put yourself in a public speaking situation.

- Develop technical expertise in an area.

- Learn to interview people to gain information.

- Learn to listen so you really hear and understand what people are telling you.

- Learn to present your ideas professionally, using effective speaking techniques so your ideas are accepted.

After you are satisfied with the work you have done in these areas,

- Practice until you cannot stand to hear yourself talk anymore.

- Listen to yourself on tape. Observe your gestures and mannerisms on video.

- Constantly seek to improve your skills.

- Learn not only by watching yourself but also by observing others:

- Spend money to go watch the masters of the profession . . . they are your best teachers.

- Learn how they touch the audience with their voice, gestures, feelings, and words.

- Emulate them, but do not copy them. Be an original, not a copy. People always pay more for an original than a copy.

Finally, and perhaps most important,

- Care about what you do so much that you will not accept anything but excellence.

---

through *experiencing* (doing a task to see what it is).[12] We are more likely to remember things that have relevance to us. We remember information that will somehow make our life easier, that helps us to know something we did not know before, or that we will be rewarded for knowing. In other words, we will remember when we see a reason to do so. We also remember because an idea makes sense to us—the order in which concepts are presented makes the idea easy to understand, or the examples and other developing materials make the idea clear.

Understanding how people learn can assist you in planning your informative speech. Consider using supplementary aids to help your listeners remember your message. It is estimated that we learn 1 percent through taste, 1.5 percent through touch, 3.5 percent through smell, 11 percent through hearing, and an astonishing 83 percent through sight.[13] Once you know this, you will realize that your best chance of getting people to remember is to have them hear and see the content of your presentation. Such devices as slides, charts, illustrations, pictures, and models help to reinforce and clarify what you say.

Here are several pointers to keep in mind when developing an informative speech:[14]

1. *Order your ideas clearly.* Select a method of organization that helps your audience follow the step-by-step development of the speech.

2. *Use chronological arrangement if the speech lends itself to a progression (first, second, and third) or sequencing (years or ages).* Sample subject: explaining a science experiment that proceeds from step 1 to step 6.

3. *Use spatial arrangement if the speech has a geographical basis (for example, from east to west, from top to bottom, or from the inside out).* Sample subject: tracing the voyage of Christopher Columbus from Spain to the New World.

4. *Use topical arrangement if the subject divides into specific parts.* Sample subject: describing the life cycle, characteristics, and environmental effects of the gypsy moth.

5. *Use comparison-contrast arrangement when the topic illustrates similarities and differences.* Sample subject: comparing Nebraska's unicameral (one-house) legislature with the two-house legislative system of all other states.

6. *Use the familiar to explain the new.* To present a new idea, use an analogy based on an idea the audience already understands. For example, you could explain how an FM radio signal travels by comparing it to the way a bow and an arrow work. The arrow goes as far as the bow projects it and then drops. If something gets in its way, however, the arrow stops moving. Similarly, the FM signal goes as far as its signal power allows it to move unless something, such as a building or a mountain, gets in its way and stops it. The analogy is one of the most impressive clarifying devices available to an informative speaker.

7. *Use vivid illustrations.* Descriptions, stories, comparisons, contrasts, and verbal pictures increase your chances of gaining and holding the audience's attention. A listener who can visualize an idea is more likely to remember it.

8. *Avoid being too technical.* If you have ever tried to follow directions for using a computer program when you knew nothing about computer language, or tried to repair a piece of electrical equipment using a technician's manual, you know the difficulty of understanding materials that may be fine for an expert but are not geared to the layperson. If your subject is at all technical, evaluate the vocabulary level of audience members. Based on their backgrounds and experiences, choose terms that are not likely to confuse, or clarify the technical terms you do use. Remember, the purpose of the speech is not to impress the audience with your vast vocabulary; the purpose is to accomplish the informative objective of the speech. Select words that will help, rather than hinder, your task.

9. *Personalize your message.* Audiences are more attracted to real examples than to fictional or hypothetical examples. If at all possible, use illustrations that allow your audience to identify with

❖ ❖ ❖ ❖

the plight of a victim, to understand and share in someone's joy, or to realize how an event changed someone's life.

10. *Do not speak down to your audience, but do not overestimate audience knowledge.* There is no set guideline for evaluating an audience's level of knowledge other than to learn as much as you can about what your listeners know specifically and generally. For example, many professors who grew up during the Kennedy era often forget that most students now in college were not even born at the time of JFK's presidency. Instructors who want to draw parallels between then and now usually must provide some historical background. Alternatively, references to the Clinton presidency might serve as appropriate illustrations for this type of audience.

11. *Use as much clarification and detail as you feel are necessary to ensure listener understanding.* If anything, err on the side of overexplanation. Most audience members appreciate a speaker who makes an effort to communicate clearly.

12.4 Developing the Question-and-Answer Session

Before you enter into a question-and-answer session, set the ground rules. Ask the program chairperson about the process to be used and the time limit, and specify any restrictions you wish to place on this segment of the speech. Some speakers like to call on the participants. Others prefer to allow the chairperson to entertain the questions. Some presenters want all questions written out beforehand and want to select the questions they will answer. If you have any restrictions, let the chairperson know before you give the speech, and inform the audience of the rules.

Use Nonverbals to Aid Q&A

Here are some nonverbal signals you can use to make sure your question-and-answer session adds power to your presentation:

- Raise your hand when you ask for questions. *Reasons*: This signals that you're in charge. And it tells people how they should seek your attention.

- Break eye contact with questioners when they finish asking a question and shift your gaze to another person. *Reason*: This signals the audience that your answer will interest—and is intended for—everyone.

- Look at questioners again as you answer, and tie your answer to your presentation. *Reason*: You can check the reaction to your answer and reinforce the main points of your presentation.

- Fix your eyes on questioners as you finish your answer only if you want to continue that discussion. If you don't want another question or have said all you want to on that subject, look at someone else as you close.

- Raise your hand for the next question. Your gesture signals that you consider the question answered and invite others to speak up.

Source: *Communication Briefings,* as adapted from Kevin Daley, CEO, Communispond, 300 Park Ave,., 22nd Floor, New York, NY 10020.

> ## Tips for Dealing with Questions
>
> - Turn negative questions into positive answers.
> - Use your answers to bridge into points you want to make.
> - Don't let words be put into your mouth.
> - Answer multiple questions one at a time.
> - If you are interrupted, it's usually best to stop talking. Always stay calm.
> - Don't guess. It's OK to say you don't know, but will check on it and get back.
> - Correct false premises in questions.
> - Don't be pressured into estimates or judgments that make you uncomfortable.
> - When dealing with the press, remember reporters do not want boring stories and are looking for "sound-bites."
>
> Source: "The Fine Print," *Washington Post Magazine*, Dec. 7, 1997.

The most difficult part of many question-and-answer sessions is to encourage audience members to ask the first question. Once this hurdle is overcome, questions seem to flow naturally. To break the ice, you may want to have someone in the audience prepared to ask a question. Another technique is to ask a question yourself. This can be accomplished by stating, "I've often been asked my views concerning . . . ," and then proceed to indicate your views.

Here are some additional suggestions for managing the question-and-answer session:

1. *Before you answer a question, restate it so that everyone knows what it is*. If the question is complicated, simplify it in the restatement.

2. *Do not speak only to the questioner; speak to the whole audience.*

3. *Be patient*. If you have to repeat material you have already covered, do so briefly.

4. *If a question goes on and on, prompt the asker to summarize the question.*

5. *Keep your answers short*. Restate the question, give your response, clarify any vocabulary if necessary, give an example if appropriate, and then stop. Following the response, some speakers ask the questioner whether the answer was satisfactory.

6. *Back up your responses with examples, statistics, and quotations.*

7. *If the question is overly complicated or of interest only to the asker, suggest a discussion with the questioner after the speech or via correspondence.*

8. *If the question is irrelevant, indicate that it is interesting or thought provoking but does not seem appropriate to the presentation*. Do not get sidetracked or pulled into a private debate with the questioner.

9. *If you do not know an answer, say so*. You can offer to find out the answer and report back accordingly.

10. *Limit the discussion to one question per person, and avoid getting caught in a dialogue with one person*. Others who have questions will become frustrated, and those who do not will get bored.

11. *Be willing to be corrected or at least to recognize another person's viewpoint*. Thank the questioner for the clarification or acknowledge that more than one point of view is possible ("That's an interesting idea" or "The idea can be viewed that way"). You may win the battle of words by attacking or insulting the questioner, but you will lose the respect of the listeners in the process. Indeed, it is futile to get involved in a battle of words with a heckler or a person with a preconceived attitude or bias.

12. *Know when to end the session*. Do not wait until interest has waned or people begin leaving. You can lose the positive effect of a speech by overextending the question-and-answer session.

12.5 The Informative Process in Action

It is helpful to study the process of preparing an informative speech. Figure 12.1 shows the steps a successful speaker took in developing a speech.

Figure 12.1   Outline for a Sample Informative Speech

I. Introduction

Attention material to arouse the listeners' interest

    A. Attention material: My friend John is dying of AIDS. He's not like Magic Johnson, who has gotten all sorts of national attention since he discovered that he, too, is suffering from the disease.

Orienting material to relate the topic to the listeners and get them involved

    B. Orienting material: AIDS has become everyone's disease.

Central idea of the speech
Partitioning step to reiterate the thesis and list the main points to be covered in the body

II. Central Idea

    A. AIDS is a major health problem.

    B. In examining this health problem, let's consider:
      1. What AIDS is.
      2. Why AIDS has become such a critical problem.
      3. What is being done to overcome this health crisis.

III. Body

First main point

Discussion of AIDS as a complex disease through explanations and medical information

    A. AIDS is a complex disease.
      1. AIDS is acquired immunodeficiency syndrome.
      2. It is caused by a virus that destroys the body's ability to fight illness.

      3. You can contract AIDS through unprotected sex with an infected partner or from sharing drug needles or syringes with an infected person.

(As medical researchers seem to progress slowly in finding the key to treating this complex disease, AIDS is an increasing health problem.)   *Transition*

B. AIDS has become a major problem in the world.   *Second main point*
    1. Once viewed primarily as a disease among homosexuals, AIDS has spread to the heterosexual population as well.   *Discussion of how AIDS has become a major world problem, with statistics and explanations*
    2. More than 118,000 Americans have died of AIDS. Victims are men, women, rich, poor, white, black, Hispanic, Asian, and Native American.
    3. College students are considered a major at-risk population by the Centers for Disease Control.
    4. The problem is not limited to the United States. AIDS has become a problem of worldwide proportions. Some call it this century's bubonic plague.

(This major world health problem continues to mystify medical researchers, who are striving to find ways to conquer the problem.)   *Transition*

C. What is being done to solve this problem?   *Third main point*
    1. Researchers believe that it may take years before a vaccine can be developed to treat AIDS.   *Discussion of what is being done to solve the problem of AIDS*
    2. Scientists today are reevaluating their theory as to the cause of AIDS, suggesting that one or more co-factors may be working with HIV (human immunodeficiency virus) to trigger AIDS.

IV. Conclusion

A. Summary   *Summary of major points*
    1. It is clear that AIDS is a very complex disease.
    2. AIDS has become a major world health problem.
    3. Though researchers are attempting to do something about AIDS, a vaccine and a true understanding of the disease are years away.

B. Clincher   *Clincher*
    1. There may be no hope for my friend John.   *Tie back to attention material*
    2. However, understanding the nature of this health problem may be helpful to the rest of us.

As you develop your own informative speeches, remember that this form of communication occupies a prominent place in today's information age. Because listeners must turn to information sources in increasing numbers, informative speakers must present information in a clear, meaningful, interesting way so that the message is understood and the audience wants to listen.

❖ ❖ ❖ ❖   ## 12.6 Listening to Information

When confronted with information, the public communication recipient must listen for *comprehension*—to understand the information and to recall that information at a later time. As listeners, we are challenged with listening comprehension throughout our lives. The educational process is based on listening to and recalling information from lectures and oral reports. On the job, we listen to briefings, instructions, and professional/technical papers. Comprehensive listening is a central part of what we do as communicators.

To be effective, the comprehensive listener needs a great deal of motivation and self-discipline. A significant barrier to listening with comprehension is the easy dodge, "Oh, this isn't interesting" or "This isn't relevant," as the excuse to tune out on the speaker. A speaker indeed might not be very interesting in his or her presentation format or style, or the material may not be immediately useful, but the information may well be important to you at a later time. You need to determine if and why the material is relevant. If the answer is positive, then you need to dedicate yourself to comprehension. A review of the materials discussed in the Improving Listening section of Chapter 2 should help you.

Have you ever found yourself daydreaming in class? Have you sat through an entire sermon and had no idea of what was said? Do you slump down in your seat and stare off into space when a briefing is taking place? Concentration is one of the keys to comprehension. Since the normal person's attention span is short, focusing your attention on the speaker, by looking at the person and observing facial expressions, gestures, and keying into the ideas being expressed, are important.

Another technique is to realize that not all listening can or should be done on the same level. A complicated technical presentation would require more attention energy than a familiar speech restating familiar material.

Do you find your mind searching to solve a problem outside the speech topic or remembering something that you want to do after the presentation? You can't deal with two issues at once: one will hold center stage. If the material you are listening to should be getting all the attention, you can enhance your concentration by the technique of **bracketing**. As you take notes on the speaker's ideas, write down the ideas competing for your attention and put brackets around them. You have recorded them; you will remember that they are important, and you can come back and deal with them later. If you aren't taking notes, jot down the idea some place and come back to it at an appropriate time. If other needs present themselves, do the same thing. That allows you to concentrate on the speaker's message now and the other needs later.

Keying in on the speaker's main points is another helpful strategy for listening with comprehension. As you focus your attention on the presentation, pick out the main points that the speaker is presenting and keep those in your short-term memory. Listeners find that jotting down the points or engaging in mental summaries can be useful. Listen for the **speaker's sign posts**—the transitions, vocal emphases, and forecasts of main points. These sign posts are structural cues that can assist your focus on the points.

While notetaking technically is not listening (you become a writer when you take notes), and while the research does not correlate notetaking with effective listening, our educational system perpetuates notetaking as a major listening strategy. When taking notes, most listeners develop their own techniques. Just because you have been using a particular method does not mean it is best for you.

You might want to use the **Cornell System of Notetaking** (see Figure 2.3). Divide your page in half. On one side, jot down the speaker's main points as they are presented. On the other side, jot down the speaker's supporting ideas as they develop the main points. This format will give you, essentially, a flow chart of the information as it unfolds.

Some listeners who are more visually oriented find it helpful to create mind maps as they take notes. Put the main points and supporting ideas into circles and connect them to each other as the speaker discusses the information. The resulting visual display can trigger recall by assisting you in visualizing the material. (For a discussion of mind maps, see Section 10.2 of Chapter 10.)

To store the information in your long-term memory, you probably have developed some memory techniques that help you in recalling information. Some people rely on associations such as **mnemonic devices**, combining the first letter of a series of words in order to allow you to remember the idea. For example, using the word *HOMES* to remember the names of the Great Lakes—*H*uron, *O*ntario, *M*ichigan, *E*rie, *S*uperior. Another association strategy is to link the information together. For example, visualize the map of the east coast of the United States, with all the state names written on the map in order to remember the original 13 colonies.

If you are confronted with a vast amount of information, **chunking** is helpful. Chunking results when you break down the information in subunits and work with the smaller units one at a time. You group things according to their common description and then put the names of each division together. Rather than trying to just remember the names of the new alignment of the professional baseball leagues that the representative of the baseball commissioner's office is speaking about, chunk them according to the two leagues, and then arrange the names under each the division designations. That gives you chunks of information to remember, rather than an extensive single list. The mind seems to grasp small chunks rather than massive lists.

A major memory strategy is rehearsal. To ensure that the information gets stored in the long-term memory so that it can be recalled, you have to repeat it and rehearse it over and over until it can be brought back into consciousness. In order to remember information, such as the lecture you just heard in class, it is best to review your notes, or recount your mental thoughts, as quickly after the listening experience as possible. That reinforces what you have heard and places it into your long-term memory.

It is possible to improve your ability to listen for comprehension. This list identifies several characteristics of listeners who effectively comprehend speakers' messages.

1. *The listener is honest with the speaker when he or she is not able to attend fully.*

2. *The listener maintains a diet of healthy food, which stimulates an active, energetic mind.*

3. *The listener takes measures to reduce stress, which diverts one's energy and attention.*

4. *The listener monitors his or her own listening behavior.*

5. *The listener works to control external distractions.*

6. *The listener works to control his or her own internal distractions through self-discipline and bracketing other concerns to go back to them at a later time.*

7. *The listener schedules a time each day to deal with concerns, reflections, and even daydreams.*

8. *The listener is energized by a desire to learn.*

9. *The listener does not fake attention but, rather, enters into the communication with honest concentration.*

10. *The listener creates penetrating, meaningful questions to ask the speaker.*

11. *The listener listens in order to share the speaker's message with another person.*

12. *The listener listens as if the speaker were speaking to him or her individually.*

13. *The listener practices the appropriate listening skills in each communication situation as an active participant.*[15]

Summary

In this chapter on informative speaking, the key ideas presented were:

♦ *Informative speaking imparts new information, secures understanding, or reinforces accumulated information.*

♦ *Informative presentations depend on audience analysis.*

♦ *Informative speeches may be about objects, processes, events, and concepts.*

♦ *Types of informative speeches are informative briefings, technical reports, lectures, and question-and-answer sessions.*

♦ *The challenge for an informative speaker is to get the audience to understand and retain the information presented.*

♦ *To develop an informative speech, order ideas clearly, use the familiar to explain the new, use vivid illustrations, avoid being too technical, personalize the message, and do not speak down to the audience.*

♦ *To present a successful question-and-answer session, the speaker should establish the ground rules for the session and be able to effectively answer the questions asked.*

♦ *When confronted with information, the public communication recipient must listen for comprehension—listening to understand the information and to recall that information at a later time.*

Key Terms

informative speaking
speeches about processes
speeches about concepts
technical reports

speeches about objects
speeches about events
informative briefings
lecture

question-and-answer session
speaker's sign posts
mnemonic devices

racketing
Cornell System of Notetaking
chunking

Learn by Doing

1. As a homework assignment, list two topics that you are interested in speaking about for an informative presentation on objects, processes, events, or concepts. In class, your instructor will match you with a partner. With the assistance of your partner, select a topic for a speech based on audience analysis (your class), setting (your classroom), and purpose (an informative speech of three to five minutes). After you and your partner have selected your topics, meet with another group. Present a short informative speech indicating what topic you have selected and why this topic suits you, the audience, the setting, and the purpose. The speech should use a structure that includes an introduction, statement of central idea, body, and conclusion.

2. Bring to class an object or piece of machinery (e.g., a camera, food processor, or microscope) that members of your class may not know how to operate or that you have a different way of operating. Be prepared to teach someone else how to use the equipment. In class you will be placed in a group with four of your classmates. Decide the order in which you will present the material. Then, the first speaker should give a two- to four-minute presentation on how the object works. Then the second speaker should demonstrate how the object operates, then the third speaker, and so forth. Your success as a speaker is measured by whether the speaker following you can operate the object.

3. You are going to give a "what-if" speech. On each of three 3- by 5-inch notecards, indicate something that could go wrong immediately before, during, or after a speech (e.g., you drop your speech outline in a puddle of water just outside your classroom building; the bulb goes out in the projector halfway through your slide presentation; an audience member challenges your statistics during the question-and-answer period). The instructor collects the cards, shuffles them, and hands them out one by one. When you get your card, give a restatement of the possible occurrence and a contingency plan for dealing with the situation.[16] (This assignment may take place when a short amount of time remains at the end of any class period.)

4. All students present one-minute speeches in which they describe a pet peeve, something that bothers them in daily life. They should tell what the peeve is, why it is a peeve, and what they would like to see done about it, if anything.

5. Investigate some phase of a career you are interested in and present an informative speech on it. The presentation must include the use of a supplementary aid. Sample speech topics: a future audiologist explains the differences among several brands of

hearing aids; an accounting major illustrates how a balance sheet is prepared; an aspiring musician demonstrates how music is scored.

Endnotes

1. Connie Koenenn, "The Future Is Now," *Washington Post*, February 3, 1989, p. B5.
2. Ibid.
3. Michael F. Warlum, "Improving Oral Marketing Presentations in the Technology-Based Company," *IEEE Transactions on Professional Communication*, 31 (June 1988), p. 84.
4. Richard Hoehn, *The Art and Practice of Public Speaking* (New York: McGraw-Hill, 1988).
5. These categories are based on those reported in James H. Byrns, *Speak for Yourself: An Introduction to Public Speaking* (New York: Random House, 1981), chapters 14–17.
6. H. Lloyd Goodall and Christopher L. Waagen, *The Persuasive Presentation* (New York: Harper & Row, 1986), p. 105.
7. John T. Molloy, "Making Your Point, Not Burying It," *Self*, April 1981, p. 92.
8. Ibid.
9. These suggestions for structuring a technical report are based on Richard Weigand, as reported in *Communication Briefings* (January 1986).
10. This discussion is adapted from Maureen Haningan, "Master the Game of Q&A," *Working Woman*, December 1984, pp. 34–35.
11. Hoehn.
12. G. H. Jamieson, *Communication and Persuasion* (London: Croom Helm, 1985), pp. 5–16.
13. Hoehn.
14. Ibid.
15. Andrew D. Wolvin and Carolyn Gwynn Coakley, *Listening* (Madison, WI.: Brown and Benchmark, 1996), p. 210.
16. This activity is based on John Alfred Jones, "Preparing Contingency Plans for Public Speaking Situations," *Communication Education*, 30 (1981), pp. 423–424.

The Persuasive Speech

Chapter Outline

Learning Outcomes

After reading this chapter, you should be able to:

- *Explain how people are influenced by persuasive messages.*

- *Explain how people are influenced by coercive messages.*

- *Describe how speaker credibility, logical arguments, and psychological appeals can affect listeners.*

- *Analyze a persuasive speech to ascertain its potential effectiveness based on logical arguments and psychological appeals.*

- *Prepare a persuasive speech using credibility, logical arguments, and psychological appeals.*

- *Be aware that while listening to a persuasive speech one must monitor the oral, physical, and verbal techniques in order to make a wise decision in buying into the speaker's ideas.*

Every day we are bombarded with messages intended to convince us to take some action, reinforce some commitment, accept some belief, or change some point of view. And almost every day we also send such messages as speakers. The process of influencing the decisions other people make is complex and involves many communication variables. **Persuasion** is "the process by means of which one party purposefully secures a change of behavior, mental and/or physical, on the part of another party by employing appeals to both feelings and intellect."[1] It is an important process. Through persuasion, we affect others and they affect us.

A persuasive speech may have as its end goal either conviction or actuation. In a **speech of conviction**, the speaker is attempting to convince the listener to believe as the speaker does. Topics that fall into this category could include: "There is no real danger of nuclear fallout from atomic plants," or "XYZ Corporation has developed a clear set of equal opportunity guidelines."

A **speech of actuation** should move the members of the audience to take the desired action that the speaker has proposed: buy the product, sign the petition, go on strike, or adopt the plan presented. Topics for this type of speech could include: "Each person should sign a donor card, thus making arrangements to give their usable body parts for transplantation after their death," or "Sign this petition to indicate your displeasure with the proposed tuition increase for the next academic year."

Persuasion, which allows listeners to choose for themselves whether to change what they think or how they behave, should not be confused with coercion. **Coercion** is influence that leaves the listener no desirable alternative but to adopt the change of mental or physical behavior the speaker proposes. Despite the negative aspects of coercion, speakers sometimes use it when other persuasive methods fail, fully aware that backlash may occur.

For example, in the early 1970s, in an effort to bolster and stabilize a sagging economy, President Richard Nixon gave a speech recommending that industries should freeze wages and prices on most consumer products and that corporations should voluntarily adopt wage-price guidelines appropriate to their particular products. When this persuasive approach did not work, Nixon made a second speech in which he set up a wage-price control board to force compliance with the guidelines. The public reaction to this second speech was strong and negative: union workers protested, big business objected, and the stock market faltered. Indeed, the reaction was so strong that some economists believe that the inflation and recession of the mid-1970s were a direct result of a negative backlash from these coercive economic policies.

13.1 Influencing Through Persuasion

The purpose of the persuasive process is to influence. A field representative from a data-processing company who stresses her product's lower cost and ease of operation is using persuasion to make a sale. A shift supervisor who tells a group of workers, "You have a choice—work nights or quit," is using coercion. This strategy may be effective in bringing about change, but it usually leads to resentment, discouragement, and lack of respect and trust on the part of the person who has been coerced. For this reason, parents, teachers, salespeople, managers, and others in a position of influence usually find

❖ ❖ ❖ ❖   that they receive more cooperation and more positive responses when they use persuasive techniques rather than coercive tactics.

Profile: Senator George McGovern, President, Middle East Policy Council and Former Candidate for President of the United States

"Without my abilities as a public speaker, I would not have made it to Congress, the Senate, or have received the nomination for President of the United States."

There are not many Americans capable of making such a statement, which is why when Senator George McGovern talks about the impact of public speaking on his career, it is apparent that the information is coming from an expert.

Senator McGovern's career in the public spotlight began long before he ran for a congressional seat in 1956. He began as a champion debater on his high school debate team and went on to pursue his passion for oratory by competing on his college debate team, a team which won a national debate tournament. McGovern proved that he could shine on his own by winning the National Collegiate Oratory Contest.

These victories foreshadowed a stunning political career that has included two terms in the U.S. House of Representatives, three terms in the Senate, and the democratic nomination, in 1972, for President of the United States. Throughout his career, the senator has

never doubted the need for a politician to be a competent public speaker. He says, "Communication is an important part of success in politics. The capacity to persuade, inspire, and educate through public speech is crucial to a career in public life."

As president of the Middle East Policy Council, Senator McGovern recognized how his public speaking abilities have changed over the years. Decades of experience have given him the ability to handle extemporaneous questions on live television and radio and the capacity to speak to a wide variety of audiences. In fact, the senator acknowledges that his competency as a speaker continues to grow as he becomes ever more comfortable and confident in his ability.

For Senator George McGovern, though, the capacity to be an effective public speaker lies with more than just basic skills and knowledge of the subject. He adds that it is important to "concentrate on being a good person and believe in what you are saying." It is those qualities that, in the end, will make you worth listening to.

Even influence that is not coercive can sometimes be dangerous, because powerful speakers can make people do what they may not want to do or endorse an idea they may not fully support. One of the best defenses against persuasive manipulation is for listeners to recognize that persuasion has the potential to be unethical or to distort the truth. Persuasive communication strategies are essentially amoral—neither good nor bad. It is only how particular speakers use these strategies, and to what ends, that gives communication a dimension of morality. By knowing this and by being equipped to recognize manipulative and coercive methods, you may be able to protect yourself as a listener from being "taken." Likewise, persuasive speakers have a responsibility not to manipulate their listeners' motivations for unethical ends.

Coercive speakers often use psychological appeals aimed at inspiring fear, hatred, social pressure, and shock to cause people to perform acts they might never have done if they had objectively evaluated the potential consequences of their actions. A particularly horrifying example of manipulation was Adolf Hitler's emotional appeal to the German nation to build a "master race." Many people responded to this appeal, thereby knowingly or unknowingly participating in the destruction of other human beings, only later to regret their actions deeply.

Persuasion is often accomplished through repetition, since one message seldom results in any real change on the part of receivers. As a result, individuals and organizations typically spend massive amounts of money waging persuasive campaigns for all sorts of consumer products, social causes, international efforts, and government projects. This approach to persuasion relies on systematic, repeated exposure to the message with the objective of enhancing retention by listeners.

13.2 The Process of Persuasion

The persuasive speaker makes a claim and backs it up with motivating reasons and emotional appeals that encourage the listener to accept it. To do this, you must plan your speech by analyzing the audience and presenting arguments that will find favor with your particular listeners. The **theory of field-related standards** suggests that not all people reach conclusions in the same way and thus may react differently to the same evidence or appeals. Therefore, in establishing your arguments, you may want to include as many different types of appeals as you can to cover the various thought processes of the audience members. For example, to establish arguments for why your listeners should vote for a particular candidate, you might describe the candidate's positions on several issues rather than just one. Specific types of psychological appeals are described at length later in this chapter.

Identifying **group standards**, the habits of thinking or the norms of a particular group also may help you develop your arguments. For example, if you are speaking to a group of labor union members, you can assume that on labor-related issues they will have views that favor the union rather than management. If you are going to propose a change in the present style of plant operation, show how it will be good for the union and its membership.

Try to determine the **individual standards** held by certain people within the group who have influence over other members. If you can persuade these influential members to go along with the proposal, will the entire group then go along? Who are the leaders? Who holds the most influence? If possible, try to key your appeals to that person or group of people. For example, if labor leaders support a proposal, the union membership probably will also. If the president of a club agrees, so may the rest of the club. If the student body leader, or the captain of the football team, or the head of the interfraternity council accepts an idea, the members of that person's group are likely to accept the idea too.

To be persuasive, you must develop your materials so that listeners feel the solution, plan of action, or cure that you are presenting is reasonable. Two methods of reasoning that you might consider using are critical and comparative-advantage reasoning. In applying **critical reasoning**, you establish criteria and then match solutions with the criteria. Let's say for example, that you are developing a plan of action for solving a club's financial problems. You set the following criteria: members' dues must not be raised, and any fund-raising activity must generate money quickly without extensive plan-

> When making a presentation at a . . . meeting, start with the recommenda-
> tions or conclusions unless there's a compelling reason not to. Then explain
> how you got to the conclusions or recommendations. Too much
> backgrounding that leads to a climax can be dull.
>
> Source: *Communication Briefings,* as adapted from Richard Wiegand, writing in
> *Business Horizons,* School of Business, Indiana University, Bloomington, IN
> 474405.

ning. To match these criteria, you propose that the club stage a lottery and
sell raffle tickets.

In applying **comparative-advantage reasoning**, you begin by stating the
possible solutions, including the status quo (the present mode of operation).
You then demonstrate how the proposal you are presenting is the most workable (how it can solve the problem), the most desirable (why it does not cause
any greater problems), and the most practical (how it can be put into operation). You also show that your proposal has fewer disadvantages than any
other.

To use comparative-advantage reasoning to solve the fund-raising problem, you would explain why a lottery is a workable plan by indicating that
other organizations have used it, and by presenting statistics on the amounts
of money they have raised. You then would indicate that the lottery is desirable because it will not cost club members a great deal of money, it is not illegal, it will probably not lose money, and it does not place a heavy responsibility on any one club member. Next, you would show that the proposal is practical because a local printer can have the tickets ready by the next week and the
finance committee of the club has already worked out a plan for distributing
the tickets and handling the money. Finally, you would explain why this solution is better than other options: raising dues, dissolving the organization,
continuing the status quo, or having a bake sale.

13.3 Components of the Persuasive Message

In Western cultures there is a long tradition of using what is termed a logical approach to develop the persuasive message. It is based on the work of
the Greek philosopher and rhetorician Aristotle, who first prescribed the development of getting an audience to accept the persuasive recommendation
of a speaker as being a three-part package.[2] In today's terms (and Aristotle's
terminology), these components are identified as speaker credibility (**ethos**),
logical arguments (**logos**), and psychological appeals (**pathos**). Though Aristotle wrote more than two thousand years ago, his theories still characterize
the development of an effective persuasive message in the Western world.

As was discussed in Chapter 1, not all cultures use the same means to
reach conclusions. Research shows that culture affects the way people use,
present, and regard public speaking. The Confucian concept of self strongly
affects many Asians. Instead of the Western logical system of stating what is
wrong and then proving what should be done, these cultures often delay arguments, include narration, and use statements that to Western ears seem
unconnected. Appeals to history and tradition can make the Western listener

confused because the information does not appear to have direct relationship to demonstrating why the recommendations are correct.

Arabic arguments often include reference to the Koran and include parables as well as proverbs, which, in the Western logic system, are meaningless proofs. The Navajo's tradition of assuming that all people are rational beings and should know everything in order to make decisions means that *all* the information available for decision making is presented in the speech. In contrast, the American mainstream a speaker exposes only that information which can be used to sway the listener to reach the solution proposed by the speaker. While, African American persuasion includes storytelling and a high degree of emotional language to persuade; again, this is not the traditional Euro-American mode.

Be aware of cultural differences and be ready to adjust your listening expectations if you are in an audience in which the speaker is from a different culture. As a speaker, be aware that the recommendations that are being made regarding how to develop a persuasive speech may not be applicable if you are speaking before an audience composed of persons who do not use or are unfamiliar with the Western logical tradition.

Accepting that the majority of this book's readers are from Western cultures, or are interested in learning to hone their logical skills, let's examine the three elements that Aristotle stressed were so important for persuasion. Consider how important each of them is in affecting your ability to persuade others or the ability of others to persuade you. Also consider how these three elements must interrelate for a persuasive message to be as effective as possible. Note, however, that listeners responding to a persuasive message do not necessarily separate (and may not be able to separate) the logical arguments from the psychological appeals. Research has illustrated that listeners rarely distinguish the rational from the emotional.[3] Indeed, because people may respond on an emotional level to a well-reasoned argument, each person will have different interpretations of and reactions to the persuasive techniques speakers use.

Speaker Credibility

The reputation, prestige, and authority of a speaker as perceived by the listeners all contribute to **speaker credibility**. In most persuasive speaking situations, listeners need to accept the speaker before they will accept the message. Thus, a speaker's credibility is related to the impact of the message and may in fact be the most potent of all means of persuasion. If you as a listener dislike, mistrust, or question the speaker's honesty, you will have a difficult time accepting what the speaker tells you.

A speaker's prior reputation with an audience can help or hinder the persuasive task. For example, if Dr. David Ho, the AIDS researcher selected by *Time* magazine as their 1996 Man of the Year, and generally considered the most versed researcher on immune deficiencies, addressed the American Medical Association about the need for a national program to develop an AIDS vaccine, he would have had initial credibility, and his ideas would probably have been accepted. But a speaker who has no reputation as an expert in AIDS, or who has been accused of research fraud, would have had a much more difficult persuasive task.

If you are unknown in a public speaking setting, you can build your credibility by advance publicity or by adjusting the introduction to your speech. Try to determine what your listeners know about you before preparing your speech. You must be aware of whether your credibility is nonexistent, positive, or negative. In a beginning speech class, you may find you have little or no credibility early in the semester. One of the ways to compensate for this is to describe the research you have done to develop the speech or the personal connection you have to the material. Presenting your material confidently may also lead the audience to perceive you positively. The more you speak and the less you read, the more you use eye contact and the stronger the documentation that develops your ideas, the more confidence your listeners will have in you.

If you feel your credibility is positive, enhance that advantage by developing a well-documented and logical presentation. If your credibility is poor, compensate for it. Try to alter your listeners' perceptions by emphasizing qualities about yourself they may respond to positively. A former convict who was attending college as part of an educational release program started his presentation about the need for altering prison procedures by saying:

> *I am a paroled convict. Knowing this, some of you may immediately say to yourself, "Why should I listen to anything that an ex-jailbird has to say?" Well, it is because I was in prison, and because I know what prison can do to a person, and because I know what negative influences jail can have on a person, that I want to speak to you tonight.*[4]

If you know that your listeners have a negative perception of you, make a special effort to develop a well-documented speech, one that admits areas of disagreement and asks the audience to give you a fair chance to be heard. A Democratic candidate, speaking before a predominantly Republican audience, might state:

> *I realize that I am a Democrat and you are Republicans. I also realize that we are both after the same thing—a city in which we can live without fear for our lives, a city in which the services such as trash and snow removal are efficient, and a city in which taxes are held in check. You, the Republicans, and I, the Democrat, do have common goals. I'd appreciate your considering how I propose to help all of us achieve our joint objectives.*

Factors of Credibility

Several factors contribute to a speaker's credibility: occupation, education, clothes, personal looks, personality, respect for others, sensitivity to trends, knowledge of the problem being discussed, ability to verbalize, vitality, trustworthiness, and general expertise.[5] Some of the factors in this list, such as clothing and personal appearance, may surprise you, but dress, voice, and manners truly do affect an audience's attitude toward a speaker. Because persuasion is cumulative—because many factors combine to urge listeners to reach conclusions—each factor in the process is important.

Politicians recognize that physical appearance, clothing, and hair style contribute to their public image, and they pay close attention to these factors. The Kennedy-Nixon television debate during the 1960 presidential campaign illustrated how extensively such physical factors can influence speaker credibility. The rhetorical analysis following the debate centered on Nixon's waxen, perspiring appearance and Kennedy's vigorous, healthy, and suntanned look. Since then, political critics have claimed that proper make-up and attire could have improved Nixon's image significantly. This important historical event has guided political consultants ever since in carefully tailoring a candidate's image to appeal to voters, especially if the candidate will appear on television, a major means of political persuasion.[6]

Perceived trustworthiness also affects credibility. Listeners appear to be more willing to consider new ideas when they perceive the speaker to be a trustworthy source.

Establishing Credibility

An unknown speaker has little initial credibility. If you are a beginning speaker, it is wise to consider some techniques for gaining personal acceptance from the audience. Above all, you should demonstrate that you are trustworthy, competent, and dynamic. These three factors operate as dimensions of a speaker's credibility during a speech.

Trustworthiness follows from a person's integrity. You want to convince your audience that you are honest, reliable, and sincere. For example, if you are attempting to persuade your listeners to sign pledge cards to donate their eyes to an eye bank upon their deaths, show them a card that certifies you yourself as a potential donor. If your personal experiences show that you follow your own recommendations, your audience is more likely to accept your advice as reliable. As a listener, you should be aware that you tend to perceive speakers as persuasive if you feel they are trustworthy.

Competence, another component of credibility, refers to the wisdom, authority, and knowledge a speaker demonstrates. Prepare yourself to be an expert on your topic so that listeners will have confidence in what you are saying. You can demonstrate competence by including up-to-date research findings, documenting sources of information, and connecting yourself to the topic.

You can also strengthen your position by quoting recognized experts in the field. In this way, listeners will draw the conclusion that if experts agree with your stand, then your stand must have merit. Quotations from experts let your audience know that you have taken the time to probe the attitudes and findings of others in the field before reaching conclusions.

For this reason, when you use supporting material, be certain to document your sources. Tell the audience the source and date of your material as well as the identities of the people responsible for creating or developing the information. If the sources are unfamiliar to your listeners, establish their credentials. For example, if you are attempting to persuade your listeners that there are advantages to living in our age of change and uncertainty, you can quote an expert:

> *Dr. Rollo May, a practicing psychotherapist and professor at Harvard, supports my contentions in his book* Love and Will *when he writes, "One of the values of living in a transitional age—an age of therapy—is that it forces upon us the opportunity, even as we try to resolve our individual problems, to uncover new meaning in perennial man and to see more deeply into those qualities which constitute the human being."*[7]

If possible, associate yourself with the topic. For example, if you are proposing a plan of action concerning safety regulations at construction sites, refer to your experience on a construction crew. Your listeners will more readily accept your point that the construction industry needs more stringent safety regulations because of your personal experience.

Physical factors can influence credibility.

Although you want to reinforce your qualifications while developing your presentation, your audience may lose interest if you begin with a lengthy review of your research, experiences, or general qualifications. The person who introduces you should highlight your expertise. Since you will be providing the information for the speaker, make sure that you provide the kind of information that will help develop your credibility. Then, let your credibility emerge directly throughout your speech with such phrases as: "It has been my experience that . . ."; "I have observed that . . ."; "My research indicates that. . . ." Remember that specifics documented by time, place, and description are usually perceived to be more valid than personal opinion, especially if the presenter is inexperienced in the field.

As you listen to persuasive speeches, evaluate what the speaker is saying. Does he or she appear to be competent? Does the presentation include up-to-date research findings and documented sources of information? If it is appropriate, does the speaker connect himself or herself to the topic?

Another characteristic of credibility is **dynamism**, the projection of a vigorous, concerned, powerful image. President Ronald Reagan, sometimes called the Great Communicator, developed his reputation as a speaker not necessarily from what he said but from how he said it—his oral dynamics. Many years as an actor had taught him how to present words and ideas in a forceful and convincing manner. Despite the media's intense focus on his character, President Clinton's ability to speak directly to the audience, be animated, and appear relaxed and comfortable enabled him to capture and sway audiences.

As a listener, be aware that some audience members are fooled by speakers who are dynamic but actually say very little of substance. What is said should be more important than how it is said. Understand that an audience can be carried away by a well-presented speaker.

By demonstrating trustworthiness, competence, and dynamism throughout your speech, you can help listeners accept you as a person of credibility and move them toward accepting your message. Calculate carefully—on the basis of your audience analysis—what will most enhance your trustworthiness, prestige, and authoritativeness, and use these factors to build your message. As a listener, try to be a discerning and critical listener of persuasive messages.

Logical Arguments

In Western cultures, critical thinking is the foundation on which most persuasive messages are built. Thus, if you want to present a well-thought-out speech, you must determine what your audience believes about your central idea and build your arguments on that information. Remember that although listeners may be swayed by a highly credible, dynamic speaker, over the long run they may forget the impact of the presentation style and remember only the basic premises. Consequently, you must make certain that your arguments are well substantiated.

There is some evidence in communication research to suggest that listeners cannot distinguish sound arguments and evidence.[8] However, especially when confronted with information that is new or that they are skeptical about, most listeners probably look for logical connections in the messages they receive.[9] Communication analysts have suggested that a well-reasoned message can have a decided impact on the speaker's credibility. As one source noted, "When listeners want reasons spelled out, they mercilessly put down as stupid or too sloppy to be trusted communicators who do not reason or who do it badly. It is easy to show that general absence of clarity, consistency, completeness, and consecutiveness in discourse is, in the world's eye, the mark of the fool."[10]

Remember that all factors in the persuasive speaking situation ought to be centered on the audience and that an audience is influenced by clarity of ideas, vividness of language, examples, and specifics that illuminate the reasons for the chosen solution. Consequently, organize and package your materials in such a way that they lead to the conclusion that only one solution is possible—the solution you are proposing. As a listener, you should be concerned about whether a persuasive speaker's contentions lead to the proposed solution. As a critical listener, evaluate whether the conclusion proposed is logical and in your best interest.

Patterns of Logical Argument

Your audience analysis should help you determine whether to use the inductive or deductive pattern of argument development. As a listener, evaluate the impact of a speaker's persuasive message by being aware of how inductive and deductive arguments work and whether the development of the speech is logical and sequential. Realize that you don't have to commit to changing your beliefs or buying an idea that doesn't make sense to you and is not in your best interests.

Inductive Argument. An **inductive argument** is based on probability—what conclusion is most likely to be expected or believed from the available evidence. Thus, the more specific instances you can draw on as evidence in an inductive argument, the more probable and believable your conclusion will seem to the audience. Inductive arguments can take one of two patterns: the generalization conclusion or the hypothesis conclusion.

In the **generalization conclusion**, the speaker examines a number of specific instances and attempts to predict some future occurrence or explain a whole category of instances. Underlying this is the assumption that what holds true for specific instances will hold true for all instances in a given category. For example, speaking in Atlanta to the National Conference on Corporate Community Involvement, the vice-president of the American Association of Retired Persons described the "graying" of America. He developed an inductive argument by a series of claims:

> Because of better medical care, nutrition and activity, more people are gliding into their 60s and beyond in good physical shape. . . .Mental ability does not diminish merely because of age, according to researchers. In fact, it may improve. . . .The economic health of today's older generation has improved to the point where advertisers are already targeting the "Maturity Market." [Using evidence to support each of the claims, he drew an inductive conclusion:] The upshot of all this change in better physical, psychological and economic well-being is that we are looking at a new breed of older person vastly different from former negative stereotypes.[11]

In the **hypothesis conclusion**, the speaker uses a hypothesis to explain all the available evidence. For such an argument to have substance, however, the hypothesis must provide the best explanation for that evidence. Reviewing a number of cases in which terrorists had been tried and convicted throughout the world, the U.S. Department of State Ambassador-at-Large for Counterterrorism offered the hypothesis that "the rule of law is working against terrorists and fewer terrorists are being released without trial." His aim was to convince his audience that "we, the people of the world's democracies, will ultimately prevail over those who would through terror take from us the fruits of two centuries of political progress."[12]

Deductive Argument. The **deductive argument** is based on logical necessity. In other words, if one accepts the premise of the deductive argument—the proposition that is the basis of the argument—then one must also accept its conclusion. One type of deductive argument is the **categorical syllogism**, an argument that contains two premises and a conclusion. For instance, you might argue:

- *All "A" students study hard.* (premise)

- *You are an "A" student.* (premise)

- *Therefore, you study hard.* (conclusion)

If your listeners accept the premises of this argument, then they must accept the conclusion because it is the only one that can be drawn.

In developing an argument using the categorical syllogism, make sure you present a clear set of premises and that these lead to the conclusion. For example, in a speech with the purpose of persuading the audience that specific symptoms lead doctors to diagnose chronic fatigue syndrome, a speaker might state:

- *A proven sign of chronic fatigue syndrome is an off-balance immune system, with a positive diagnosis of Epstein-Barr disease.* (premise)

- *A proven sign of chronic fatigue syndrome is a positive diagnosis for human herpes virus 6.* (premise)

- *A proven sign of chronic fatigue syndrome is a positive diagnosis for human B-cell lymphotropic virus.* (premise)

- *Therefore, a person diagnosed with Epstein-Barr disease, human herpes virus 6, and human B-cell lymphotropic virus can be diagnosed as having chronic fatigue syndrome.* (conclusion)

Public speakers typically use a special form of deductive syllogism, the **enthymeme**, in which one premise is not directly stated because the speaker and listener both accept the premise.[13] For example, while speaking to those attending a conference on writing assessment, a speaker concluded, "If we can teach our children, from all backgrounds, to write with joy, originality, clarity and control, then I don't think we have much else to worry about."[14] This conclusion is based on the premise accepted by both speaker and listeners that children should be taught effective writing skills. Make sure when using the enthymeme that your audience does, indeed, share common premises. As a listener, be wary of a persuasive speaker who leads you to a conclusion by assuming that you share acceptance of the premise. If you don't accept the premise, don't be led to the conclusion.

The **disjunctive argument** is an either/or argument in which true alternatives must be established. Talking about America and the collapse of the Soviet Empire to a university audience, then-Secretary of State James Baker pointed out that the United States faced an either/or choice:

> To follow our fears and turn inward, ignoring the opportunities presented by the collapse of the Soviet Empire, or to answer the summons of history and lead toward a better future for all.[15]

The **conditional argument** sets up an if/then proposition. In this pattern of argument, there are two conditions, one of which necessarily follows from the other. For example, the chief executive officer of a major accounting firm proposed that the federal government adopt a new accrual accounting system so that the public and Congress could monitor the federal budget. He argued that

> if citizens were to demand the financial information to which they are clearly entitled, incentives would be created for sound fiscal manage-

ment—and, perhaps, for more enlightened political leadership. We could then expect to see better-informed decision making—less fiscal reckless-ness—and a reduction in the risks caused by the misallocation of capital.[16]

Persuasive Evidence

The persuasive speaker must not only structure the argument to meet the listeners' needs but also must support these contentions persuasively. The most persuasive form of supporting material—**evidence**—includes testi-mony from experts, statistics, and specific instances. If you can offer solid data to support your contentions, they will serve both to strengthen your per-ceived credibility and to lend substance to the argument you present. For ex-ample, a speaker who attempts to persuade listeners that the U.S. Food and Drug Administration (FDA) needs more funds to hire inspectors might cite specific instances from the agency's files. Real cases are on record of potatoes that were contaminated with insecticide, turkey stuffing that contained glass particles, and ginger ale that contained mold—all of which were sold to con-sumers. For additional support, the speaker might cite statistics from con-gressional budget hearings indicating that only 500 FDA inspectors are avail-able to monitor 60,000 food-processing plants in the United States; thus, each inspector must monitor 120 plants!

Essentially, your evidence should support the central idea, connecting it, if possible, with the listeners' beliefs about the topic. Persuasive evidence should be carefully tied to the argument at hand and accurately reported from authoritative, reliable sources. For example, the speaker who argues for additional FDA inspectors would connect evidence from FDA files and the congressional budget hearings to the generally held belief that uncontami-nated food is necessary for public health and welfare. It seems fairly safe to assume that most of the audience would agree with the need for uncontami-nated food, but not all speaking situations are so clear-cut. Before trying to build a persuasive case, speakers must ascertain through audience analysis that their assumptions are consistent with those held by the audience.

Reasoning Fallacies

In addition to presenting carefully structured and supported arguments, you should ensure the validity of your arguments so that your listeners can reasonably draw the conclusions you wish them to reach. To accomplish a valid argument, you must avoid some common reasoning fallacies.

One reasoning fallacy that can trip up persuasive communicators is the **hasty generalization**. A speaker who makes a hasty generalization reaches unwarranted, general conclusions from an insufficient number of instances. For example, a speaker who argues that gun control legislation is necessary by citing a few freeway shootings in Los Angeles is probably making a hasty generalization. Such limited instances may not provide the listener with enough of a foundation on which to base an all-inclusive conclusion.

Another reasoning fallacy that limits the persuasiveness of a message is **faulty analogical reasoning**. No analogy is ever truly complete because no two cases, however comparable, are ever identical. Speakers use faulty analo-gies when they assume that the elements two items or events share are similar in every respect. The speaker who argues, for example, that the current AIDS crisis is completely analogous to the bubonic plague that ravaged medieval Europe overlooks the scientific advances that make the AIDS crisis a very dif-ferent (although no less serious) medical problem.

Faulty causal reasoning occurs when a speaker makes an overstated claim that something caused something else. A speaker would probably be overstating the case by arguing, for example, that the bank scandal in the House of Representatives, in which many congresspeople wrote bad checks, directly resulted from a lack of moral accountability on the part of all federal public officials.

An entire set of reasoning fallacies can result if the speaker tries to ignore the issue. By **ignoring the issue**, the speaker uses irrelevant arguments to obscure the real issue. A common form of this is to attack the personal character of a person, which is irrelevant to the topic under discussion. Political campaign speeches often center on this approach. For instance, Bill Clinton was the recipient of such attacks in his campaigns for president. Accusations of marital infidelity, draft evasion, marijuana use, and political influence on the part of his wife's law firm were lodged against him. Some political observers questioned whether these issues were at all related to Clinton's ability to be president.

Appealing to people's prejudices and passions, rather than on the basis of the issue at hand, is another way of ignoring the issue. For example, despite the vast amount of negative publicity resulting from the financial scandal surrounding Jim and Tammy Bakker's PTL ministry in the late 1980s, devotees of PTL, stirred by passionate appeals from their leaders, continued to contribute millions of dollars to keep the religious organization going.

Yet another example of the fallacy of ignoring the issue is claiming that a statement is true because it cannot be disproved. For example, proponents of pit bull terriers argue that pit bulls are not dangerous pets because dog-bite statistics show that pit bulls rank ninth in number of bites—after poodles and cocker spaniels. Such a claim ignores the fact that pit bulls do cause harm. The issue is not whether poodles and cocker spaniels bite.

All reasoning fallacies can interfere with the persuasiveness of a message and can diminish the total impact of the speech. A discerning audience member can see through most smoke screens. Therefore, as a speaker, analyze your arguments to make sure that the structure and supporting evidence lead to valid conclusions that your listeners can accept. As a public listener of persuasive messages, be aware that speakers sometimes use fallacious reasoning in developing arguments and be on guard so that you don't fall for misinformation.

Developing Persuasive Arguments

When developing a persuasive speech, you must consider the order in which to present the arguments. Two possibilities are available. Some studies support the idea that the strongest argument should come first so that it will have the greatest impact on listeners at the outset. Other studies, however, support the idea that the strongest argument should come last to ensure that listeners remember it.[17]

You also must decide whether to develop both sides of the argument (and thus refute opposing arguments) or to present only your own stand. One potential problem in developing both sides of the argument is that you may raise issues and present ideas your listeners had not previously considered. If you are unable to refute these issues effectively, you may give your listeners a solution other than the one you intended—one they might not have considered if you had never mentioned it!

❖ ❖ ❖ ❖   Because the research on argument selection is not definitive, it is sometimes difficult to decide how best to develop the issues in a persuasive speech. It is safe to assume, however, that the order of your arguments must be based on careful audience analysis. If you feel that the audience is on your side, state your arguments first and bring your listeners along with you for the rest of your presentation (a deductive mode of reasoning). However, if you perceive your audience to be hostile to your position, build the background first, and then present your arguments when you feel your listeners are ready for them (a more inductive mode of reasoning). This strategy requires thorough prior analysis as well as process analysis during your presentation so that you can make any necessary adaptations based on listeners' responses.

Speakers should be aware of the **inoculation strategy**, which suggests that just as people can be protected from disease through immunization, so too can listeners be inhibited from accepting subsequent counterarguments if they are armed with the means to refute them.[18] Let's say you plan to attend hearings favoring rezoning a residential area in your neighborhood. If your local citizens' association bombards you with arguments against changing the neighborhood, you will go to the hearings more prepared to recognize the weaknesses in the opposing arguments and, ideally, strengthened in the support of your own stand.[19]

Another factor to consider in developing your arguments is **cognitive dissonance**, the mental discomfort that occurs when we accept an action or an idea that does not coincide with our previously held attitudes.[20] For example, if you are trying to persuade a group of new investors to purchase stock in a mutual fund, you should give reasons that reinforce the benefits of mutual funds, allay any fears about such funds, and diminish the attractiveness of alternative investment procedures. Your persuasive task will be especially challenging if your listeners have seen a decline in the value of mutual funds. If you present strong arguments and reassure your listeners that mutual funds are a sound, long-term investment, they will have more commitment to purchase the mutual fund after they reassess what you have said.

Here again, prior analysis can help you determine which persuasive strategies will best reinforce your position. If the potential buyers have young children, then your argument can center on the long-term proven profit increase of mutual funds over savings accounts, increased profits that can be used for the children's college educations. You can appeal to persons of limited finances by emphasizing that a mutual fund broadens the opportunity for profit and lessens the possibility of financial loss because clients are spreading their investments over more than one company.

Structuring the Body of a Persuasive Speech

The structure of a persuasive speech should allow the listener to reach the behavioral or mental change the speaker desires. The most common method of developing a persuasive message is to use the problem-solution arrangement (see discussion of problem-solution arrangement in Chapter 9).[21] The speaker identifies what is wrong and then presents the cure or recommendation for its cure.

The structure of the body of a speech which develops inductively would be: ❖ ❖ ❖ ❖

III. Body

    A. Identify the situation (what is wrong).

    B. Identify the problem (what has to be changed).

    C. List the possible solutions to the problem.

    D. Evaluate the solutions for workability, desirability, practicality.

        1. Workability—Can the solution solve the problem?

        2. Desirability—Can the solution cause bigger problems?

        3. Practicality—Can the solution be put into effect?

    E. Recommend the solution that is most workable, desirable, and practical.

An alternative to this, the see-blame-cure-cost method develops the speech by stressing the evil or problem that exists, determining what has caused the problem, investigating possible solutions, and then presenting the most practical solution. The see-blame-cure-cost technique allows the audience to see the problem, know who or what is to blame, hear of the possible cures, and then realize the costs involved in making the change—such as increased taxes, giving up personal rights, and the emotional confusion that often accompanies any alteration.

Psychological Appeals

Psychological appeals, which constitute the final component of the persuasive message, enlist listeners' emotions as motivation for accepting arguments. Just as you must select your arguments and enhance your credibility on the basis of what you know about your listeners, so must you select psychological appeals on the basis of what you think will stir your listeners' emotions. The purpose of incorporating some emotional appeals in your speech is to keep your listeners involved with you as you spell out your persuasive plan, even though they may not discern the emotional from the rational in your presentation.[22] One way to develop psychological appeals is to use Maslow's hierarchy of individual needs.

Maslow's Hierarchy of Individual Needs

Abraham Maslow, the psychologist noted for developing the concept of self-actualization, proposed a hierarchy of human needs (Figure 13.1) that can help speakers analyze the emotional needs of an audience. To use this theory, a speaker must determine the level of need of a particular group of listeners and then select appeals aimed at that level.[23] Although Maslow's theory is hierarchical, in reality these levels of need can function simultaneously. Therefore a speaker need not appeal to listeners on only one level at a time.

Maslow suggested that all human beings have five types of need. At the first, most basic level are **physiological needs**—hunger, sleep, sex, and thirst. These needs must normally be satisfied before a person can be motivated by appeals to other levels of need. Recognizing this, the U.S. Agency for International Development appeals to the physiological needs of people in developing nations as a means of persuading them to adopt a democratic

Figure 13.1 Maslow's Hierarchy of Human Needs

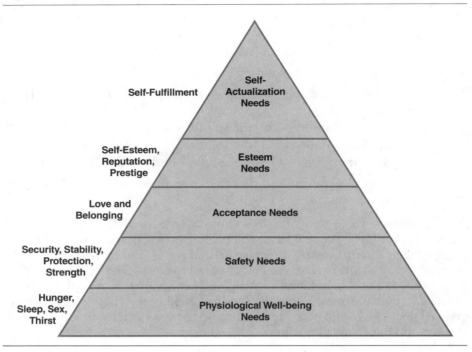

form of government. A speaker might address a group of potential organ do-
nors by pointing out the physiological needs of transplant patients, or persuade a group of homeless people to go to a shelter or an assistance center by
appealing to their physiological needs.

The second level, **safety needs**, encompasses security, stability, protection, and strength. In presenting speeches to laid-off workers, employers may
soften the blow by sharing information on job-search seminars, resume preparation, and other career skills. Successful political candidates often target
this second level of human needs when tailoring persuasive campaign
speeches. An incumbent who can claim responsibility for a high level of police protection, for efficient trash disposal and snow removal, and for a vi-
brant economy is very likely to get reelected. However, if an opponent can
prove that the present officeholder is not satisfying these types of needs, the
incumbent may well be voted out.

The third level consists of **acceptance needs**, for love and a sense of be-
longing. Americans are highly motivated by the need to belong, as evidenced
by their affiliations with many different types of social and work-related
groups. Persuasive speakers may appeal to a listener's desire to be "a good
American" in order to motivate audiences. **Esteem needs**, at the fourth level,
involve both self-esteem (desire for achievement and mastery) and esteem
from others (desire for reputation and prestige). A coach giving a half-time
speech is appealing to the esteem needs of team members.

Self-actualization needs, the desire for self-fulfillment or the achievement of one's greatest potential, is the fifth level in Maslow's hierarchy. This is
a lofty level that few people ever reach but many strive for. A persuasive
speaker can appeal to listeners' needs for self-actualization by setting high
goals to reach. For example, entertainer Bill Cosby, in a commencement

speech at the University of Maryland, challenged the graduates to make a difference in the world and in their own lives.

Group Needs

The needs of audience members may be strongly influenced by the needs of the groups to which they belong. Many Americans who have gone through the 1970s "me" decade of self-indulgence and the 1980s "no" decade in the wake of smoking, drunken driving, and AIDS are now into the 1990s "back to basics" decade of a simpler lifestyle.[24] Adapting to trends in group needs thus becomes a challenge for the persuasive speaker.

The desire to motivate a group may be a legitimate objective of the speech itself. Organizations are booking motivational speakers for meetings and conventions in record numbers. The main goal of these speakers is to inspire self-improvement or financial improvement in salespeople, marketing personnel, and other staff groups. An official of the Washington Speakers Bureau observed that "The thousands of motivational speakers currently in the circuit make up the largest segment of the speaking industry."[25]

Appeals to Motivate Listeners

Once you have determined your audience's needs (perhaps using Maslow's hierarchy), you can then build into your speech the psychological appeals that will help you persuade listeners to accept your point of view. A considerable variety of motivational appeals are available.[26]

Many speakers experience success by making an appeal to:

1. *Adventure*. Here the speaker stresses the listener's desire to explore new worlds, see exciting places, take part in unusual experiences, or participate in different events. A speaker representing the travel industry might motivate potential travelers by describing what it would be like to go on a tour.

2. *Companionship*. Speakers often tap our desire to be with others. A speaker might make this appeal in an attempt to recruit volunteers for a local youth center.

3. *Deference*. Showing respect for a wiser, more experienced authority can be a successful speaking strategy. A speaker on international issues might defer to an officer in the Foreign Service for an assessment of a thorny international situation. Such deference can assure an audience that the speaker is in touch with key people who do make a difference. Speakers often use this appeal when they refer to a knowledgeable researcher who supports their point of view.

4. *Fear*. This appeal is used to raise apprehension in an audience. Identifying fears that threaten listeners or their values can motivate an audience to take action to overcome a potential danger. For example, speakers for the American Cancer Society's antismoking campaign stress the negative effects of smoking not only on the smoker but also on those in the same household and on a developing fetus. Though the fear appeal can be powerful, research shows that a speaker must be careful not to overdo it. A listener can become too frightened to accept the proposed action because the situation is perceived as hopeless, or the listener

**Appeals to psychological needs help motivate
listeners to accept arguments.**

may become desensitized because of oversell. This is the case of
some overeaters who decide that they have already jeopardized
their physical health.[27]

5. *Gender.* This can be a powerful persuasive tool. Appealing to
women's rights, stressing the need for more women leaders in
upper levels of management, and criticizing sexual harassment
have all been useful approaches for speakers who attempt to
rally support for women's causes. On the other hand, the speakers promoting the 1996 Million Man March on Washington and
the 1997 Promise Keepers Washington Rally appealed to men
specifically by talking about what males needed to do to be better
people, and how attendance at these events would aid them to be
better people.

6. *Guilt.* Religious speakers often use this approach to persuade
people to change their ways, or to feel badly about actions they
have committed or might wish to commit.

7. *Humor.* Speakers who appeal to a listener's sense of humor demonstrate that they do not take themselves or their subject
overseriously, and that everyone can relax a bit. Note the number
of humorous advertisements you see daily on television. These
ads are attempts to persuade you. Advertising agencies realize
that if humor is appropriate and helps make the point, it can be
an effective motivating tool. However, some speakers hesitate to
use humor in a persuasive speech, especially one on a serious

topic, because they feel the audience may be offended and more difficult to persuade.

❖ ❖ ❖ ❖

8. *Loyalty*. Our feelings of loyalty—to nation, to friends and family, and to organizations—are important to us. During Operation Desert Storm in 1991, appeals to national loyalty made by President Bush and others constituted probably the greatest persuasive motivator in getting near-unanimous approval for the military action. The same is true of the "Buy American" speech campaign conducted by representatives of the U.S. clothing and automobile industry. We demonstrate loyalty to and defend those things and people of whom we are proud and with whom we identify.[28]

9. *Power and authority*. People often want to hold positions of power over others, to be the leader, to be in charge. The speaker who emphasizes American military initiatives may well appeal to the power and authority many Americans want to maintain as a world-leading nation.[29]

10. *Reverence*. Audiences are sometimes motivated by hero worship of sports figures, performers, astronauts, and other prominent figures. Referring to heroes or important people who back your cause can convince others to accept your ideas. For example, in attempting to get a large turnout for a national "Freedom of Choice" rally held in Washington, D.C., in 1992, the president of the National Organization for Women stressed that marchers would include Hollywood stars Jane Fonda, Joanne Woodward, Cybill Shepherd, Molly Ringwald, Morgan Fairchild, and Mary Steenburgen.[30]

11. *Revulsion*. If used with care, the appeal to disgust can be effective. A speaker might illustrate the effects of water pollution by showing the listeners some samples from Chesapeake Bay, and then ask them to support legislation to clean up the bay. Astute speakers do not, however, arouse such a strong sense of revulsion that listeners tune out the message. Anti-abortionists and anti-vivisectionists sometimes overwhelm their listeners with revolting photographs of aborted fetuses and maimed laboratory animals.

12. *Worship*. Concern for the religious beliefs of people is a powerful persuasive tool. Thirty percent of American adults attend church or synagogue in a typical week.[31] Using this information, persuasive speakers can appeal to a listener's religious convictions as a way to gain support for their side. The founder of a major anti-abortion organization, in a speech intending to persuade an audience, said, "We want to define for you the nature of the battle. And the nature of the battle is this: Whose God and whose God's laws will dominate the culture? It's good versus evil, good guys against bad guys."[32]

13. *Sympathy*. By showing photographs or films of starving children, impoverished elderly, or the homeless poor, a speaker can compel listeners to give time, money, or other resources. A sym-

pathetic bond, often coupled with guilt, is thus created with those less fortunate.

As this list reveals, speakers have a wide variety of options from which to choose in developing persuasive appeals. Speakers must analyze the audience to determine need levels, select appeals that will meet these needs, and place the appeals in the speech at points where they will have the greatest persuasive impact. For example, if you determine that your listeners are operating at the level of acceptance needs, you would select appeals that motivate them at this level. Let's say you wish to persuade the employees of a particular organization to form an employees' association. You might explain how the association will satisfy their needs for meeting and interacting with other people and for participating in group decision making.

13.4 The Persuasive Process in Action

Psychological appeals, coupled with speaker credibility and well-reasoned and supported arguments, provide a sound approach to influencing others to change their beliefs or actions. The sample persuasive speech in Figure 13.2 illustrates the interaction of these components.

13.5 Listening to Persuasive Speeches

The listener to persuasive speeches must understand and comprehend the speaker's message before making a critical assessment of it. Unfortunately, too many listeners make that critical judgment prematurely—before receiving the complete message. They tune out the speaker's message, based on little or no understanding of the speaker's arguments, evidence, appeals, and even credibility.

As discussed in the "Critical Level" section of Chapter 2, there are factors which a listener should take into account when determining whether or not to be persuaded. These include the personal appeal of the speaker, the speaker's arguments and evidence, the speaker's motivational appeals, assumptions on the part of the speaker, what is not said, and the use of the passive language.

Listeners of persuasive speeches should remember that it is the purpose of the speaker to influence your opinion or behavior by

Photo: Amy Peng/Daily Bruin

It is the purpose of the persuasive speaker to influence the listener's opinion or behavior.

Figure 13.2 Outline for a Sample Persuasive Speech   ❖ ❖ ❖ ❖

Purpose statement: To persuade audience members to do their part to save the environment by listing the environmental problems this nation faces and how problems of the environment can be addressed through a combination of concern and control.

I. Introduction

    A. Attention material: Humans have the power to destroy all life on the earth. As environmental specialists have observed, "That power may be released at any time, for it is harnessed only by fallible humans, and, increasingly, by fallible machines."   *Attention material to gain audience interest*

    B. Orienting material: The future of our environment should be of concern to all of us.   *Orienting material to get listeners involved in the topic*

II. Central Idea: Do your part to save the environment   *Central point of the speech*

III. Body

    A. Here are the environmental problems facing us: *First main point*

       1. Nuclear winter—the detonation of even a small number of nuclear weapons could send enough nuclear fallout into the atmosphere to trigger major climatic disruptions and create a global nuclear winter.   *Discussion and development of the first point with statistics, factual information, explanation, persuasive appeals*

       2. Energy—78 quadrillion BTUs of energy were consumed in 1992 in the United States alone.

       3. Water—more than 50 percent of the nation's wetlands have already been destroyed.

       4. Air—more than half of the U.S. population lives in areas where air pollutants still exceed health standards at least part of the time.

       5. Wildlife—the world faces a major threat of the loss of wild species, destroying the balance of nature.

       6. Land—natural areas today are lost to development, further upsetting the balance of nature.

       7. The destruction of the natural environment is the result of many factors—population expansion, industrial demands, and unplanned and uncontrolled urbanization and development.

    (The problems of our environment are staggering. However, there is much that we can do to begin to address these problems.)   *Transition*

    B. The problems of the environment can be addressed through a combination of concern and control.   *Second main point*

       1. All of us, decision makers and taxpayers alike, need to recognize the impact of governmental decisions and actions on the environment.   *Discussion and development of the second point with suggested strategies*

       2. Sound resource management and careful protection of the environment are critical.

3. The nation needs a new agenda that takes a global approach to dealing with population growth that is exceeding world capacity, toxic chemicals, burning of fossil fuels, and nuclear destruction.
4. What you can do as an individual—conservation consciousness and strategies, recycling, consumer and taxpayer pressure.

IV. Conclusion

Restates major points of the body of the speech

A. Summary
1. The environmental problems facing us include nuclear winter, the overuse of energy, the destruction of the nation's wetlands, unclear air, the destruction of the balance of nature, and the destruction of the natural environment.
2. These problems can be addressed by citizen demand for government environmental decisions, sound resource management, a global agenda to deal with the problems, and individuals becoming conservation conscious.

Appeals for action on the part of the listener

B. Clincher
1. Carrying out the environmental agenda will require the cooperation of individuals from all walks of life. The involvement and assistance of industry, labor, educators, scientists, lawyers, students, government workers, homemakers, etc., will be needed.
2. You can do your part by becoming involved. Write your political representatives, become an environmental doer rather than an environmental destroyer. Recycle rather than trash!

convincing you to believe as the speaker does, or to move you to take the desired action that the speaker has proposed. Speakers often will do anything, including acting unethically, to get you to act as they wish you to act. Be aware of this as you listen to persuasive speeches. All of the techniques covered up to this point of this chapter are intended to teach persuasive speakers how to craft an effective speech. Knowing these techniques, you, as a listener, are better able to figure out what the speaker is attempting to do, and to monitor the oral, physical, and verbal techniques in order to ensure that you are making a wise decision in buying into the ideas. An educated consumer is a wise consumer.

Summary

In this chapter on persuasive speaking, the key ideas presented were:

♦ *Persuasion is "the process by means of which one party purposefully secures a voluntary change of behavior, mental and/or physical, on the part of another party by employing appeals to both feelings and intellect."*

❖ ❖ ❖ ❖

♦ *The basic process of persuasion requires that the speaker make a claim and back it up in such a way that listeners accept the claim.*

♦ *Successful persuasive strategies center on the use of speaker credibility, logical arguments, and psychological appeals.*

♦ *A speaker's credibility incorporates trustworthiness, competence, and dynamism.*

♦ *Effective arguments can be structured inductively or deductively, depending on the listener's prior acceptance of the argument.*

♦ *A speaker should avoid such reasoning fallacies as hasty generalization, faulty analogical reasoning, faulty causal reasoning, and ignoring the issue.*

♦ *In arranging the issues in a persuasive speech, a speaker should take into account the positioning and development of arguments, inoculation strategy, and cognitive dissonance.*

♦ *Effective use of psychological appeals requires careful analysis of listeners' needs.*

♦ *Maslow's hierarchy of needs—physiological, safety, acceptance, esteem, and self-actualization—provides a framework for understanding listeners' needs.*

♦ *The speaker has a wide variety of psychological appeals from which to choose.*

♦ *The effective persuasive message combines ethos, logos, and pathos in an honest, straightforward presentation.*

♦ *An aware listener will monitor the oral, physical, and verbal techniques used by a speaker in order to ensure that the listener is making a wise decision in buying into the speaker's ideas.*

Key Terms

persuasion	speech of conviction
speech of actuation	coercion
theory of field-related standards	group standards
individual standards	critical reasoning
comparative-advantage reasoning	ethos
logos	pathos
speaker credibility	competence
dynamism	inductive argument
generalization conclusion	hypothesis conclusion
deductive argument	categorical syllogism
enthymeme	disjunctive argument
conditional argument	evidence
hasty generalization	faulty analogical reasoning
faulty causal reasoning	ignoring the issue
inoculation strategy	cognitive dissonance
psychological appeals	physiological needs
safety needs	acceptance needs
esteem needs	self-actualization needs

❖ ❖ ❖ ❖   **Learn by Doing**

1. Prepare a speech on a topic about which you have strong feelings. Propose a change in present procedures, take a stand on a view concerning the subject, or propose a plan of action. The topic should be one to which your listeners can relate and react so that you can persuade them. A sample central idea for this speech might be "_____ College/University should not raise tuition."

2. Select a controversial topic and prepare a speech in which you advocate a particular solution to the problem. Your task is to persuade your listeners to accept your solution. A sample central idea for this speech might be "Euthanasia should be a legal option for terminally ill patients."

3. Prepare a speech analyzing the persuasive strategies used by some group in advocating a particular cause (for example, women's rights, gay rights, Native American rights). Select a number of persuasive messages by spokespersons for the group you choose, and use examples from these messages to illustrate your analysis of the persuasive strategies.

4. Find print, radio, or television ads illustrating the various psychological appeals described in this chapter. Prepare to describe and analyze the use of the appeals in the ads you select.

5. Consider the components of a persuasive message—credibility, logical arguments, and psychological appeals—and determine what you perceive to be the most influential persuasive strategies with American listeners today. Why do you think so?

6. What do you think is the difference between preparing persuasive speeches and preparing informative speeches?

7. Analyze the "credibility crisis" of any of the recent American presidents or presidential candidates. What do you think an official could or should do to maintain credibility in the eyes of the American public?

8. Attend a persuasive speech by someone in a public forum, or analyze a persuasive manuscript in *Vital Speeches of the Day*. Prepare a descriptive analysis of the use of persuasive strategies by this speaker.

9. Your class is going to have a discussion on the topic: "What I need to remember when listening to a persuasive speech." You are responsible for making a list of "warnings" which you will share with your classmates.

Endnotes

1. Based on definitions conceived by Robert Goyer.
2. Aristotle, *The Rhetoric of Aristotle*, trans. Lane Cooper (New York: Appleton-Century-Crofts, 1932).

3. Stanley F. Paulson, "Social Values and Experimental Research in Speech," *Western Speech Communication*, 26 (Summer 1962), pp. 133–139.

4. From a speech by an inmate from the Grafton Prison Farm, Grafton, Ohio, May 1976. Name withheld by request.

5. For a classical discussion of the dimensions of credibility, see James C. McCroskey, *An Introduction to Rhetorical Communication*, 7th ed., (Boston: Allyn and Bacon, 1997), chapter 5.

6. See, for example, Joe McGinniss, *The Selling of the President, 1968* (New York: Pocket Books, 1970), and Patrick Anderson, *Electing Jimmy Carter* (Baton Rouge: Louisiana State University Press, 1994).

7. Rollo May, *Love and Will* (New York: Norton, 1969), p. 20.

8. Wayne Thompson, *Quantitative Research in Public Address and Communication* (New York: Random House, 1967), pp. 50–53.

9. Carroll Arnold, "What's Reasonable?" *Today's Speech*, 19 (Summer 1971), pp. 19–23.

10. Ibid., p. 22.

11. Robert B. Maxwell, "The 'Graying' of America," *Vital Speeches of the Day*, September 15, 1987, p. 710.

12. Jim Courter, "Step by Step," *Vital Speeches of the Day*, July 15, 1987, p. 581.

13. The role of the enthymeme as a rhetorical syllogism has been reassessed by Thomas M. Conley, "The Enthymeme in Perspective," *Quarterly Journal of Speech* 70 (May 1984), pp. 168–187.

14. Donald M. Stewart, "Good Writing," *Vital Speeches of the Day*, August 1, 1987, p. 633.

15. James A. Baker III, "America and the Collapse of the Soviet Empire," speech presented at Princeton University, December 12, 1991, and published in *Vital Speeches of the Day*, January 1, 1992, p. 167.

16. Duane A. Kullberg, "Accounting and Accountability," *Vital Speeches of the Day*, July 15, 1987, p. 608.

17. For a discussion of some of these research studies, see Raymond S. Ross, *Persuasion: Communication and Interpersonal Relations* (Englewood Cliffs, N.J.: Prentice-Hall, 1974), pp. 187–193.

18. William J. McGuire, "Inducing Resistance to Persuasion," in Leonard Berkowitz, ed., *Advances in Experimental Social Psychology* (New York: Academic Press, 1964), pp. 196–203. Also see W. Richard Ullman and Edward M. Bodaken, "Inducing Resistance to Persuasive Attack: A Test of Two Strategies of Communication," *Western Speech Communication*, 39 (Fall 1975), pp. 240–248.

19. Thomas B. Harte, "The Effects of Evidence in Persuasive Communication," *Central States Speech Journal*, 27 (Spring 1976), pp. 42–46.

20. Leon Festinger, *A Theory of Cognitive Dissonance* (Stanford, Calif.: Stanford University Press, 1963).

21. For a discussion of problem-solution arrangement, see Chapter 9 of this text.

22. Paulson.

23. Abraham Maslow, *Motivation and Personality* (New York: Harper & Row, 1970), pp. 35–58. How Maslow's hierarchy reflects today's societal needs is demonstrated in M. Joseph Sirgy, "A Quality-of-Life Theory Derived from Maslow's Developmental Perspective," *American Journal of Economics and Sociology*, 45 (July 1986), pp. 329–342.

24. Bob Spichen, "New Attitude: AIDS, Crusades Promote Change of Habits," *Norfolk Virginian Pilot*, August 12, 1987, pp. 1, 3; and David M. Gross and Sophfronia Scott, "Proceeding with Caution," *Time*, July 16, 1990, pp. 56–62.

25. Michael Adams, "Motivational Speaking: Is It Just a Quick Fix?" *Successful Meetings*, June 1987, p. 27.

26. This discussion is adapted from Bruce E. Gronbeck, Raymie E. McKerrow, Douglas Ehninger, and Alan H. Monroe, *Principles and Types of Speech Communication*, 13th ed. (New York: Longman, 1997), chapter 6.

27. A comprehensive summary of research on fear appeals is provided by C. William Colburn, "Fear Arousing Appeals," in Howard Martin and Kenneth Anderson, eds., *Speech Communication: Analysis and Readings* (Boston: Allyn and Bacon, 1968), pp. 214–226. Also see Ronald W. Rogers, "Attitude Change and Information Integration in Fear Appeals," *Psychological Reports*, 56 (February 1985), pp. 179–182.

28. For a discussion of the problem with loyalty in work, see Wayne Sage, "The Discontented Worker," *Human Behavior*, 2 (June 1973), pp. 64–65.

29. For a discussion of power as a motivator, see David C. McClelland, "Love and Power: The Psychological Signals of War," *Psychology Today*, 9 (January 1975), pp. 44–48.

30. "Major Rallies Return Focus on Abortion," *Baltimore Sun*, April 4, 1992, p. 3A.

31. Frank Newport and Lydia Saad, "Religious Faith Is Widespread but Many Skip Church," (Princeton, N.J.: Gallup Poll, March 29, 1997).

32. "U.S. in Life-death Struggle, Terry Says," *Baltimore Sun*, April 4, 1992, p. 4B, quoting from a speech by Randall Terry given in Columbia, Md.

CHAPTER FOURTEEN

Ceremonial
Speeches

Chapter Outline

❑ 14.1 Introductions

❑ 14.2 Welcomes

❑ 14.3 Farewells

❑ 14.4 Award Presentations

❑ 14.5 Acceptances

❑ 14.6 Thank-yous

❑ 14.7 Toasts

❑ 14.8 After-Dinner Speeches

❑ 14.9 Sermons

❑ 14.10 Prayers

❑ 14.11 Commemorative Speeches

❑ 14.12 Listening to Appreciate

Learning Outcomes

After reading this chapter, you should be able to:

- *Understand the role of ceremonial speeches in public communication.*

- *Recognize what constitutes an effective ceremonial speech, including introductions, welcomes, farewells, award presentations, acceptances, thank-yous, after-dinner speeches, sermons, prayers, and commemorative presentations.*

- *Know how to prepare and present an effective ceremonial speech.*

- *Know how to listen appreciatively to a ceremonial speech.*

Speakers are frequently called on to present **ceremonial speeches**, special types of short speeches on various social or civic occasions. Traditionally, these presentations have had three functions: (1) *to explain a social world to listeners*, as in commencement addresses; (2) *to display the speaker's eloquence*, as in entertaining speeches; and (3) *to shape and share community ideals*, as in inaugurals and keynotes.[1] White House speechwriters tend to dismiss ceremonial remarks that U.S. presidents usually present in the White House Rose Garden as "Rose Garden Rubbish," but such presentations serve important functions.

Public speakers should be able to develop and present ceremonial speeches, for they can play a role in both career and social responsibilities. When preparing a speech for a special occasion, it is essential to analyze the audience carefully and to adapt the speech specifically to those particular listeners. Remember that listeners will have expectations as to what the occasion requires; it is important for the speaker to know what these expectations are. Common types of ceremonial speeches include: introductions, welcomes, farewells, award presentations, acceptances, thank-yous, toasts, after-dinner speeches, sermons, prayers, and ceremonial speeches such as tributes, keynotes, inaugurals, and commencement speeches.

Listeners of ceremonial speeches will have expectations as to what the occasion requires.

❖ ❖ ❖ ❖   ## 14.1 Introductions

A **speech of introduction** precedes a public presentation. Its purpose is to give the audience the information they need to have about the speech or speaker. In addition, it fills in any details that the audience must be aware of, such as whether a question-and-answer session will follow the speech and the format of that session.

Too often, these introductions are poor because the speaker has not carefully prepared the remarks to be appropriate to the listeners' needs. In introducing a speaker, be sure to include such material as who the speaker is, where the speaker is from, what the speaker's accomplishments are, and when these accomplishments took place. Try to establish the credibility of the speaker, highlighting significant aspects of his or her background that relate to the speech topic. It is just as important, however, to portray the speaker as a person in whom the listeners will be interested. You might want to offer comments on how important the topic is and how significant the speaker is. Do not overstate your own connection to the speaker. (If you've just met the person, it seems inappropriate to introduce her as "my old friend.") Above all, a speech of introduction should be short and to the point. Remember, the listeners have come to hear the speaker, not the person making the introduction.

One note of caution: be careful to prepare the listeners to be interested in the speaker, but avoid overpraising the speaker so much that he or she cannot possibly live up to the expectations you have raised. Probably we have all looked forward to hearing a speech by someone praised as "the best speaker you'll ever hear"—who then fell far short of that label!

If possible, get the necessary information from your speaker in advance of the presentation. If you can't interview the guest in advance, telephone or write. Request specific information, including how to pronounce the speaker's name and what background material to highlight.

If there are special circumstances concerning the speech or the speaker, it is the responsibility of the introducer to ease the speaker's way. For example, when Wellesley College invited First Lady Barbara Bush to present the June 1990 commencement address, the announcement sparked considerable controversy. Writer Alice Walker had been the first choice for speaker, and some Wellesley students felt that Mrs. Bush was not an appropriate speaker, for she is most known as "wife of . . ." rather than as a professional woman in her own right. While Mrs. Bush's speech itself was a masterful example of rhetorical strategy in deflecting the criticism, the president of Wellesley, Nannerl Keohane, established the proper rhetorical tone for the address in her splendid introduction:

> In a sermon delivered at the opening of Wellesley in 1875, Henry Fowle Durant directed that Wellesley should prepare women for great conflicts, for vast reforms in social life, for "noblest usefulness." And to instill that message, the chosen motto of the College, still constantly familiar to all of us today, was "Non ministrari, sed ministrare"—not to be the passive recipient of good works, but to do them. And thus service to other human beings, to family and community and the world became (and has remained) an integral part of the Wellesley tradition. Barbara Bush clearly exemplifies that tradition of "noblest usefulness." The most popular First Lady in our time, Mrs. Bush has used the visibility and clout of her position to work untir-

ingly to heal wounds and combat evils—AIDS, drugs, homelessness, and the breakup of families. Her work is best known in the field of literacy. . . . She has worked in public, and she has worked behind the scenes, caring more about what she accomplishes than what she is given credit for. . . . Barbara Bush exemplifies what she believes: "to live a complete life, you need to help other people. . . . You have a choice: you can love your life, or not, and I have chosen to love my life."[2]

Notes and Suggestions for the Introduction of a Speech

An introduction speech is one in which a chairman or other person introduces a speaker to an audience. The purpose is to bring an audience and speaker together in the proper spirit. Several of the requirements are:

1. The speech should be short. Use a limited amount of material. (STAND UP, SPEAK UP, SHUT UP!)
2. The audience and speaker should feel comfortably acquainted.
3. It should put the speaker at ease.
4. It should include the who, what, and why of the speech.
5. It should never embarrass the speaker. (*Unless for special effect.*)
6. The person introducing a speaker should not call attention to himself.
7. Discover enough of the speaker's background to interest the audience.
8. Be sure that the speaker's name is correctly pronounced.

Suggestions for presenting the speech of introduction:

1. Take your place on the platform.
2. Pause until the room grows quiet.
3. Address the audience in an extemporaneous style.
4. Use natural gestures, eye contact, and movements.
5. Indicate to the speaker when he or she is to come forward.
6. Return to your seat.

Avoid:

1. Trite, hackneyed phrases.
2. Unnecessary verbiage.
3. Not setting the correct mood for the speaker.
4. Reading the introduction.
5. Insincerity of verbiage and tone.
6. Apologies.
7. Making a production out of a simple speech. (You are not the speaker.)

14.2 Welcomes

A **speech of welcome** is in order if you are called on to provide greetings to a visitor to your organization, to new members, or to make your own remarks on joining a group. Essentially, you will want to extend your greetings, pointing out that it is important or appropriate for the persons being welcomed to be with the group at this particular time. Remember that a good speech of welcome is sincere and personal.

If you are asked to present brief remarks upon joining a group, you may want to take the opportunity to extend your own personal greetings to the members of the organization. A newly confirmed secretary of state addressed U.S. Department of State employees with these words:

As I looked into your faces, and heard your greetings, and felt your touch, you've made me feel very much at home already. . . . I don't know how much of a future together we have. But I would like that future to be active, creative, innovative, positive. I hope and expect to be learning a great deal from you about what is going on in this building—but more importantly what is going on around this planet that affects us, our interests, and our people.[3]

14.3 Farewells

A **farewell speech** can take two forms. You may be saying farewell as you move on to another position or retire; or, you may be extending your group's farewell to a departing member. Regardless of the approach taken, the farewell speech should be characterized by sincerity, warmth, and brevity and should give a memorable message. Good speakers will express true feelings, or sentiments, that will not embarrass themselves or someone else, and offer an uplifting, optimistic speech. Using humor or a dramatic statement, recounting common experiences with those assembled, recalling events or people you'll remember—all these options are very appropriate. (Figure 14.1)

Figure 14.1 Sample Speech of Farewell

Magic Johnson, considered by many to be one of the finest professional basketball players ever, gave this speech of farewell to announce that he was infected with the HIV virus and would retire from the Los Angeles Lakers team.

> Because of the HIV virus I have obtained, I will have to retire from the Lakers today. I do not have the AIDS disease. My wife is fine. She's negative. I plan on going on living for a long time and going on with my life. I guess I get to enjoy the other sides of living.
>
> I'm going to miss playing. I'm going to be a spokesman for the HIV virus, helping young people to realize they can practice safe sex. You can be naive. You think it will never happen to you. It has happened. I'll deal with it and my life will go on.
>
> My life will change. I'll still be a part of the game, working with the Lakers and the league. Basketball will still be a part of my life. I want kids to understand that safe sex is the way to go. We think only gay people get it and that it's not going to happen to me.
>
> I feel really good. My wife is healthy and I'm going to go on. I'm still going to pursue my dream of owning a team. I took the test due to a life insurance policy. They found nothing in terms of the flu, and they kept testing.
>
> I think everybody will be more careful. That's what I want to preach. Most of all, what I'm going to miss is the camaraderie. I can do all the things a normal person can do.
>
> I'm going to come out swinging. All I can do is have a bright side. That's why I am here right now.

(Source: From Earvin "Magic" Johnson, press conference, November 7, 1991.)

In 1991, Magic Johnson, one of the most popular players in the history of the National Basketball Association, showed composure in the face of a terrible personal tragedy when he announced that he was retiring from basketball because he had tested positive for HIV, the virus that causes AIDS . Later that day, his former Los Angeles Lakers coach, Pat Riley, fought back tears in leading an arenawide prayer. Riley grabbed the microphone at midcourt. He asked for everyone, "in your own voice, in your own beliefs, in your way, to pray for Earvin and for the one million people who are afflicted with an insidious disease who need our understanding."[4]

14.4 Award Presentations

When an individual or a group achieves some distinction, officials are usually called upon to give an **award presentation**—a commendation to the recipient. The presentation of an award should include some discussion of the award itself, including the basis for selection, its history, and its significance. The speech should also detail the achievements of the person or group receiving the award so that it is clear to the listeners that the recipient is qualified. As the award is actually presented to the person, it is a nice touch to read the inscription so that everyone can share in this honor.

Photo: Courtesy of University of Missouri—Kansas City, Communication Studies Department

An award presentation honors an individual for achieving some distinction.

President George Bush joined Walter Massey, then the director of the National Science Foundation, in presenting the National Medal of Science and Technology to a number of recipients in the White House Rose Garden on September 16, 1991:

> Today, your Nation recognizes your monumental accomplishments, honors the differences you have made: Advancing human understanding, improving the human condition, helping mankind conquer ignorance and illness, helping this Nation compete and prosper. . . . In honoring each of you, this Nation honors the boundless horizons of the human mind, the soaring spirit of inquiry, the special genius of the architects who fashion today's fantastic idea into tomorrow's usable tool. Your work stands as its own reward; so let me simply add your Nation's thanks.[5]

14.5 Acceptances

A **speech of acceptance** normally follows an award presentation, an election victory, or a success. A good acceptance speech should include a sin-

When an individual or group achieves some distinction, an award is often given.

cere thank-you to those responsible for your recognition. It is also appropriate to discuss the significance of the award or victory. An acceptance should also be brief.

Hollywood producer and director Steven Spielberg received the Irving G. Thalberg Memorial Award at the 59th Academy Awards in 1987. While many Academy Award acceptance speeches are ineffective rambles, Spielberg's remarks showed thought and preparation:

> The Thalberg Award was first given 50 years ago in 1937. . . . I'm told Irving Thalberg worshiped writers. And that's where it all begins. That we are first and foremost storytellers. And without, as he called it, "the photoplay," everybody is simply improvising. He also knew that a script is more than just a blueprint. That the whole idea of movie magic is that interweave of powerful image, and dialogue, and performance, and music that can never be separated. And when it's working right, can never be duplicated or ever forgotten. I've grown up—most of my life has been spent in the dark watching movies. Movies have been the literature of my life. . . . [The] audience, who we all work for, deserves everything we have to give them. They deserve that fifth draft, that tenth take, that one extra cut, and those several dollars over budget. And Irving Thalberg knew that. . . . I am proud to have my name on this award in his honor. Because it reminds me of really how much growth as an

artist I have ahead of me, in order to be worthy of standing in the company of those who have received this before me. So my deepest thanks to the board of governors of the Academy, and the audience out there in the dark. . . .[6]

14.6 Thank-yous

The **speech of thank-you** is your acknowledgment of services or aid given to you by others. Like the acceptance speech, a heartfelt thank-you will be appreciated by your listeners, especially if they have been instrumental in supporting you, doing a good job, and so on. In such a presentation it is customary to include a tribute to those you are recognizing. General Norman Schwarzkopf, who led the U.S. military in Operation Desert Storm in the Persian Gulf, thanked America for its support in a speech before a Joint Session of Congress at the close of the operation:

> I am awed and honored to be standing at the podium where so many notable men and women have stood before me. Unlike them, I do not stand here today for any great deed that I have done. Instead, I stand here because I was granted by our national leadership the great privilege of commanding the magnificent American service men and women who constituted the Armed Forces of Operation Desert Shield and Desert Storm. . . . I must . . . tell each and every one of those extraordinary patriots that . . . I will never, ever in my entire life receive a greater reward than the inspiration that I received every single day as I watched your dedicated performance, your dedicated sacrifice, your dedicated service to your country.[7]

14.7 Toasts

The **toast** is a recognition of or tribute to a person or a group, in which a short speech is given and a celebratory liquid is sipped. It is an important form of communication at certain occasions, such as governmental functions. Diplomats, for instance, find that an effective toast is sometimes integral to their work with foreign dignitaries. Toasts are also common at celebrations such as weddings and anniversaries, as well as at dedications. An effective toast, like many special forms of speeches, should be short and to the point. The U.S. Department of State Office of Protocol suggests that toasts at White House state dinners not exceed three minutes in length.[8]

As the speaker presenting the toast, you will want to highlight the reason that the guests are gathered together and establish some bond in the speech you make. Some toasts are humorous, others dramatic. If the gathering is in honor of some person or event, this should certainly be mentioned. For example, in marking Columbus Day at a luncheon at the Italian Embassy in Washington, President Ronald Reagan responded to a toast by the Italian ambassador with a toast honoring Italian-American ties:

> It's particularly fitting that we gather here on a day honoring Christopher Columbus, a remarkable Italian who altered the course of history by exhibiting great moral character and individual courage. . . . Our precious liberty, so important to Italians and Americans, depends on the quality of character that we honor on Columbus Day. Italy has long been a particularly close and important ally of the United States. In our commitment to

genuine arms reductions and to the maintenance of a stable balance of power so necessary for peace, Americans and Italians are of one mind.[9]

14.8 After-Dinner Speeches

Another speech frequently used at luncheons, dinners, and banquets is the **after-dinner speech**, whose purpose is usually to provide an entertaining or compelling message on a theme. Common settings are athletic banquets, personality roasts, retirement dinners, and fund-raisers. The speaker should decide on a theme and then structure a speech around that theme. The case method of organization is appropriate for this type of presentation (see Chapter 9). In this way, a speaker can set out a unifying thesis and then put together a series of examples, anecdotes, or jokes. After-dinner speeches are often humorous. As an expert on humor observed, "Humor has often been the key that unlocks an audience's receptivity."[10]

It is important to recognize that not everyone can be an effective humorous speaker. It takes a good sense of timing. There is nothing more embarrassing than trying to be funny but failing; it will make both you and your listeners uncomfortable. As a result, not all after-dinner presentations ought to be humorous. It should be possible to develop other types of speeches—speeches that use mystery, suspense, or adventure, for example—as effective ways of entertaining an audience.

For a sample of an after-dinner speech, read the presentation made by Art Buchwald, the columnist, humorist, and television and movie commentator. (Figure 14.2).

Figure 14.2 Sample After-Dinner Speech

My Fellow Americans,

My name is Art Buchwald and I am in the movie business. It is a great honor to be your speaker this evening. I got a call last week from one of the people involved with this program. He said, "Please don't speak more than twenty minutes."

I was ready to follow orders when I got a call from David [Wolper, the person to whom the tribute was being made] who said, "Look, if you're going to talk about me take as long as you want."

This is the one thousand two hundred and thirty-third dinner where we've paid tribute to David Wolper. As a matter of fact, you get 10,000 miles on your frequent flyer account if you attend a David Wolper Dinner.

I don't plan this evening to point out what a fine and revered family man David Wolper really is. That will be done next week at the dinner honoring David given by the National Conference of Christians and Jews.

And I do not intend to tell you what David has done for race relations in the country. You will hear more about that next month when David is honored by the Malibu Anti-Defamation League.

And it is not my role this evening to tell you what a great and wonderful filmmaker David Wolper really is—David will tell you that later.

This evening I will tell you about USC, where David and I both went to school. I first met David in front of the Student Union when he was selling tables for a dinner he was giving himself to celebrate his getting a "C" in freshman English. We hit it off immediately. David scalped tickets for the gridiron games—and I took the English tests for the football team. I did pretty good until a tackle complained that I had gotten him a "D" in Shakespeare and was hurting his chances of getting into medical school.

Figure 14.2 Continued

I was the editor of the humor magazine *The Wampus* and David became my business manager. David was in charge of the magazine's money and I should have learned a lesson from him which would have saved me a lot of trouble. David always insisted on taking the gross profits for himself and giving me the net. After we left school in 1948 David took all the gross from *The Wampus* and bought a movie company. I took my net and bought a map of the movie stars' homes.

I went to Paris to make my career and David chose to stay in Hollywood. I could tell you how David took the fledgling Flamingo Films and turned it into one of the great tax shelters of all time. But, if you attend the City of Hope Prayer Breakfast for David next Tuesday, you will get a much more detailed picture of that part of his life.

Also, I wish to announce there will be a David Wolper cookout on June 1st at the John the Baptist Savings and Loan in San Marino with the money going for victims who had money invested in Drexel Burnham.

Who is David Wolper and why do we keep honoring him with dinners? He is an artist who has made pictures about presidents, spacemen, and just ordinary people like Ronald Reagan and Gerry Ford.

Needless to say, David's great triumph was Roots. The story of how Wolper acquired that property is part of this nation's history. I was going to tell it at the Night of a Thousand Stars honoring David Wolper in Ventura, but I'll tell it to you tonight instead.

Some years ago Wolper was at the National Archives in Washington hoping to find a hot property in the public domain, so he wouldn't have to pay for it, when he heard a man in the next cubicle mumbling, "And the first one from our family to come to this country was the African. His name was Kunte Kinte and he called the river Kamby Bolongo. He was captured when he went into the woods to make a drum—and he later married Bell—and their child was a girl named Kizzy."

Wolper said, "What on earth are you doing?"

The man replied, "I am looking for my roots. I can only trace them back as far as a slave ship in Annapolis. If I could find out where the Kamby Bolongo River is I could sell my book to the Literary Guild."

"No sweat," David said, "The Kamby Bolongo River is in Gambia."

"How do you know that?"

"That's the first thing we learned at USC."

"If you're right," the man said, excitedly, "I'll sell you the TV rights to my story."

"I know I'm right," David replied. "My uncle comes from there."

The rest is history. Alex Haley's chance meeting with David Wolper, a USC alumnus, was serendipity because the University of Southern California is the only school in the nation that has made the study of the Kamby Bolongo River a required course.

After *Roots*, David decided to try something different. He was asked by Peter Ueberroth to put on the show for the Olympics in Los Angeles. Although you saw a great show, Wolper's original ending fell through. As a finale he wanted to have Rafer Johnson take the Olympic torch and set Michael Jackson's hair on fire. Jackson was willing to do it, but he wanted to be paid for it, and David said, "I've never paid for anything in my life."

After the Olympics, David went on to launch the Statue of Liberty festival. How could David Wolper afford to devote so much time to public service? How could he give so much to charity? It's quite simple. Throughout his entire career, David has always taken the gross and given everyone else the net. That's why the Hollywood accountants are honoring him at a dinner tomorrow night.

Source: Speech presented by Art Buchwald at a roast for David Wolper, May 2, 1990. Reprinted with permission of the speaker.

When Preparing to Use a Joke

If you're going to include a joke in your next speech, you might want to consider these suggestions from Lilly Walters, executive director of an international speakers bureau:

- Be sure to memorize the punch line.

- Practice the story and see if you can cut it in half.

- Use the story only to make a point that you want people to remember. Be sure the story relates to the point you're trying to make. If it doesn't provoke laughter, the point will still be made.

- Wait for the laugh. It takes the audience longer than you to process a joke. You know the punch line.

Some comments you might want to make if the story bombs:

- "That was a joke designed to get a silent laugh—and it worked." (Roger Langley)

- Look at someone in the audience whom everyone else knows and say: "_____, that's the last time I use your material!" Be sure you clear this with the person ahead of time.

Source: *Communication Briefings*, as adapted from *What to Say When You're Dying on the Platform*, by Lilly Walters, McGraw-Hill Inc., 1221 Avenue of the Americas, New York, NY 10020.

14.9 Sermons

Religious services typically include some form of **homiletics**, or **sermonizing**, presented by a member of the clergy or of the congregation. An effective sermon has several characteristics: (1) unity, a sense of coherence around a theme; (2) memory, recalling the traditional beliefs of the religious community; (3) recognition, to enable members of the congregation to affirm their own faith; (4) identification, a sense of familiarity and relevance for the listeners; (5) anticipation, to sustain listener attention; and (6) intimacy, to create a personal relationship between the speaker and the listener.[11]

A sermon is usually placed in the context of some scriptural reference and developed to extend a religious thesis for the listeners in the congregation. Sermons usually center on a passage from a sacred text or on a moral or ethical issue and follow the basic structure of any informative or persuasive speech, with emphasis on statements that are backed up with supporting material. One of the most common negative perceptions about sermons is that they are too long, but sermons need not be long to be effective. Both ordained and lay ministers are increasingly developing a conversational style in the preparation and presentation of sermons.

On the occasion of her niece's bat mitzvah (a ceremony in which a girl, on her 13th birthday, dedicates herself to being an adult member of the Jewish faith), a speaker connected the message of the Torah to the congregation at both the personal and the group level by stating:

> The message of Haazinu is a communal and national one. It serves as a paradigm for Jewish history, and roots a sense of Jewishness in a recognition that Jews are not just a community of faith, but a people with a past. But, can we

make some personal connections to Haazinu as well?. . . Perhaps like the children of Israel on the edge of the Jordan, a rite of passage like this [the bat mitzvah] closes the pages of one chapter of a life and inexorably leads to the next. . . .Each stage has its own pitfalls and responsibilities. In order to come to terms with oneself, one should listen to and understand the voices from the past which root you in the present and guide you to the future. Those voices can perhaps help in keeping you from becoming involved with the "new" gods, but instead anchor you to that which has endured for generations.[12]

14.10 Prayers

In addition to presenting sermons, members of a congregation may be called upon to present **prayers**—statements of faith and concern addressed to the congregation's God. A prayer should be worshipful, setting the proper tone and mood and also expressing the joy or the concern that may be at the center of the religious occasion. Though some presenters use prayers written by others, some people prefer to develop their own. The typical prayer opens with an address to God and concludes with a meditation that expresses thoughts that the listeners share. A well-presented prayer can be a true work of art, requiring all the speaker's resources to fashion an eloquent call to worship.

The late Mother Teresa, noted for her selflessness, afforded an example of a simple but meaningful prayer when she said:

> Dearest Lord, may I see you today and every day in the person of your sick, and whilst nursing them minister unto you. Though you hide yourself behind the unattractive disguise of the irritable, the exacting, the unreasonable, may I still recognize you. . . . Lord, give me this seeing faith, then my work will never be monotonous. I will ever find joy in humoring the fancies and gratifying the wishes of all poor sufferers. . . . Sweetest Lord, make me appreciative of the dignity of my high vocation, and its many responsibilities. Never permit me to disgrace it by giving way to coldness, unkindness, or impatience. . . . Lord, increase my faith, bless my efforts and work, now and for evermore.[13]

14.11 Commemorative Speeches

Commemorative speeches are presented to recognize a person or an event. These types of speeches offer brief, memorable remarks about the focus of the commemoration and draw some type of point for the individual listeners.

A **tribute** should stress the reasons the recipient is being honored and point out the recipient's accomplishments. Its function is "to deepen the appreciation and respect of the listeners for the person, persons, event, institution, or monument" and to "impress them with the worth of the ones to whom you pay tribute."[14] It is tempting in a tribute to become overly sentimental and to exaggerate the praise. Keep in mind that the listeners are in attendance because they understand the need to honor the recipient, so the focus of the speech should be on offering honor and drawing some point from it.

A **eulogy** is a tribute presented in recognition of an individual who has died. One of the most moving eulogies in contemporary history was President Ronald Reagan's televised speech commemorating the crew of the space shuttle *Challenger*, which exploded on January 28, 1986, killing all aboard. Televised news reports of the explosion had captured the world's attention throughout the day, but Reagan's speechwriter used her rhetorical skill to develop an eloquent tribute to the crew and their pioneering efforts:

> I know it's hard to understand, but sometimes painful things like this happen. It's all part of the process of exploration and discovery. It's all part of taking a chance and expanding man's horizons. The future doesn't belong to the fainthearted. It belongs to the brave. The *Challenger* crew was pulling us into the future, and we'll continue to follow them. . . . The crew of the space shuttle *Challenger* honored us by the manner in which they lived their lives. We will never forget them nor the last time we saw them—this morning—as they prepared for their journey and waved good-bye, and slipped the surly bonds of Earth to touch the face of God.[15]

Tributes may also commemorate a beginning. The keynote speech, inaugural address, and commencement address are all types of tributes and are intended to motivate listeners in some way. The key to effective speeches of this type is to identify the appropriate appeals for the intended listeners so that they are sufficiently involved in and responsive to your ideas.

A **keynote speech** usually serves as the focus of a conference or convention and typically is presented early in the proceedings to function as the "rallying cry" for those involved. The keynote speaker sets the tone for the entire conference, so it is important to target the appeals and present the speech effectively. Political conventions, for example, normally start with a keynote speech that informs the delegates and the television audience of the party's philosophy.

As the keynote speaker for the American Institutes of Chemical Engineers meeting in Houston, the chief executive officer of Occidental Petro-

Noted athletes, such as Olympic Gold Medalist Dominique Dawes, are often called upon to give motivational speeches to inspire others to achieve their goals.

leum Corporation spoke about the need for U.S. industry to create not only environmental awareness but also environmental literacy through increased cooperation:

> As we look for environmental solutions in the 1990s we're going to be challenged as never before to have better dialogue among industries. Industry cooperation, both horizontally and vertically, will be necessary to undertake the technological remedies needed to overcome formidable environmental problems. Look at the synergy that is taking place between the automotive, petroleum and chemical industries in the search for cleaner burning fuels. This is an excellent example of the type of cooperation I'm talking about.[16]

An **inaugural speech**, given when a new officeholder assumes responsibilities, is also designed to set the tone for new beginnings. A good inaugural speech must establish the transition from the old to the new and highlight expectations that accompany that transition.

Sharon Pratt Kelly presented a stirring inaugural when she assumed the office of mayor of Washington, D.C. stressing that her motto—"Yes We Will!"—should be considered more than a theme for a day: "It is an attitude and an ethic we must embrace to move our city beyond the troubles of drugs and crime, racial polarization and mounting financial problems."[17] Mayor Kelly characterized her transition to office in the sense of "a time and a season for everything and everyone":

> So it is with our great city. In their time and in their season, Commissioner John Duncan, Mayor Walter Washington and Marion Barry, each in his own way, made a telling contribution to the progress and growth of our community. Now, we begin a new time; a new season of coming together. A season where the international city, the federal city, the many neighborhoods, the many constituents, move to become one. For in this togetherness we have the power to meet the staggering challenges we face and do more to allow this city to become all of what she was meant to be—a great cosmopolitan community—a beacon for a 21st century America.[18]

A **commencement address** commemorates old events and new beginnings for members of a graduating class. The traditional commencement speech offers praise for members of the graduating class and encourages them to greet their future. The speech is difficult to present, for it must be targeted both to graduates and to families and friends who are attending the ceremony. A commencement speech, while usually the central point of the ceremony, is not really the focus; the awarding of the degrees is the main purpose for all in attendance.

Joel Conarroe, president of the Guggenheim Foundation, speaking at a commencement ceremony at the University of Maryland, used his own address to poke fun at the traditional format of a commencement speech:

> First, he (or she) should say something funny so as to win over the graduates and their by now penniless parents. Second, he is supposed to say something agreeable about the host institution, then, third, offer some advice, and in so doing work in an anecdote about his own college years. Fourth, he should say something challenging. And finally, he is required to quote from somebody who is smarter than he, thus ending the talk on an elevated note that leaves everyone not only pleased that it's over but also impressed by his reading habits.[19]

A sample commencement speech is presented in Figure 14.3.

Figure 14.3 Sample Commencement Speech

Eric Berko, a student at Elyria (Ohio) High School, presented this commencement speech, which stressed his perceptions of the past, present, and future of his classmates:

Looking In, Looking Out: The Legacy of Us All

I stood looking in through the window. It was the afternoon after our senior prom and a group of us had gone to Put-in-Bay for some fun in the sun. Unfortunately, it rained most of that day. Everyone else was really tired, but for some reason I wasn't. I wandered outside into the gentle mist, walked around, came back to the cottage, and looked in through the window. Sleeping bodies littered the floor. They seemed content to remember the great prom night we had all experienced. I came back inside and looked out the same window. My breath fogged up the pane and this, added to the rain gently running down the window, made the scene outside rather blurry and hard to see.

That after-prom experience forms the basis for what I'd like to share with you today. Looking inside the house, seeing the people, and remembering the experiences we've had, was not difficult. It is symbolic of our past. The four years of high school that we've shared seem so clear. This is especially true today when the experiences all come together. High school has brought us many things, including many memories. Some of these will be remembered with joy, and others we will wish to forget. High school has also provided us with knowledge. But we have gained more than just book knowledge—we have gained more than facts and figures, names of famous people, and dates of important events. We have gained values, life skills, and maybe most significantly, meaningful relationships.

The values that we've gained will help us throughout our lives. You may remember a bit of sage advice given to us by one of our English teachers: "Hard work guarantees nothing, but the lack of it does." It's a motto that, in reality, teaches us all that we are responsible for our own destiny, and if we fail to succeed, it will probably be from a lack of desire to succeed, and a lack of effort on our part. And then there's a science teacher's chemically inspired battle cry, "You can't mix apples and oranges together, because all you get is fruit salad." We are responsible to make sure that what we do, and the way in which we do it, has a clear purpose. If not, the result will be a lack of unity.

During the past four years, through participating in extracurricular activities, in school functions, and the requirement of going to classes, we have gained lifelong skills. Our class has had a series of successes that have been the direct result of our working together and striving for excellence. Whether it was winning the spirit week competitions, the excellence of the senior-led athletic teams, the participation in the activities of the music department, the Academic Challenge team's success, or the effort that resulted in selection to such organizations as the National Honor Society and Thespians, we have gained the knowledge of working together. Without this spirit of cooperation, we could not and would not have been able to succeed. There's a song in the movie *Fame* that says, "We're always proving who we are, always reaching for that rising star to guide me far and shine me home, out here on my own." Often, this could have been considered the motto of our class.

From the responsibilities we've assumed as leaders of the various school clubs and organizations, we have learned the importance of setting goals and following through on our responsibilities. These patterns will hopefully continue with us throughout our lives. Even those who assumed the responsibility for playing practical jokes, thus making entrance into school each morning a challenging and often frustrating experience, have added to our understanding of who and what we are. How many of you have heard your

Figure 14.3 Continued

name called by the phantom voices, or looked for the turtle tracks on the ceilings, or leaned down to tie your socks? Ridiculous? . . . maybe. A learning experience? Of course. The practical jokers pulled it off each and every day with dedication and creativity—qualities that people who succeed in life carry with them and exercise.

And then there were classes. How often did each of us feel that these were the less important part of school? As Mark Twain put it, "I have never let schooling interfere with my education." The last-minute cramming for exams, getting balled out by the teachers for doing our homework for the next class in the class right before, and the headaches and sore throats that magically appeared the day term papers were due all seem like normal parts of everyday life. Through these experiences we *have* learned. We have learned the facts and figures; we have learned the names of famous people; we have learned the important dates in our history; and, most important, we've hopefully learned to be responsible human beings. We've learned that "the world steps aside to let any person pass if that person knows where he or she is going."

Look around you. You are surrounded with some of the most important people in your life. When you think back years from now, the most significant thing you will remember about your high school years won't be an event or a class, it will probably be the people with whom you shared these experiences. It could be the friend you turned to when things weren't going right, or the person who helped you when you had troubles with your parents, or the person who sat next to you in class and comforted you when a teacher unfairly picked on you. Most likely it will be the people who acted as your bridge over troubled waters. Who gave you the feeling that,

I'm on your side, when times get rough
And friends just can't be found
Like a bridge over troubled water
I will lay me down.
I will comfort you.
I'll take your part.
When darkness comes
And pain is all around
Like a bridge over troubled water
I will ease your mind.

Thinking back now about that day at the cottage, I realize that trying to look out through the steam-covered window was a lot more difficult than looking in. It's the future, the uncertain, the unknown. It's blurred. It's scary. For the first time in many of our lives, our paths are not clearly marked for us. The decisions we make will affect our lives forever. Our class poet, Laurie Reinker, expressed this beautifully when she wrote,

Now we've reached the Crossroads,
Many ways from which to choose.
It is a time to make decisions
Which will help us win or lose.
The time has come to take the chance,
We've earned through work and care,
To reach our goals, to meet our needs,
To climb the final stair.

When we reach that final stair, then you and I, the members of the Elyria High School class of 1984, will truly be able to find a way to use the

Figure 14.3 Continued

values, skills, relationships, and knowledge that we've gained in high school to make the window clear, so that our future will be as bright as our past.

> *I got faith in our generation*
> *Let's stick together and futurize our attitudes*
> *I ain't looking to fight but I know with determination we can challenge the*
> *schemers who cheat all the rules*
> *If we take pride*
> *A fair shot here for me and for you*
> *Knowing that we can't lose.*

If we succeed, then we will leave a legacy of us all.

(The excerpt from "Bridge Over Troubled Water," by Paul Simon. Copyright © 1969 by Paul Simon. Poem by Laurie Reinker. Used by permission of the authors.)

Ceremonial speeches are an important part of the ritual of human life. A memorable speech can be exactly the right touch needed for any special event. As a result, speakers should take their ceremonial role seriously and spend time preparing the most effective presentation possible.

14.12 Listening to Appreciate

A school graduation ceremony just wouldn't be the same without a commencement speaker. But have you attended a speech on such an occasion and

To truly appreciate a ceremonial speech, the good listener will tune in to the speaker.

not been able to recall what the speaker said? What is a church or synagogue service without a sermon, or a funeral without a eulogy? But, again, have you left those occasions without being able to indicate the theme or the highlights of the presentation? Being a receiver of ceremonial speeches generally takes the form of listening at the appreciative level.

Many people are appreciative listeners. The popularity of poetry readings, books on tape, authors' book signings, and networks like CNN which feature the spoken word, reflect the interest that many people have in language and style. As a result, we can enjoy a speaker's use of language as the centerpiece of the message and gain from the experience. This type of listening is not the same as trying to remember the facts of a lecture or a briefing on how to operate the new computer system.

To truly appreciate a ceremonial speech, the good listener will tune in to what the speaker is doing with the language and allow that language to be the focus of attention. Further, you need to allow the language to have its emotional impact. Use your empathy to understand where the speaker is coming from and what effect he or she is attempting to achieve. Listening appreciatively is listening to the music of the language. It "requires that we fasten our whole attention upon the sounds as they come floating through the air; that we observe the patterns' key form, and respond to the thought and feeling out of which those patterns have emerged."[20]

A speaker who uses eloquent language may very well create a compelling speech that can be appreciated for the musical nature of the language style. Often eloquent language becomes the by-words of a generation or a movement. Phrases such as "Ask not what your country can do for you, ask what you can do for your country," the epic phrase from John F. Kennedy's inauguration speech; or "We have nothing to fear but fear itself," from Franklin Delano Roosevelt's first inaugural address, are classical examples of eloquent language. The Reverend Martin Luther King, Jr., was considered a master of turning the eloquent phrase. Many consider this talent the key to his success in ascending to leadership in the civil rights movement. His rhythm, tone, and color of the words created a sense of beauty of language that had a poetic effect on his listeners. Consider for example, his often quoted "I Had a Dream" speech:

> So let freedom ring from the prodigious hilltops of New Hampshire.
>
> Let freedom ring from the mighty mountains of New York.
>
> Let freedom ring from the heightening Alleghenies of Pennsylvania!
>
> Let freedom ring from the snowcapped Rockies of Colorado!
>
> Let freedom ring from the curvaceous peaks of California!
>
> But not only that; let freedom ring from the Stone Mountain of Georgia!
>
> Let freedom ring from every hill and mole hill of Mississippi.
>
> From every mountainside, let freedom ring.[21]

In listening appreciatively, allow yourself to be taken in by the words. This is not a critical or a comprehensive experience—you don't have to evaluate or be on guard. Just listen for the language, the effect of the presentation, the feelings that are invoked in you.

Do not let your public communication guard down, however. Be aware that some ceremonial speakers use their time at the podium to switch purposes and move from an appreciative listening experience to an attempt at persuasion. As with all types of speeches, if you find that the speaker is using the language to manipulate you to act as he or she desires, or to take an action of some type, switch to a different listening mode. Being a wise public communicator listener carries with it responsibility to recognize and withstand manipulation.

Profile: Chris Zorich, NFL Player and Motivational Speaker

As a professional football player, Washington Redskin Defensive Tackle Chris Zorich has been recognized for his fierce determination and commitment on the playing field. Raised in Chicago by his single mother, Zorich earned a football scholarship to the University of Notre Dame, where he won three consecutive All-American titles. He has earned numerous honors since he began his professional career including a place on John Madden's (Fox-TV color analyst) "10th Anniversary All Madden Team," a distinction presented to players who give "150% on the playing field." Zorich's accomplishments, though, go far beyond his football career. In fact, he has contributed so much through his nonprofit charity, the Chris Zorich Foundation, that in 1995 he was named one of USA Weekend's "Most Caring Athletes."

It was through this charitable foundation, which awards scholarships, runs youth programs, and aids impoverished families in the Chicago area, and his association with professional sports that "people began calling with requests for speaking engagements." Now, speaking approximately three times each month at conventions, banquets, conferences, and schools, he is able to motivate business professionals and students by addressing issues such as "teamwork, [the] importance of community involvement, [and] success beyond professional aspirations."

Zorich has never taken formal public speaking classes but, he says, "While at Notre Dame a professional speaking coach visited and I attended some of her sessions. As I have a stuttering problem, it really helped a lot [and] we still keep in touch." Experience has also been a large factor in his success as a speaker. Zorich has observed that over the years he has loosened up his approach. This has led to more animation in his speeches and an improvement in the delivery of his ideas.

Zorich believes that there are three crucial elements of an effective speech:

- Stay focused on your theme—It is important to avoid getting sidetracked.

- Keep your speech concise—If you speak for too long the audience will lose interest.

- Make your opening and closing remarks memorable.

By observing these rules, Chris Zorich is able to inspire and motivate audiences of all ages to get involved and give back to their community. For this reason he is a speaker in demand and, as a Chicago middle school teacher says, "a positive role model for the impressionable young people of today."

Summary

This chapter investigated the types and formats of ceremonial speeches. The major ideas presented were:

♦ *There are many types of ceremonial speeches: introductions, welcomes, farewells, award presentations, acceptances, thank-yous, toasts, after-dinner speeches, sermons, prayers, and commemorative speeches such as tributes, eulogies, keynotes, inaugurals, and commencement speeches.*

♦ *Ceremonial presentations have three functions: to explain a social world to listeners, to display the speaker's eloquence, and to shape and share community ideals.*

♦ *Public speakers should be able to develop and present such speeches, for they can be part of both career and social responsibilities.*

♦ *When preparing a speech for a special occasion, analyze the expected audience carefully and adapt the speech specifically to those particular listeners.*

♦ *A speech of introduction precedes a public presentation.*

♦ *A speech of welcome is in order if you are called on to provide greetings to a visitor to your organization, to new members, or to make your own remarks on joining a group.*

♦ *An award presentation is a commendation to a recipient of a citation or recognition.*

♦ *In a farewell speech you may say good-bye as you move on to another position or retire, or extend your group's farewell to a departing member.*

♦ *A speech of acceptance normally follows an award presentation, an election victory, or a success of some kind.*

♦ *The speech of thank-you is your acknowledgment of services or aid given to you by others. It should include a tribute to those being recognized.*

♦ *The toast is a recognition or tribute to a person or a group, in which a short speech is given and some liquid sipped as a means of acknowledging the recipient.*

♦ *The after-dinner speech is frequently used at luncheons, dinners, and banquets. Its purpose is to provide an entertaining or compelling message on a theme.*

♦ *The characteristics of an effective sermon are unity, memory, recognition, identification, anticipation, and intimacy.*

♦ *Prayers are statements of faith and concern addressed to the congregation's God.*

♦ *The purpose of a tribute is to deepen the appreciation and respect of the listeners for the person, persons, event, institution, or monument.*

♦ *A eulogy is a tribute presented in recognition of an individual who has died.*

♦ *A keynote speech usually serves as the central point of a conference or convention and typically is presented early in the proceedings to function as the "rallying cry" for those involved.*

♦ *An inaugural speech, given when a new officeholder assumes responsibilities, is designed to set the tone for new beginnings.*

♦ *A commencement address commemorates old experiences and new beginnings for members of a graduating class.*

♦ *Being a receiver of ceremonial speeches, generally, takes the form of listening at the appreciative level.*

Key Terms

ceremonial speeches   Speech of introduction
speech of welcome   farewell speech
award presentation   speech of acceptance
speech of thank-you   toast
after-dinner speech   homiletics
sermonizing   prayers
commemorative speeches   tribute
eulogy   keynote speech
inaugural speech   commencement address

Learn by Doing

1. Secure the text of or a video- or audiotape of a ceremonial event. Analyze the style of the speech. Ceremonial presentations may be obtained by researching in professional journals or newspapers, or asking sources such as religious leaders and politicians for copies of presentations they have made.

2. Select a type of ceremonial speech and prepare it for presentation in class.

3. Find a copy of a famous presidential inaugural speech. Analyze the speech to determine what characteristics made this such a memorable speech.

4. Your instructor will assign you the name of a person in your class whom you will later be introducing as a speaker. Interview that person and collect all the information you will need to prepare a speech of introduction (topic of the speech, some background information on the speaker, why the speaker chose the topic, the qualifications of the speaker to present a speech and so on). On the appointed day, introduce your partner.

Endnotes

1. Celeste Michelle Condit, "The Functions of Epideictic: The Boston Massacre Orations as Exemplar," *Communication Quarterly*, 33, no. 4 (Fall 1985), pp. 284–300.

2. From text of speech by Nannerl Keohane, President of Wellesley College, given at Commencement Ceremonies of Wellesley College, Wellesley, Mass., June 1, 1990. Reprinted by permission of the author.

3. Edmund S. Muskie, speech to U.S. Department of State employees, Washington, D.C., May 9, 1980. Department of State Press Copy of Remarks.

4. Mark Asher and Dave Sheinin, "NBA Offers Its Prayers to a Friend," *Washington Post*, November 8, 1991.

5. George Bush, Presentation Ceremony for the National Medals of Sciences and Technology, Washington, D.C., September 16, 1991. Reprinted in *Weekly Compilation of Presidential Documents*, 27 (September 23, 1991), Washington, D.C.: Office of the Federal Register, National Archives and Records Administration, pp. 1277–1288.

6. © Copyright Academy of Motion Picture Arts and Sciences, 1987. Reprinted with permission.

7. H. Norman Schwarzkopf, "Operation Desert Storm," *Vital Speeches of the Day* 57, June 1, 1991, p. 482.

8. Rudy Maxa, "Here's to the Toast," *The Washingtonian*, September 1986, p. 159.

9. Ronald Reagan, luncheon toast at the Italian Embassy, Washington, D.C., October 12, 1983. Reprinted in *Weekly Compilation of Presidential Documents*, 19 (October 17, 1983), Washington, D.C.: Office of the Federal Register, National Archives and Records Administration, p. 1421.

10. Bob Orben, "How to Spice Up Those Dull Speeches," *Current Comedy Newsletter*, 440 (February 19, 1981), p. 4.

11. Fred B. Craddock, *Preaching* (Nashville: Abingdon Press, 1985), Chapter 8.

12. From sermon presented by Dr. Hasia Diner at the Bat Mitzvah of Rebecca Fink. Used by permission of the author.

13. Daily Prayer of Mother Teresa, from *Morning, Noon and Night*, edited by Rev'd. John Carden (London: The Church Missionary Society). Reprinted with permission.

14. Robert G. King, *Forms of Public Address* (Indianapolis: Bobbs-Merrill, 1969), pp. 64–65.

15. Ronald Reagan, text of speech, January 28, 1986. Reprinted in *Weekly Compilation of Presidential Documents*, 22 (February 3, 1986), Washington, D.C.: Office of the Federal Register, National Archives and Records Administration, pp. 104–105. For insight into the background and development of this speech, see Peggy Noonan, *What I Saw at the Revolution* (New York: Random House, 1990), Chapter 14.

16. Ray R. Irani, "Environmental Literacy," *Vital Speeches of the Day* 57, (June 15, 1991), p. 543.

17. Sharon Pratt Kelly, "Inaugural Address," Washington, D.C., January 2, 1991. Text of speech, p. 2.

18. Kelly, p. 1.

19. From "Books and the Good Life," by Joel Conarroe, presented at the Commencement Exercises of the University of Maryland, May 25, 1989. Used by permission.

20. J. Machlis, *The Enjoyment of Music* (New York: Norton), p. 3.

21. Martin Luther King, Jr., "I Have a Dream," Washington, D.C., August 28, 1963, audio recording.

Glossary

After-dinner speeches are used at luncheons, dinners, and banquets to provide an entertaining or a compelling message on a theme.

Assignment of meaning occurs when a listener receives a stimulus, processes it, and mentally puts the stimulus into some predetermined category.

Attention represents the focus on a specific stimulus that is selected from all the stimuli we receive at any given moment; at this point, all other stimuli recede in our consciousness so that we can concentrate on a specific word or visual symbol.

Attention devices are illustrations, specific instances, expositions, statistics, analogies, testimony, and humor that a speaker uses to focus the listener's concentration on one stimulus over all others in the environment.

Attention span is the focusing that occurs in an individual's short-term memory. The capacity of the short-term memory to gain and retain information is about 60 seconds.

Attitudes are predispositions to respond. They are positive or negative expectations.

Audience analysis is the act of collecting the necessary information about the audience so that the speaker can adapt the speech to the needs and interests of the audience; prior analysis for a speech.

Audio aids such as records, tape recordings, and other sound duplication mechanisms used to demonstrate a point accurately to speech listeners.

Audiovisual aids such as films, videotapes, and audiotapes combined with slide shows mix sight and sound, used to demonstrate a point accurately to speech listeners.

Awards presentations are given when an individual or a group achieves some distinction.

Body of a speech develops the major points of the speech and subpoints that pertain to the speaker's central idea.

Bracketing is a technique used in research recording in which as ideas are written down, brackets are put around them to remind the researcher that the ideas are important. It is also used in listening to put "brackets" around competing stimuli so that you can mentally set them aside for the moment in order to focus on the message being presented.

Broad development for a speech is formatting a speech by investigating several ideas rather than a single idea.

Case method of organization is less complex than the partitioning and unfolding methods because the speaker discusses the central idea without breaking it into subpoints in the body.

Categorical syllogism is a deductive argument that contains two premises and a conclusion.

Causal arrangement for a speech is the process of showing how one event made another event happen; how a cause (the first event) led to an effect (the second event).

Ceremonial speeches special types of short speeches on various social or ceremonial occasions explain a social world to listeners, display the speaker's eloquence, and shape and share community ideals.

Central idea of a speech explicitly reveals the goal of the speech and implies what type of response the speaker wants from listeners.

Channel is the sensory medium that is used to convey a message from a sender to a receiver; the channels are speaking, hearing, seeing, smelling, tasting, and touching.

Chronological or time arrangement for a speech orders information from a beginning point to an ending one, with all the steps developed in numerical or time sequence.

Chunking takes place when a speaker or listener groups things according to their common description and then puts the names of each division together.

Circular response are the feedback responses that audience members provide back to the speaker. They set up a chain reaction as the speaker adjusts to the audience's feedback.

Clarity is a factor of speaker style that is identified as clearness; the selection of words and phrases that communicate the speaker's intent to be understood by listeners.

Clincher of a speech is used to make a final appeal to the audience and to ensure that they remember your message.

Code is the appropriate verbal and/or nonverbal language with which to symbolize a message.

Coercion is influence that leaves the listener no desirable alternative but to adopt the change of mental or physical behavior the speaker proposes.

Cognitive dissonance is the mental discomfort that occurs when a listener accepts an action or an idea that does not coincide with previously held attitudes.

Colorfulness is language that helps the listener visualize the speaker's message. A good speaker tries to create word pictures that enhance the listening experience.

Commemorative speeches are presented to recognize a person or an event.

Commencement addresses commemorate old events and new beginnings for members of a graduating class.

Communication transaction is the simultaneous sending and receiving of messages; a description of what truly occurs when speakers and listeners communicate.

Comparative advantage reasoning takes place when the speaker begins by stating the possible solutions, then demonstrates how the proposal is the most workable (how it can solve the problem), the most desirable (why it does not cause any greater problems), and the most practical (how it can be put into operation).   ❖ ❖ ❖ ❖

Comparison-contrast arrangement for a speech organizes the body of a speech by discussing both the similarities and the differences of two or more things.

Comparison method for a speech organizes the body of a speech by describing how two or more things are alike.

Competence a component of credibility, refers to the wisdom, authority, and knowledge a speaker demonstrates.

Comprehension level of listening is the listening stage at which the listener recognizes and retains information.

Computer output microfiche (COM) is the library's electronic computer catalogue which lists sources, such as books, under the title, the author's name, or the general subject.

Computer-based retrieval system allows a researcher to compile a bibliography or a set of facts relevant to a specific topic.

Computerized presentation graphics such as *PowerPoint, Astound,* and *Action*, incorporate word processing, outlining, graphs, tables, logos, clip art, illustrations, photography, video images, audio clips, and Internet connectivity; used to develop images for use during a speech which can be projected directly from a computer, printed on transparencies for use on an overhead projector, made into hard copy for use with an opaque project, or to produce slides.

Conciseness is a factor of speaker style which encompasses the use of language that is specific and to the point.

Conclusion of a speech is the section of the presentation in which a summary restates the major points of the speech and a clincher leaves a final message of intent.

Concrete supporting materials are illustrations, specific instances, expositions, statistics, analogies, testimony, and humor used in a speech which are specific rather than general or abstract.

Conditional arguments set up an if/then proposition; in this pattern of argument, there are two conditions, one of which necessarily follows from the other.

Conflict techniques are attention devices such as illustrations, specific instances, expositions, statistics, analogies, testimony, and humor that illustrate strife and confrontation.

Contrast method for a speech organizes the body of a speech by describing how two or more things are different.

Cornell System of Notetaking a technique in which the page is divided in half. On one side, jot the speaker's main points as they are presented and on the other side, the speaker's supporting ideas as they develop the main points; this creates a flow chart of the information as it unfolds.

Cough meter the sounds a speaker hears from a disinterested audience as the people clear their throats, cough, and become restless.

Critical level of listening is the listening stage at which the listener comprehends and evaluates the message that has been received; a critical listener assesses the arguments and the appeals in a message and then decides whether to accept or to reject them.

Critical reasoning takes place when the speaker establishes criteria and then matches the solutions with the criteria.

Critical thinking is the thinking process that is reasonable; thinking that is focused on deciding what to believe and do.

Cultural noise occurs because the sender or receiver has a set of preconceived, group attitudes that individuals from differing nationalities, races, and genders have and that limits their openness to the ideas or beliefs of those from other cultures; it often prevents a receiver from dealing objectively with a message.

Culture consists of those individuals who have a shared system of interpretation.

Cutaways are models used to supplement the oral part of a presentation that show the inside of an object, which an audience would otherwise have to imagine.

Charts are visual representations of statistical data that give information in tabular or diagrammatic form.

Deductive arguments are based on logical necessity; if one accepts the premise of the deductive argument—the proposition that is the basis of the argument—then one must also accept its conclusion.

Demographics are characteristics of audience members, such as their age, gender, and interests.

Developing outline expands the planning outline by adding the details that will flesh out the speech.

Dilemmas of principles centers on how, in various situations, a person may be torn between conflicting moral obligations that cannot be fulfilled at the same time.

Discrimination level of listening is the listening stage at which the listener distinguishes auditory and visual stimuli.

Disjunctive argument is an either/or argument in which true alternatives are established.

Dynamics centers on the fact that communication is continuous and ongoing.

Dynamism the projection of a vigorous, concerned, powerful image by a speaker.

Electronic catalogues such as computer output microfiche, are accessed through on-line computers to search for library resources.

Enthymeme is a special form of deductive syllogism in which one premise is not directly stated because the speaker and listener both accept the premise.

Environment is the context, place, or setting in which the speech occurs; where the speaker is and who is there affects a message.

Environmental noise is an outside interference that prevents the listener from receiving the message.

Esteem needs the fourth level in Maslow's Theory of Hierarchy of Needs, involves both self-esteem (desire for achievement and mastery) and esteem from others (desire for reputation and prestige).

Ethical public speakers are generally defined as those who conform to the moral standards the society establishes for its communicators.

Ethical value system forms the basis for a person's decision making and for a personal understanding of why a person will or will not behave in a certain way.

Ethics are the values that have been instilled in a person; they have been knowingly or unknowingly accepted and form the basis for how the individual acts, and dictate how a person determines right from wrong.

Ethos is speaker credibility.

Eulogy is a tribute presented in recognition of an individual who has died.

Evidence the most persuasive form of supporting material, includes testimony from experts, statistics, and specific instances.

Evidence in critical thinking is all the means by which any alleged matter of facts is established or disproved; includes testimony, records, documents, and objects that assist in building a logical case.

Expectancy restructuring is based on the idea that if a person expects to do well, then he or she will do well.

Experts are individuals who through knowledge or skill in a specific field gain respect for his or her opinions or research.

Exposition in a speech gives the background information that allows listeners to understand the material being presented; types of exposition include definitions, historical information, and the speaker's relationship to the topic.

Extemporaneous speaking is a mode in which speakers take time to think about personal information they have that would help develop a well-thought-out speech and, if necessary, do research.

Eye contact is looking into the eyes of your listeners as you speak.

Eye span involves training your eyes to glance down quickly, allowing you to pick out a meaningful phrase and deliver it to the audience.

Fabrication is making up information or guessing at information and making it appear to be true.

Factual illustrations are used in a speech to explain ideas by referring to a real situation or event.

Familiar supporting materials are illustrations, specific instances, expositions, statistics, analogies, testimony, and humor used in a speech which refer to ideas or objects about which the audience already has some knowledge.

Farewell speeches are presentations that say goodbye as people move on to another position or retire.

Faulty analogical reasoning is a fallacy that attempts to prove that one concept is correct because it is comparable to another; however, no analogy is ever truly complete because no two cases, however comparable, are ever identical.

Faulty causal reasoning occurs when a speaker makes an overstated claim that something caused something else.

Feedback is a verbal or nonverbal reaction (or both) to the message, the speaker, the channel, or even the rest of the audience itself.

Feeling-doers those who act on information impulsively, respond well to emotional appeals.

Forecasts are statements that alert the audience to ideas that are coming; transitions that tell the listener what is coming next.

Forecasts of ideas are statements used by a speaker to indicate that a series of ideas will follow, such as "there are three ideas," and "the next point is."

Freedom of expression is the right to present one's views in a public forum.

General American speech the language spoken by well-educated Americans and Canadians of the central, midwestern, and western regions of North America; tends to be the most acceptable of the regional dialects.

Generalization conclusion is a technique in which the speaker examines a number of specific instances and attempts to predict some future occurrence or explain a whole category of instances.

Gestures are hand and body motions and facial expressions.

Goal of a speech is the part of the purpose statement that expresses the expected outcome; the expected goals for a speech are to inform and to persuade.

Group standards are the habits of thinking or the norms of a particular group,

Hasty generalization is a form of reasoning fallacy in which a speaker reaches general conclusions from an insufficient number of instances.

Hearing is a biological activity that involves reception of a message through sensory channels

Homiletics are sermons or speeches at religious services.

Humor the quality of being funny or witty, is a speaking strategy for gaining and holding the audience's attention.

Hypothesis conclusion is the result of a speaker listing evidence in a sequential order that leads the listener to conclude that the inference reached is correct.

Hypothetical illustrations are used in a speech to explain an idea by asking the listener to imagine a situation or a series of events.

Ignoring the issue takes place when the speaker uses irrelevant arguments to obscure the real issue.

Impromptu speaking is a mode of presentation that requires the speaker to organize ideas while speaking because there was very little time for preparation.

Inaugural speech given when a new officeholder assumes responsibilities, is designed to set the tone for new beginnings.

Inciting words are words that trigger strong feelings within a person, either positive or negative.

Individual standards are those attitudes held by certain people within the group who have influence over other members.

Inductive argument is based on probability—what conclusion is most likely to be expected or believed from the available evidence.

Informative briefings are speeches intended to share data and insights among people with common interests.

Informative speaking is discourse that imparts new information, secures understanding, or reinforces accumulated information.

Inoculation strategy suggests that just as people can be protected from disease through immunization, so too can listeners be inhibited from accepting subsequent counterarguments if they are armed with the means to refute them.

Internal summaries are restatements of ideas a speaker uses regarding something just explained such as "and so we have seen that;" they summarize each major point before proceeding to the next major point,

Introduction to a speech has the purpose of gaining the listeners' attention and orienting them to the material that will be presented.

Issue arrangement for a speech centers on the method of development specified in the presentation's purpose statement and the type of issue arrangement used for the overall organization of the speech.

Keynote speech speeches of a conference or convention, presented early in the proceedings, to function as the rallying cry for those in attendance.

Lectures are the formal presentation of material to facilitate learning; an integral part of academic life, they serve as the main vehicle for the presentation of information in almost all subject fields.

Left-brain dominance is a speaker's or listener's tendency to perceive ideas best when they are presented in a logical and structured format; it is characteristic of speakers and listeners who prefer to listen to a lecture rather than be an active participant, require handouts to review the presentation, and favor serious and logical ideas.

Listenable speaker style is the way a speaker presents material that commands audience attention; three important qualities of listenable speaker style are clarity, conciseness, and colorfulness.

Listener sign posts are phrases that tell a listener what is coming next (e.g. "First, I would like to point out . . ." or "A familiar story can illustrate . . .").

Listening involves reception, perception, attention, the assignment of meaning, and response by the listener to a message.

Logos are the logical arguments.

Manuscript mode of delivery is written out and delivered word for word; it provides accurate language, solid organization, and a permanent written record of the speech.

Memorized mode takes place when a speech is written out word for word, committed to memory, and presented.

Message of public communication the speech itself, is composed of verbal and/or nonverbal symbols and supplementary aids, such as visual aids, selected by the speaker to convey his or her ideas.

Method is the process to be employed in developing the goal of a speech. In an informative speech, methods include "by analyzing," "by demonstrating," and "by explaining;" while in a persuasive speech, key words in the purpose statement might include "to accept that," "to attend," or "to join."

Mind mapping is an alternative to using an outline for the extemporaneous mode of presentation, in which the speaker makes a list of all the ideas to be included in the speech, places each major idea in a circle, and then the subpoints are grouped around the major heading circles and connected to the circles with spokes.

Mnemonic devices combine the first letter of a series of words in order to allow for remembering the idea; for example, using the word *HOMES* to remember the names of the Great Lakes—*H*uron, *O*ntario, *M*ichigan, *E*rie, *S*uperior.

Mockup is a model constructed in sections which is used in a speech to supplement the oral part of a presentation; typically it is used to show how an object is put together.

Movement such as walking back and forth in front of an audience, is influenced by the emotional distance a speaker wants to establish, the amount of emotional energy within the speaker, and the speaker's need to stay near the lectern to refer to notes or use a microphone.

Narrow development for a speech is formatting a speech by investigating a single issue in great detail.

Nationality refers to the nation in which one was born, now resides, or has lived or studied in for enough time to become familiar with the customs of the area.

Noise is any internal or external interference in the communication process; it is also referred to as interference.

Organizational confusion occurs when the source fails to present ideas in a structured order.

Orienting material to a speech the second part of an introduction, is designed to give the audience the background necessary to understand the basic material of the speech.

Outside knowledge is information from sources outside of our own experiences and direct observations that are used by speakers to develop a speech.

Paralanguage are vocal dynamics such as rate, volume, and pitch of speech and the length of pauses, that are used by a speaker to help the listener understand the points being developed.

Paraphrases are someone else's ideas put into your own words.

Paraphrasing is making a summary of the ideas that have just been received; a concise restatement of the speaker's message.

Participants are the persons engaged in the communication event—the speaker and the members of the audience.

Partitioning method of organization for a speech is the most direct ordering of ideas for listeners to follow and depends on a great deal of repetition.

Partitioning step centers on forecasting the main points of the body before beginning with the first point in the body itself.

Pathos are psychological appeals.

Pause is a temporary stop or hesitation.

Perceptions are the basis for the way a person views the world; they affect a speaker's choice of topic and style of composing the message.

Personal knowledge is the personal experiences, observations, or learning acquired through sources such as school, the media, and reading, which give us the knowledge needed to develop some speeches.

Personal speaking inventory is a listing of a speaker's life experiences and interests in order to aid in the selection of a topic for a speech, as well as determine what personal resources the speaker has .

Persuasion is the process by means of which one party purposefully secures a change of behavior, mental and/or physical, on the part of another party by employing appeals to both feelings and intellect.

Philosophical thought centers on the concept that the positive value of certain levels of human existence lie beyond the province of conceptual analysis and the practical uses of intelligence altogether, and should be given their due weight in an adequate philosophy of life.

Physiological impairment is the lack of ability to use any or all of the senses; unless compensated for, it can block the effective sending or receiving of a message.

Physiological needs the most basic needs in Maslow's Theory of Hierarchy of Needs, are food, sleep, sex, and drink.

Plagiarism is using the ideas and words of others, while offering them as the speaker's own without giving credit to the originator of the material.

Planning outline is a brief framework used to think through the process of the speech. It contains the major ideas of the speech, without elaboration.

Polarization takes place as the individual members become an audience and begin to center their attention on the speaker and the message.

Postspeech analysis is paying attention to the reactions of the audience after the speech in order to gain information that might be used in future speech presentations.

Posture is the way a person stands.

Prayers are statements of faith and concern addressed to a religious congregation's God.

Presentational outline is the material the speaker takes before the audience.

Prior analysis is the investigation done before a speech to determine potential topics and the types of supplemental materials, language, and examples needed to be included in a speech based on analysis of the audience, the setting, and the purpose of the speech.

Problem-solution arrangement identifies what is wrong and determines how to cure it or make a recommendation for its cure.

Process analysis is the speaker's watching the audience during a speech for feedback to allow for alterations of the presentation.

Pronounce means to form speech sounds by moving the articulators of speech—chiefly the jaw, tongue, and lips.

Psychographics are the attitudes of the members of the audience, such as positive or negative predispositions toward the speaker, the speech, and the occasion.

Psychological appeals enlist listeners' emotions as motivation for accepting the speaker's arguments.

Psychological noise is the result of either a speaker or listener not being able to function effectively in his or her role because of stress, frustration, or irritation.

Public speaking is the act of communication that occurs between one person and an audience.

Public speaking competency is the ability to create appropriate and effective messages; it is based on an understanding of the symbolic, dynamic, and transactional nature of communication.

Purpose is what the communicator is trying to accomplish (e.g., answer a question, change a point of view, influence others to take an action).

Purpose statement is a planning device for a speech in which the speaker defines the subject; it then allows for the development of the criteria by which the material for the speech will be evaluated.

Quality is the characteristic tone of a speaking voice.

Question-and-answer session that follows many speeches is a type of informative speech itself. It is an on-the-spot test of unrehearsed answers that measures the speaker's knowledge, alerts the speaker to areas in the speech that were unclear or needed more development, and gives the listeners a chance to probe for ideas.

Quotations are material written or spoken by a person in the exact words in which it was presented.

Random sampling is a technique that allows researchers to survey less than the entire population while assuring a great degree of accuracy; it recognizes the probability of error.

Readability is the ease of comprehension as measured by the number of words per sentence of a manuscript speaker or a writer.

Real objects are the actual articles being discussed used to clarify, support, and illuminate the oral segments of presentations.

Receiver the listener to a speech, receives the verbal and nonverbal signals and translates them.

Reception is the initial step in the listening process, which includes both the auditory message and the visual, nonverbal message.

Redundancy is the repetition of points made in a speech in order to foster listening comprehension.

Response is an intellectual or emotional reaction to a message.

Restatement is a declaration made after a speaker presents an idea or assertion which is inserted before proceeding to the next point; it is accomplished by rewording key points so that major ideas stand out for the listeners.

Rhetoric is persuasive discourse.

Rhetorographics are the setting of a speech, including its situational and environmental aspects.

Right-brain dominance is a speaker or listener's tendency to desire examples rather than technical explanations, to need word pictures to remember ideas, to like to explore ideas individually rather than be lectured to, to prefer metaphors and analogies to facts, to like humor, and to want to know how information can be specifically useful or applied.

Safety needs the second level in Maslow's Theory of Hierarchy of Needs, encompass security, stability, protection, and strength.

Scale model is supplementing the oral part of a presentation by using a substitute for a real object that is in exact proportion to the dimensions of the actual article.

Schema are scripts that a person uses to organize and interpret information.

See-blame-cure-cost method in speechmaking, is a four-step organizing technique for problem solution in which the evil or problem that exists is examined (*see*), what has caused the problem is determined (*blame*), solutions are investigated (*cure*), and the most practical solution is selected (*cost*).

Self-actualization needs the desire for self-fulfillment or the achievement of one's greatest potential, is the fifth level in Maslow's Theory of Hierarchy of Needs.

Semantic problems result from speakers or listeners not using words in a comprehensive way; problems may arise because of the lack of clarity of meaning of words.

Sermons are speeches at religious services.

Setting consists of the place, time, and emotional climate of the speech.

Social facilitation takes place as individual listeners become part of an audience and lose some of their individual identity as they pick up on reactions and responses from other listeners in that audience.

Sound bites are 15- or 30-second messages that communicate the theme or main point of an entire speech.

Spatial arrangement sets a point of reference for a speech and then presents the major ideas in terms of their geographical location; it is a common method for giving directions.

Speaker credibility is the reputation, prestige, and authority of a speaker as perceived by the listeners.

Speaker's sign posts are transitions, vocal emphases, and forecasts of main points for assisting the speaker to retain focus on the points of a presentation as the person speaks.

Speaking style is the qualities—the person's verbal and nonverbal communications—that constitute a person as a speaker; every individual's speaking style is distinctive and communicates much about the speaker as a person.

Specific instances are condensed examples that are used to clarify or to prove a point in a speech.

Speech of actuation is a persuasive speech that should move the members of the audience to take the desired action that the speaker has proposed.

Speech of conviction is a persuasive presentation in which the speaker attempts to convenience the listener to believe as the speaker does.

Speech to inform imparts new information or reinforcing information and understandings that the listener already has.

Speech to persuade gets the listener to take some action, accept a belief, or change a point of view.

Speeches about concepts examine theories, beliefs, ideas, philosophies, or schools of thought.

Speeches about events inform the audience about something that has happened, is happening, or is expected to happen.

Speeches about objects describe a particular thing in detail. The object may be a person, a place, an animal, a structure, a machine—anything that can be touched or observed.

Speeches about processes instruct the audience about how something works, is made, or is done so that the listeners can then apply the knowledge themselves.

Speeches of acceptance follow an award presentation or a success.

Speeches of introduction precede a public presentation and give the audience the information they need to have about the speech to be presented.

Speeches of thank-you acknowledge services or aid given by someone to others.

Speeches of welcome extend the speaker's greetings.

Speechmaking the presentation of speeches, is recognized as a chief means for social control.

Speechophobia is a psychological condition that describes people who are terrified by the prospect of giving a speech.

Statements of declaration propose the major contentions of a speech.

Statistical surveying is a method for collecting data that provides some degree of assurance that the resulting information will be correct.

Statistics are any collection of numerical information arranged to indicate representations, trends, or theories.

Summary of a speech restates the main points of the body of the speech.

Supplementary aids   are visual, audio, and audiovisual materials that clarify, support, and illuminate the oral segments of presentations.

Supporting materials   such as illustrations, specific instances, expositions, statistics, analogies, testimony, and humor are used to back up a speaker's major and subordinate points.

Suspense techniques   are attention-getting devices such as illustrations, specific instances, expositions, statistics, analogies, testimony, and humor that aid a speaker to create expectation and uncertainty in the audience.

Symbolic language   is the words that a speaker uses to represent the ideas, objects, and events that he or she wants to express.

Syntactical problems   are caused by flawed grammatical usage that causes problems in decoding a message.

Synthetic model   is a substitute for a real object that is not in proportion but is nevertheless representational of the actual article. It is used to supplement the oral part of a presentation.

Technical reports   are concise speeches explaining a process, detailing a technique, or discussing new elements either to people within a business or industry or to people outside it.

Testimony   is a direct quotation of an actual statement or a paraphrase, a rewording of a quotation, from an authority; it is used by speakers to clarify ideas, back up contentions, and reinforce concepts.

Theological reasoning   determines whether an action is right or wrong by relying on a rule, a law, or the outcome of a moral debate. It presupposes the existence of a prime mover, such as God, a natural force, or some other supernatural instigator.

Theory of field-related standards   suggests that not all people reach conclusions in the same way and thus may react differently to the same evidence or appeals.

Therapeutic level of listening   is the listening stage at which the listener acts as a sounding board so that a speaker can talk through a problem and, ideally, reach his or her own solution.

Toasts   are recognitions of, or tributes to, a person or a group.

Topic   is the subject of a speech.

Topical arrangement of a speech   explains an idea in terms of its component parts according to an identifiable pattern of information.

Transitions   are bridges that provide the listener with a connection between the points, such as restatement of the previous issue and the forecast of the next one. Transitional words or phrases are used by a speaker to indicate a change of idea or topic, such as "therefore," "another idea is," and "finally."

Triangle stance   is a physical position in which a person places foot A at a slight angle and foot B at about a 45-degree angle, with the heel placed roughly even with the arch of foot A for the purpose of balancing the body so that the speaker can be relaxed.

Tributes   have the function of deepening the appreciation and respect of the listeners for a person, persons, event, institution, or monument.

Trustworthiness is a characteristic that follows from a person's integrity—honesty, reliability, and sincerity.

Unfolding method of organization can be used for a speech with any purpose, but is best for persuasion; it differs from a partitioned organization in that it does not restate the central idea or include the division step.

Verbal illustrations are detailed stories used in a speech to explain an idea.

Visual aids are supplemental aids that appeal to the audience's sense of sight and are intended to clarify, support, and illuminate the oral segments of presentations; they include real objects, models, photographs, pictures, diagrams, charts, cutaways, and mockups.

Visualizations are pictures or images created by the speaker in the mind's eye of the listener.

Vivid techniques are attention devices such as lively descriptions, colorful choice of language, and a vigorous style intended to encourage listeners to pay attention to a speaker's message.

Volume is the fullness or power of the sound, ranging from loud to soft, and ***rate*** is the speed at which words are spoken.

Watcher-thinkers, those who need to ponder decisions, respond best to facts and logical appeals.

INDEX